Authentic Childhood

Experiencing Reggio Emilia in the Classroom
Third Edition

Susan Fraser

NELSON / EDUCATION

NELSON / EDUCATION

Authentic Childhood: Experiencing Reggio Emilia in the Classroom
Third Edition

by Susan Fraser

Vice President, Editorial Director:
Evelyn Veitch

Editor-in-Chief, Higher Education:
Anne Williams

Acquisitions Editor:
Alwynn Pinard

Senior Marketing Manager:
Amanda Henry

Development Editor:
Jessica Freedman

Permissions Coordinator:
Melody Tolson

Content Production Manager:
Claire Horsnell

Production Service:
KnowledgeWorks Global Ltd.

Copy Editor:
Gail Marsden

Proofreader:
Anandhan

Indexer:
Kevin Broccoli

Senior Manufacturing Coordinator:
Joanne McNeil

Design Director:
Ken Phipps

Managing Designer:
Franca Amore

Interior Design:
Sue Peden

Cover Design:
Martyn Schmoll

Cover Image:
David Nunuk/All Canada Photos

Compositor:
KnowledgeWorks Global Ltd.

Printer:
RR Donnelly

Library and Archives Canada Cataloguing in Publication

Fraser, Susan, 1934–

Authentic childhood : experiencing Reggio Emilia in the classroom / Susan

Fraser.—3rd ed.

Includes bibliographical references and index.
ISBN 978-0-17-650136-5

1. Early childhood education—Philosophy. 2. Early childhood education—Case studies.
3. Early childhood education—Italy—Reggio Emilia. 4. Early childhood education—British Columbia. I. Title.

LB1139.23.F72 2011 372.21
C2010-905439-3

ISBN 13: 978-0-17-650136-5
ISBN 10: 0-17-650136-3

Woodpecker

Contents

Preface

In the last few years, because of the powerful influence of Reggio Emilia, a significant shift has occurred in early childhood theory and practice. All over the world, early childhood educators have been inspired by the high-quality early childhood education developed in the municipal preschools in Reggio Emilia. As a result, preconceptions related to theory and practice in the field of early childhood education have been reexamined and a new approach has emerged inspired by Reggio Emilia and based on our own values and culture.

The new material included in the third edition of *Authentic Childhood: Experiencing Reggio Emilia in the Classroom* demonstrates that Reggio Emilia still continues to have a powerful influence on early childhood educators and children's programs. This can be seen in the way the educators in Reggio Emilia have inspired a greater respect for children and their intelligence and in the way teachers are increasingly creating beautiful classrooms for children's learning. Reggio Emilia's influence is evident in the way relationships are nourished and promoted among children, parents, and teachers in the classroom and in the understanding of how important natural and cultural experiences are for grounding children in a changing world.

In the third edition, teachers are introduced to a process inspired by Project Zero at Harvard University. This process, called deconstruction, will help teachers collaborate with children, parents, and colleagues to heighten awareness of classroom practices that are not fair and equitable for all families and children involved. Hopefully this will lead to changes and encourage teachers to think critically about their work with children and inspire them to make the world of education a better place for children.

ACKNOWLEDGMENTS

I would like to thank all the educators, students, parents, and young children in the early childhood education programs, kindergarten, and child-care centres I have visited and learned from in writing the third edition of *Authentic Childhood*. Without the help of this amazing group of people these three editions would not have been possible. In writing the Third Edition, I would especially like to thank Kathy Price, Laurie Kocher, and Alejandra Sanchez, who invited me to attend Children Teaching Teachers at Douglas College in the fall of 2009. The faculty of the ECE program at Douglas College shared with me many of their resources and theories about early childhood education in the post-modern world. I learned so much from all of them!

In the last two years I have also been privileged to visit a number of early childhood programs, especially Heather Fraser's family childcare in West Vancouver, Katherine Maclean's kindergarten class at Edgehill Elementary School in Powell River, Linda Murdoch and Natsuko Motegi's preschool class at Marpole Oakridge Community Centre, Pamela Wallberg at Alderwood House School, and the teachers Dee Conley, Barbara Lee, Susan Emery, and Lise Burnett at Quadra Island Children's Centre. All these people have been an inspiration for me in writing the third edition. I could not have done it without them. My grateful thanks to all of them.

I would also like to thank all the members of the Reggio Emilia Book Club and Network in Vancouver and Pat Tarr at the University of Calgary, who keeps me informed about Reggio-inspired experiences in elementary school. She invited me to participate in the Calgary Reggio Network Association whenever I visited Calgary. Participating in both the Vancouver and Calgary Reggio Network's discussions and their suggestions for books to read taught me a great deal about Reggio Emilia and how it has inspired so many early childhood educators to do what the educators in Reggio Emilia always wanted us to do, which is "to make Reggio our own" in Canada.

Foreword

Dr. Alan Pence
School of Youth and Child Care,
University of Victoria*

Sue Fraser's account of her journey of learning and transformation, following her contact with the preschools of Reggio Emilia, Italy, is a valuable contribution to early childhood education (ECE) literature. Not only do we find in her book a thoughtful and thought-provoking picture of reflective practice in ECE, but we also see in Sue the embodiment of lifelong learning of the sort we hope the children in our care will experience in their own lives.

Sue came to her Reggio experience in the early 1990s, following a distinguished career as an early childhood practitioner and instructor. At a time when some of her contemporaries were more focused on retirement than on re-formation, Sue, along with her colleagues at Douglas College and in several early childhood programs, set out to transform their programs. Inspired by the work in Reggio Emilia, Sue describes the challenges and the possibilities that emerged as a result of efforts to rethink their practices. The result is a unique and useful Canadian portrait of change in ECE, a change that can be understood as part of an emerging global effort to reconceptualize ECE and to examine its underlying assumptions.

The influence of Reggio Emilia on North American early childhood thought and practice is one of the most interesting chapters in a history that stretches back to the Canadian and U.S. infant schools of the 1820s. Many in the field of early childhood education, including Sue, ascribe an evolutionary linearity to this story of the educators' development of a relatively more sophisticated understanding of children and their development and appropriate care. To those who hold such a modernist view of "progress," the Reggio Emilia approach, like the work of Piaget and other earlier influences, represents an incremental step on the upward spiral of ECE knowledge. There are others, however, who understand the history of ECE and the potential of the chapter on Reggio Emilia quite differently.

I am one of those who sees in the programs of Reggio Emilia a paradigmatic rather than incremental difference—a type of difference that allows us to discuss Reggio Emilia as a postmodern approach to early childhood care and education. Reggio Emilia is, I believe, the first ECE approach broadly

*Reproduced courtesy of Dr. Alan Pence.

accessible in North America that is capable of stimulating a discussion of ECE in a postmodern era. Seen in this light, the programs of Reggio Emilia and the words of its principal architect are more revolutionary than evolutionary. As revolutionary concepts, they challenge the basic assumptions upon which the ECE establishment in North America has been erected. Potentially, the greatest gift that Reggio Emilia can confer is not in assisting the construction of ECE in North America but in enabling the deconstruction of that edifice. It is through deconstruction that ECE will be able to better understand the limitations of its modernist history and open itself up to an appreciation of the diversity of children, families, and communities that constitute the essence of ECE's postmodern world.

> The program of making everything knowable through the supposedly impersonal norms and procedures of "science" has been radically questioned. The hope of constructing a "grand narrative," either intellectual or political, that will give us the ultimate truth and will lead us to freedom has been shattered in many ways. Reality it seems is a text, subject to multiple interpretations, multiple readings, multiple uses. (Michael Apple, in Lather 1991, vii)

The "program of making everything knowable" that Michael Apple refers to has also been described as the "project of modernity" (Harvey 1989, 12). The influence of modernity is ubiquitous in Western (and many non-Western) societies. Although some writers identify its rise with Enlightenment thinkers of the 18th century, its belief in a universal and ultimately knowable truth has strong associations with much older traditions, including religions such as Judaism, Christianity, and Islam. Precepts of "knowability" are long established in Western thought and activity, as is the related concept of progress.

Early childhood education, no less than any other area of thought and practice in North American social sciences and human services, has been formed in the image of modernity. Cahoone's introduction to *From Modernism to Postmodernism* notes,

> The positive self-image modern Western culture has given to itself, a picture born in the eighteenth-century Enlightenment, is of a civilization founded on scientific knowledge of the world and rational knowledge of value, which places the highest premium on individual human life and freedom, and believes that such freedom and rationality will lead to social progress through virtuous, self-controlled work, creating a better material, political, and intellectual life for all. (1996, 12)

Cahoone, however, continues in the next sentence,

> This combination of science, reason, individuality, freedom, truth, and social progress has, however, been questioned and criticized by many. Some critics see modernity instead as a movement of ethnic and class domination, European imperialism, anthropocentrism, the destruction of nature, the dissolution of community and tradition, [and] the rise of alienation.

For much of the world the benefits of modernism carried a steep price. This price is perhaps no more apparent than in the rationalizations that drove colonization.

> The core of the concept [is that] with a few temporary deviations, all societies are advancing naturally and consistently "up," on a route from poverty, barbarism, despotism and ignorance to riches, civilization, democracy, and rationality, the highest expression of which is science.... The endless and growing diversity of human societies [that Europeans encountered] had to be made sense of, or at least ordered and categorized, in a way acceptable to its discoverers.... What produced diversity? The different stages of development of different societies. What was social change? The necessary advance through the different social forms. (Shanin 1997, 65–66).

The excesses of modernism are not restricted to the international sociopolitical stage. There are strong echoes in Shanin's critique of development and progress that reverberate through the halls of developmental psychology and knock at the door of early childhood education. Psychologist Michael Cole points out one such problematic association: "It is a natural step to assume that there is a serious analogy to be drawn between the thinking of primitive adults and that of 'modern' children, by virtue of their shared lack of complex experiences" (1996, 15).

Although child psychologists such as Cole and Erica Burman (1994) and child sociologists James and Prout (1997) and others have begun to critique and deconstruct assumptions underlying the traditional image of children as weak, incomplete, and incapable, ECE has been resistant to change (for further discussion see Dahlberg, Moss, and Pence 1999 and Moss and Pence 1994). Early childhood educators must begin to question their long-cherished constructions of "best practice," child-centred curriculum, professional behaviour, and developmentally appropriate practice. Such self-examination can be intimidating, and even terrifying. But it can also be liberating in allowing us, as well as the children, parents, and communities with whom we work, to see the world in new and creative ways.

Some in ECE have already trod a nonmodernist path, and there is much we can learn from them. Foremost among these pioneers are Loris Malaguzzi and his colleagues in Reggio Emilia. But if we are to see as they have seen, we must discard our modernist lenses and hear their words as revolutionary, not "progressive." Rather than being understood as incrementally different, their contributions need to be seen as paradigmatically different. If the ECE profession succeeds in fitting Malaguzzi and the Reggio experiences into its established "boxes," we will have lost the greatest gifts they have to offer—innovation and transformation. And if we ourselves are not transformed, then neither will be our programs, nor our relationships with children, families, and communities.

Postmodernism is largely about the loss of certainty, control, and predictability. It is about the presence of many voices and many views and the need to engage with those other views and open oneself to exploring a world of profound diversity. In a postmodern world, process, engagement, dialogue, and co-construction take precedence over routines, best practice, exclusivity, and the safe haven of predetermined outcomes.

Malaguzzi's words are not those of a modernist. He thinks outside the established boxes. His ideas are not exclusionary, reductionist, or safe. They recognize diversity and seek out the unknown. They appreciate the power of uncertainty and the possibilities that lie in the ninety-nine languages of children that have been lost. As Malaguzzi said, "The child has a hundred languages (and a hundred, hundred, hundred more) but they steal ninety-nine" (Edwards, Gandini, and Forman 1993, vi). Malaguzzi challenges us to reconceptualize early childhood education, care, and development:

> To learn and relearn with children is our line of work. We proceed in such a way that the children are not shaped by experience, but are the ones who give shape to it. (82)

> Our image of the child is rich in potential, strong, powerful, competent. (50)

> Teachers must possess a habit of questioning their certainties. (63)

> We had to preserve our decision to learn from children, from events and from families to the full extent of our professional limits, and to maintain a readiness to change points of view so as never to have too many certainties. (45)

Once children are helped to perceive themselves as authors or inventors [they] come to expect discrepancies and surprises. As educators we have to recognize ... the same within ourselves. (60)

[Our] teachers follow the children, not plans. (85)

It is curious how resilient is the belief that educational ideas and practices can derive only from official models or established theories. (51)

We think of school as a sort of construction in motion, continuously adjusting itself. (56)

Sue Fraser's account is just such a construction in motion. She describes how on her first visit to Reggio Emilia, "My years and years of teacher training peeled away and suddenly I was back remembering how it felt to be the child I once was." Sue has not sought to reconstruct Reggio Emilia in Canada, but she has been inspired by the words and actions of Reggio and Malaguzzi to deconstruct her own practice and engage in a creative co-construction with others for whom she cares deeply. Sue's epiphany evidences the power of Reggio Emilia to transform, to see things differently, to open one's ears to what postmodernist author Patti Lather (1991, xvi) describes as the "polyvocal complexities" of the world, a world of diversity, a world of one hundred languages that the forces of modernity reduce to one. But Malaguzzi objects, "No way. The hundred *is* there."

REFERENCES

Burman, E. 1994. *Deconstructing developmental psychology.* London: Routledge.

Cahoone, L., ed. 1996. *From modernism to postmodernism: An anthology.* Cambridge, MA: Blackwell Publishers.

Cole, M. 1996. *Cultural psychology: A once and future discipline.* Cambridge, MA: Harvard University Press.

Dahlberg, G., P. Moss, and A. Pence. 1999. *Beyond quality in early childhood education and care: Postmodern perspectives.* London: Falmer Press.

Edwards, C., L. Gandini, and G. Forman 1993. *The hundred languages of children: The Reggio Emilia approach to early childhood education.* Norwood, NJ: Ablex Publishing Corporation.

Harvey, D. 1989. *The condition of postmodernity.* Oxford: Basil Blackwell.

James, A., and A. Prout, eds. 1997. *Contemporary issues in the sociological study of children*. London: Falmer Press.

Lather, P. 1991. *Getting smart: Feminist research and pedagogy within the postmodern*. London: Routledge.

Moss, P., and A. Pence, eds. 1994. *Valuing quality in early childhood services: New approaches to defining quality*. New York: Teachers College Press.

Shanin, T. 1997. The idea of progress. In *The post-development reader*. Edited by Majid Rahnema. Halifax: Fernwood Publishing, 65–71.

Prologue

One day in 1991, my colleague Cathleen Smith in the early childhood education program at Douglas College in New Westminster, British Columbia, brought to work an article from *Newsweek* magazine that announced that the Diana School in Reggio Emilia, Italy, was the best nursery school in the world. It seems amazing today, but we had never heard of Reggio Emilia then. We began to search for more information, and after reading *Excellent Early Education: A City in Italy Has It* (New 1990, 4–10), Cathleen made plans to visit Reggio Emilia and see the municipal preschools for herself. She was so excited by what she saw and heard that on her return she began to plan the first visit of a Canadian delegation to Reggio Emilia, which took place in 1993. I was a member of this delegation, and as I toured the municipal preschools and listened to the educators tell us about their programs, I knew that they had achieved what I had always believed possible but had never actually seen put into practice.

I remember on that visit standing in the field at La Villetta school with tears in my eyes, looking at the imaginative contraptions the children had made with Giovanni Piazza in creating the Amusement Park for Birds. My intense emotional response was triggered, I think, because on seeing the children's work and watching them interact with the teachers, I was taken back to my own childhood, when I lived with my grandmother in South Africa. She had been an art teacher in England before she married a doctor and settled in Thaba N'chu, a small village in the Orange Free State. I became her pupil in a class of one as the two of us walked for miles on the African veld, sketching the scenery and the wild flowers. We sometimes worked together in creating three-dimensional representations of what we had seen on our walks. The one I remember best is an African landscape we built on a four-foot sheet of wood. After we had covered the surface of the board with papier-mâché to make the undulations of the African veld, we built mud huts out of clay and then thatched the roofs with dried grass. We modelled animals and placed them where they would be found on the veld; hippos, for instance, went in the river, and leopards on the kopjes made of small rocks and grass. We found some small moulded tin farm animals and made a European farmstead in the African veld, creating a microcosm of our South African culture. This landscape became a favourite toy for many children who visited us over the years.

As I stood there I also remembered a remarkable woman, Madame Colonna, an Italian princess who was given refuge in my boarding school as

World War II was ending. She told us that during the war she had escaped from Italy and joined the French Resistance. After being captured and brutally beaten, she escaped a second time, this time to South Africa, where she lived with us in the school and taught us French. We loved her French classes. We put on fêtes and masked balls, and we cooked French food. We visited a French restaurant and learned about etiquette. We listened to endless stories about her life in Italy and her later experiences fighting the Fascists. We learned about European history and culture, and she shared with us her appreciation for beautiful things. We learned about passion and courage and the importance of fighting for what was right. Her legacy to us was priceless. She is the reason I wanted to become a teacher and make learning an exciting experience for children.

There was also another reason I was overcome emotionally as I watched the children with the teachers in the field in La Villetta school. I was flooded with memories of how in 1964 I had started a small nursery school that I ran in West Vancouver for the next 20 years in which children had the freedom and materials to be as creative and imaginative as the children I was watching in Reggio Emilia. However, as I watched the fountains and windmills the children had made with Giovanni Piazza, I knew we would never have been able to create something as impressive as the Amusement Park for Birds because we believed in *never* intervening in the children's play. Certainly, we had made ponds in the playground on which children sailed paper boats on rainy days, like the pond I saw at La Villetta school, but then we stood back and watched the children as they played. I wish we had known about the work that the educators were doing in Reggio Emilia at that time so we could have learned about the importance of collaborating with children and engaging with them in investigations. I think we would have acknowledged the competence of young children, but we never knew then how important it was to listen closely to their conversations and collaborate with them in realizing their ideas, as the Reggio Emilia educators did.

I also remembered how discouraging our struggle had been over the years to get the local, provincial, or federal government to make a truly meaningful commitment to early childhood education. In Canada the funds allocated to early childhood programs are never enough to achieve the consistently high quality at all levels of the program that is evident in the Reggio Emilia system. I was envious of the success that the educators in Reggio Emilia had in forming a partnership with the municipality to administer the preschools. The parents of the children and I had also tried to interest the local school board and the municipality in forming a partnership with us to take some responsibility for early childhood education in our town. We did succeed in getting their support in providing space and services for the preschools, but nothing else. The idea of the government taking full responsibility for child care in Canadian society remains a controversial subject. In the early 1980s I decided to leave my job of working directly with young children and move into teacher education, where at least there is a recognition of society's responsibility to provide public funding for the education of teachers of young children.

With all these thoughts in my head, I envied the children in Reggio Emilia, who had the good fortune to live in a culture that valued them, took responsibility for their care, and gave them wonderful opportunities to work closely with adults who had the interest, patience, and ability to help them achieve their ideas. I remembered again how it felt to be a child, the excitement of being intensely involved in the creative process. It came to me, with a sudden flash of insight, that this was exactly what I had been missing in the 20 years I had been a preschool teacher and the 15 years I had worked as a college instructor. My years of teacher training peeled away, and suddenly I was back remembering how it felt to be the child I once was, working alongside an adult who provided me with authentic art experiences, who helped me appreciate the beauty in my environment, and who encouraged me to visually represent my ideas using different media such as clay, paint, and pencil. I remembered how it felt to have a teacher who was passionate about life and made learning so exciting. I remembered with sadness all those times spent supervising students on practicum, when I wondered what in the world we were doing to children by putting them through meaningless routines like circle time. I had spent years observing children daydreaming or being disruptive as teachers tried to teach them such things as the day's date on the calendar. I thought about the activity sheets that teachers were expected to prepare and how these activities interrupted the important things children were doing for themselves. So many of these activities, especially in the art area, were based on an adult's conception of what curriculum should be provided for children. I remembered with horror the many caterpillars made out of egg cartons, Thanksgiving turkeys, and reindeer hats, all identical, that I had seen displayed on the classroom walls in the kindergartens, child cares, and preschools I had visited over the years. Now, in Reggio Emilia, as I watched the children engaged in learning in La Villetta school and the other schools we visited that week, I knew I needed to understand the principles behind the Reggio Emilia approach and see if I could implement them in the education of teachers of young children.

CHILDREN TEACHING TEACHERS

I was fortunate that at Douglas College we had earlier, with Cathleen Smith's guidance, begun a method of teacher preparation based on the theoretical foundation of social constructivism. This theory is based largely on the work of Lev Vygotsky, who stated that children learn best when they co-construct their learning within the social group. This theory is also at the heart of the Reggio Emilia approach. This similarity in our theoretical foundations made it easier to integrate the principles learned from the Reggio Emilia approach into our ECE program at Douglas College.

In the early childhood education program, the theory of social constructivism is most evident in the curriculum when students begin to work in a core experience in our program called Children Teaching Teachers. Children who attend the local preschool, the child care, and the elementary school across the street are invited to visit the college once a week to spend two hours working with our ECE students. A group of approximately four students then collaborate in preparing an environment and presenting experiences to the visiting children, based on previous observations of the children's interests. The groups take turns working with the visiting children. The teams observe and videotape the session and later analyze and discuss their documentation, using their conclusions to ensure consistency in the planning for the following week's session. One group of students, for instance, after making playdough with the children, noted from their observations that the children were interested in what happened to the flour when they added water. The following week they decided to see if they could further develop the children's interest in mixing dry and wet ingredients by reading *In the Night Kitchen,* by Maurice Sendak, and setting out on a table the ingredients to make muffins. The children weighed and measured the dry and wet ingredients and chanted "milk in the batter, milk in the batter" as they mixed them together. The children later observed how the liquid batter had changed and become solid after the muffins were baked.

On our return from Reggio Emilia in 1993, we decided to explore the principles learned from Reggio Emilia in Children Teaching Teachers. We began slowly at first because we realized we still had a lot to learn about the theory, philosophy, and practices. Cathleen visited Reggio Emilia nearly every year and brought back with her fresh ideas and suggestions. In 1994, in fact, she brought to Vancouver *The Hundred Languages of Children,* an exhibit of the children's work in the preschools of Reggio Emilia. At Douglas College, one of the sites where the exhibit was on display, this exhibit gave us more inspiration to explore the approach in our program.

By now not only Children Teaching Teachers but all the courses in the ECE program at Douglas College have begun to reflect the principles learned from the Reggio Emilia approach. Cathleen retired several years ago, but we keep closely in touch with her, and as a faculty we read as much material and attended as many workshops and conferences on the Reggio Emilia approach as we could, despite our distance, living as we do in the northwest corner of North America. We are also invited to present workshops at many conferences held in Canada. The most amazing and exciting thing for us is that each year since we began using the Reggio Emilia principles in our program, the students have become more and more enthusiastic about their training and especially about their participation in Children Teaching Teachers. One student* wrote the following evaluation of her experience in Children Teaching Teachers in her journal:

> Children Teaching Teachers is a valuable experience. Not only does it allow us to put our theory to work through practical experience; it challenges us to create environments that are appealing and that engage the children. It is a learning environment not only for the children but the students as well.... I felt it very important that we provide the children with a warm and welcoming atmosphere where they were free to discover the activities that we provided for them. I realized that to engage the children we needed to first catch their attention, and what better way than to have the room visually appealing?

As a faculty we have become more collaborative as the program has become more integrated, and the dividing lines between the content in each of our courses have become increasingly blurred. The faculty members observe the students working with the children and use these observations as a source of curriculum content for their courses. The deconstruction of the CTT experiences that happen after each session is a powerful tool for student's learning and pedagogical change. The most exciting thing of all, I think, is the connection the program has made with the ECE community outside our college, to the teachers, the children, and their families in the preschools, child cares, and local elementary school in our neighbourhood. I believe that social relationships are at the heart of our work, and through collaboration we have created at Douglas College "a circle of we," as Carolyn Edwards (1993) calls it, which gives students experience in the value of creating positive human environments for children, families, and the wider community.

---

*Reproduced courtesy of Corinne Wallaton, Douglas College.

EXPLORING THE REGGIO EMILIA APPROACH IN THE CANADIAN CONTEXT

Quadra Island Preschool and Children's Centre

Quadra Island Children's Centre

Quadra Island Preschool

After integrating the Reggio Emilia ap-proach in the early childhood education program at the college level, I began to feel a need to see for myself how these principles could be used to inspire teachers in an early childhood setting. Early in 1997 I met a group of teachers who worked in the preschool and the children's centre on Quadra Island, off the coast of British Columbia, and four teachers from the Vancouver Child Study Centre, who were interested in working with me in exploring the approach in their classrooms. Therefore, I had the opportunity to observe the process of exploring the approach in three very different environments: a preschool and a child care in a rural setting and a preschool on a university campus in the city of Vancouver. All three centres are nonprofit, so the parents and the local community are very involved in their management. I was fortunate that this essential element of collaboration among the community, teachers, and families was already well established in all of the programs that agreed to work with me in exploring the Reggio Emilia approach.

The preschool and child care are situated in two beautiful wooden buildings surrounded by forest and farmland on Quadra Island, a large island at the northern tip of the Gulf of Georgia. Quadra Island lies across from Vancouver Island on the east side of a narrow channel, Discovery Passage, which forms a narrow bottleneck between the Gulf of Georgia and Johnstone Straits. The island is surrounded by turbulent waters on both sides, surging either north or south depending on the flow of the tide. This environment gives the people who live on the island a rugged individualism, but also a need for community, as violent storms and dangerous seas can cut them off from the outside world. There are 3500 permanent residents on the island, the population growing to about 5000 in the summer. On a typical 15-minute early morning ferry ride to Campbell River, the nearest town, a passenger would see business people carrying leather briefcases, workers wearing thick boots and hardhats and carrying lunch pails, women wearing long, wispy skirts and backpacks, and hordes of noisy high-school students on their way to catch the bus to school. A few farmers might be transporting the vegetables, beef, or lamb raised on the island. Many of these people would have left their children in the child care or preschool on their way to the ferry to work. Not everyone on the island, however, commutes to work. A number of people have started small home industries, including some in computer technology. There is also a large artistic community, which gives the island the rich culture that is evident in the local craft stores and at the market on Saturday mornings, where many of the local artists, especially potters, sell their work.

Quadra Island has a rich history of human habitation. There are petroglyphs on the beaches at the southern tip of the island that date back thousands of years. Captain Vancouver made contact with the First Nation band on Quadra Island over two hundred years ago. The Kwakiutl band now lives in the village at Cape Mudge. One of the residents, who has lived on the island for 40 years, said in his speech at the centennial celebration of May Day in 1998, that despite the earthquakes, wars, and fires, through all the good and the bad times, the islanders have never missed a May Day celebration. The two fine child-care programs, the preschool and the child care, which the families, the community, and the teachers have created for the children on Quadra Island, reflect this strong sense of community spirit.

During my first meeting with the teachers of the preschool and child care in the summer of 1997, they said that they had been feeling a need for more inspiration to guide their work. They had heard positive things about Reggio Emilia, and some of them had seen the exhibit when it came to Vancouver. I suggested they read *The Hundred Languages of Children* (Edwards, Gandini, and Forman 1993), and I gave them some articles about the Reggio Emilia municipal preschools. Baerbel Jaeckel, the teacher in the Quadra Island preschool, attended the Reggio Emilia symposium with me in Whistler in August 1997 and met Lella Gandini and Louise Cadwell. Dee Conley, the director of the Quadra Island Children's Centre, went to see *The Hundred Languages of Children* exhibit in Calgary in October 1997 and heard Lella Gandini speak on the Reggio approach. They returned from these conferences inspired and determined to try to explore the approach in their programs. All seven teachers from the child care and preschool attended the three-day Reggio Emilia symposium at Capilano College in North Vancouver in May 1998 to hear presentations by Lella Gandini and Carolyn Edwards.

Baerbel Jaeckel has since retired and the Preschool and the Quadra Island Children's Centre have become amalgamated into one program. The same team of teachers at the Quadra Island Children's Centre continues to be inspired by the Reggio Emilia approach and still embrace it enthusiastically in their work with young children.

I visited the island as often as I could, at least once a month from 1997 through 1999, to observe the process of exploring the Reggio approach in the classrooms and to meet the teachers to discuss their experiences and their successes and challenges. Each teacher filled out a detailed questionnaire at intervals during the process to give me insight into their experience integrating the principles learned from Reggio Emilia. In 2009 in updating the information for the 3rd edition I Interviewed the teachers again to find out after ten years if they had continued to be inspired by the Reggio Emilia approach. The teachers stated that they felt the Reggio Emilia approach had changed much of their program, but especially it had inspired them to change their relationships with children and their image of the child. They continue to be amazed at how much children have to add to the curriculum when they are listened to and encouraged to contribute their ideas. Over the years the environments in the classrooms have become more and more beautiful especially with the children's work on display in all areas of the classroom. A visitor is drawn into a busy productive classroom of happily engaged teachers and children. In the last ten years, the teachers in the Quadra Children's Centre have truly made Reggio Emilia their own.

The Vancouver Child Study Centre

The Vancouver Child Study Centre also agreed to work with me in exploring the Reggio Emilia approach in their program. In the spring of 1997 the Faculty of Education at the University of British Columbia decided to close the Child

Study Centre as a laboratory school. This was a terrible blow to early childhood education in British Columbia. The centre, especially in the 1960s and 1970s, had been the heart of early childhood education in our region and had achieved an international reputation. The parents and some of the teachers at the centre, with the support of many of us in the early childhood community, made the brave decision to keep the preschool in operation. Some of the Child Study Centre staff, however, stayed at the original site and ran the preschool under the administration of the university campus day-care group.

The parents and seven of the Child Study Centre's staff began in the spring and summer of 1997 to raise funds to reopen the centre and to search for new premises close to the university campus. In the fall of 1997, the Vancouver Child Study Centre reopened in a spacious church basement at the entrance to the university campus. Although it is in the basement, the room has large windows along one wall, which let in plenty of light and sunshine. The classroom itself is L-shaped, which allows for a busy area for blocks and dramatic play at one end of the L, a meeting area, bookshelves, and tables for children to do puzzles and other activities in the angle of the L, and a kitchen and art area at the other end of the room. There is adequate wall space to display the documentations of the children's work. A mixed group of three-, four-, and five-year-olds meets for two and a half hours in the morning and afternoon four days a week. A group of toddlers and their parents (the Anchor project) uses the space on Friday mornings.

I had been connected with the Child Study Centre since 1964 when I was a student-teacher in one of the classrooms, and later in the 1980s I did the research for my master's degree in a multicultural preschool associated with the centre. At the opening of the new centre, I asked the teachers if they would be interested in exploring the Reggio Emilia approach in their program, and they agreed to discuss this possibility with the parents at their next meeting. The Child Study Centre had hosted part of *The Hundred Languages of Children* exhibit in 1995, so the teachers and some parents were already familiar with the Reggio Emilia approach. The parents were enthusiastic about our proposal, and in collaboration with them we began to explore the approach in both the morning and the afternoon preschool programs.

Having served as a laboratory school for the university, the centre reflects a very high-quality and clearly articulated early childhood education program. Collaboration among parents, teachers, and the community is an essential component of the Reggio Emilia approach; thus, the centre proved an ideal place to explore this approach, as there has always been strong collaboration between the parents and the teachers, especially during this difficult time when the centre lost its support from the university. As I have done with the teachers on Quadra Island, I observed the program as often as I could, at least once a month, and have held meetings with the teachers. The teachers filled out a survey, as well, to describe their experience in exploring the Reggio Emilia approach in their programs. In both the Quadra Island centres and the Vancouver Child Study Centre, on each of my visits, I documented the children's activities with photographs and written commentaries.

There have also been big changes since the 2nd edition was completed. Three of the four teachers have retired and Vivian Urquhart is the only person left from the old team (However, she also retired in June 2010). The centre has moved again into another church basement not far from the old centre and the newly formed team continues to provide children with a preschool program inspired by the Reggio Emilia approach.

"Where Do We Go from Here?" is the title of the last chapter in the book *The Hundred Languages of Children*. The faculty in the ECE program at Douglas College, the teachers in the child care and preschool on Quadra Island, and the teachers at the Vancouver Child Study Centre have attempted to find some of the answers to this question. Our adventures have indeed been "dense with moments of confusion and illumination, conflict and progress" (Edwards, Gandini, and Forman 1993, 309). By 1999 I decided the time had come to write our story, although it was not yet complete—it still isn't, and probably never will be. The chapters in this book are only a reflection of our current understanding of the Reggio Emilia approach as we attempted over the last ten years to integrate the principles we learned from the educators in Reggio Emilia into the two child care centres on Quadra Island, the Vancouver Child Study Centre, and the Early Childhood Education Program at Douglas College.

It is now ten years since I wrote the first edition. Before beginning the second edition, I again visited all the schools I worked with to write the first edition. They have all continued to be inspired by the Reggio Emilia approach and have made it their own in different ways. The environments in the child care centres on Quadra Island have grown even more beautiful over the years. The teachers there told me that if there is one thing that has endured and changed their whole approach to early childhood, it is their view of the image of the child as powerful, resourceful, inventive, and full of ideas. They see this view as the foundation and touchstone for everything that happens in their program. The teachers at the Vancouver Child Study Centre continue to do inspiring work with children. The original four teachers visited Reggio Emilia in February 2002 with the Canadian delegation, and made changes in their program. Their environment over the last ten years has become an even more effective third teacher. Visitors from all over the world leave inspired by the Centre's program and documentation of rich learning made visible. In the third edition, I have included information from other centres inspired by Reggio Emilia; for instance, there are more examples of the work of the teachers and children in the Marpole Oakridge Community Preschool. There is an account of the beautiful natural environment and the children's use of natural materials in a kindergarten class in Powell River. And there is also a final word from Pamela Wallberg at Alderwood Preschool in Richmond, B.C.

Where do we go from here? Our journey inspired by Reggio Emilia continues. The Reggio Network that we started in Vancouver in 2000 has continued to grow. It offers teachers interested in Reggio Emilia an opportunity to share their work with all of us. The meetings have grown from a small core group who met twice a year to about eighty or more regulars. The group started a book club which continues to flourish.

More and more teachers in preschool and primary school are finding ways of including ideas learned from Reggio Emilia in their programs. Teacher education programs at both the college and university level are including the Reggio Emilia approach in their curriculum. Some, such as Capilano College and the Faculty of Education at the University of Calgary, are inviting children to participate in their teacher education programs.

Not only in Canada but all over the world, teachers want to find out more about the Reggio Emilia approach and attend courses and workshops inspired by Reggio Emilia. In the last few years since I retired from Douglas College I have had the good fortune to be invited to do presentations and visit child care centres in the United States, Taiwan, China, Abu Dhabi, and across Canada to talk to teachers about the Reggio Emilia approach. In the second edition I describe my experience with two teachers in Vancouver, Linda Murdoch and Michelle de Salaberry (joined by Natsuko Motegi in 2005), who invited me to participate in their preschool program, housed in the Marpole Oakridge Community Centre. I visited the preschool regularly to observe how the Reggio Emilia approach inspired them to make changes in their program. Many of the children they teach are from immigrant families, and I was interested to see the approach interpreted in their setting. I wove their story throughout the following chapters. I have also got to know another wonderful child care centre in Regina, Saskatchewan. Anne Luke is the director of the Early Learning Centre, which serves a population of mainly Aboriginal children. They too embraced the Reggio Emilia approach and gave me permission to tell some of their story.

Since writing the first edition, my own personal journey has led me to find out more about how children think and represent their ideas with the support of teachers who see children as competent contributors to the curriculum and provide them with intelligent materials. I have been inspired by reading *Making Learning Visible: Children as Individual and Group Learners,* especially the ideas of Carlina Rinaldi, Howard Gardner, and Mara Krechevsky. I have expanded my knowledge in the last few years of the hundred languages of children and found the information in *Beautiful Stuff! Learning with Found Materials* by Cathy Weisman Topal and Lella Gandini has helped me to go much deeper into investigating the role of materials in the classroom.

I asked Carlina Rinaldi (the head of the schools in Reggio Emilia) and Lella Gandini (their representative in North America) how I could write this story in a way that is respectful to all the educators in Reggio Emilia who developed the approach over the last 50 years. They advised me to emphasize in this book that what we have done in exploring the approach in British Columbia preschools and teacher education programs has been inspired by the Reggio Emilia approach and that what you read in the following chapters is our inter-pretation of the approach in our context. We have not tried to replicate the preschool programs of Reggio Emilia, as our history and culture are so different. What we have tried to do is understand the philosophy and principles of the Reggio Emilia approach and adapt them to our own situation. We hope that sharing our experience will be helpful for others who are trying to do the same.

In the third edition, I will describe how each program has in its own way continued to make Reggio Emilia its own, which is what the educators in Reggio Emilia told us in 1993 needed to happen. Throughout the following chapters, I will also thread ideas and thoughts about keeping children aware and conscious of their responsibility in caring for our natural environment. This is a topic that I believe is of vital importance to all of us at a time when so much of the natural world is under threat of extinction. Many children live in urban settings and as a result have fewer and fewer opportunities of engaging with nature and learning to care about the natural world.

In the third edition, I will include throughout the text examples of peda-gogical documentation, especially the process of deconstructive analysis (Deconstruction). I have included more information about exploring the Reggio Emilia approach in a toddler setting. There is also new material describing inter-esting projects carried out in toddler, preschool, and kindergarten classrooms. Finally, I have increased the discussion about the hundred languages of children to describe a project that investigates "the language of map making."

The information in this book is laid out not in a linear fashion but rather in the form of a spiral. The principles learned from the Reggio Emilia approach, for instance, are introduced in Chapter 1 and are revisited in increasing detail in later chapters. This format is inspired by the educators of

Reggio Emilia, who believe that learning does not take place in a linear direction. They liken children's learning to a web, in which the strands are formed and reformed with increasingly complex connections and in which changing one part has the effect of changing all the other parts too. This metaphor describes our experience in exploring the Reggio Emilia approach. I have given the words of the children, students, teachers, and parents a strong voice, so that readers can hear for themselves the many different ways that they have experienced the Reggio Emilia approach. We hope that our experiences will help others who are inspired by the wonderful schools of Reggio Emilia and wish to try out some of the ideas learned from them in their own programs. A final word of warning to those who want to explore the principles learned from Reggio Emilia. We have found, and we should have known this all along, that in trying to integrate what we have learned from Reggio Emilia into our own programs, we thought we would begin by changing only one small piece but, lo and behold, all the other pieces shifted too!

Reggio Emilia continues to be a leader in the field of early childhood education. We are all facing huge changes in our lives, whether it is in changes to the environments in which we live, or in our political, economic, and social systems and especially in communication and information technology. All these changes affect every aspect of education. Reggio Emilia was one of the first early childhood programs to adapt to these changes and as such it has acted as a guide for many of us as we struggle to cope with our changing world. It has inspired us in early childhood to examine "taken for granted ideas" in our theory and practice and find different ways of relating to children, families, colleagues, and the environments in which we work. In the third edition, I will attempt to view each chapter through a poststructural lens to see what new perspectives emerge in our thinking and practice. I will also pose some questions in each of the chapters about "taken for granted ideas" that we act upon without thinking about their relevance in our daily work teaching and caring for children. If we are able to make the "taken for granteds" in our practice visible then, it will be possible to think of some questions that may help us discover a new and better way of being teachers in the future world of early childhood education.

The Reggio Emilia approach is cohesive; the philosophy and theory have evolved over the last 50 years into a strong practice that provides children with what Loris Malaguzzi said is a program that "works within a network of cooperation and interactions that produces for the adults, but above all for the children, a feeling of belonging in a world that is alive, welcoming, and authentic" (Edwards, Gandini, and Forman 1993, 58).

Chapter 1

Penguin

Reggio Emilia in the
Classroom

[The Reggio Emilia approach] produces for the adults, but above all for the children, a feeling of belonging in a world that is alive, welcoming and authentic.

—Loris Malaguzzi

Questions to Consider:

- What led the Canadian delegation to visit Reggio Emilia, a small city in northern Italy?

- What made the greatest impression on the Canadian delegation as they observed the preschools and listened to the educators in Reggio Emilia describe and explain their approach?

- What are the major historical and cultural factors that have shaped the Reggio Emilia approach?

- Which theorists have influenced the educators in Reggio Emilia in developing their approach to early childhood education?

- What pedagogical principles are specific to the Reggio Emilia approach?

- After reading the following chapter, what new perspectives emerge about the things we take for granted in our theory and practice?

FIRST IMPRESSIONS OF THE REGGIO EMILIA PRESCHOOLS

After a long plane journey and an hour's bus ride from Milan across the fertile plains of the Po Valley, we arrived at last in Reggio Emilia, a small city in northern Italy. It was May 1993, and I was travelling with a group of early childhood educators who had come from Canada to learn about the child-care system that had been developed in this city over the last 50 years. We had heard and read a great deal about the Reggio Emilia approach and had been waiting impatiently for an opportunity to see the preschools for ourselves.

The Canadian delegation arrived in Reggio Emilia on a Sunday evening, and as it was still early when we finished checking into our hotel, a small group of us decided to try to find the famous Diana School. We walked out into the piazza and through a covered archway, which led to the square behind the hotel. We were amazed when we visited this peaceful square the next day to find it transformed into a bustling market for goods of all sorts, from fresh vegetables to elegant clothing. That evening, however, the square was very quiet as we stared in awe at the two majestic stone lions, with their enigmatic expressions, playfully guarding the entrance to an ancient church at the far end of the square. These statues are very old and are believed to have been brought to Italy from Egypt by the Romans. The statues of the lions held particular interest for us, as these were the ones the children in Diana School had studied in the lion project that we had read so much about and had seen on video. For many of us it was the photographs of the children's amazing representations of these lions in pencil, ink, and clay that had made us want to come to Reggio Emilia and see the schools for ourselves.

After gazing at the lions and touching the ancient, worn surface of the stone, we continued our walk through the narrow, winding streets of the city, passing many small shops. We stopped to gaze at the goods beautifully displayed in the windows, marvelling at the value placed on aesthetics in this culture. We entered the public gardens that surrounded the famous Diana School and walked through the dusty grass to the far end of the park. We lingered to look at an old stone fountain covered in moss, recognizing it as the one we had seen the children from La Villetta school studying, in the videotape *Amusement Park for Birds*.

The children in La Villetta school had shown particular interest in the birds that visited the large meadow surrounding the school. In 1990–91, the children had made bird houses and built, with the help of their teachers and their *atelierista*, Giovanni Piazza, an environment showing the meadow from a bird's perspective. George Forman visited Reggio Emilia in 1992, and he and Lella Gandini asked Giovanni and Amelia Gambetti, one of the La Villetta teachers, to help them understand how a project, or *progettazione,* is carried out. The teachers realized from their conversations that the children were interested in making things that the birds would enjoy. One child suggested building an amusement park for the birds. Other children then came up with ideas, such as fountains, a ticket booth, a waterwheel that the birds could use as a diving board, an elevator to return baby birds to their nests, and a lake for the birds to sail on. Giovanni and the teachers made a flow chart of all the ideas, from which they selected two main ones, fountains and water wheels, that they felt would be particularly interesting for the children to develop further.

They took the children to the park to see and sketch the fountains. When they returned to school, they encouraged the children to draw their ideas about fountains and how they worked. The teachers projected onto an easel a slide of the fountain the children had sketched in the park so the children could draw their ideas of how the water circulated inside the fountain. The children built clay models from their drawings of the fountains. They made graphic designs of waterwheels and then transferred their ideas by building wheels, first with paper and then with construction materials. They tested their wheels in an indoor water tank they had constructed earlier, which was attached to the sink in the atelier. Giovanni helped the children solve problems, such as how to attach the paddles at the correct angle so the water turned the wheel. They built pinwheels to help them understand how water and air could act as a source of energy to make wheels turn. Eventually, the weather was warm enough to start building the amusement park outside in the meadow. More and more people became involved in the project. The municipality provided water pipes to the meadow so the children could attach hoses to fill the lake they made for the birds, work the fountains, and turn the waterwheels. The children and Giovanni built a large table to feed the birds and a blind for birdwatching. Members of the local Audubon society helped the children place bird houses high up in the trees to attract more birds to the park. The parents also helped build many of the pieces of equipment the children had designed. An invitation was placed in the local newspaper announcing the time when the mayor would open the Amusement Park for Birds. People in the community, families, children and teachers from all the other schools in Reggio Emilia, and even the children's pets came to the opening of the park. The cooks made an enormous layer cake in the shape of a fountain to celebrate the occasion. A year later, when the Canadian delegation visited La Villetta school, we saw the amusement park and were able to read from the documentation displayed on the walls the story of its construction.

Later in our walk through the park, we came upon a squat building surrounded by a fence. Could this be the famous Diana School, designated by *Newsweek* magazine in 1991 as the best nursery school in the world? Peering over the fence, we recognized it from photographs we had been shown by earlier visitors, and through the foliage of the trees we could see Scoula Diana written on the wall. We walked around the building and were surprised at how similar the building was to many of the child-care centres with which we were familiar in Canada. Diana School was housed in an unpretentious building that might have been designed for any purpose. There was a playground, but unlike the centres we knew in North America, it had no large, brightly coloured plastic climbing equipment. Through the fence we saw gnarled trees that would be ideal for climbing and a large concrete tunnel covered with a mound of earth. Our excitement mounted, and we could hardly wait to visit some of the schools, meet some of the teachers, and learn about their programs.

We were not disappointed as we toured five of the schools—Rodari, Michelangelo, Panda, La Villetta, and Diana—in the following days and listened

Diana School, Reggio Emilia

to the *pedagogisti* (team leaders), teachers, *atelieristi* (curriculum specialists), and the head of the schools, Loris Malaguzzi, explain the program and the philosophy. We were overwhelmed by how much there was to see and learn. I knew it would take a long time to even begin to understand the approach. What impressed me the most then and now was how well the philosophy, theory, and practice were integrated in a cohesive program that so clearly reflected the values of the Italian culture.

Over the next ten years I began to realize how Loris Malaguzzi and the educators in the preschools in Reggio Emilia had been the first to lead us into the postmodern world. I did not realize in 1993 how in the years ahead we would have to question our understandings embedded in the theories and practices we took for granted as the foundation of early childhood education. Now as we deconstruct our theories and practices and create a new and dynamic approach to early childhood education for the 21st century, we are able to follow the leadership of the educators in Reggio Emilia who began the process so many years ago.

They warned that it would be impossible to duplicate the approach elsewhere because the Reggio Emilia approach evolved in a particular cultural context, was shaped by historical forces, and was nurtured by social conditions present only at that time and place. These forces came together to enable the educators in the municipal preschools in Reggio Emilia to develop what is likely the highest-quality early childhood practice in the world today.

THE HISTORY OF REGGIO EMILIA SCHOOLS

Before I left for Italy, I read as much as I could find on the history of the municipal preschools in Reggio Emilia and their approach to early childhood education. I knew, for instance, that the first school had been built by a group of women in 1945 or 1946. Reggio Emilia, like many Italian cities, had been devastated during World War II. In order to go to work and help rebuild the economy in their region, the women needed care for their children. These women wanted not only child care but also rights for themselves and for their children. They were determined to make fundamental changes for women in the workforce, and they wanted to provide quality learning experiences for their children.

Political equality enabled women to play a powerful role in the community in this part of Italy. The women of Reggio Emilia used their experience of working in informal networks to organize and seek rights for themselves and for their children. As well, an organized group, the Union of Italian Women (UDI), contributed to the formation of the first schools by providing child care for the children of working women.

On hearing what the women of Reggio Emilia were trying to do, Loris Malaguzzi, then a young teacher, rode his bicycle to the outskirts of the city to offer them his help. He tells the story of how the women sold "an abandoned army tank, a few trucks and some horses" to buy building materials (Malaguzzi in Edwards, Gandini, and Forman 1993, 42). From the beginning Loris Malaguzzi played a central role in the development of the schools, providing much of the inspiration and leadership as the schools evolved their own philosophy over the years.

The Sociocultural Perspective

The municipal preschools in Reggio Emilia evolved in a unique social system. For a long time there had been a strong movement toward democracy in this region of Italy; in fact, the first declaration of democracy in Italy was made from a balcony of our hotel, La Posta, in 1797. Since World War II, Reggio Emilia has had a socialist municipal government. The philosophy that is the foundation of the Reggio Emilia system has emerged from this sociocultural perspective. The social constructivist approach to education, the high level of community participation in the preschools, and the emphasis on collaboration among children, teachers, families, and the community are examples of the Reggio Emilia philosophy put into practice.

The belief in society's collective responsibility for young children is apparent in the importance given to issues such as child care in Reggio Emilia. Many of the practices in the schools, such as the lack of a hierarchy among the staff and the emphasis placed on collaboration, reflect the policies of the elected municipal government and the socialist leanings of the people of the region.

In 1967 a national law was passed that entitled every child between three and six years of age to attend a publicly supported early childhood education program. Parents were given the choice of enrolling their children in national, municipal, or private preschools. That same year, the municipality of Reggio Emilia took the lead in Italy by assuming the administration of the parent-run schools.

In 1970 Reggio Emilia educators also became innovators by opening the first infant–toddler centres (called *asilo nido*) one year before the provision of child care for children under three became law in Italy (Edwards, Gandini, and Forman 1993, 44–54). By 2010, the municipality supports 46 centres. However, although the municipality seems to have a strong commitment to early childhood education, the teachers told us in 1993 that they have had to become strong advocates and fight for funds and services that support the quality of education they believe young children are entitled to. In 1998, 12 percent of the city budget was spent on providing child care for children six years and under. The school committee, *La Consulta,* which includes administrators, teachers, and community members, debates many of the issues relating to child care. This committee is able to influence policy at the municipal level (New 1998). Recently, the city has converted an old cheese factory into an international centre (named after Loris Malaguzzi) for the study of childhood. Conferences are held here for delegations who come from many countries all over the world to learn about the Reggio Emilia approach.

In February 2002, Carlina Rinaldi told the Canadian delegation that a rising population, due to immigration and an increased birthrate, have led to changes in school administration. Some parents, because of the long waiting lists are starting and administering schools in collaboration with the municipality.

Reggio Children, founded in 1994, is responsible for liaison with the outside world. For instance, it manages publications and the touring exhibit, *The Hundred Languages of Children*. Reggio Children has also developed the recycling centre, *REMIDA*. Volunteers from the Friends of Reggio Society sort materials donated by businesses in the city and organize them into aesthetically pleasing arrangements. Teachers and children visit the recycling centre to select materials for classroom projects.

Theoretical Influences

Loris Malaguzzi, in his lecture to the Canadian delegation in 1993, said, "Here all theories are put together in an unusual way." This was our first indication that the educators in Reggio Emilia had begun to view early childhood theory and practice through a new lens, one that we later learned to call poststructuralism. He told the delegation that the educators in Reggio Emilia had used many theoretical perspectives in building their philosophy. He said that they were interested in studying Piaget to learn how individuals construct knowledge within themselves, but that they were also interested in studying Vygotsky to understand how children co-construct knowledge in social situations.

Loris Malaguzzi had visited the United States early in his career, and he brought back to Reggio Emilia many of the principles he had seen put into practice there, including the ideas of John Dewey. Dewey (1859–1952) believed that a child should learn "through and in relation to living." Dewey developed a child-centred curriculum, in which children were educated for living in the reality of the modern world. He felt that education was a process of living, rather than a preparation for future living. Like Friedrich Wilhelm Froebel, who founded the first kindergarten in 1837, Dewey believed in the value of play in education; however, Dewey's concept of play was more open. He felt that the "gifts," such as the spheres, cubes, and cylinders, that Froebel teachers used with children were too artificial and abstract for children to relate to. He recommended that teachers create a dramatic play corner in the classroom and that children be given real materials, such as carpentry tools and cooking utensils, to dramatize everyday living experiences. He called these "real, familiar, direct, straightforward materials." Dewey also believed that children should be encouraged to reproduce their own experiences in imaginative play. He stated that children should be allowed to practise and learn how to live in a democratic society. Dewey encouraged teachers to plan the program based on the children's interests and, at the same time, to be responsible for weaving traditional subject matter into the child's school experiences (Dewey 1897). He felt that children would develop the inner motivation to learn if teachers gave children the freedom to construct knowledge from their own investigations. This was the beginning of the project approach, a method implemented in many early childhood programs today.

These ideas of John Dewey would have been apparent in many of the early childhood programs that Loris Malaguzzi visited in the United States. For instance, Malaguzzi probably saw children actively involved in play and using real materials and tools. He would have noted "democracy in action" as children interacted in the social group and were encouraged to solve their own problems with the teachers' support. He would have seen the children engaged in activities, such as using a carpenter's bench in constructing a bird cage or setting up a grocery store for dramatic play in the classroom. The teachers would have chosen these experiences because they had relevance in the children's lives. Malaguzzi shared these ideas with the teachers in Reggio Emilia, and eventually Dewey's principles became an important part of the philosophy of the schools in Reggio Emilia. Malaguzzi told the Canadian delegation in 1993 that "Dewey and Reggio Emilia are similar [because] ... the unity of the social life and subject matter are related."

The connection that Malaguzzi made with Dewey was crucial. It embedded the Reggio Emilia approach within the mainstream of educational ideas, which reach back to Jean Jacques Rousseau (1789–1802), Johann Heinrich Pestalozzi (1746–1827), and Friedrich Wilhelm Froebel (1782–1852). This connection with other philosophies gives the Reggio Emilia approach an organic root that is shared with early childhood education in other parts of the world. Instead of becoming a closed system, as in the Waldorf and Montessori schools, the Reggio Emilia approach is free to grow and develop, and cross-fertilization can happen between programs. The principles that have evolved in the preschools in Reggio Emilia, therefore, have meaning to many other early childhood programs. This has enabled Reggio Emilia to become a leader in the development of early childhood philosophy, theory, and practice all over the world. They have led the way in deconstructing old theories and practices and provoked us to re-examine our "taken for granted ideas" and understandings in light of a changing world.

GUIDING PRINCIPLES OF THE REGGIO EMILIA APPROACH

The following principles of the Reggio Emilia approach became increasingly evident during our visit to Reggio Emilia:

- *collaboration*—working together at every level through collaboration among teachers, between children and teachers, and with parents and the larger community

- *the image of the child*—conceptualizing an image of the child as competent, inventive, and full of ideas

- *environment as a third teacher*—preparing an environment that acts as a third teacher (In Reggio Emilia, classes always have two teachers.)

- *relationships*—seeing the importance of relationships (1) physically, in the way objects are displayed in the classroom, (2) socially and emotionally, in the interactions of the people in the environment, and (3) intellectually, in the approach to learning that is always seen in context

- *transparency*—creating transparency through the light that infuses every space and in the mirrors, light tables, and glass jars that catch and reflect the light around the classroom, as well as metaphorically in the openness to ideas and theories from other parts of the world and in the availability of information for parents and visitors

- *documentation*—providing a verbal and visual trace of the children's experiences and work

- *pedagogical documentation*—teachers becoming researchers and examining their work from multiple perspectives.

- *provocation*—listening closely to the children and devising a means for provoking further thought and action

- *progettazione*—making flexible plans for the further investigation of ideas and devising the means for carrying them out in collaboration with the children, parents, and, at times, the larger community

- *one hundred languages of children*—encouraging children to make symbolic representations of their ideas and providing them with many different kinds of media for representing these ideas

- *respect*—showing respect for children, families, teachers, environment and materials

- *reciprocity*—valuing interaction and the exchange of ideas

This is not a finite list of the principles fundamental to the Reggio Emilia approach but, rather, a selection of some of the important ones that many visitors bring away with them after visiting the preschools in Reggio Emilia.

The Environment as a Reflection of Reggio Emilia Principles

Each of the schools we visited has a different flavour. For instance, the buildings the schools are housed in vary; some, like Diana School, are public buildings, and others, like La Villetta, are formerly private houses. The educators in Reggio Emilia have created environments for children that are truly beautiful. Every space, whether it is the floor, the ceiling, the windows, or the hallways, reflects a concern for providing children with an aesthetic and stimulating environment. There are many surprises, including unusual arrangements of furniture, such as the placement of two small armchairs in a curtained alcove in front of a series of large pictures telling the story "Little Red Riding Hood," where later in the day the municipal puppeteer will perform the story for the children. The use of materials is also unexpected—coloured tubes connect classrooms, spinning disks hang on walls, masks hang from the ceiling, and leaves are pressed against the window panes. Mirrors are placed everywhere, including on the ceiling, on the floor, and lining the sides of a large prism-shaped house built for children to climb in and see unexpected images of themselves.

Food plays an important part in Italian culture, and this value is reflected in the time spent making the presentation of food attractive and enjoyable for the children. Tables are set with brightly coloured tablecloths and small bowls of flowers. A water container shaped like a wine bottle and glasses are provided at each table for the children to serve themselves. The menu, consisting of large photographs of different kinds of pasta and fruit, is displayed prominently on the wall. One menu we saw showed a photograph of tuna moulded into the shape of a fish, with eyes and fins made from sliced red peppers.

Respect is shown for the families of the children, for instance in the way the space is planned to welcome their presence in the school. The schools are easily accessible from the street, rather than surrounded by vast parking lots. Many children arrive on foot or on the back, but more often the front, of a bicycle so they can see where they are going. The entrance hall is furnished with comfortable chairs for parents to give them the message that they should take the time to make the transition gently between home and school. Shelves display the children's work, and a portfolio for each child is available in the infant and toddler classrooms so parents can see what their children have been doing in school. Documentation displayed on panels on the walls of the classrooms also shows parents and visitors the children's experiences in school. These documentations include commentaries, photographs, and examples of the children's work to provide a record of the process the children and teachers follow as a learning experience unfolds. On the floor below the documentation or on shelves nearby are indoor plants, bowls of flowers, or a few beautiful objects to examine. Windows in the interior walls of the buildings allow parents and visitors a view of the classrooms within. Light is everywhere—clear natural light or light reflected by mirrors and through coloured glass infusing every space—for transparency is an important principle in Reggio Emilia schools, as well as a metaphor that explains the philosophy of openness to families, to the community, and to ideas.

Another principle reflected in the design of the environment is the importance of social relationships. Reggio Emilia, like other Italian cities, has a piazza, or public square, that is the hub of the city. Here, people gather for events, meet to discuss politics or other issues, or just linger to socialize. At lunch time and in the evening the piazza is filled with groups of people absorbed in earnest discussions and families strolling around, chatting, and greeting friends. This social practice is clearly reflected in the way the schools have been designed. Many of the classrooms open onto a piazza, providing a familiar place for children, teachers, and visitors to meet socially. The piazza allows freedom of movement between the classrooms and other areas of the school. The children are not confined to their own classroom, but rather can mingle with the children in other rooms in the school. For instance, the children from all three classes in Diana School are able to use the piazza and, if they wish, to dress up in the clothes arranged on circular dividers in this central meeting place.

The arrangement of space has been carefully thought out so that every part of the building has a purpose. There are places where children can work together in small groups or in larger groups with a teacher. For example, platforms are built in corners of the room to provide a separate space for small groups of children to build with blocks of various sorts. Clear plastic strips hanging from the ceiling form a transparent curtain that separates the platform from the rest of the open space in the room. Low bleachers are built in the classrooms, providing an area where larger groups of children and teachers can meet to share experiences and discuss their plans for the day. Loris Malaguzzi, in emphasizing the importance of interaction, said, "I believe there is no possibility of existing without relationship. Relationship is a necessity of life" (Kaufman 1993, 287).

Routines are minimal in the Reggio schools. The children are not interrupted by unnecessary transitions from one activity to the next, as so often happens in schools in other parts of the world. In a Reggio Emilia classroom, there are times to eat and sleep and meet with the group, but there are few unnecessary interruptions in the children's day. This is thought to be one of the reasons the children can become so absorbed in a lengthy project, such as the Amusement Park for Birds. The teachers and children arrive in the morning, spend some time socializing or playing, and then gather to plan the day. Some children may already be working on a project and after the group meeting leave together to carry on with it. Other children may have a new idea they want to pursue or may decide to do one of the activities that are available every day, such as painting at the easels, building with the many different kinds of blocks available, or playing with the beautiful natural objects set out in the housekeeping area of the classroom.

The children who have been chosen to help the cook leave the classroom a little earlier than the others to help set up the lunch tables or to prepare and serve the food. Some teachers eat with the children, but most teachers eat on their own or, sometimes, with visitors to the preschools. The auxiliary staff supervise the children during this time.

After lunch the children usually have a long siesta and spend a relaxing afternoon playing outside if they stayed inside during the morning. Most children are picked up by four o'clock, unless parents have made special arrangements for them to stay later. The teachers then have additional time to meet and discuss the observations they made of the children and to go over any problems that may have arisen. This is also a time to make future plans based on their observations during the day.

The environment in all the classrooms gives the visitor a sense that it is a good place for children to be. There are many activities that are similar to those in early childhood centres in other parts of the world, such as blocks, housekeeping materials, games, and puzzles on shelves beside low tables, but some areas, such as the *atelier,* or studio, were new to us. The atelier, such as the one on the top floor of the house at La Villetta school, is filled with interesting materials and work that the children are doing with the *atelierista,* or curriculum specialist, who is a part of the teaching team in every school in Reggio Emilia. Each atelier seems to reflect the unique character of the atelierista. At La Villetta, for instance, the atelier is filled with mechanical constructions that the children built with atelierista Giovanni Piazza, whereas at Diana School, the atelier displays the beautiful clay pieces the children were doing with atelierista Vea Vecchi. The documentation on the walls of the ateliers and in the classrooms tells the story of the children's and teachers' investigations. The viewer sees not only the finished products, but the steps in the process as well.

The teachers are intensely involved in what the children are thinking, saying, and doing. They are present for the children and actively engaged with them in their activities. The teachers are either helping the children as they work with the materials, sitting beside them discussing something of interest, or sitting close by, observing and recording their actions and conversations. Sometimes the teachers set up a tape recorder to capture the children's conversation. We also saw them videotaping the children as they explored percussion instruments in the studio at Diana School. This level of awareness and involvement of the teachers with the children contributes to the high quality of the programs that amazes visitors to the Reggio Emilia schools.

The social relationships that are developed in the schools of Reggio Emilia are the fabric into which everything else is woven. These social relationships go beyond the classroom walls to reach out to families and the community. For example, Loris Malaguzzi told us in 1993 that he invited a group of parents who were recent immigrants from Turkey to use a classroom and the kitchen facilities in one of the schools for a place to meet in the evenings. Each school has a parent–teacher committee that meets every month. There are also meetings arranged throughout the year to provide an opportunity for parents and teachers to get to know one another and exchange ideas. The teachers try to create a community that uses the parents' particular skills. Lella Gandini, in a speech in Whistler, B.C., in August 1997, said that in Reggio Emilia, "parents have a sense of belonging and their voices are visible. We believe in the potential of parents and we as teachers should help this to emerge."

SECOND IMPRESSIONS OF THE REGGIO EMILIA PRESCHOOLS

The second Canadian delegation to visit Reggio Emilia arrived in the city on February 8, 2002. Some of us wondered how we would feel about Reggio Emilia the second time around. Soon after we arrived, a group of us set off to visit the lion statues in the Piazza san Prospero, to confirm that we really were in Reggio Emilia. How much smaller everything looked than I remembered from my first visit! This happened again and again during the following week, especially when we visited schools like Diana and La Villetta. The classrooms were just as beautiful but seemed much smaller than I remembered them. I certainly missed the presence of Loris Malaguzzi. Nothing will ever affect me as profoundly as did his lectures about early childhood education during that first visit in 1993. His ideas inspired me to reexamine everything I knew about early childhood education and start the long hard process of deconstruction and then reconstruction of my early childhood practices.

Those of us who had been to Reggio Emilia with the first delegation found many changes on our second visit, including the founding of Reggio Children, discussed earlier, and the volunteer organization, the Friends of Reggio Society, through which community members support the preschools. A group of past and present parents, for instance, gave our delegation a presentation to inform us of their role in the system. The volunteers explained how they are able to participate at many different levels from being a part of discussions on educational issues to being a part of work bees preparing materials in the classroom. On another occasion, two parents took us on a guided tour of the city.

The delegations one participates in now are huge, hundreds of people as opposed to 24 in the first delegation we were part of in 1993. In the last ten years the municipal preschools in Reggio Emilia have had over 12 000 visitors. Inevitably, although the educators make every effort, a visitor now feels more remote from the program. Sheer volume of visitors makes experiences more distant and less subjective. We met with teachers, pedagogisti and atelieristi on our visits to the schools, but these conversations were much more formal than in 1993. I remembered nostalgically the long evenings during our first visit spent talking to teachers about all sorts of interesting subjects and philosophies.

Carlina Rinaldi, in her address to the second Canadian delegation, emphasized the importance of teachers seeing themselves as researchers and becoming more aware of the process of learning in children. She said that if we used multiple languages in teaching children we would broaden our understandings. She emphasized the importance of documentation to make the learning process visible and shareable. Rinaldi's leadership has, I believe, reaffirmed Malaguzzi's educational vision but also consolidated and refined it. For instance, she has introduced the value of organization for the system. This more recently stated value seems to have had a major impact on preschools. For instance, every preschool now develops a statement of intent at the beginning of the school year. The overall effect of the statement of intent seems to have brought curriculum development closer to the process followed in North America. We were told that in 2001 teachers in Reggio Emilia had identified mathematics as a subject neglected in their curriculum. As a result, many of the schools we visited emphasized activities that promoted mathematical and logical thinking skills. In Diana School, for instance, we saw children inventing and writing rules for math games. We were told they would later explain the rules of how to play their math game to the children who were entering their class the following year. At one of the tables in the classroom a group of children were using a three-dimensional grid made from sturdy wire to classify small clay objects they had made themselves. On our second visit to Reggio Emilia we observed more of an emphasis on children mastering discrete skills, such as matching and classifying, that teachers had identified as significant at that point in the children's cognitive development. In contrast, on our previous visit we had seen more emphasis on the expressive arts and on large projects, like A Longterm Project about Dinosaurs, described by Baji Rankin (Edwards, Gandini and Forman 1993).

Children, Spaces, Relations: Metaproject for an Environment for Young Children was published in 1998 by Reggio Children. In 2002, I could see many of the design concepts described by the authors, Giulio Ceppi and Michele Zini, reflected in the municipal preschools. The classrooms in the preschools in Reggio Emilia now offer an even wider variety of sensory experiences than I remembered from our first visit. We were amazed then at the visual richness of the environment, but on our second visit we saw how this had been expanded to heighten the children's sensory awareness. Welcoming visitors at the entrance to Diana School, for instance, was a mound of bright red apples piled high on a large tray. We observed the children investigating elements such as texture and sound. Colour is a very typical conceptual learning activity in our North American schools, but the investigation of colour in Reggio Emilia took a much more imaginative path than I had ever observed before. When we visited the Diana School, for instance, we saw the children exploring a variety of yellow materials. The atelierista told us the children were "exploring all the nuances of yellow." Some children were on a quest to find out if yellow had a smell; to help them discover the answer there was a sprig of yellow flowers set out on the light table with perfume, lemon juice, and yellow paint for the children to use to paint a picture of the flowers. On the light table children were also able to explore the scent of orange peel, slices of kiwi fruit, and gingko leaves. A group of children were using yellow pencil crayons, yellow chalk, and wax crayons to make a yellow mural. The year before, many of the teachers had seen an exhibition by Alberto Burri; an artist from the region who uses fabric to portray colour and texture. The exhibition had inspired the teachers to carry out an in-depth classroom exploration of the relationship between colour and texture. In the Diana School there was a large panel titled "white, white and white," made with white textured materials. In La Villetta school the teachers had isolated sound as an element for the children to investigate. We were told the children were building "an alphabet of sound." We saw the children walking around the school with clipboards, recording the different sounds they heard in different parts of the school building. The data they collected were then entered into the computer for later analysis. These kinds of experiences, based on isolating elements to heighten awareness, were different from the all-encompassing projects we had seen in 1993, like Visit to the Poppies and Amusement Park for Birds. However, when we heard Giovanni Piazza, the atelierista in La Villetta school, describe Windows and Landscape, a project he had recently completed with the children in his school, we could see that progettazione as we remembered them are still very much a part of the Reggio Emilia approach. We realized, as we listened to him explain in detail every step of the project's development, that we still had much to learn from the educators in Reggio Emilia.

Piazza told us the project began because he and the teachers had observed the children's interest in landscapes. "We noticed," he said, "the children were very interested in constructing and narrating landscapes. The children had been up to the mountains, they had been to town. There were some beautiful paintings and drawings which emerged from these experiences." The teachers decided to develop this interest further by giving the children each a small paper bag and asking them to collect interesting objects and bring photographs, drawings, and stories from their summer holidays. Giovanni said that this was done so that when the children returned, the material they brought back with them would provide an anchor to help the children remember their experiences and create the possibility of "a path to travel along." The children had many stories to tell on their return to school. One discussion about train windows and what could be seen from them eventually led to an investigation about windows and landscape. The teachers set up a sheet of plexiglass in a frame for the children to investigate windows in the classroom. The children told him, "I am going to make a window (from the) outside." "I am going to do mine (from the) inside, but I can see you inside there as if you were really inside a window; it's exactly the same!" Giovanni said, "Think how children are thrown off balance by these ideas; they realize they can be both inside and outside a window." He asked us to think about children coming to this realization and how we as teachers could support them to investigate the idea further by giving them the materials to respond to it in creative ways and expand their understanding. He said, "This is something that is very important for children. In this process they are living through, the children construct a new relationship with each other, and also with the landscape."

Ideas that emerged during discussion of the holiday materials and stories included:

- an interior and an exterior landscape

- seasonal change as seen through the window

- different landscapes as seen from windows on all the floors of their school building, from the ground floor to the skylight in the attic

- what the birds see, feel, and think (perhaps as they look *in* the window)

Giovanni told us that for a topic to be important enough for children to develop into a larger project, or progettazione, it must

- arouse emotions

- provide opportunities for the children to collect lots of information verbally, by drawing or taking photographs, or by using a variety of materials such as collage, clay, and three-dimensional construction materials

- provide lots of opportunities for collaboration

- provide opportunities to create representational work using a wide variety of materials.

Giovanni spoke to us about how we as teachers often underestimate the depth of children's thinking. He noted that children are interested in big ideas like life and death. In the project about windows and landscape, what held the children's interest and sustained the topic were overarching ideas like friendship, which came from the idea of two windows side by side opening and closing. Children also explored the big idea of changing points of view, as they thought about looking in and out of windows at different landscapes.

Giovanni emphasized that for a project to be successful it must have such big, overarching ideas, which generate passion and sustain the children's interest. It must also have a lot of "surface area"; that is, it must offer many possible different paths.

Giovanni's account showed us the complexity involved in the development of a Reggio Emilia project. In this case the project began with a provocation, the materials and stories that the children brought back from their holidays. The children's contributions gave teachers an idea of how to organize the children into groups to do further research. For instance, small groups of children were given paper, pencils, and cameras to visually express their thinking about landscapes. Teachers also listened to their conversations for ideas as to which direction the project might take. The teachers observed the children talking about unusual windows like the skylight, comparing different points of view seen through windows, wondering what a bird would see flying over the town. The teachers wondered what would happen if they made windows the protagonist for the project. A table was set in front of a window, which, Giovanni said, "told the children that something important is happening here." The children were excited by the materials—the sheets of plexiglass and clay he had put out for them to work with. They responded by making suggestions about what they might do with the materials:

"It could be a bird's window."

"A green window smells lovely."

"It could be one for the school cat."

Giovanni said, "For me one of the most important things is to see together what they will decide to do; we could give them the title (for the project) or let them choose."

Teachers began to think about what kind of materials would be best to use to represent windows. Giovanni explained that a teacher selects materials by thinking about the aesthetics inherent in the topic. For instance, when thinking of materials to represent landscape, he would ask himself "If the wind is cold and harsh, what materials would be appropriate to choose? Perhaps a piece of twisted wire—it looks like the window—and wiggly wire could be the wind working its way up the school, and we could attach little pieces of paper for the breeze." He pointed out that children can think like artists and consider aesthetics in designing their art work.

Consideration too must be given to the "affordances," or possibilities inherent in the materials chosen for the project. Giovanni explained that clay was chosen because "a window is a three-dimensional structure, too difficult for children to represent graphically, but clay is already three dimensional."

The image of the child, the environment as a third teacher, and the "hundred languages of children" all played an essential part in the project. Giovanni emphasized the importance of observation, interpretation, and documentation. Observation of the children led the teachers to pursue the children's interest in landscape. "I've got some photographs, and I have got some drawings. These instruments help me to show the child that there is a longer story, not something finite in the moment, but we are inside the narrative." And then the children knew that something important was happening.

Principles of respect for the child and reciprocity are still much in evidence. Giovanni stated that in Reggio Emilia, children are seen as "competent, capable of constructing, a child who is not an empty container but who brings knowledge to the learning process and therefore needs a different kind of attitude from the teacher … one that avoids hiding the children's processes and substituting the adult's own processes … we need a teacher who learns and constructs knowledge with the children." "Irony emerges as an element of our work," he added, and teachers have to be able to "enter into the irony," to enter imaginary worlds with children (address to the Canadian delegation, February 12, 2002).

When adults and children are able to enter imaginary worlds together, there can be amazing "transcendencies." To give a Canadian example, the preschool children at North Shore Neighbourhood House were concerned that the children in the infant–toddler program would be afraid of monsters, so they decided to make a dream catcher and hang it in a window to protect them (Carr 2004).

Principles that we had first become aware of in 1993, such as respect, relationship, reciprocity, and transparency, were still much in evidence in all the schools we visited. The principle of transparency, which had made such an impression on us on our first visit, was still evident in every aspect of the program. Light is used in ways we had never thought of. We saw coils of tube lights winding their way up staircases or curling through the display of clay figures on a shelf. We were intrigued by the way teachers used light projectors and coloured acetate sheets or plastic discs in the construction area to project on the walls coloured shadows of the buildings constructed by the children.

We saw some of the same documentation we had seen in 1993 still up on the walls: for instance, the coiled clay pictures of dancers the children had made in the early 1990s. This was wonderful to see; it gave us a sense of history and showed how much the work of preschool children is valued in Reggio Emilia, even long after the children themselves have left the preschools.

We saw children using computers in many of the classrooms we visited, which I do not remember from 1993. In La Villetta school, we saw a small group using a computer to design a geometrical pattern for the weaving they were planning to do on the loom. We were interested to see the computer being used by a group of children working together to do something creative, as opposed to an individual child playing a solo computer game, which is a more common sight in North American preschools.

As the Canadian delegation did in 1993, we returned from Reggio inspired by what we had seen and heard, amazed at the depth and breadth of their vision of early childhood education, and determined once again to strive for a similar level of excellence in our own programs in Canada. We began to realize that we like the educators in Reggio Emilia were going to have to undergo the process of deconstruction and examination of "taken for granted ideas." Practices such as scheduling, old formulas for circle time, and program planning would all need to be examined to find if they were relevant in the 21st century. Above all it became apparent that we would have to look very carefully at our "image of the child" and the cultural values of the families and communities with whom we worked. All this would likely lead us to new ways of relating to others and different understandings about our work in early childhood education.

Chapter 2

Robin

The Image of the Child

The cornerstone of our experience, based on practice, theory and research, is the image of the children as rich, strong and powerful. The emphasis is placed on seeing the children as unique subjects with rights rather than simply needs. They have potential, plasticity, the desire to grow, curiosity, the ability to be amazed, and the desire to relate to other people and to communicate.

—Carlina Rinaldi

Questions to Consider:

- What are the major theoretical perspectives that have influenced the image of the child in Reggio Emilia?

- What image of the child emerges from our understanding of each of these theoretical perspectives?

- How can we help adults focus on children's strengths as opposed to their needs or weaknesses?

- How do teachers from diverse cultural backgrounds view children?

- Who is silenced and who is privileged in inclusive settings?

- How does the reconceptualization of early childhood programs from a poststructural perspective influence the image of the child?

INFLUENCES ON THE REGGIO EMILIA APPROACH

Each of us holds deep down an image of the child. This image has many reflections. First, there is the subjective, personal one, the one we know from our own experiences as a child. Then there is the objective, empirical one, the one that we construct from observing and thinking about the children we meet in our journey through life. But the strongest image of all is the cultural one, the one that is shaped by the values and beliefs about what childhood should be at the time and place in which we live.

Loris Malaguzzi told the Canadian delegation in 1993 that "all theories are put together in Reggio

Emilia in an unusual way." This statement is significant for those of us studying the Reggio Emilia approach, but it is particularly important for those of us wishing to understand the image that the educators in Reggio Emilia hold of the child. The philosophies and theories of a number of people, including Erik Erikson, John Dewey, Jean Piaget, Barbara Biber, and Lev Vygotsky, have been integrated into the Reggio Emilia approach. It is necessary, therefore, in trying to understand the approach, to first understand the image of the child at the core of each of these theories or philosophies.

The first section of this chapter will attempt to define the image of the child from the perspective of the developmental theorists that Loris Malaguzzi identified as important in the evolution of the Reggio Emilia approach. The chapter then turns to how teachers, parents, and community members can define a common image of the child, including the child with disabilities, in early childhood settings. Finally, we consider the image of the child from a poststructural perspective and how this influences the way we view children.

John Dewey's Image of the Child

John Dewey has influenced the educators in Reggio Emilia with his positive view of human nature. Dewey saw the child as "spilling over with activities of all kinds," and he saw education as "taking hold of his activities, of giving them direction." He felt that a child should be given the materials to "reproduce in imaginative form his own experience" (Dewey 1915).

There is an echo of Dewey in the way teachers in Reggio Emilia listen closely to children to help them take hold of their ideas and give them direction. The educators in Reggio Emilia have expanded Dewey's emphasis on the role of play in representing ideas in their concept of the hundred languages that a child can use for symbolic representation. John Dewey also stressed the importance of viewing the child in the context of the family and society, which has become a key principle in the Reggio Emilia approach. Dewey believed that children who experience the processes of democracy early in their lives, for instance, as they participate in discussions in group time and work together with teachers planning and carrying out projects in the classroom, are learning to be responsible, participating citizens in a democratic society.

Erik Erikson's Continuum of Achievement

Erik Erikson was a theorist who wrote about children from both a cultural and developmental perspective. His theory is examined in detail here because, like the Reggio Emilia approach, its roots are European, but it too continued to evolve after it was transplanted to North America.

Erikson began his work with children in Germany in the 1930s. As a young man he was interested in becoming an artist and spent some time wandering around Europe. However, after meeting Anna Freud, the psychoanalyst and daughter of Sigmund Freud, he began to study psychoanalysis, especially child analysis. Anna Freud introduced him to a group of teachers who ran a small American school in Vienna. He agreed to teach art to the children in the school, but in the 1930s when the threat of the Nazis became too overwhelming, he and his Canadian-born wife, Joan Erikson, left Germany to live in the United States, where he continued to practise psychoanalysis. In the following years he began to expand his image of the child as his awareness increased of the role culture plays in the child's developing personality.

After studying the child-rearing patterns of Native Americans, Erikson wrote *Childhood and Society,* in which he outlined his theory of the eight ages of man. The first four stages of Erikson's theory deal with childhood from birth to the teenage years. Each stage identifies the task the child needs to achieve for healthy personality development to occur, as well as a description of the consequences if the challenge is not met. Erikson believed that each task in the eight ages of man could be metaphorically measured on a continuum of achievement. Erikson's image of the child is based on identified personality traits that can be measured on a continuum from positive to negative. In the development of a healthy personality, children need to have traits found at the positive end of the continuum, balanced by a small amount of the traits found at the negative end. These personality traits are as follows:

Trust vs. Mistrust

Autonomy vs. Shame and Doubt

Initiative vs. Guilt

Industry vs. Inferiority

The first stage of development involves achieving a balance of trust and mistrust. In the first two years, the infant develops a basic trust if the people who care for him are responsive to his needs. The child's sense of security grows as he develops "the recognition that there is an inner population of remembered and anticipated sensations and images which are firmly correlated with the outer population of familiar and predictable things and people" (Erikson 1950, 247). If, however, the child is never allowed to cry and every wish is anticipated, he grows up to be too trusting. A little mistrust is healthy, but if too much mistrust develops, the child may have difficulty forming close relationships later in life. The healthy personality, therefore, is more trustful than mistrustful. The educators in Reggio Emilia have adapted this idea of a balance between trust and mistrust by emphasizing responsive interaction with children, which can be symbolized by a game of ping pong. Imagine a teacher repeatedly throwing the ball to the child and then catching it when the child throws it back. This turn taking, or responsive interaction, with children is essential in the development of trust, the foundation for healthy development at this stage.

Autonomy versus shame and doubt is the second of the eight ages of man. Erikson stated that "this stage, therefore, becomes decisive for the ratio of love and hate, cooperation and willfulness, freedom of self-expression and its sup-pression. From a sense of self-control without loss of self-esteem comes a lasting sense of good will and pride; from a sense of loss of self-control and of foreign control comes a lasting propensity for doubt and shame" (1950, 254). It is during this stage that the child who is growing up in an environment that "allows him to stand on his own feet" and is "firmly reassuring" develops a strong sense of self, balanced by a willingness to cooperate (Erikson 1950, 252). This stage lays the groundwork for a sense of right and wrong. If the child has been given opportunities to explore within safe limitations and to develop autonomy, the child begins to show pride in doing what is right and shame for doing wrong. Eventually, this trait will become a sense of fairness, tempered by a realistic doubt that everything in life will work out perfectly. A sense of security enables the child to act autonomously, which is an essential component of an image of a child who is competent. The toddlers, for instance, in the asilo nido in Reggio Emilia are put to sleep in baskets on the floor with a small opening through which they can climb in and out. This practice respects the toddlers' right to be autonomous and responsible for their own rhythms of sleeping and waking. As well, the toddlers are not con-fined to cage-like cribs, as is the case in most other toddler centres.

In the third stage the child builds on autonomy to develop a sense of ini-tiative. "He is eager and able to make things cooperatively, to combine with other children for the purpose of constructing and planning, and he is willing to profit from teachers" (Erikson 1950, 252). This stage adds to the image of the child the ability to be inventive and full of ideas. Baji Rankin describes the process that unfolded as the children in the Anna Frank School in Reggio Emilia study and represent their ideas about dinosaurs. She describes how, after much discussion and research, four girls selected materials and used their initiative and inventiveness in collaborating to create a three-dimensional representation of *Tyrannosaurus Rex*:

The girls chose styrofoam as their medium. The material turned out to be rather easy to work with as it was easy to handle and the shape and size of the styrofoam pieces suggested to them different parts of the dinosaur.... A satisfying, three-dimensional, approximately 4-foot high, highly decorated *Tyrannosaurus Rex* resulted along with a stronger friendship among these particular girls. (Edwards, Gandini and Forman 1998, 223–24)

In the fourth stage, industry versus inferiority, the child adds the quality of deep and sustained engagement. According to Erikson, "the child must now be a worker, he learns to win recognition by making things" (1950, 252). This image of the child accurately describes the children in Reggio Emilia as they collaborate with the teachers to create the amazing work on display in the municipal preschools.

The educators in Reggio Emilia believe that if parents and teachers focus only on the negative traits, the child will be viewed as needy, and a dynamic will be set up that responds mainly to the child's deficits, rather than strengths. If the child is viewed in a positive light, teachers will focus on her strengths and build on these. Erikson's positive image of the child and his view of the child in the context of the family and society have been integrated into the Reggio Emilia approach. These two perspectives, in particular, give Erikson's theory and the Reggio Emilia approach relevance to early childhood educators in the North American setting.

Jean Piaget's Stages of Development

Jean Piaget was born in Neuchâtel, Switzerland, in 1896. Initially, he was interested in biology, and by the time he was 21 years old, he had published over 20 scientific papers on mollusks. On completing his Ph.D. in 1921, he was hired to work with Alfred Binet in France on the development of intelligence tests for children. His early work in the natural sciences led him to make many important inferences from his observations of the children taking these tests. He found, for instance, that children were able with experience to adapt to the testing procedure, and when he compared the performance of older and younger children, he found that the older children did not know quantitatively more than the younger children. Instead, there was a *qualitative* difference in their results; that is, they thought differently about problems. This discovery led him to explore the field of epistemology: the study of the process children and adults undergo in becoming knowledgeable.

Three key parts—order, structure, and process—to Piaget's cognitive developmental theory form a basic framework on which other ideas can be built.

1. *Order.* Children progress through four stages of development, sensorimotor (birth to 2 years old), preoperational (2 to 7 years old), concrete

operational (7 to 11 years old), and formal operational (11 years old and up). Children progress through each stage in the same order, but their rate of progression varies depending on cultural factors, previous experience, and individual differences.

The sensorimotor stage is the preverbal stage. Children before the age of two use their senses and physical actions to explore and make sense of the environment. The second stage, the preoperational stage, is divided into two substages, preconceptual and intuitive. In the first substage, children use symbols, especially language, to order and derive meaning from their experiences; however, they still use their own perspectives as a frame of reference. In the second substage, children use their intuition to solve problems, as in the example shown on the following page of a child creating a bubble-making machine. By the third stage, the concrete operational stage, children have formed simple concepts and can begin to use thinking skills, such as classification and seriation, to organize their environment and solve problems. Finally, the formal operational stage is reached when children use logical and abstract thinking processes.

2. *Structure.* Intelligence develops as children build notions or ideas from their experiences in the environment. At first, they form the information from these experiences into preconcepts, or schemas, that are somewhat workable but primitive views of the world. Later, with more experience, children refine these schematic understandings to form more complex, abstract concepts.

3. *Process.* Assimilation, accommodation, and equilibration are three parts in the process of learning. Assimilation occurs when children absorb information from experience to form schemas. When the child adapts these schemas learned from previous experiences to meet new assumptions, this is known as accommodation. Equilibration is a self-regulatory process children employ in an attempt to maintain a balance between their cognitive structures and their experience of the external world. When children strive to reach equilibration by seeking satisfactory solutions to problems arising in their environment, they develop intelligence. This dynamic process creates a spiral of learning that is experienced differently in each of the four stages of development. In the first stage, the child will explore, for instance, a square block physically by putting it in the mouth. When the block is no longer a novel experience, the child has reached a state of equilibration. In the second stage, however, the child's desire to label the block and use it in symbolic play will cause a new state of disequilibration, as the child strives to meet the challenge of transforming the block into a symbol. At the third stage of cognitive development, the concrete operational stage, the school-age child will be

A child creates a bubble-making machine.

presented with the challenge of performing simple operations, such as measuring the six external surfaces of the cube. In the fourth, formal operational stage, the child will again experience disequilibrium when challenged to carry out abstract operations such as determining the cubic area of the block.

Thinking originates, according to Piaget, in a gradual internalization of action. Children in the sensorimotor period of development use their senses to explore the environment. Their actions on objects and the world around them form the basis for concept development in later stages. The child, like the one discussed above, who has had many opportunities to discover all the properties of a square block, will develop an awareness of angles and planes, equidistances between points, area, and volume, which eventually will develop into an in-depth understanding of cubic properties. "The learner's structures, as they interact with the environment, first do simple assimilations and accommodations but eventually—at a nonpredictable threshold or bifurcation point—combine to make a sweeping change (*toute ensemble*) transforming themselves into new and more sophisticated structures" (Doll 1993, 71).

Piaget was the first to pay serious attention to what children could do, as opposed to focusing attention on what they lacked. He also demonstrated that learning is qualitative rather than quantitative. For educators, the open-endedness of this image of the child required a change in the teacher's role from directing the learning to facilitating it. The kind of environment that teachers provide for children, therefore, has changed from being a structured environment in which the teacher delivers the content to one that fosters the children's exploration and investigation. This new environment, in turn, has generated an image of the child as an active discoverer and inventor, who constructs her knowledge from experiences in the environment. The following observation of children, recorded at the Vancouver Child Study Centre in 1998, illustrates how active exploration of materials provides children with many opportunities for learning about physical science*.

> Patrick and Douglas stand opposite each other at a water table. Patrick is filling a cylinder with water, pushing his arm into the cylinder, and watching the water squirt out of the top of the cylinder.
>
> The teacher passes by and asks, "Is that a bubble machine? What do you think a bubble machine would be like?" Patrick starts squeezing a soapy sponge and looks at the bubbles forming on his hand. He empties a bucket of soapy water into the water in the water table. "Look! A bubble machine!"
>
> Douglas connects two long plastic tubes together, puts one end in the bucket, and starts to blow. He makes a face, but he continues to blow through the tube. He attaches the two ends to make a circle and pushes it down into the soapy water in the water table, carefully positioning the circular tube to keep it horizontal. He gently raises the tube to the surface, and there is a soap film attached to the circumference of the circle. He blows an enormous bubble downward from the soap film.
>
> "Look, Chava," he calls out to his teacher.
>
> Chava asks, "How did you make it? Aaron, come here and check this out." She calls another child over to look at the bubble. Aaron gently pokes it with his hand. The bubble bursts, and Patrick lowers the circular tube gently under the soapy water, raises it, and blows a bubble, which connects to a bubble in the water, making a long, tubular shape.
>
> Adam joins him.
>
> Patrick says, "Watch this, Adam. Don't spoil it! See the bubble. You put your hand in the bubble. Look, you do it."
>
> Adam tries to raise the tube but is not successful in forming a bubble.
>
> Patrick says, "Adam, go in my spot." They change places, but Adam still can't get a bubble to form. They leave the tube in the soapy water and pour water in the water wheel. They start to spin the water wheel, squealing as it splashes their faces.

These two boys clearly reflect a Piagetian image of the child. They investigate the water, soap, and tubes. Patrick eventually invents a bubble machine, which he tries to teach Adam to use. He demonstrates intuitive

*Reproduced courtesy of Chava Rubenson.

thought (specifically, transductive reasoning) by suggesting that they change places; presumably, he thinks the position at the table will have an effect on Adam's ability to make the bubble. The teacher, Chava, by asking the boys the question, "What do you think a bubble machine would be like?" provokes the boys to think about different methods of making bubbles, which leads Douglas to invent the pliable hoop and successfully blow a long, tubular bubble. This invention, in turn, led to more discoveries of how soap film could be manipulated. The episode ended with disequilibration, as Adam was still unsuccessful in blowing his bubble, even though he changed places with Patrick.

Loris Malaguzzi acknowledges the contribution that the cognitive-developmental theory of Piaget has made to the Reggio Emilia approach. The Piagetian view that development occurs in conjunction with experience is well supported in the schools in Reggio Emilia. The rich and stimulating environments in these schools provide many opportunities for children to transform materials and to use symbolic representation to express their thoughts and ideas. These opportunities are part of the generative curriculum, which is fundamental to the schools in Reggio Emilia.

Malaguzzi lists a number of aspects of Piaget's theory with which the educators in Reggio Emilia disagree. They agree with the Piagetian image of an active, self-motivated child, but they contest the view of an egocentric child who constructs knowledge in isolation from the social group and without the support of adults. Malaguzzi and the educators in Reggio Emilia also question a basic tenet of Piaget's theory: the lockstep progression through the four developmental stages. Their experience in supporting children in the realization of their thoughts and ideas led them to agree with Lev Vygotsky's theory that children have a zone of proximal development that enables them with the support, or "scaffolding," of adults to achieve more mature levels of functioning than Piaget identified as possible (Edwards, Gandini, and Forman 1993, 75–80).

Teachers in considering each of the above theories of Dewey, Erikson, and Piaget will need to remember that each of these theories represents a view situated in the modernist tradition that states that there is a universal truth supported by scientific evidence that shapes knowledge of a young child's development. When teachers view these theories through a poststructural lens, they will reflect critically and question how these theories might be influencing their observations. For instance, they will ask themselves if the time, place, gender, and racial biases present when the theories were constructed affect their observations. Perhaps, in the observation of Patrick, Aaron, and Douglas above, they will question issues of gender and race. "Why were there only boys involved in this scientific exploration? Are teachers giving girls equal attention for their explorations? Was each of the boys given an equal opportunity to be listened to? For instance, was Patrick, a child from the Solomon Islands, given equal recognition for his discovery as Douglas was for his success in blowing a bubble from his bubble machine? As Glenda MacNaughton states, teachers in a poststructural world need to "confront a will to truth" and "know differently and justly." (MacNaughton 2005, 63).

Lev Vygotsky's View of the Child's Learning

Lev Vygotsky was born in Orsha, Belarus, in 1896 and grew up in a prosperous Jewish family in Gomel, Russia. He was a successful student and graduated as a lawyer from Moscow University in 1918. Because racism made it difficult for a Jew to practise as a lawyer at that time, he returned to Gomel and taught at the secondary and post-secondary levels. He was passionately interested in psychology, and in his short career, before he died of tuberculosis at the age of 38, he wrote seven books and numerous articles. His ideas were suppressed in Russia after 1936 but were rediscovered in the 1960s and, in the last 30 years, have gained increasing attention all over the world.

Four of Vygotsky's ideas are particularly important for educators of young children. The first is that children actively construct knowledge. Vygotsky studied Piaget and agreed with this aspect of his theory. The second point, however, conflicts with Piaget's theory. Piaget stated that development is invariant and that learning follows development. For instance, Piaget wrote that children must first have a foundation of sensorimotor experience on which they can then build concepts, which, in turn, are shaped by language. The child in the sensorimotor stage of development needs many opportunities to explore elements such as texture, shape, and colour before he can learn the words to describe these elements. Vygotsky, however, stated that learning leads development. Vygotsky believed that if the child is first given labels, for instance, the names of colours, this will hasten the child's ability to understand the concept of classifying by colour. Learning, according to Vygotsky, is not invariant, as Piaget believed, but relevant to experience. If an adult, therefore, tells the child the name of the colour of the pencil she is drawing with, this information will enable the child to recognize other red objects and to become aware of relationships of objects grouped by colour.

Vygotsky's third point is that learning cannot be separated from its social context. Learning is enhanced when children are able to interact with others who assist and support them in the learning process. His fourth point is that language plays a central role in intellectual development because it is through language that the higher mental functions, such as symbolic thought, are transmitted. Vygotsky identified three lower and three higher mental functions.

The lower functions are inborn and similar to those functions found in more advanced species of animals, such as mammals. The three lower funtions are reactive attention, associative memory, and sensorimotor thought. The higher mental functions are unique to humans and are developed through interactions with other humans. The higher mental functions are focused attention, deliberate memory, and symbolic thought. In the example above, an adult would support a child's greater understanding of the concept by focusing the child's attention on the colour of the pencil, asking questions to help the child recognize the colour in other situations, and encouraging the child to use the concept at the symbolic level.

According to Vygotsky, the child has two levels of performance: the first is the level that the child is capable of achieving independently, and the second is the level of performance that the child reaches with assistance. The distance between these two levels is known as the *zone of proximal development*. For instance, an adult sitting beside a child who is drawing with coloured pencils might focus the child's attention on the green colour of the grass in the child's picture. The adult might then ask the child what colour the leaves will be on the tree that the child has begun to draw. In this way, the adult moves the child from the level of unassisted learning to the level of assisted learning within the child's zone of proximal development. The child, with help from an adult, may now begin to use accurate representational colours in drawing, whereas previously he would have randomly chosen the colours for depicting objects in the picture (Bodrova and Leong 1996).

Vygotsky, like Piaget, acknowledged the importance of play in a young child's development. Both theorists saw value in play, especially for the opportunities it provides for children to engage in symbolic representation and symbolic action. However, whereas Piaget saw the value of play in the freedom it provides children for active engagement, Vygotsky believed that play is important for the constraints it imposes on free expression of the child's will. Vygotsky felt that the greatest value of play lies in the demands it imposes on children to master their own behaviour. Each episode of play has a set of roles and rules that children are required to follow if they are to be successful participants. His views differed from those of Piaget, therefore, in that he believed that play is not entirely spontaneous. He asserted that play imposes certain constraints and limitations on children that are essential in the development of what he terms *self-regularization* (Bodrova and Leong 1996, 125).

Malaguzzi told the Canadian delegation in 1993 that "learning is a collaborative process ... and Vygotsky showed us the importance of the social aspects of learning." The view of the child from a Vygotskian perspective is of a *social* child who is intelligent, strong, creative, and competent. The image of the child in the Reggio Emilia approach is of a child who is securely embedded within the social and cultural group.

Barbara Biber and the Whole Child

Barbara Biber, an educator and psychologist in the United States, was instrumental, particularly during the 1960s and 1970s, in forming a link among Erikson, Piaget, and the evolving educational philosophy in the preschools in Reggio Emilia. Biber was among the early educators to first perceive development from the perspective of the "whole child." She integrated the psychosocial view of Erikson with the cognitive constructionist view of Piaget, in an attempt to discover "how to make knowledge and the experience of learning available to growth processes; how not merely to keep children interested in their lessons but to make the process of learning functional at deeper levels of the total process of integration; in other words, how to make the experience of learning (1) yield ego strength and (2) contribute to positive feelings and attitudes toward self and others" (Biber 1972, 313–14).

Biber believed that relationships are central to the child's education; thus, she stressed the importance of a child's sense of belonging and active participation in the social group as critical factors in the development of a positive sense of self and in the ability to learn successfully. The important principles of collaboration and a positive image of the child in the Reggio Emilia approach have been influenced by her work. Further connections between the educators in Reggio Emilia and the work of Barbara Biber exist in the kind of learning environment considered important for children. She writes about the importance of providing children with rich sensory experiences, helping them to become aware of "the light of the afternoon in wintertime; the bong of drums and the whisper of triangles" (1972, 315). She and the educators in Reggio Emilia believe that children need a rich sensory environment to heighten their aesthetic awareness, to develop their thinking skills, and to encourage representation at many levels. Her contribution to the Reggio Emilia approach is apparent in her statement that "by helping the child penetrate experience, concrete and abstract, to the level of relationships, the school is preparing the child to order and deal with his world in terms of his society's logic and perception of reality.... The child creates and recreates the world around him, building a pattern of coherence for his impressions, concepts, roles, and relations, and integrating knowledge and feeling" (Biber 1972, 316).

The teacher's relationship with children in the schools in Reggio Emilia is echoed in Biber's view of a teacher as "the intellectually resilient teacher, the one who can enjoy the intriguing course that the young mind takes in ordering the world of ideas, can perceive and accept the importance of the underlying thought processes while she supplies information and experience relevant to the correction of errors of fact and inference.... On this level, teacher and child are interacting cognitively: communicating" (1972, 317–18). She spoke of the teacher "mediating" the learning environment for children and supporting the children in "transforming information, knowledge, skill, and competence into ego strength" (1972, 321). This statement also describes the relationship the teachers in Reggio Emilia develop with the children in their classes. However, the teachers in a Reggio Emilia classroom view the child as competent, whereas Biber saw the teacher as leading the child toward competence.

Barbara Biber's major contribution to early childhood education was in integrating the separate areas of development, psychosocial and cognitive, into a holistic image of the child. Also, by placing relationships at the centre of the child's learning experience, she saw the teacher as taking a supportive rather than authoritative role in the classroom. This change in perception allowed the teacher to play a partnership role with children, as in the Reggio Emilia preschools. It also enabled educators to appreciate the work of Lev Vygotsky, who had established earlier the importance of the adult's role in supporting the child's learning.

Poststructuralism

Poststructuralism is a move away from the 20th century dominant constructivist theories that we have examined above. Hillevi Lenz Taguchi and others, such as Glenda McNaughton, Luigi Iannacci et al., urge us to expand our understanding of early childhood beyond the "still prevalent modernisation of articulating one grand learning theory for post modern education" (Lenz Taguchi 2006, 257). In questioning our knowledge of child development from a poststructural perspective, we come to understand that there is no universal truth that we can rely on to analyze child behaviour. The theories that we have believed in so implicitly in the past are only one way of understanding children. These theories are governed by the particular lens the theorist in question chose to look through at a particular time and place. Further, we need to be aware of the language traditionally used to analyze children's behaviour. If we use the language of the dominant discourses of the 20th century, our understandings are shaped and as a result limited by viewing child development from a single perspective. The educators in Reggio Emilia were perhaps the first to use multiple perspectives in their analysis of the children's learning. Included in this too were the teacher's observations and documentations so that the final analysis was a co-construction of ideas and theory generated through reflection and discussion. Lenz Taguchi states that in Reggio Emilia, we see an approach to early childhood education that is created by a "selection of excellence" from a multitude of theories representing many different disciplines as well as artistic and poetic languaging and imagery that cannot be scientifically classified." (Lenz Taguchi 2006) Further, the educators in Reggio Emilia urge us to deconstruct our thinking about children and in collaboration with others construct a view of children that is responsive to the families, community, and culture of our time and place.

THE EXPERIENCE OF CHILDREN TEACHING TEACHERS

The students in the ECE program at Douglas College participate, during the second and third semester of their training, in a core curriculum experience called Children Teaching Teachers (CTT). The class is divided into groups of approximately three or four students, who plan and present activities to the small groups of children from local child cares and preschools who visit the college once a week to participate in CTT. This experience provides the ECE students with many opportunities to explore the principles learned from the Reggio Emilia approach.

The ECE students in the child growth and development course are asked first to observe children and to consider the image of a child from the perspective of three developmental theorists: Erikson, Piaget, and Vygotsky. The following extracts are selected from the students' observation reports.

Example 1—Erik Erikson

N. (30 months) grabs the airport from another child who has started to play with it since N. left it. The other child starts to cry.

N.: "Mine, mine!" She gets into a tug of war over the airport. The other child shouts back, "No, mine!"

N. Pays no attention to this child's words and continues to pull.

The above example presents a powerful image of two young children both trying to establish their autonomy.

Example 2—Jean Piaget

M. (42 months) is able to recognize and use a variety of symbols. Dressing in a fancy dress and shoes symbolizes getting married to her. A wooden block is used as a gun on another occasion and cornmeal in a container represents variously apple juice and a cupcake.

The image portrayed by this student is of a child who engages in rich episodes of pretend play. The child is able to function effectively at a symbolic level, transforming herself and objects as she engages in imaginative play.

Example 3—Lev Vygotsky

S. (teacher) to **N.** (30 months): "You're playing with the lift, N. You'll have to wait your turn."

N. Goes back to examining the lift; she seems puzzled as to how it works.

S.: "I am going to try something." She puts a car into the lift. "Here's the car, down, down."

N.: "Let me, let me, it's inside." She carefully lets the car come down the ramp.

This image shows how the teacher supports the child, refocusing her attention on the task, enabling the child to overcome frustration and begin to solve the problem by learning how to make the toy work.

When students have understood the image of the child from different theoretical perspectives, they can begin to absorb this information into their own image of the child. Many of the students in a typical early childhood class at Douglas College are immigrants who come from all over the world; from countries such as China, Taiwan, Iran, India, the Philippines, Africa, and South America. They bring with them their own memories of childhood, school experiences, and child rearing patterns. "[I]n their child growth and development courses they are encouraged to reflect and question various theories and philosophies in ECE with the goal of gaining a deeper understanding of them. A further goal is to think in terms of a positive image of the child, one that may be unexpected and beyond the theories we have learned to apply." (Sanchez 2009) Through a process of collaborative/critical reflection the small group of students present their experiences and observations of individual children or groups of children to the rest of the class for discussion. Finally, they write a report which responds to the questions and comments from the audience and from teachers and parents with whom they have shared their observations. (See page 321 for a description of the Collaborative Critical Reflective Protocol [inspired in Rounds for Teachers, Project Zero, Harvard Graduate School of Education]).

The students, during the process of developing a shared understanding of the image of the child, begin by reflecting on their own views of children and the way children are perceived in the significant theories they have studied in class. Through discussions in their small groups and from their observations and presentations of documentation to the audience after each session of Children Teaching Teachers, the students begin to consider their own and other perspectives of children. This means their thinking will go beyond viewing children solely from a subjective and/or objective modernist perspective. For some students this will mean freeing themselves from seeing children as fitting exactly into a certain stage of development based on developmental psychology. For others it will mean expanding their views on children to include multiple perspectives of images of children. One student in her reflection paper in April, 2009, wrote, "During CTT, there is <u>always</u> a moment when I am really astonished at how the children express their thoughts on the things they were exploring or the things that were happening around them. I always ask myself … 'Are these children scientists, theorists, inventors, artists, educators or significant leaders trapped inside their little bodies with cute smiles … they make me question myself … how I see and think of many things now.' "

Each student will in time, and in collaboration with others, begin to deconstruct and co-construct an image of the child that matches their core values and the values of the families, community, and culture of the children they care for. Folded into this image of the child are ideas gleaned from their readings of poststructuralist thinkers such as Dahlberg (1999), McNaughton (2005), and Hillevi Lenz Taguchi (2006) who provoke students to consider how to help children develop a strong sense of social justice, equity, and responsibility for caring for each other and for the natural environment.

SHARING AN IMAGE OF THE CHILD

The view of what a child is and ought to be has deep roots in the culture, society, and family values of the people involved. Because we live in a multi-cultural society, and the people we work with come from many different backgrounds, the images we hold of children will reflect this diversity. This disparity in point of view makes it difficult for the adults working with the children in the centre to share a common vision of what a preschool child is really like. However, a shared understanding of the preschool child is essential in designing programs that are congruent with the values and beliefs of all the parents, teachers, and members of the community who are involved in the child-care centre.

Image of the child

The key question to ask teachers, parents, and others who are involved in the program is, "What is your image of the child?" The answers to this question should be given after careful reflection, as the labels that first come to mind often need to be explored further to get to the truth of their meaning. Later, when everyone has had a chance to reflect on the answers, they can begin to work as a group to develop their shared understanding of the image of the child. This may be time consuming because there may have to be much negotiation before the group as a whole reaches a common vision of their image of the child.

The Quadra Island Preschool provided an example of how teachers, parents, and the community evolved a common vision. The group of parents in the preschool worked very closely with the teacher and took turns working as the parent assistant in the classroom. It was essential for them, therefore, to explore as a group their image of the child to ensure consistency in the program. After they had discussed each person's ideas about children, they drew up the following list of characteristics that defined their image of the child.

They stated that preschoolers are imaginative and curious, but whereas three-year-olds tend to be observers, four-year-olds are much more energetic. They noticed that preschool children are forgiving of adults' mistakes. The children's behaviour has the quality of fluidity. For example, they observed the group of children becoming more sociable as they turned four. One parent said, "They [preschoolers] are clever, more so than you think." Another parent noticed how excitable behaviour contrasted with "deep and sustained activity." The parents noted how the children liked to play with language and how their ideas, at times, were surprisingly sophisticated. One parent said, "The amount of creative play the children engage in and how much they learn by imitation is a continual source of amazement to me." The group stated that the overriding characteristics of the preschooler are powerfulness, loudness, and forcefulness. This image of the child matches the Reggio Emilia educators' image of the child as "rich, strong and powerful" (Rinaldi 1993, 102).

The parents and teacher in this preschool worked as a team to provide the children with a program that matched the list of characteristics they drew up together. For instance, they removed barriers, such as long circle times and adult-imposed theme lessons, which interfered with the children's natural bent for fast-paced, energetic, and fluid activity. The daily schedule they devised allowed the children to engage in deep and sustained activity. It was flexible to avoid unnecessarily interrupting the children's natural rhythm and engagement in learning and play. However, the schedule also provided time for the teacher and the "parent assist" to meet in small and large groups to discuss ideas and topics of interest with the children.

The participants also agreed with the parent who said that children are more clever than we think, so they decided that it was essential that the adults took the time to listen to the children and support them in finding a means of expressing their ideas. Loris Malaguzzi stated that children have a hundred languages of expression. The teacher and the parents decided that one of their goals for the year would be to provide the children with many different media for expression.

Culture and environment in North America are widely diverse depending upon where in the country you are living. On the West Coast of Canada, for instance, children, even in large urban centres like Vancouver, live close to nature. The mountains, ocean, and forests loom larger than the city itself. At the Vancouver Child Study Centre, for instance, children are surrounded by forest, they are within a few minutes of the beach, and across the Bay one can see the towering North Shore Mountains. They have to cross the bridges linking areas of the city and are often in full view of volcanic mountains, like Mount Baker.

The kind of environment children experience in their day-to-day lives has to be taken into consideration in considering the image of the child in whatever part of the world one is living. The children in Italy are exposed to an ancient civilization that has produced some of the most beautiful art and music in Western culture. Teachers wanting to include ideas learned from Reggio Emilia so often bemoan the fact that their children don't have the same exposure to art as do Italian children. Observations of children in Western Canada, however, show how responsive they are to their environment and culture. For instance, in observing the children in child-care programs on the West Coast of Canada, teachers note how passionately they explore sand, water, and volcanoes and love to construct roads, bridges, and buildings. This kind of activity is happening all around them as the towns and cities expand into the countryside. Teachers will need to reflect, therefore, on the kind of environment and experiences the children in their care will have been exposed to as they construct their image of the child and prepare an environment that responds to their interests. It is also important to reflect on the values that teachers will want children to be exposed to, such as care and nurture of the natural environment, that on the West Coast is so much part of their lives.

PRINCIPLES OF INCLUSION

The educators in Reggio Emilia have been instrumental in shifting the image of the child from a child with needs that adults strive to meet to a child with strengths and rights. The Reggio Emilia educators stress the image of a competent child who is a producer, as opposed to a consumer, of resources and one who has a right to a quality early childhood education: one that provides the child with relationships and experiences that promote learning and foster development. This shift in image has had a powerful impact on the education of children who are challenged in one or more areas of development. It has forced educators, for instance, to think carefully about how they can provide children with disabilities with an education that enables them to reach their full potential. These educators have become aware of how important it is to *include* these children with their peers, giving them the same opportunities to form relationships and the same quality educational experiences as other children have. The educators in Reggio Emilia have become world leaders in their advocacy for the rights of *all* children to experience a quality early childhood education. The phrase "children with special rights" has come to stand for inclusion of all children in preschool programs and for a guarantee that they will receive the support they need to maximize their potential development. This phrase invokes awe in people who have been trying to figure out how to support their children, especially children with disabilities (Smith 1998).

Italy was one of the first countries in the world to recognize that all children have the right to a quality education. From the time in 1960 when orphanages and institutions for children with disabilities were closed and the children returned to their families, the rights of these children have been given increasing consideration. At first, they were educated in special classes, but in 1971 children between the ages of six and fourteen were given the right to a desegregated education. In 1995 a law was passed that guaranteed infants under the age of three a place in infant–toddler centres.

Children with special rights are given priority in being accepted into the municipal preschools in Reggio Emilia, and only one child with disabilities is accepted in each class. Once the child is enrolled, the two classroom teachers meet the psychologist-pedagogista to decide if they will need the support of a third teacher to work with *all* the children in the classroom.

The process of orientation, or *inserimento*, is carried out slowly and carefully. Ivana Soncini told the Canadian delegation in 1993 that in Reggio Emilia beginnings are considered very important and that a long time is spent to ensure that the child and family will experience no stress as a result of the separation. Soncini went on to say that the child's behaviour is observed for a long period, and no diagnosis is made before the team has a thorough understanding of the child's situation. Even then no special curriculum is developed for children with disabilities, and they are expected to participate in the same program as the other children in the class at a level that is comfortable for them. An agreement, or statement of intent, is written to ensure that communication is ongoing with other health professionals, with families, and with the teachers working with the child. The educators in Reggio Emilia have found it helpful to videotape the child's progress in the school and to share and discuss these tapes with the family.

Ivana Soncini stated that one of the biggest advantages in the Reggio Emilia system is that the different learning styles of children are accommodated because the hundred languages of children allows children a wide variety of ways to express themselves. This is particularly important for children with special rights. "The teacher's primary objective," he told the Canadian delegation, "is to bring out the full potential of the child." He ended his talk by emphasizing the importance of social learning. He said that the child's difficulties are best handled in social situations. The child should want to come to school, and the family should feel positive about their child's experience in school. As Carlina Rinaldi stated, "...we in Reggio Emilia view children as active, competent, strong, exploring and finding meaning, not as predetermined, fragile, needy and incapable" (*Innovations*, 2001).

Ben and the Gargoyles

The following story of Magda Buczynski and Ben at North Shore Neighbourhood House illustrates how a teacher who sees children in a positive way can enable a child to become a fully participating member of the group. Magda said that initially she had been apprehensive about having Ben join her class because he had been diagnosed with attention deficit hyper activity disorder (ADHD) and she had been told that his behaviour had been challenging for the teachers in his previous class. Magda wrote, "When I considered all these statements they still did not capture who Ben is or how my relationship and his relationships with other children would be. I like it when both I and the children are faced with a challenge and I have to learn together with them."

Just prior to Ben's entry into Magda's class, Ana, one of the children, had told the class about the night her apartment block had burnt down. This led to discussions about bad dreams, and a parent offered to help the children make dream catchers "to catch the monsters." The children began an investigation of monsters and this eventually led to a field trip to the Hotel Vancouver to see the gargoyles high up on the roof of the building. Ben entered into the project enthusiastically. His increasing ability to focus attention for long periods of time and to become part of the learning group is shown by the following observation notes recorded at the time.

> As soon as the Gargoyle book was introduced and made available through transparencies at the light table he began to spend longer periods of time refining his tracing. Magda watched and listened to his interest and responded to his emotions ... He became very vigilant about being present at small group discussions concerning the field trip. He would gain entry to the group by offering to show his tracings to Magda and his peers.

Finally, it was agreed to take Ben on the field trip with seven of his peers to investigate the gargoyles at the Hotel Vancouver.

Anne Carr, in her summary of the field trip experience, wrote: "(Ben) required minimal extra support to participate. He spent a long time sitting beside and drawing the lions outside the Vancouver Art Gallery. It appears that Magda chose to value Ben's uniqueness or subjectivity and break the neutrality of using certain psychopedagogical strategies that had been suggested by other professionals. She seemed to value the relationship between Ben's subjectivity and the intersubjectivity of his peers. During this period, at least, Ben would be more truly described through his relationship with his peers and their interest in gargoyles rather than a particular clinical label" (Carr, 67).

The above anecdote illustrates how important it is for a teacher to have a positive image of the child and to know how to support a child's entry into the social group. Magda, who is open to taking reasonable risks and who sees possibilities, allows a child like Ben to demonstrate his competence and participate successfully in the classroom. This is particularly important in the case of a child who needs extra support. Once the child becomes accepted by the other children, other problems the child might be having tend to melt away or at least become less of a focus. This was clearly demonstrated as Magda found ways for Ben to become an accepted member of the group.

Sometimes, however, it is not only the children who have difficulty in accepting a child into a group; teachers, students, or even sometimes a parent can be the stumbling block. Inviting adults to a puppet-making workshop can help change attitudes. Everyone makes a puppet of a child and then small groups create a mini-puppet show of a *positive* incident that they have observed at school. As each group presents their scenario of some amazing incident they have observed happening at school, the focus is shifted from children's weaknesses and problem behaviours to their strengths and capabilities. The teacher can then collect the puppets and over time present the scenarios to the children in the class so they too can celebrate each other's strengths.

WORKING WITH CHILDREN FROM DIVERSE CULTURAL BACKGROUNDS

Linda Murdoch*, who teaches children from many different cultural backgrounds in Marpole Oakridge Preschool, noted how her image of the child had changed since she had begun to embrace the Reggio Emilia approach in her program. She said, "I really don't think of kids the same now. I used to think of those who could do and those who could not. Now I recognize their capabilities as individuals and how they can contribute to the group" (interview, April 9, 2004).

Children from diverse cultural backgrounds can function very successfully in a group when the teachers hold an image of the child that values their differences and welcomes the diversity they bring to the class. Teachers who understand that children communicate in a hundred different languages will ensure that the children in the class who do not speak the major language of communication will function successfully if they are able to use play and the materials in the classroom as a means of communication. The children also need teachers who are responsive and know just what materials and support the children need to move ahead with the project the group is interested in pursuing. For instance, in the Circus project (discussed on page 160), and the Castle and Knight project (page 229), although the children did not speak English as a first language, they were able to communicate clearly to the teachers through their play what topic interested them. It was important, too, that the teachers were able to read the children's nonverbal messages. Michelle said, "We would listen to the children's conversations and watch their play and then set up materials." The teachers also responded to the children's interests by providing information. For instance, Linda and Michelle** brought in books and videos about topics of interest, such as castles, knights, and the circus. The teachers were also resourceful in drawing on the knowledge of people they knew. They invited a clown to give the children ideas for the circus project and medieval character actors to show the children what it was like to live during the middle ages. As the projects developed the teachers were skilled in sustaining the children's interest through conversations,

---

*Reproduced courtesy of Linda Murdoch
**Reproduced courtesy of Michelle de Salaberry

supported with illustrations from books, interesting artifacts, or photographs. For instance, one child brought in a sword to show the class, which led to the children cutting and designing swords and shields. Linda used the digital camera to take photographs of interesting block constructions the children had made. She printed these, labelled, and mounted them to create vignettes, which the children looked at and discussed later during group meeting time. The vignettes were made into a book illustrating the children's growing understanding of castles, which was sent home and shared with the families.

The children seemed to understand from these strategies that they were now contributing members of the group and, as a unit, moving forward together. "Though few words are spoken, the mutual understanding is profound … all seem to perceive the essence and rules" (Rinaldi 2001, 93). This is an exciting phenomenon to observe happening in a group of children. It seems that at some critical point the children take ownership of the topic under investigation. Carol Anne Wien calls this "The windhorse effect." "[This] term is borrowed from the secular Buddhist tradition called Shambhala and refers to raising positive energy, the life force that whirls through us" (Trungpa in Wien 2008, 15). In emergent curriculum a different mental state develops for those collaborating on a project, and this altered intention, motivation, and energy carries individuals and eventually the whole group in the way that the metaphor "windhorse" suggests. The energy has the power of a horse carrying a rider at great speed (Wien 2008).

This windhorse effect seemed to be happening in both the Circus and the Castle and Knight projects. As the projects began to unfold, the children seemed to understand the goal and began to participate as a group in achieving it. It is particularly exciting to see it happening in a group of children who do not share a common language because suddenly they begin to communicate with each other across cultural and linguistic barriers. All the children, some it is true need more support than others, but gradually everyone including the families gets caught up in the process.

A child sometimes took individual ownership of different aspects of the project. For instance, Vanessa, who became the ringmaster for the circus, said, "I have got to make that hat today!" Ian took responsibility for designing and making the drawbridge for the castle. At other times the children all worked together to achieve the group's purpose. For instance, the children decided as a group to make a roof for the circus tent and organized themselves into pairs who took turns painting the fabric for the roof. The activity flowed by itself; there was no need at this point for the teachers to direct the action. At times, however, the teachers took the lead.

Sue Fraser

Ian's drawbridge

Michelle said, "I rarely needed to direct the children; they just seemed to know when and who would do the next task. However [during the castle project], I became aware that a few children hadn't had an opportunity to take part, so they were invited to do the next part, which was the 'points' [turrets]. They merely needed a place to start for them to become more involved. They spent a long time on their 'points'—there were lots of conversations [co-constructive learning] and when they added the turrets to the castle two other children quickly made flags to add to them. Some children just seem to know what needs to be done next. Jashanjot [one of the youngest children], who often seemed to be on the outside watching the others play knights, one day created a 3-D knight from paper tubes. It was quite remarkable and became the catalyst for the exploration of knights. Other children also wanted to make a knight and Jashanjot became the expert. When we asked the children if they would like to build a knight that was bigger than any dad for an upcoming Father's night, all were eager. Jashanjot was fast at selecting the materials to make the head and visor and demonstrated skill in wiring it all together. He was now part of the group and proved himself to be a competent contributor."

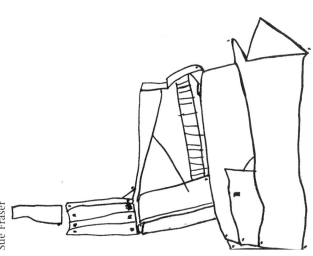

Sue Fraser

Ian's plan for the drawbridge

Documentation roles for drawbridge

Ian had drawn a plan for a drawbridge at home. He studied this carefully and from it was able to make a wooden bridge for the castle. He kept telling us we would need a drill to fasten it and some ropes. We brought these in, and, with a definite idea in mind, Ian was able to tell us where he needed to drill the holes. With a little help Ian was able to drill the holes on his own. He discovered that the ropes were too big for the hole, and so suggested we drill another one beside the first to make it bigger. This idea did not prove too successful, as instead of one big hole, we now had two little ones. One of the other children who was watching suggested he might need a smaller rope. From the bucket of strings we offered he was able to choose the ones that fit, and managed to tie them to the bridge.

The next step required him to decide where the other end of the ropes were to go. At first he wanted them to go through the crenellations, but I thought this might break them off. He chose two other possible locations, and after I held the ropes up so he could see which he preferred, he made his decision. After making little pencil marks where he would need to drill, he was able to successfully drill the holes right through the castle walls. He threaded the strings through and tried it out—IT WORKED!

He then drilled and wired the bridge to the castle at the bottom as he told me it would slip side to side if we didn't. The other children gathered around to see the bridge in action. Ian let them all have a turn to pull it up and down. The children were all thrilled and seemed amazed that it worked. "WOW!"

When the book Linda created of the block-play vignettes began to go home, the parents became involved and interested in the daily additions to the Castle project. Soon they were sending in books, rocks, metal, wood, as well as supporting their child in making box castles and drawings for the project. When Nicole's castle arrived it was the catalyst for the making of the big castle. A project has many facets; sometimes the speed is overwhelming, and at other times the lulls make us question what we are doing. Each time this hiatus in the project happened, one of the above events would point the way for further exploration. The projects seem to come to a natural end when no new ideas are being generated or when the school year is over. A finale of

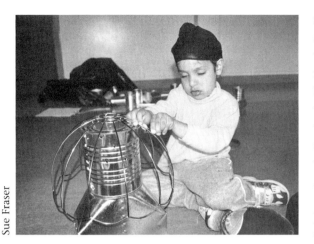

Sue Fraser

Jashanjot making the visor for the knight

some sort is always planned as a way of wrapping up the work. For the Circus project it was a circus performance by the children, complete with lions, horses, and tightrope walkers. For the Castle and Knight project it was a trip to see a castle and a visit by a Chinese dragon.

Michelle summed up her experience working with children and families from diverse cultural backgrounds in a program inspired by Reggio Emilia: "A successful program creates a 'circle of we'; that is, it provides opportunities for the children, teachers, families, and the community to build relationships. When the environment is set up as the third teacher and the children are free to interact with that environment in a way that is meaningful to them, with teachers that listen and respond to children and believe them to be competent, then children will do remarkable things. In such an environment children are able to self-organize. Some children have big ideas; others help carry them out, almost like threads weaving back and forth to create a tapestry. The proverbial ball is passed from child to child to teacher and back again over and over, creating a whole. The teachers support the learning by providing materials, documentation, provocations, and time to enable the children to go deeper in their thinking and understanding. When parents and even the community are involved they learn to value what the children are learning, they become aware of their child and all the other children as part of a group. They come to understand that their child is not an island but a valuable piece of the mosaic within the 'circle of we'" (interview, October 2004).

Anne Luke, director of the Early Learning Centre in Regina, Saskatchewan, said in a conversation that her work with families from different cultural backgrounds has helped her to understand that "the more diverse someone gets from you, the more self-aware you need to be, and you have to understand that your own perspective is influencing the relationship. Multiculturalism is understanding yourself and getting away from what you expect" (conversation, June 28, 2004). In working with children and families from diverse cultural backgrounds, teachers become increasingly aware of how important it is to make explicit "taken for granted ideas" that dominate attitudes and perceptions of others. When teachers, through a process like critical reflection are given the opportunity of discussing stereotypes of race and gender, they become aware of the need for change in their own attitudes and beliefs. Further, during the process of documenting the children's experiences in the classroom, different understandings emerge of children and their potentials. This, in turn, lessens the likelihood that some children will be listened to more than others in the group. Practice becomes more equitable and fair, and the children's confidence in themselves grows as they know they are each a valued member of the group.

The Asian Image of the Child

On visiting preschools and working with students in Taiwan and China, I was always amazed at how quickly the children and students got down to work, how efficiently they conceptualized the task in hand, and how skilled they were in carrying it out. Education in Asia is based on a centuries-old Confucian tradition. Teachers are respected for their wisdom and knowledge, and their role is to establish order and to be the authority in the classroom. The method of teaching is often through drill and repetitive activities. The teacher will demonstrate a task and the children are expected to take the role of an apprentice, to watch and listen and follow the rules. This contrasts with Western pedagogy, especially with constructivist theory, in which the teacher is seen as a partner with the children in the co-construction of learning in the classroom.

We have always believed in the West that taking a very structured approach to learning destroys inventiveness and creates conformity. George Forman, however, states that the Asian students he has got to know in his classes are "inventive, have deep understanding of the material and excel in complex disciplines such as math and science" (Forman 2003).

Sue Fraser

Puppet face made by Ken in Tainan, Taiwan

I was always amazed in the classes I taught in Asia at how creative and skilled students were in the use of materials. In a puppet-making class I taught in Taiwan, one student used a zipper to make the mouth for a puppet. He called his puppet "Mr. Shut-up" and in the puppet show produced by the students at

Mural painted by the children and parents at
Sunny Montessori Children's House, Taiwan

the end of the class, every time the puppet was cheeky he had his mouth zipped shut. In the preschools in Reggio Emilia, I watched teachers demonstrate how to use materials; the children, like the Chinese children I observed in Asia, would watch and listen. The Asian children and the Italian children we saw in Reggio Emilia were all very skilled in the use of materials. They were also able to use materials in very creative ways.

In Taiwan I worked with a group of parents and children who were painting murals to decorate their classrooms at Halloween. I was amazed at how efficiently as a group they achieved such a complex task. The murals, which combined images from Asian culture and Halloween, were spectacular hanging in the classrooms at the Halloween party that night.

Susan Lee*, who grew up in Taiwan and who is familiar with the Reggio Emilia approach, has observed teachers' growing interest in Reggio Emilia in Asia. She said:

> I think the teachers in Asia would agree with the view that children are competent, resourceful, inventive, and full of interesting ideas. When planning curriculum, the teachers need to consider if the contents would interest the children and stimulate their curiosity and learning desires. The teachers need to trust the children and believe they have the ability to do any task. The teachers also need to be humble enough so they can have open minds to see new things and learn from the children. I have seen this happening in many schools in Taiwan because many teachers nowadays have had the chance to study in foreign countries and learn new ideas and have new experiences. They are able to apply what they learned and have integrated their experiences into their teachings.

*Reproduced courtesy of Susan Lee

I have seen many changes in the way the teachers are planning their classroom space so that it does become "the third teacher in the classroom." In the past, most teachers decorated the room with commercial materials or adult images. Nowadays the teachers know how to plan the environment by using the children's ideas or works to reflect the children's strengths, interests, and culture. Although most of the display ideas still do come from the adults, the teachers have made obvious progress in incorporating children's ideas.

I think the idea of "negotiated curriculum" has started to take root in Asia. However, I think it will take time to put the concept into practice because it takes great courage and is still a challenge for teachers to try this approach. It also requires strong support from the educational system. When planning curriculum the teachers do consider the children's interests and learning objectives as the most important factors; but, in practice, the plans are still based on the teacher's view and opinions. Most teachers would be hesitant to negotiate curriculum because it's a new idea for them and because they don't have the confidence to see how it would work in their teaching.

Most schools and teachers in Asia use documentation to make their program visible. However, the documentation panels display only the end products that children have made. They rarely show the process of how children did the work or project. Most schools use communication books to inform parents about the program, but they contain written information only. I think it's hard for parents to grasp the whole picture of how their child learns in school. It would make more sense to parents if teachers included the children's drawings and showed the steps in the development of the project. Parents then could see the stages in the project displayed on the documentation panels.

I think both Montessori and the Reggio Emilia approach have their values. People also value them differently. Although Montessori programs are very popular in Asia, people have begun to see the value of Reggio Emilia. Some schools have even combined the two approaches. Education plays a very important role in Asia. Any programs that improve the educational system will be popular in that society (Lee 2004).

The Reggio Emilia Approach in China

by Jennifer Wang*

There is a common saying in China that "A child is a piece of white paper, and the educators can draw the most beautiful picture on it." This dictum reveals the traditional Chinese view of education. For thousands of years, the teacher's role was to pass on knowledge from the great thinkers of the past to the students. The students were required to absorb their ideas and learn them by heart. The student was thought of as a container waiting to be filled. In early childhood education, it is generally the teacher's right to decide what and how to learn and then to draw up a lesson plan and implement it in the classroom. In the past, the teacher was the authority in the classroom and could not be challenged. The children were expected to be passive and obedient in the classroom, although their creativity was encouraged. Curriculum was organized into separate subject areas—language, math, art, music, and so on—and the teaching emphasis was on acquiring knowledge and skills.

In the past decade, the theories of John Dewey and Jean Piaget have been introduced into China, and more and more Chinese teachers have come to realize that a child is not only a piece of paper, but also a painter himself, and that children have the ability to learn and have plenty of ideas. Some educators accepted this child-centred theory, but found it hard to make changes because when they practised it in the classroom, they faced opposition from traditional thought. In the past ten years, educators have been struggling to find a balance between teacher-centred and child-centred education.

Reggio Emilia is an excellent example for Chinese teachers of the role of children in education. More and more educators, especially among the younger generation, agree with the Reggio Emilia image of the child as "rich, strong, and powerful." These teachers are giving the children more opportunities to express their own ideas and are paying more attention to discovering the children's real interests.

The role of the teacher in Reggio Emilia is to be an observer, a learner, and a researcher as well as a partner, supporter, and co-constructor with the children in the classroom. The teacher is neither a leader in the traditional way nor just an observer in the classroom, but is closely involved with the children at their level. The most valuable part of the Reggio Emilia approach, especially for Chinese teachers, is that the theory is carried out in daily classroom practice. The image of the children

*Reproduced courtesy of Jennifer Wang

and the role of the teacher in Reggio Emilia have had a very powerful influence on teachers and even on policy makers. The new Curriculum for Early Childhood Education developed by the Department of Education now puts the children and their interests in first place. It also defines the role of the teacher as one of "supporter, cooperator, and guide."

However, teachers trying to change their role are still facing problems in determining how to discover the children's interests and then develop them into a project; when to get involved and how much guidance to give the children; and how to achieve educational and curriculum goals in daily practice.

There are now many kindergartens in China, especially in big cities like Shenzhen, Nanjing, Shanghai, and Beijing, following the spirit of Reggio Emilia. They have set up Reggio Emilia–style learning centres and art studios, brought in more natural materials, and provided more learning possibilities. Documentation of projects shows how the children are learning. There are fewer fancy teacher-made decorations on the wall and more displays of the children's work.

The teachers and children are now introducing traditional Chinese culture and literature into their projects. For example, in our kindergarten, Golden Maple Sunshine Bilingual Kindergarten, the children worked on a project investigating moon cakes. Before the coming of the Moon Festival, the children showed us they were interested in the moon cakes displayed on grocery shelves. They had many questions; for instance, they asked why people eat moon cakes during the Moon Festival, and how the beautiful decorations on the top of the cakes were made. The teachers and children decided to do research on this topic. They started from the history of the moon cake. The children questioned their parents and even their grandparents and developed more ideas for the project. Then the teachers found some resources and story books. They discussed the stories and noted the different versions of the history of the Moon Festival. They

Sue Fraser

Exploring materials at the Golden Maple Sunshine Bilingual Kindergarten in Beijing then visited the kitchen in the kindergarten and observed the process of making moon cakes. They studied the different moon cakes carefully and designed their own decorations for moon cakes. They showed the teachers that they wanted to bake them themselves, so the teachers invited the cook to guide them in making the moon cakes in the classroom. They found the right temperature and baked the cakes by themselves. The children observed how the moon cakes changed when they were baking. They were so proud of their own moon cakes. Then they decided to sell them and went to the market to find out the price of a case of moon cakes. They recorded the price range and found out the normal price. Although they ended up giving their moon cakes to their parents at the Moon Festival Party as a surprise, they learned how to evaluate a commercial product and how to set a price.

In our experience, although the teachers and the children really enjoy the Reggio Emilia projects, they still have a long way to go. First, the Reggio Emilia approach needs highly qualified teachers who know how to discover the children's interests and how to give them help when they need it. Second, the cost is a concern to most of the kindergartens in China. To apply the Reggio Emilia approach, the teachers must provide plenty of materials in the classroom and do the documentation. Tight budgets mean some kindergartens may not have the equipment to do it. Third, the traditional ways are still valued. Education is still under the control of a system that attaches great importance to the acquisition of knowledge and skills rather than to the importance of children developing abilities.

Compared with the Montessori program, the Reggio Emilia approach still needs time to become accepted. Montessori was introduced to China in the first two decades of the 20th century. It became very popular in the 1980s. The Montessori approach of dividing the curriculum into different areas, such as language, science, and math, more closely matches traditional Chinese methods. The use of set materials also makes the Montessori program easier to understand and implement. Both the process and the results of learning are more obvious than in the Reggio Emilia approach. That is why most big-city kindergartens use the Montessori program and most of them are still hesitant about introducing the Reggio Emilia approach.

Despite the difficulties, more and more educators would like to experience the happiness Reggio Emilia brings. We are gathering information and improving our understanding. I believe the Reggio Emilia approach will gradually be accepted by more and more kindergartens in China.

The foundation of an early childhood education program is a shared understanding of the image of the child—an image that is informed by theory and co-constructed through observation, reflection, and discussion. When teachers, in collaboration with their colleagues, take the time to examine their own and their collective images of the child, a process of change is set in motion that reaches into every aspect of their work with young children. For instance, their understanding of the learning process deepens and their relationships in and out of the classroom change. When teachers realize that the children have interesting ideas to share and points of view to investigate, they begin to listen to children, plan curriculum differently, create environments that support collaborative investigation, and even change the kind of materials offered to children. For instance, when teachers become interested in children's ideas and interests, they will want to provide children with tools, such as pens, paint, and clay, to make their thinking visible. Documentation becomes an essential part of this process as teachers strive to uncover the learning paths that are emerging in the room. All these ideas are examined in more detail in the following chapters. When the child is seen as "a producer of culture, values, and rights, competent in living and learning" (Ceppi and Zini 1998, 117), the adults who are creating the spaces in which children learn will ensure that "children's learning paths and processes thus pass through the relationship with the cultural and scholastic context which, as such must be a 'formative environment,' an ideal place for development" (Ceppi and Zini 1998, 117).

Chapter 3

Hooded Merganser

The Role of the Teacher

Questions to Consider:

- What philosophical and theoretical principles shape the role of the teacher?

- What ideas inspired by the teachers in Reggio Emilia will influence changes in the teacher's role in North America?

- How are these ideas about the role of the teachers interpreted in practice?

- What is the job description of an early childhood educator today?

- What does a teacher implementing the Reggio Emilia approach need to understand about the role of the teacher in the Reggio Emilia system?

- What are the benefits of the teacher's role in the Reggio Emilia system? What are the challenges?

- In a poststructural world, how has the role of the teacher changed?

The central act of adults ... is to activate, especially indirectly, the meaning-making competencies of children as a basis of all learning. They must try to capture the right moments, and then find the right approaches, for bringing together, into a fruitful dialogue, their meanings and interpretations with those of the children.

—Loris Malaguzzi

THE CHANGING ROLE OF THE TEACHER

A hundred years ago, no one would have been able to foresee how much growth and change there would be in early childhood education in the 20th century. In the second half of the 19th century, industrialization and immigration brought many families to work in the cities of North America. Many of the women in these families became working mothers and no longer had the support of the extended families who traditionally had taken care of their young children.

The first to respond to the needs of working mothers in North America were the nuns in Quebec City and Montreal who opened crèches (day nurseries) and salles d'asile (shelters for older children) in the

1850s. The earliest nonreligious day care in North America, aside from orphan care or child welfare, was probably the Day Nursery of Philadelphia, which opened in 1863. The growth of day care in Canada was much slower than in the United States, probably owing to Canada's smaller population. In 1892 Canada had only three day nurseries, one in each of the cities of Toronto, Montreal, and Hamilton, whereas by 1898 the United States had 175 day nurseries. The number in Canada did not increase until 1911, when six of the seven largest cities in Canada had day nurseries (Prochner 1994, 10–15). The purpose of these early day cares was to provide children with a clean, safe environment, in which the teacher's role was to ensure the children's health and moral behaviour, a role that today would be seen as custodial caregiver. The change in the role of the teacher from custodial caregiver to early childhood educator did not begin until public school kindergartens based on Froebelian principles were opened in the United States and Canada.

The Evolution of the Role of the Teacher

In 1856 Margaretha Schurz, a student of Froebel, opened the first kindergarten in the United States in Watertown, Wisconsin. Although this was a private school for German-speaking children, it inspired educators such as Elizabeth Peabody to study the Froebel method. After her return from observing Froebel kindergartens in Germany, Elizabeth Peabody persuaded William Harris, the superintendent of schools in St. Louis, Missouri, to open in 1873 the first public school kindergarten in North America. Susan Blow, who had trained in the Froebelian method, was hired as the first teacher. In 1876 James L. Hughes, the superintendent of the Toronto public school system, visited the kindergarten exhibits at the Philadelphia Centennial Exhibition and saw demonstrations of Froebel's methods. On his return to Toronto he set out to find a teacher to help him start a kindergarten based on Froebelian principles. In 1883 Ada Marean, who later became Mrs. Hughes, was hired as the head teacher in the first kindergarten in Canada, which opened in the Louisa Street School. Soon after, in 1885, the Toronto Normal School began a teacher-training program for kindergarten teachers, and by 1895 there were 40 kindergartens in the public schools in Toronto. The following excerpt from a lesson notebook from 1881 presents a typical schedule for the morning in one of these schools:

Opening exercises (prayer, hymn "God Is Love")

Songs ("Good Morning, Kind Teacher," "Thumb & Fingers")

General ball exercise

Modelling

Third gift with children

Sticks and tablets

Folding

Sewing (vertical in red, connect with sticks)

The circle

Games

Closing song (Dixon 1994, 8)

The Froebelian interpretation of the importance of learning through play, as can be seen from the schedule above, allowed the children hands-on experience in using materials, such as paper folding, sewing, and weaving using paper cut into strips. Teachers, however, were required to follow a carefully prescribed procedure in presenting activities to the children; thus, the learning was a structured experience for children. Froebel designed didactic tools called *gifts* and *occupations,* which teachers used to teach concepts such as colour, shape, number, symmetry, and proportion, as well as skills such as weaving, threading, and paper cutting. In his system there were ten gifts, consisting of materials that children were to use in specific ways. For instance, the third gift, mentioned in the lesson plan above, consisted of eight one-inch cubes. A child received the gift from the teacher and after playing with it was expected to learn number concepts, specifically divisibility, and the value of self-activity. The occupations that Froebel advocated were more open ended and designed to allow children to practise useful skills. Sewing, the occupation listed in the lesson plan above, was designed to increase the child's awareness of lines and to practise the art of embroidery (Froebel [1887] 1974, 286).

It was not until the early part of the 20th century, when John Dewey adapted Froebel's methods in founding the progressive school movement, that the role of the teacher became less directive, and children were allowed more freedom to follow their own ideas.

The child study movement also had an impact on the role of the teacher. In the 1920s and 1930s many college and university campuses in Canada and the United States opened laboratory schools. Disciplines such as home economics, psychology, and education needed a setting where children could be studied in order to gain more knowledge about child development and child psychology. It was during this period, for instance, that Dr. Arnold Gesell founded the Gesell Institute at Yale University for the purpose of studying children and identifying the "norms" of development. In Canada, the Institute of Child Study at St. George's School on the University of Toronto campus was established as an autonomous faculty. Many graduates from the institute spread out across Canada, filling important positions in early childhood education. Not only did the child study movement create a solid theoretical foundation for early childhood education, but it also provided teachers with a greater sense of professionalism in their work. As teachers began to study theories about child development and methods for observing children, they increased their understanding of children's behaviour and development. This knowledge, in turn, enabled them to see children as individuals and to plan programs to meet the needs of each child. The grounding student teachers receive in the study of child development and in the philosophy of learning through play (reaching back to Froebel and Dewey) are the tenets that make early childhood education a discipline separate from teaching older children.

World War II provided the next impetus for early childhood education. Day cares were opened across the United States and Canada to care for the children of mothers who were recruited for war work. The most famous of these day cares were the Kaiser Nurseries in Portland, Oregon, which were established to enable mothers to work in the shipyards. At the end of the war, many of these high-quality day cares were closed, and women returned to their homes. It was not until almost two decades later that there were any further advances in the field of early childhood education.

In the 1960s the work of Jean Piaget became more widely known in North America. His theory of cognitive development caused major changes in every aspect of early childhood education, such as in the delivery of the program, the use of space, and the kind of educational materials used in the classroom. His theory also caused a major change in the role of the teacher. Jean Piaget said that "if the aim of intellectual training is to form the intelligence rather than to stock the memory, and to produce intellectual explorers rather than mere erudition, then traditional education is manifestly guilty of a grave deficiency" (1971, 51). These words had a powerful impact on the way teachers delivered the content of their lessons. In the second half of the 20th century, teachers increasingly began to change from seeing children as empty containers who need to be filled with information to viewing them as active agents who construct their own knowledge from their experiences in the environment.

As a student at the Child Study Centre at the University of British Columbia in the mid-1960s, I found it interesting to watch this change in the role of the teacher take place. The Child Study Centre was a laboratory school for children age three to five, which closely followed John Dewey's principles. (In the early 1960s the theories of Jean Piaget were only just beginning to have an impact on early childhood education.) The program at the Child Study Centre was based on the theory that children learn through play, but the curriculum also provided the children with many real experiences, such as cooking in the classroom and cultivating a garden in the outdoor playground. The classroom was divided into areas for specialized activities such as art, woodworking, block building, and dramatic play. The room had a library corner, water and sand play areas, and shelves stocked with puzzles, games, and small blocks for fine motor development. The first hour of each morning and afternoon session was scheduled as free play with special activities, such as preparing fruit to make a salad, set out on one or two tables in the classroom. Children then gathered together for about half an hour for circle time, when they listened to the teacher read a story, sang a few songs, and had a short discussion about some topic of interest. Finger plays such as "Eenzy Weenzy Spider" were frowned upon, as were books that were not didactic. The stories by Lucy Sprague Mitchell, which dealt with the "here and now," and the books of Ezra Jack Keats, such as *The Snowy Day,* which explored a specific concept, were considered the most appropriate books for children. The last hour, no matter what the weather, the teachers took the children outside to play.

It was during circle time that the conflict in the role of the teacher emerged. The head teacher in the five-year-olds' class believed that it was the teacher's responsibility to teach the children specific skills and content; for instance, she believed it was important to teach children how to develop memorization strategies. She set up an exercise during circle time in which she required the children to memorize the names of the animals whose pictures she had pinned on a board. She would take one picture away, and the children would have to identify the missing animal. She taught the children strategies to help them with this activity, such as sorting the animals and counting the number of animals in each group. Each day she also had a specific lesson plan based on a concept she wanted to teach the children. In one lesson, she asked the children to come up to the front, one by one, and place pictures of vegetables in the correct position on a chart that was divided into two sections, the lower half representing underground, and the upper half above ground. At the staff meeting later that day, the other teachers in the centre noted that they thought these lessons were too structured because she had allowed very little opportunity for the children to actively engage in the activity. They suggested that a more appropriate aid to memory would be to help the children remember when they harvested the vegetables from their garden in the summer and what seeds they had planted in the spring. As well, they felt that a more appropriate time for the children to learn the concepts would be when they were picking or digging the vegetables out of the ground. The debate went on for a long time, and the argument became heated. I could see how hard it was for the teacher to give up the responsibility of teaching the children content and instead to allow them the freedom to investigate and develop skills on their own. I remember one of the teachers quoting from J. McVicker Hunt's book *Intelligence and Experience,* which emphasized that children's active interaction with real materials is essential for the growth of intelligence.

The work of Diana Baumrind, which looked at different styles of parenting, also had an impact on the role of the teacher in the latter half of the 1960s. She termed these styles authoritative, authoritarian, and permissive (she later divided permissive into permissive/indulgent and permissive/neglecting). Authoritative parents, according to Baumrind, are consistent, affectionate, interested in their children as individuals, and able to communicate clearly their expectations for responsible behaviour. Authoritarian parents are controlling and offer little nurturance and affection, whereas permissive parents are inconsistent in their expectations and expect less of their children. Baumrind stated that authoritative parents are the most effective in raising children who have good social skills and are self-confident and self-assertive (1967). This research helped teachers find a balance between having a too-authoritarian role and being too permissive as the style of teaching became less structured in the classroom. The 1960s were an exciting time for early childhood education. Everything the teacher did seemed to come into question, especially any form of authority. What emerged was a new role for the teacher, one that was far more democratic and less didactic. The emphasis changed from teaching children content to preparing a stimulating environment and then standing back and observing the children's play.

The 1970s added a new dimension to the role of the teacher in Canada and the United States. This was a time when issues such as poverty and multiculturalism came to the fore. In the United States the Headstart program, which had begun in the mid-1960s, began to have a major impact on early childhood education. It began as an attempt to give children who were outside the cultural mainstream an opportunity to catch up with children who entered school better prepared to cope with the demands of public school education. In Canada preschools such as the Sexsmith Multicultural preschool were started to help children who did not speak English as a first language to adjust to a new language and culture. Advocacy became an important part of the teacher's role as educators struggled to get adequate resources to provide children with quality early childhood education programs. The freedom of the 1960s began to disappear, and *accountability* became a key word. Planning programs based on themes such as spring or community helpers enabled teachers to demonstrate that they were doing more than just providing baby-sitting services.

This brief history of early childhood education in North America shows how the change over the last hundred years from an image of the child as needy to a view of the child as competent has raised questions about the teacher's role. Before the turn of the century, the child in the early crèches and day cares was seen as needing protection. This view was followed by an image of an ignorant child who needed instruction, and more recently by a view of the child who learns by finding things out for herself. There are, however, still strong echoes of an earlier age when children were seen as weak and needing protection, such as when we call children who need extra support "children with special needs" and when we use the phrase "meeting the needs" as opposed to considering the abilities of children in our care.

At each phase in the history of early childhood education, there was a major change in the role of the teacher. First, teachers were mainly concerned with the child's health, safety, and moral development; then for a long time teachers emphasized prescribed information and skills. More recently, teachers focused on providing children with an environment that stimulated exploration. Finally, teachers added the notion of rights for the child to their image of the child, as teachers found they had to act as advocates for children in need of resources. The educators in Reggio Emilia believe strongly in the right of children to a fair share of the resources in an affluent society and in the right to an "authentic" childhood, one in which children are expected to be, as Gianni Rodari said, "no longer a consumer of culture and values, but a creator and producer of values and culture" (1996, 116). In Reggio Emilia schools, children have the right to a world in which they are respected, and their childhood is valued as a time when they lay down the foundation that will enable them to grow into adults who are creative and critical thinkers and responsible citizens in a democratic society.

In the 21st century we are encountering major changes again in the role of the teacher as we move into the postmodern world. Many of these changes have been inspired by ideas learned from Reggio Emilia, but also through questioning the knowledge and theories prevalent in the modernist scientific era. Writers, such as MacNaughton (2005) and Hillevi Lenz Taguchi (2006), urge us to think critically about the scientific truths we have previously taken for granted and to come to understand that "...the same object or phenomena is understood differently in different meaning making contexts" (Lenz Taguchi 2006, 258). For instance, the stages of development as clearly outlined by theorists such as Erikson and Piaget need to be considered in light of the fact that they were developed from observations of children in the West in the last century. We now have to question whether these stages of development can apply to all children, for instance children reared in aboriginal communities in Canada and elsewhere in the world. When we are faced with the possibility that there is no "universal truth" applicable to all cultures in a poststructural world, we have to go further and question the role of assessment tools, program planning, etc. The answers to these questions have a profound effect on the role of the teacher and the changes we begin to see happening in relationships in the classroom and with the family and community as a whole.

THE STRUCTURE OF REGGIO EMILIA SCHOOLS

The Reggio Emilia municipal preschools have developed in the last half century into a clearly delineated educational system with defined roles and responsibilities. The elected superintendent of the department of education in Reggio Emilia oversees fourteen infant-toddler centres (for children four months to three years old) and twenty-two preschools (for children three to six years old). A department director is head of two sectors—the administrative and the pedagogical sectors. The administrative manager heads a team of ten administrative personnel, and the director of the pedagogical sector coordinates the team of nine pedagogisti, one of whom is an expert in special education. Each pedagogista supervises three or four schools and infant centres, supporting the teachers and staff in each school team, interpreting the philosophy, and acting as consultant and mediator when necessary. There are eleven teachers, one cook, and three full-time and three part-time auxiliary staff in each infant–toddler centre. The preschools usually have three classrooms, one each for three-, four-, and five-year-old children. There are two co-teachers for each preschool classroom, one cook, and two full-time and three part-time auxiliary staff members. Also, each preschool employs an atelierista, or studio teacher, who specializes in the visual arts curriculum and in how young children relate to materials and use them to represent their ideas. Parents play an important role in Reggio Emilia schools, participating in activities and serving on classroom or school committees. They also have representation on the school advisory council, which is composed of ten to fifteen parent representatives plus members of the school staff in rotation. The advisory council does not have decision-making powers, but it is influential as it is represented by the general coordinating committee, which works together with the municipal administration to determine the educational, political, and cultural aims and objectives of the infant–toddler centres and preschools.

The Teacher's Role

Central to the role of the teacher in the schools in Reggio Emilia is the responsibility for forming a circle of relationships. Teachers work with one another, with the parents, and with the children to form "a mutual community of learners." This means that the children's learning becomes a shared responsibility. When this basic tenet is understood, other essential components of the teacher's role become obvious, especially the importance of communication. Communicating with children means listening carefully to their ideas, participating with them in conversation, and documenting their experiences. Communicating with teachers and other staff involves a high level of collaboration at every level, such as in discussing the observations of the children, interpreting these observations, and making progettazione, or flexible plans, through negotiation with children for future directions. Documentation has to be done in collaboration with all the participants involved to capture a complete picture of the experience. Collaboration and communication are essential skills when relationship is at the core of a teacher's role.

Another important part of the role of the teacher is to act as co-constructor of knowledge. The teachers at the Michelangelo School, in a discussion of the role of teachers in the preschools in Reggio Emilia, told the Canadian delegation in 1993 that for children to be able to co-construct knowledge they must be able to find the right environment and a partner who can facilitate this learning. The adult in this partnership cannot be a teacher in the traditional sense; he has to be a provocateur who can support and help the children in building their own knowledge. Jerome Bruner states,

> So back to the innocent but fundamental question: how best to conceive of a subcommunity that specializes in learning among its members? One obvious answer would be that it is a place where, among other things, learners help each other learn, each according to her abilities. And this, of course, need not exclude the presence of somebody serving in the role of the teacher. It simply implies that the teacher does not play that role as a monopoly, that learners "scaffold" for each other as well. (1996, 21)

This statement illustrates a major shift in the traditional relationship between the teacher and the learners. The teacher in Reggio Emilia is not viewed as the expert or the sole dispenser of information; rather, the role of the teacher becomes one that is shared equally among members of the group. There is an implicit acknowledgment that all the participants can make a worthwhile contribution to the learning experience. The teacher's role is to create a partnership with the learners, to walk beside them as together they launch themselves into the experience and as together they begin the process of the co-construction of knowledge. At times, however, the teacher will have to act as a provocateur, to prod the learners to move forward or in a new direction. Sometimes, it may become necessary to take stronger action, to put children in crises so they can come up with solutions. This idea is similar to Piaget's concept of disequilibrium, when a teacher sets up a situation in which the child has to adapt to a new set of circumstances. Carolyn Edwards used the term *traffic jam* at the Reggio Emilia Symposium in North Vancouver in May 1998 to describe the same idea of disentangling all the jumbled pieces so that the child is free to move forward again, perhaps in a different direction.

Sometimes the teacher has to break up a temporary idea that may not be a lasting solution. Amelia Gambetti demonstrated this notion at La Villetta school in the early stages of the Amusement Park for Birds project. The children had been building their theories about how a fountain works, when suddenly they were sidetracked into talking about electric currents.

Filippo: Or one can die because the current [electricity] can get into the water.

Andrea: And one gets a shock. The current is in the water because the current comes, gets wet, and then one dies.

Simone: In the fountain there is water that runs, not the current [electric].

Amelia: How does the water arrive to the fountains?

Filippo: There is a pipe underground. [Forman and Gandini 1994]

Amelia did a number of things here: she listened carefully to the children's discussion, intervening when she felt she needed to break up the temporary idea of electric currents; she provoked the children to think beyond the limit of the fountain itself; and she questioned them about how the water gets into the fountain. This example demonstrates that a teacher who inspired by the Reggio Emilia approach has to be more than just an observer. She takes an active role in the discussion, provoking the children to think more deeply about the ideas they are working on.

The educators at Michelangelo School told the Canadian delegation study tour in 1993 that the teacher's role is to observe children and judge when to supply the technical information they require to carry out their ideas. We observed, as an example, how a teacher worked with a child to help her make a clay drawing of a dancer. It was a challenging task for the child to place the rolled coils of clay to form the dancer's body, showing how the legs, feet, arms, and hands moved as she danced. The child also had made the dancer's long hair from thin coils of clay. We watched how the teacher discussed with her how to place these coils on the dancer's head, making them appear to swing above her shoulders to suggest the movement of the dancer's body. The teacher stayed beside the child for almost half an hour, offering support and giving technical suggestions. She showed the child how to mix slip, a soupy clay mixture, which acts like cement in joining pieces of clay together. When the clay figure was complete, she helped the child carefully lift it onto a sheet of cardboard to dry.

The teachers at Michelangelo told us that the adult has to understand that children do not have "the strength to sustain work." It is the role of the teacher, therefore, to help the children stay interested in their work and bring their thoughts and ideas to fruition. The theory of Vygotsky is at work here. "The discrepancy between a child's actual mental age and the level he reaches in solving problems with assistance indicates the zone of his proximal development ... with assistance, every child can do more than he can by himself— though only within the limits set by the state of his development" (Vygotsky 1962, 103). Bruner uses the term *scaffolding* to describe this process (1996, 21).

The teachers at Michelangelo concluded the discussion by pointing out that it was not easy for teachers to work with an emerging curriculum. "Many teachers," they said, "are too rigid in expecting what children will do. The teacher must wait, live with uncertainty, but in the end, the children may do things that may be a surprise. It means to be open to listening to children, and sometimes the adult must accept that the project is only going to be a short one."

The Atelierista's Role

The atelieristi in the municipal preschools in Reggio Emilia have specialized training in the visual arts. They also have a deep understanding of children's relationship with materials and how they learn from them. In each of the schools there is an atelier, where children work with the atelierista. These areas are richly supplied with art materials. Here, groups of children work on progettazione such as the lion project and the Amusement Park for Birds. The atelieristi work closely with the other teachers, becoming part of the circle of relationships in each school. It is the atelieristi's particular responsibility to help in the development of the children's aesthetic awareness. They also provide the children with opportunities for using the hundred languages of children and collaborate in developing and displaying the documentation of the children's experiences.

Giovanni Piazza, the atelierista at La Villetta school, in his speech to the second Canadian delegation, gave us insight into the complexity and depth of an atelierista's job. He said small and large projects take a great deal of preparation, "looking at it first, analyzing it well, planning and constructing together with the children." Before a project is about to begin, he asks himself, "How can I fill myself up to be ready to see [the right path to take]?" He stressed the importance of taking ample time, listening to children, giving them opportunities using a variety of different media to express their thinking, and then waiting for interesting ideas to emerge. He said that the observation material (the written notes, photographs, and collected materials) that he shares with the children lets them know "that we are in a narrative," that the project is beginning to evolve!

The Pedagogista's Role

The pedagogisti play an essential role in the Reggio Emilia system. For the last few years, I have had the opportunity to act in an informal way as a pedagogista for a number of preschools and child-care centres that have begun to embrace the Reggio Emilia approach. I have found that only after teachers have decided amongst themselves to deconstruct their practice and begin the slow process of co-constructing a different approach to early childhood education inspired by Reggio Emilia can the pedagogista begin to have some real impact in supporting the teachers.

The process of changing beliefs and practices cannot be hurried. The pedagogista's first task is to build a relationship with the teachers. This may take time, depending on how soon trust is established between teachers and pedagogisti and how willing teachers are to change their beliefs. The pedagogista builds trust by first taking on the role of the listener and then asking key questions. Putting oneself in the role of the learner as opposed to the expert is essential until trust is established and the group itself begins to search for new approaches to problematic situations.

The pedagogista may begin the process of change by helping the teachers identify the values they feel are important in their work and then by ensuring that the environment conveys these values to the children, families, and community. The pedagogista will need to help the teachers articulate their image of the child so the team achieves coherence. Teachers begin the process of deconstruction when they let go of their own agendas and transfer their attention to the children. When teachers observe children closely and free themselves from preconceived notions about what they need to be taught, they become aware of the real interests and capabilities of the children they work with. This awareness causes teachers to deconstruct rituals like circle time and practices like theme planning. In my experience this is the painful part, but essential in beginning the process of reconstruction. Then teachers can begin to shape the environment to support and enhance team values and the qualities of their particular group of children. This all demands a great deal of collaboration; before teachers can successfully begin co-construction, they need to establish trust in each other and truly begin to function as a cohesive team.

Teachers often need help in identifying which topics have the possibility of developing into interesting projects. The pedagogista can help the teachers decide if a topic the children are interested in has, in Giovanni Piazza's terms, enough surface area to sustain the children's interest and enough breadth to provide a rich learning experience. "We are always pleased when a project involves a number of very different problems from different domains of knowledge, and when these are dealt with by the children for a good reason" (Rubizzi 2001, 110). The process involves listening and talking to children and providing them with the kinds of materials that enable them to make their thinking visible. Teachers may need to learn effective ways to present materials to children. Teachers may also need help with the process of negotiating or co-constructing the project. At this point the pedagogista can try to help the teachers deepen the children's learning by asking questions such as:

- What are the big ideas that are fuelling the children's interest in the topic?

- What materials would enable children to make their thinking or theories about the topic visible?

- Does the topic have enough surface area to sustain the children's interest over a long period of time?

- Is the environment acting effectively as a third teacher by enhancing their learning about the topic under investigation?

- Is the documentation providing opportunities for the group to revisit experiences and make future plans?

Documentation is essential in a program inspired by Reggio Emilia, and teachers often need the most help with this aspect of their work. When, what, and how to document have to be addressed. A pedagogista can also help teachers find the time and space to create documentation.

In the past few years the role of critical reflection has emerged as a powerful means of questioning "the taken for granted ideas" that prevail in early childhood programs. "Critical reflection is the process of questioning how power operates in the processes of teaching and learning and then using that knowledge to transform inequitable teaching and learning processes" (MacNaughton 2005, 7). The pedagogista can take advantage of her role to lead a team of teachers through the process of critical reflection. (See page 321 for a further description of the Collaborative Critical Reflective Protocol inspired by the "Rounds for Teachers" at Project Zero, Harvard University). One or more teachers would begin the process by presenting their observations and/or pedagogical documentation of an episode that occurred to the team and/or others interested. At the end of the presentation, the audience would respond with questions and comments. A discussion would follow in which different perspectives/readings would be examined as alternative ways of viewing the experience. The purpose of deconstructing the experience would be "about disrupt, destabilizations, undermining and challenging taken-for-granted notions, values, practices and pedagogy 'as usual'" (Lenz Taguchi, as cited in Sanchez 2009). The pedagogista would hope that after the teachers have undergone the process of deconstruction of the experience they would have achieved changed understandings and more equitable teaching practices. This was a particularly helpful procedure in helping a team of teachers and parents in the case of the Quadra Island Preschool construct a shared image of the child (see page 36).

At Douglas College the Collaborative Critical Reflective Protocol is used extensively with students in Children Teaching Teachers. Sanchez states that "This journey with students and colleagues of reflecting and interpreting the images of childhood using alternative discourses of pedagogy has contested the traditional teaching practices of the paradigm of developmental psychology in the Early Childhood Education Program at Douglas College (Sanchez 2009, 32). The students are able to construct an image of the child, for instance, free of the constraints of having to set a child within a prescribed stage of development.

The role of the pedagogista is complex but very rewarding as he or she has the key in early childhood programs to really affect change as MacNaughton says to do early childhood studies differently to make the world a better place (2005, 2).

From beginning to end the process of changing teachers' beliefs and practices is complex, and it is sometimes painful for them to let go of so much they have believed in. It is, however, a very rewarding journey for both the teachers and the pedagogista (Carr 2004).

The Teacher in Reggio Emilia and in North America

There are many similarities between the role of the teacher in North America and in the municipal preschools in Reggio Emilia. However, the teacher's role in Reggio Emilia is different in several significant ways, some of which are listed below.

1. *The role of the teacher as an observer is extended to documentor and researcher.* Observation is an important skill for all early childhood teachers, but the educators in Reggio Emilia have taken it a step further. Observation, for them, is only the first step in collecting the data that are used in developing documentation, which captures the story of the children's experiences in the classroom. The teacher then uses the documentation to revisit the experiences with the children and to communicate with parents and other visitors to the classroom. Documentation is taken a step further as it becomes a tool for teacher research.

2. *The role of the teacher as program planner changes to the role of creator of the environment as a third teacher.* Preparing a stimulating environment that fosters play and exploration is an essential part of the work of a teacher of preschool children. Creating an environment that acts as a third teacher in the classroom, however, is a new and challenging task for those inspired by the Reggio Emilia approach. Teachers will need to ask what has the environment as a third teacher come to mean in their context. They will consider in collaboration with colleagues what values they as a group believe should shape the kind of environment that will be responsive to the children and families in their classroom. They will examine each area of the room to ensure every space and object reflects these values. They will observe the children to discover their interests and then provide the kind of materials that will provoke further thinking and action. A classroom that is functioning successfully as a third teacher will be responsive to the children's interests, provide opportunities for children to make their thinking visible, and then foster further learning and engagement.

3. *The role of the teacher as curriculum planner changes to the role of the teacher as a co-constructor of knowledge.* Teachers usually plan experiences and activities for the children collaboratively with other teachers in the school. Inspired by the Reggio Emilia approach, however, the program is perceived as emerging from the children's

interests and ideas and in negotiation with them. This means that teachers need to meet more often to discuss and reflect on their observations and on the transcriptions they make of the children's conversations. Planning is still done in cooperation with others, but it becomes more spontaneous, it has to be done more often, and it involves more collaboration and negotiation with others.

4. *The role of the teacher as parent educator changes to the role of the teacher as a partner with parents.* Early childhood educators have always understood the importance of communicating with parents. For school to be a positive experience for children there has to be congruence between the children's experiences at home and at school. When relationship becomes a guiding principle, teachers will find themselves working even more closely with parents. The concept of transparency allows parents to enter their children's experiences at school. In turn, they will understand how valuable their contribution is to their children's education, and they will become more aware of the many different ways they can partici- pate in the program. Documentation is an important channel of communication between home and school. It not only keeps par- ents informed of day-to-day happenings in the classroom, but at a deeper level it makes the thinking of the children and teachers vis- ible. It describes the path the learning is pursuing and it helps par- ents understand the value of their children's experiences in school.

5. *The role of the teacher as communicator changes to the role of the teacher as listener, provocateur, and negotiator of meaning.* Communication, in its myriad forms—written, visual, and verbal—has always been important in early childhood settings, but the emphasis on collab- oration and documentation in the Reggio Emilia approach has greatly increased and changed the way the teacher communicates. Listening to children's conversations, knowing how to help them elaborate on their ideas, providing children with materials that enable them to make their thinking visible, negotiating with them in furthering these ideas, reflecting on practice with other teachers, interpreting the program to parents verbally, and documenting the children's experiences—all these and more have made communica- tion one of the most essential parts of the teacher's role.

6. *The role of the teacher in providing guidance changes to the role of the teacher as a supporter of the competent child.* Teachers frequently spend much of their time guiding the children's behaviour. During

indoor and outdoor play, teachers use guidance strategies to manage the children's behaviour, they supervise the children at transition times, and they help them with daily routines such as bathroom, lunch, and snack time. Bruner, in his study of Oxford preschools, noted that "a high proportion of adult-initiated interaction with children was given over to the boring stuff of petty management" (Katz 1993, 28). The greatest rewards occur for teachers when they begin to see children as competent, when the environment begins to act as a third teacher, and when collaboration is in effect. The amount of time managing the classroom diminishes as the teacher becomes a partner with the children in the co-construction of knowledge, and teachers become free to do the things they really find rewarding—engaging with children in real conversations about things that are important and pursuing exciting ideas with the children.

7. *The role of the teacher in* maintaining *the social relationships in the classroom changes to the role of the teacher in* supporting *the social relationships in the classroom.* Establishing a positive social environment in the classroom and beyond in the community is another essential part of the teacher's role in early childhood settings. A sense of belonging is at the core of every early childhood classroom; without this sense, young children simply will not thrive. The first task of every teacher is to create what Carolyn Edwards calls "the circle of we" (1998). The educators in Reggio Emilia have helped us understand how important it is to provide children with opportunities to co-construct their knowledge in the social group. This creates what Bruner calls "a mutual community of learners" (1996, 81). The social relationships, or the circle of we, not only includes children but is expanded to draw in teachers, parents, and the community.

8. *The role of the teacher in facilitating play changes to the role of the teacher as an exchanger of understandings.* Learning through play is the foundation of the majority of early childhood programs with philosophical roots reaching back to Froebel, Dewey, and, more recently, Piaget. Teachers spend time and put effort into creating environments that foster play in all areas of the program. Play is believed to be important for physical, emotional, social, cognitive, and moral development. Teachers learn how to promote early math and literacy skills through play, as well as science and social study concepts. For instance, at Douglas College the students and children spent six

weeks exploring concepts related to air. They made kites, windmills, and even an air balloon that floated above a fan in the classroom. It is important that teachers are aware that the materials and environments they set up to invite children to play are a reflection of cultural values and ideas about how children should use their bodies and what they should learn. The materials and environments they have prepared, however, may not be relevant for all children in their care. Teachers during the process of deconstruction are able to question and reflect critically on issues such as gender, racial stereotypes, and consumerism and the values and hidden agendas in the materials and environments they create for children's play. As these issues become more visible, teachers become more selective and thoughtful in the preparation of their classrooms.

9. *The role of the teacher changes from working primarily with individual children to working with children as a group.* Encouraging children to work together as a group (as opposed to working individually on a project) is an essential component in the Reggio Emilia approach. The educators in Reggio Emilia believe that the experiences children have in participating in a learning group in their early years will help them develop valuable skills and attitudes that will benefit them all their lives. Teachers who embrace the principles learned from Reggio Emilia, therefore, learn how to support children in working together successfully to achieve the group's purpose. They know how to invite children to join a group, support them as they interact with other children in the group, and help them learn how to listen, accept others' points of view, and blend their own ideas with those of other group members. Teachers also sense when to take the lead and when to hand it over to the children.

10. *The role of the teacher changes from working with children primarily from one cultural group to working with children from many diverse cultural backgrounds.* When teachers welcome diversity and genuinely enjoy families from diverse cultural backgrounds, children and their families will feel they are welcomed in the classroom and their culture is appreciated. If teachers strive to find ways to connect to parents, parents will feel encouraged to participate in their children's experiences in school. (Documentation helps, particularly because it provides non-English-speakers with a visual channel of communication.) The energy of all individuals will pour into the classroom and not drain away, providing a rich experience for all, especially the children.

11. *Teachers, inspired by ideas learned from Reggio Emilia and wanting to make changes, will need to deconstruct many "taken for granted" ideas related to all aspects of their work with young children.* One way to do this is to undergo as a team the process of collaborative critical reflection (see page 321). Engaging in this process helps teachers to deconstruct some of these practices that have become static and irrelevant and then together with their colleagues construct new ways of "being" and "becoming" in their teaching and in their classrooms.

Play is also considered an important part of the Reggio Emilia approach, but it does not seem as central to their program as in other early childhood settings. For instance, one does not hear the educators in Reggio Emilia extolling the values of learning through play. Children certainly have many opportunities to play freely in the Reggio Emilia preschools, but educators do not stress play as the most important medium for learning. What they do stress is "an exchange of understanding between the teacher and the child: to find in the intuitions of the child the roots of systematic knowledge" (Bruner 1996, 57). This emphasis encourages teachers to listen to children, to engage in conversation with them, and to observe, record, and reflect on their behaviour and words. "Listening starts with the adult trying to grasp the children's perspective and build from there, rather than starting with curriculum content" (Wien 2008, 14).

The following interview with teachers at the Vancouver Child Study Centre, which I conducted in May 1998, reveals how inspired by the Reggio Emilia approach the role of the teacher in this child-care centre has changed.

Susan Fraser: What changes have occurred in the role of the teacher as you introduced the principles learned from Reggio Emilia?

Patricia Breen*: I have had to unwind my own agenda. I have had to dispense with my old image of the teacher. We are now all equal; in fact, we are going to take turns in being the coordinator of the centre. We are learning to work together and communicate more. We are now making decisions equally. If the program is to function 100 percent we have to be mentally on board 100 percent of the time. It feels good to have ownership of our own program.

We see that in forming a partnership with parents we will have to delegate more responsibilities. For instance, when we worked on the bridge project [see Chapter 7], we involved parents by asking them to take their children to see the bridges in the city and to talk to them about bridges. This made them aware of our project, involved them in it, and gave them an opportunity to make suggestions.

---

*Reproduced courtesy of Pat Breen

Our relationship to children is also changing. We are listening more to children; we need to stand back and watch what the children do.

Chava Rubenson*: Children absorb at different levels; they often go home and process what we have talked about at school. Communication is a challenge because of multiculturalism (many of our families come from many different countries). We have to deal with different values, and many of the children do not have a large vocabulary of English words. There are also cultural factors that need to be considered, such as the difference in the image of the child in other cultures. You can compare the operations of the centre to a cake and we, the teachers, are the recipe.

An interview with a college instructor at Douglas College, in May 1998, also clarifies the changes brought to the role of the teacher.

Sue Fraser

Pat in a discussion with the children

Susan Fraser: What impact has introducing the principles of the Reggio Emilia approach into the Children Teaching Teachers and the ECE program had on helping early childhood education students learn about the role of the teacher?

Pat Brown:** The students, I think, learned the most in the Children Teaching Teachers experience. They had to put the interpersonal skills, which they had learned in theory in the second semester, into practice. They worked very closely and in collaboration

*Reproduced courtesy of Chava Rubenson
**Reproduced courtesy of Pat Brown

with their peers in Children Teaching Teachers. To make their teams work effectively, they discovered the importance of respectful communication. By the third semester of their training, they had a good, basic understanding of developmentally appropriate practice, and they applied it in their planning. A very important difference that has occurred since we began to explore the Reggio Emilia approach is seeing the child as competent and creating environments that support this competence. In planning the environment to act as a third teacher the students anticipated potential problems and took measures to prevent these from occurring. Another major difference is in their approach to guidance. When the environment works as a third teacher, guidance issues do not seem to come up to the same degree as before. When they do, however, the students remember the importance of treating the children respectfully and of encouraging them to problem-solve. Relationship is a key factor in making Reggio Emilia work well.

EARLY CHILDHOOD EDUCATORS TODAY

What is the role of the teacher in early childhood education at the beginning of the 21st century? For the first time in Western history, more children are cared for outside the home than within the home. With both parents at work in an increasing number of homes, early childhood educators are providing children with a major portion of their care. All aspects of the profession, therefore, have to be given serious consideration because of the impact this will have on future generations.

It is important to understand that the hierarchy in the work of an early childhood educator is fairly horizontal—there are not many levels in the job that require different sets of skills. The work is both complex and multifaceted. Many early childhood teachers are expected to manage the centre operations, including budgeting, hiring staff, enrolling children, and fundraising. They also plan the program and the physical space in the classroom. A large part of the job involves overseeing the social relationships in the classroom, supervising the children, communicating with children and their families, and acting as an advocate in the community for quality programs for children. The graduate of a two-year program and more recently a four-year degree in early childhood education is expected to be knowledgeable in subjects as far-reaching as child development, early childhood curriculum, multiculturalism, group dynamics and interpersonal communication, inclusion of children needing extra support, and business management.

Over the last century the role of the early childhood educator has become more clearly defined. It has evolved as a separate discipline, perhaps somewhere between social work and education. For those of us studying the Reggio Emilia approach, there seems to be another change in the wind, a shift in the paradigm, especially in looking at relationships. If we think of the role of a teacher as a prism with many different facets, it seems likely that in the 21st century, *relationship* will be the side of the prism that is turned to face us, the one that is in sharpest focus.

It is evident why the educators of Reggio Emilia place so much importance on relationship with children, co-workers, parents, and the community. The high quality of care in the infant–toddler centres and the preschools in Reggio Emilia is a result of the emphasis that has been placed on building relationships so carefully and solidly at every level of the program. The concern some people express about placing children for long periods in their early years in child care will be lessened if society sees it not as a necessity, but as a positive choice. If child care can be viewed as a natural part of the web in family relationships, then generations of young children will reap the benefits. This view means shifting the emphasis in the teacher preparation programs from learning how to manage early childhood settings to creating a community of people working together for the benefit of the children. Then as the prism takes a further turn in the 21st century, educators discover a totally new side to the prism that views early childhood through a postmodern lens. Pacini-Ketchabaw et al. state that "[if] we accept that we are in a process of becoming, of constant change, then we must abandon our idea of a static, knowable educator and move on to a view of an educator in a state of constant change and becoming (Pacini- Ketchabaw et al. 2009, 97).

THE PREPARATION OF TEACHERS

Mabel Higgins*, in her article "Come, Join the Journey" (1999, 33–39), describes how her interest in the Reggio Emilia approach began when she read the following quotation in the November 1994 edition of *Exchange:* "What we do every day celebrates children and the work of teachers. With great care, we create a friendly, responsive environment for children, an environment that invites children to action and exploration" (Gandini 1994). Higgins writes, "The words and the visions on these few pages stirred something inside me ... *this is the way it ought to be but is not always the case.*" To find out more about the Reggio Emilia approach, she travelled to

---

*Reproduced courtesy of Mabel Higgins

Winstead, Connecticut, to attend a workshop given by Lella Gandini and Amelia Gambetti. Higgins describes her response to the workshop:

> [I was] deeply moved while I heard them converse back and forth in sequence ... in harmony with one another as they shared their views with us. Their passion brought me back many years to my earlier training. Interestingly, I note that aspects of this approach did not appear foreign to me.... During the late '60s at Lambton College in Sarnia, Ontario, we were influenced by people like Netherlands-trained Elisabeth VanStam. She imparted a European influence in her classrooms, making us aware of the environment and aesthetics. She inspired us ... and her passion invoked an "open-mindedness" in us regarding education and life. Another member of that early team was Jane Danic, who graduated with Ola Munn from Ryerson's first ECE Program in Toronto. Upon graduation she and Ola Munn returned to Sarnia and opened the Riverside Nursery in 1954. It was described by Elsie Stapleford (Canada's child care mentor) as demonstrating a real understanding of the needs of young children. It became an important training ground for early graduates of the Lambton College ECE program. The rooms of the Riverside Nursery School were always filled with joyous sounds of children questioning and exploring their surroundings. These two women modeled openness and empathy, while encouraging their students to observe, document, research, explore and take risks!

One such exploration took Mabel to Ypsilanti, Michigan, in 1969 to observe the Perry Preschool Project.

Mabel Higgins has continued to expand her interest in the field of early childhood education. While attending the workshop at Winstead she met Betty Exelby from Loyalist College, in Belleville, Ontario, where they discovered their common interest in the Reggio Emilia approach. "After some five years of immersion in the Reggio Emilia approach," Mabel writes, "I have begun a *process of invitation*. I could no longer hold on to this "secret" [about Reggio Emilia] or wait until I completely understood its merit. I took a deep breath and put out the message to college students and faculty, the staff in laboratory schools and the community to '*Come, join the journey.*'"

The invitation to college students to join her in her journey of discovery of the Reggio Emilia approach required that the curriculum be built from the students' concerns and interests in the same way that the curriculum arises from the interests and questions posed by the children in Reggio Emilia.

Mabel states in her article that: "*I wanted to do this with my students while teaching within the framework of the recently established Ontario Standards for College Early Childhood Education programs.* We know that learning occurs when the learner has control over what they are learning. I once heard someone say that ... *We teach best, that which we most need to learn!* I was ready to do some learning alongside my students." As a result, the faculty began to make modifications to the curriculum design courses and field experience courses. Mabel notes that "a review of the program was occurring at the same time so the 'mood' or desire for change was already rolling in and the 'fit' became natural." One of the major changes they made in the field experience course was in the way observation is taught. They installed a video lab, where students and faculty can observe children and teachers at the campus school. "Prior to this," Mabel states, "we taught students observational techniques in a traditional classroom and then sent them off to observe on their own. Together we now work through the questions that arise as we observe."

The program began to employ Vygotsky's theory in supporting the ECE students' learning; for instance, knowing that the students were at varying levels of ability, the instructors provided them with the tools to enable them to climb from their current level of understanding to a higher threshold in the zone of proximal development.

Mabel notes that it was easy to inject lectures on Reggio Emilia into the curriculum courses because the approach had always been to offer students a smorgasbord of educational approaches. She writes, "No matter what lesson I was presenting, little bits of this approach would seep into our discourse. I soon began to bring in books on the subject, then videos and now whilst still presenting a variety of approaches, my bias [toward the Reggio Emilia approach] becomes rather evident."

The Reggio Emilia approach was also introduced into the students' final field experience in the fourth semester. In this semester students are prepared for life after graduation. The college instructors modified earlier assignments in this semester and added two new components implementing some elements of the Reggio Emilia approach: (1) community outreach projects and (2) student-initiated placement experience. Mabel writes, "*The results have been astounding. In both assignments the faculty role was one of protagonist and guide. The challenge was unleashed and the students were supported in every way possible to meet it. Our students, like the children, were given the space, time and materials to develop their project. They collaborated with faculty, peers and community.*" She describes the community outreach project of one student, Lindsay Boshell, below. Lindsay stated her plan as follows: "Through an exploration of 'The Discovery House Museum' and through Ron Broda's artistic talent, I, an early childhood education student, will stimulate children's imagination and creativity. I will encourage a lifelong joy of learning through exploration."

The Train Project

This project evolved through the children's exploration of the museum. The children examined all of the offerings in the Museum but settled in at the Train Room where a life-like model of Sarnia in days gone by had been donated by a local citizen. An elaborate railroad track and train are featured. In the neighbourhood and along the St. Clair River there is a "real" steam engine. They visited and examined this train with great interest. Lindsay asked questions and documented these along with their queries and answers. She posted these as panels for family members to view. She provided [the children] with the tools to express their learning, while the museum provided the impetus for investigation. Ron Broda, a well-known Canadian children's author and artist, supported their investigation of materials and techniques. His role was not unlike that of the atelierista in Reggio Emilia. The work of the children was assembled in the Museum's glass display cases with other objects of significance. They were afforded the same prestige as expensive artifacts.

Mabel notes that "allowing for and supporting this college student's interest and explorations have taught us that the Reggio Emilia approach can also be used in the college level classroom. This particular program has become an integral part of the museum."

After the three-week field experience, the ECE students tell their stories. They share their documentation through video presentations, documentation panels, books, and dialogue. Mabel writes, "In this way we enjoy closure of two years of weaving theory and practice and have a sense that our students leave prepared to continue their journey."

Mabel's invitation to the staff in the laboratory school to "Come, Join the Journey" led to her being invited to make a presentation to both the program faculty and the demonstration school teachers. The evening yielded many questions, which led to a deeper exploration of the Reggio Emilia practices. She writes, "Teachers are expressing their interpretations of the Reggio Emilia principles daily. Every visit to our centres becomes an adventure for me as the teachers share their ideas and pose more questions."

The community too has been invited to join the journey. A series of workshops, such as "Looking in on the Reggio Emilia approach," has been arranged. The staff from Loyalist College Children's Centre have been invited to Sarnia to present a workshop on the Reggio Emilia approach. Tours have been arranged of the Dearborn Child Development Centre and Scrapbox at the University of Michigan, in Ann Arbor; of Loyalist College Children's Centre in Belleville, Ontario; and of the Peter Greene Hall Children's Centre in Halifax, Nova Scotia. Visitors view displays of Reggio materials that the students have made and take part in roundtable discussions. Mabel Higgins concludes by saying, "Possibilities begin with dreams, then action is necessary. Injecting Canadian ECE training programs with curriculum respective to the Reggio Emilia approach may bring this dream into the daily lives of our children."

Mabel Higgins asks everyone "to come join the journey," and many teachers have. All across the continent there are teachers, in child-care centres, elementary schools, and postsecondary institutions who have introduced ideas learned from Reggio Emilia into their programs. They have found that the journey is exciting, challenging but also very rewarding. Their enthusiasm is making change happen in early childhood programs all across the country.

At Douglas College students in their second and third semester of the early childhood program plan and present a program for young children from local child-care centres and the local kindergarten who visit the college once a week for six weeks during both semesters. The students learn in a realistic situation many of the skills they will need in their future roles as teachers. For instance, they learn a great deal about the importance of collaboration and how to work as a team. For example, in small groups, they plan the activities they will present to the children and they decide as a group how to set up an environment that responds to the children's interests and reflects the kind of values they have identified as relevant for the particular group of children they are to work with each session. They learn to think critically about their work; for instance, in the fall semester in 2009, I listened to one group of students examine the possibilities inherent in the materials they were planning to prepare for the children. Was shaving soap just for sensory exploration or could children use it in a more representational way? During the morning one of the children tried to taste the soap. In the debriefing later the students discussed constraints about cleanliness, whose agenda was at work when the students intervened, and was soap an "intelligent" material that provoked children to go beyond sensory exploration in their explorations?

In Children Teaching Teachers, the students learn many teaching procedures they might never have experienced before. For instance, they practise how to scaffold children's learning, and how to identify "ordinary moments" that might have the possibility for further investigation in the weeks ahead. Each group of students creates a pedagogical documentation of an experience during the morning that they can share with the class as a whole. It is during the sharing of these pedagogical narrations and the participation in the deconstruction process in the debriefing at the end of each session that students challenge the dominant discourses of the early childhood field, such as developmental theories and "taken for granted ideas." The process of collaborative critical reflection (see page 321) has become an essential component in the student's thinking as they construct their future roles as teachers.

Great Horned Owl

Relationships

Questions to Consider:

- What are the underlying theoretical perspectives that guide our understanding about relationship?

- How is relationship woven into all parts of the program?

- What roles do communication and documentation play in establishing relationships?

- How does the emphasis placed on relationship affect the facets of the program, such as children, co-workers, community, program, play, space, time, and materials?

- What are the challenges in making relationship central to the program?

- How can we tell that relationship has become a fundamental principle in the program?

- Why is it important for children to form a close relationship with nature?

I believe there is no possibility of existing without relationship. Relationship is a necessity of life.

—Loris Malaguzzi

When teachers study children, either for the purpose of observation or in planning curriculum experiences, they consider the uniqueness of each child in the class, but they also view children in the context of their family, peer group, and community. Ask any teacher of young children what her goals are for children, and she will probably say to ensure they develop a strong sense of self and reach their full potential physically, emotionally, socially, and intellectually. This is one of the reasons play in childhood is considered so important in the West—it is in play that educators in the Western world believe the development of the whole child is fostered. Learning through play has been an important philosophical perspective in early childhood programs since Froebelian kindergartens were founded in the early part of the 20th century. Later, Piagetian theory reaffirmed the value of play, especially its role in promoting young children's cognitive development. The development of play behaviour and how it evolves from a solitary to a social behaviour has been described by Parten (1932) and Smilansky (1968). More recently, researchers such as Elizabeth Jones and Gretchen Reynolds (1997) have examined the role of the teacher in play. However, only in more recent years, as we have become more aware of the role that *relationship* plays in early childhood, have early childhood educators emphasized children's development in the context of the social group.

However, when relationship becomes the guiding principle in early childhood programs a shift in the perspective of the educators towards play occurs. For instance, teachers begin to question how children from other cultures relate to play as it is structured in early childhood classrooms. They begin to examine their own assumptions and hidden agendas as they prepare environments for play. They ask themselves questions about their own attitudes to play and whether these are limited by their own cultural perspectives. They ask themselves what topics are permitted and how are children allowed to use their bodies as they play. They think critically about the materials and equipment they select for play and whether these promote racial and gender stereotypes. They may question values, such as consumerism, inherent in many of the toys we provide for children. The purpose is to ensure that all families feel comfortable with their children's education. Play may not have the same value or meaning in some cultures so parents may be hesitant about its relevancy in their children's education. Education through play is a construct of the Western world and as such there are many "taken for granted ideas" in play that need to be deconstructed and re-evaluated in the context of today's classrooms. However, the importance of the relationships that are fostered through play builds upon all children's early social development.

One of the earliest social relationships develops between mother and infant at birth. The typical suck/pause pattern of feeding forms the basis for the turn-taking rhythm, which is an early form of communication between mother and infant. When mother and child establish a synchronous rhythm, they form a positive relationship. Development of the relationship, however, will not proceed as smoothly if factors such as early trauma or a mismatch in temperament between the mother and child interfere with the formation of this rhythm. This early relationship between the mother and child is an example of the interdependence of children and adults in all areas of development (Brazelton 1981).

The work of Vygotsky and Bruner has increased our awareness of the importance of the quality of the relationship between child and caregiver in fostering the child's intellectual development, especially language development. In the following example of an interchange between a mother and child, Bruner observes how a mother instinctively uses language to further her child's thinking. He describes how the mother uses "little 'formats' or rituals" to help the child learn the words for the pictures in the book they are reading together: "'(1) Oh look Richard! (2) What's that? (3) It's a fishy. (4) That's right.' She then encouraged the child to think about the meaning conveyed by the pictures, '(5) What's the fishy doing?'" Bruner observes how the mother seems to know intuitively when to raise the ante, or to challenge the child to think and use language at a higher level. He notes that "she remains forever on the growing edge of the child's competence" (1986, 77).

As Bruner's example shows, interactions between children and either an adult or a child who is more competent act as scaffolding to nudge children to go beyond what they can achieve on their own. They now enter what Vygotsky termed *the zone of proximal development*—the area in which the child is able to perform with assistance at a higher level of mental functioning. Vygotsky believed that when children receive the right kind of assistance from others, they reach beyond their present level of ability and move forward in their development. The major difference between the theories of Piaget and Vygotsky lies in the importance given to the role of the relationship between children and their teachers or caregivers. Whereas in a Piagetian world children construct their knowledge mainly on their own, in a Vygotskian world children co-construct knowledge with others. The quality of the relationship established with teachers or caregivers, therefore, becomes critical in the child's growth and development. In the past, early childhood programs in many parts of the world were based on the philosophy that children learn through play. But since the work of Vygotsky (and later Bruner) identified the critical role of relationship, and especially reciprocity, in the child's development, there has been a shift toward making relationship a fundamental principle in programs for young children. Before Vygotsky's theories became generally known in Western society, however, the educators in the Reggio Emilia preschools understood the importance of relationship and made it central to their programs.

The challenge for early childhood educators is to ensure that all children who receive care outside their homes are able to form quality relationships with their teachers and caregivers. Think of a child at the centre of concentric rings of relationships, the ring containing family, school, and child care being the closest. Bronfenbrenner terms this ring the *microsystem*. Surrounding this is the *mesosystem,* the ring in which different microsystems interact; for instance, the quality of the relationship between home and school or child care would be considered here. These interactions will be influenced by how adults at home and at school perceive the child and by how the child-rearing beliefs at home match the teacher's image of the child. The next ring is the *exosystem,* or the community in which the child lives. The formal or informal social structures in the exosystem affect the child's experiences within the first circle of relationships. For instance, the policies in the preschool or child care have an impact on the quality of care the child receives outside the home. The final, surrounding ring is the *macrosystem,* which comprises the culture and subculture in which the child is reared (see Figure 4–1). When links between these circles of relationships are strong and communication flows freely between them, the child benefits; however, if the links are weak or nonexistent, the child's development will suffer. For instance, if the child is secure within the ring of family relationships, communication between the school and the family is strong. In addition, if the community and culture are supportive of the child and family, then conditions for the child's development are optimal (Bronfenbrenner, in Yeates et al. 1994, 5).

Creating a sense of belonging is fundamental to the Reggio Emilia approach. For the program to function successfully, everyone involved—children, families, and teachers—needs to feel that they play an integral part in what Carolyn Edwards calls the *circle of we.* If we agree with the educators in Reggio Emilia that we will be able to provide the highest quality of child care and education only by making relationship the foundation of the program, then we will have to review every aspect of our programs to see how we

FIGURE 4.1   Multiple rings of relationships affect children*.

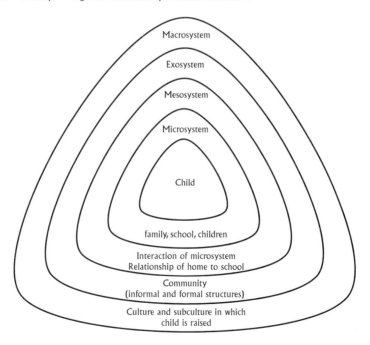

*From FRASER/GESTWICKI/ *Authentic Childhood,* 1E. © 2002 Wadsworth, a part of Cengage Learning, Inc. Reproduced by permission. www.cengage.com/permissions.

can strengthen relationships. In a preschool program, relationship takes place at many levels: between the teachers, between the teachers and children, and among the teachers, families, and community.

RELATIONSHIPS WITH FAMILIES

The initial contact that families have with the school will set the tone for future relationships between home and school. Therefore, the educators in Reggio Emilia believe that beginnings, or *inserimento,* are critical. Educators need to review the orientation procedure to ensure that at each of the stages in introducing the child and family to the school, a strong relationship between the teachers and the family is fostered. The process cannot be rushed, as there has to be enough time for the child and the parents to build trust in the teachers and the school. Teachers need to respect the attachment of the child to the parents at every stage and should separate the child from the parents only when the child feels secure in the new surroundings. The principles listed below can help teachers build strong relationships with families.

1. *Make families feel welcome.* The entranceways in the preschools in Reggio Emilia are designed to make families feel welcome and to encourage them to linger awhile, rather than rush their children's transition from home to school. These spaces are furnished with comfortable chairs. Portfolios of the children's work and experiences in school are arranged on shelves nearby, and documentation is displayed on the walls to inform parents and visitors about what the children are experiencing in school.

   In thinking of ways to make families feel more closely connected to the centre, the Quadra Island Children's Centre staff moved the children's attendance sheet that parents sign every day from an outside entrance into the classroom itself, so that parents spend a few minutes each day with the teachers and children. They hoped that in this way parents would become more familiar with the centre. As well, in the fall of 1998, the staff decided to invite parents and other people from the community to a meeting at the child care. The purpose of the meeting was to explore ways to foster greater understanding and to increase interaction among all the partners. Dee Conley*, the director of the child care, explained that they had arranged the meeting because the staff wanted to ensure that no one felt excluded from the circle of we they were creating in the child care. The meeting began with

---

*Reproduced courtesy of Dee Conley

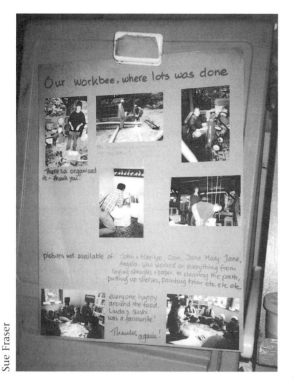

Our workbee, where lots was done

This documentation panel reveals ways that parents became involved in the Quadra Island Children's Centre program.

members of the volunteer board each explaining their roles and responsibilities. The treasurer, for instance, explained the organization of finances. In her report she noted how dependent the child care had become in recent years on fundraising to balance the budget. The parents were amazed and immediately suggested raising the fees to lessen the pressure on the staff and the board. The staff also asked the parents for suggestions on how they could improve communication and interaction. The parents suggested posting in the entrance hall a wish list of tasks that needed to be done, such as repairing furniture. They suggested that the staff set up an area where families could display photographs of themselves and the things they like to do. In this way, parents would get to know the other families. Once they became more aware of the benefits of establishing a closer relationship between themselves and the teachers in the child care, the parents suggested having at least four meetings a year like the one organized that evening.

2. *Communicate clear expectations.* Expectations are usually stated in a handbook that teachers give to parents when they enrol their children in the program. The parents in the Quadra Island Children's Centre are expected to serve on the nonprofit board that administers the school. They also contribute their skills by chopping wood for the woodstove that heats the child care, maintaining the buildings and playground, and building and repairing the equipment. Parents volunteer their time in the child care, as well, by preparing food and materials for the children to use. A number of people who serve on

the board are people in the community who do not have children in the child care but who volunteer to help in the administration of the centre.

The Quadra Island Children's Centre has a documentation panel displayed prominently at the entrance to the school, showing photographs illustrating previous parent involvement. The teachers find that it helps to remind parents of the importance of their involvement and shows them ways in which they can participate in the program.

3. *Provide parents with information about their children in the program.* Documentation of the children's experiences makes the program visible to the parents. A portfolio for each child in the program is an essential tool for communication with the parents. The teachers in the Quadra Island Children's Centre decided that to ensure this task was done, they would each take responsibility for a small group of children. Each teacher would then observe and record information about the children in her group, discussing the observations with the other staff members and communicating with the parents of the children in her group every day.

4. *Listen and communicate honestly with parents.* Open communication is possible only when trust has been established between teachers and parents. Careful orientation of parents to the program is essential to enable this trust to grow. Teachers also have to nurture trust daily by making it possible for the parents to feel a sense of belonging and commitment to the school, as the teachers at the Quadra Island Children's Centre did by communicating with the parents individually every day.

Sue Fraser

The May Day float made by the children and parents at Quadra Island Preschool.

5. *Plan creative ways of involving families in the program.* Parents often participate by doing the essential jobs of serving on committees and driving the children on field trips. It is important, however, to also involve the parents in creative ways. The parents in

the Quadra Island Preschool, for instance, designed and built a float to take part in a parade that the community had organized to mark one hundred years of celebrating May Day on the island. The parents created a replica of the *Venetura*, one of the steamships that had visited the island in the early days. Everyone, dressed in period costume of a hundred years ago, walked or rode on the float in the parade.

Peter, a parent helper, makes pizza with the children.

6. *Accept differences in the value systems of families in the school*. The diversity in modern society presents a challenge for teachers, but it can also provide a rich source for learning experiences in the classroom. When diversity is viewed as an asset, it becomes a wonderful medium for forming relationships with children and families.

In the Sexsmith Multicultural Preschool in Vancouver (a program that was developed to help children and their families adjust to Canadian culture and learn English as a second language), the teachers observed that the children's play frequently centred on pretend cooking in the housekeeping corner. The teachers asked the parents if some of them would like to volunteer to cook a simple dish from their culture with the children in the class. This cooking experience then became the basis for further learning experiences. For instance, one mother who had recently emigrated from Hong Kong offered to help the children cook stir-fried Chinese vegetables. The adults planned a field trip to buy vegetables at a nearby Chinese grocery, and the mother showed the children how to cook the vegetables in a wok. A family who owned a Chinese restaurant invited the class to have a meal at their restaurant. Following this experience, the children made egg drop soup at school. The teachers placed the recipe and materials for cooking and eating Chinese food, such as a wok, bowls, and chopsticks, in the dramatic play corner for the children to use.

A few days later, the teachers observed the children pretending to be waiters and serving the food to children who were pretending to be the customers. The children asked for a chalkboard, on which they wrote up the menu for the day, and for white napkins, which the "waiters" threw over their shoulders as they served the "customers." This group of children was particularly knowledgeable about serving food, as many of their families worked in restaurants or in the cafeteria of the local hospital. After observing the children's interest in preparing and serving food, the teachers asked them if they would like to convert the classroom into a restaurant and invite the parents to be their customers. The children helped write a simple menu of celery sticks stuffed with peanut butter or cream cheese and apple or orange juice. The teachers and children attractively set a few tables with tablecloths and cutlery, and when the parents arrived the children took their orders and served the food. This experience proved so successful that the participants repeated the activity, creating meals typical of other cultural groups; for instance, one Punjabi family helped the children make roti and curry. The parents' involvement in the program increased and became an integral part of the program as they became aware of how much their contribution was appreciated. Sometimes it is difficult to find ways to involve parents who do not speak English as a first language, but the teachers in the Sexsmith Multicultural Preschool were able to do this successfully by following the lead of the children. It was the children's interest in food and restaurants that formed the basis for inviting the families to share their skills with the children in the preschool (Fraser 1992, 27–30).

Challenges in Forming Relationships with Families

A number of factors besides culture, such as socioeconomic differences or too little time and energy because of stressful conditions in the family, the workplace, or society, make it a challenge to form strong relationships between home and school.

Accommodating Differences in Values

Differences in values of the parents and the teachers, especially if these affect the beliefs concerning how children should be raised, may block communication between the school and the family. There may be differences in the teachers' and family members' image of the child, which can lead to conflict in child–adult relationships. Even if parents and teachers agree on the view of the child as competent, how does this view translate into practice? The interpretation of competency may differ among cultures and across socio-economic groups. As Sue Bredekamp points out, "overemphasis on children's competence can lead to abuses: If infants are so competent, why is parental leave necessary? If preschoolers are so smart, why not start formal reading instruction at two? If kindergartners are competent, what could be wrong with push-down (developmentally inappropriate) curriculum?" (1993, 14). To establish relationship as central to practice, teachers need to implement the principle of the image of the child as competent with careful thought and consideration. In some cultures, for instance, parents foster children's dependence on family members and discourage children from showing initiative or asserting their independence. Teachers, therefore, may need to modify their approach in order to respect the values of the family.

Understanding Stressors on the Family

The educators in Reggio Emilia, through the support they give to working parents, have eliminated a great deal of the stress parents experience related to child care. Support begins by having a procedure in place for orientation that ensures that before the child is separated, trust has been established between the teachers and all family members. The educators in Reggio Emilia slow down the process of separation to ensure that the child and family are made comfortable in each stage of the transition from home to school. They go so far as to check that the food prepared for children at school has the same taste as it does at home. The teachers realize how important it is to establish good communication with the family. They take the time to talk to parents when they leave their child in the morning and when they pick up the child in the afternoon. The practice of documentation informs the parents about the child's experiences in school so that the family stays closely connected to what the child is doing every day. Collaboration is a strong value, and parents are expected to participate at many levels in their child's school activities, whether by serving on committees, volunteering in the classroom, or helping with the preparation of materials and construction of equipment. The strength of the relationship that is established between teachers and families serves as a support if stress emerges in other areas of family life, such as through divorce, illness, or other misfortune.

The formation of strong relationships with families also depends on the parents and teachers having enough time and energy to initiate and maintain the relationship. This is particularly hard for parents who work in stressful and demanding jobs. In an interview with some parents from the preschool and child care on Quadra Island in June 1998, I asked how they could be made to feel more involved in their children's preschool experiences. They responded by saying, "Do people who are working all week really want to be involved in child care?" "Child care provides me with the time I need to work. I will participate, but I need to feel it is for my kids, and it needs to be enjoyable, not more added work." "To get a better sense of community in the child care would take a few people really committed to community building. They would have to spend a lot of effort getting all the parents involved." The parents agreed that for the children to feel a strong sense of belonging, the parents would have to get to know the other families and begin to build a community of we.

In a discussion at the Quadra Island Children's Centre in November 1998, I asked one of the teachers, Dee Conley*, about parent volunteers. She described the changes brought by including parents in the program:

> Yes, things have improved over these last few months. One big motivation came from having a Parent Board–staff meeting and spelling out the true situation. Honest and direct communication was effective to bring about changes and involve more parents. Once we had formed a relationship with the parents we were able to phone individual parents for specific requests—for example, to ask them if they would give us photographs of their family to display in the entrance hall. Parents have liked the "Wish List" of things to do that we posted. We have found that talking to parents one on one is more personal and welcomes feedback on how they view the program. We have one mother who comes every Friday and does some housekeeping jobs for us. This fall we had two work-bee/potluck dinners. At the first one some 30 people came, mostly parents. This enabled us to complete many of our maintenance jobs.

Loris Malaguzzi stated, "Of course, education is not based solely on relationships; however, we consider relationship to be the fundamental, organizing strategy of our educational system. We view relationships not simply as a warm, protective backdrop or blanket but as a coming together of elements interacting dynamically toward a common purpose. The strength of this view of education is in expanding the forms and functions of relationship and interaction" (1993,10). As early childhood educators, therefore, we have to reassess "the form and function" that relationship plays in our programs by asking ourselves the following questions:

- Are we engaging in culturally sensitive interaction with the families in the centre?

- Are we supportive and able to make families that are under stress feel that they can still be involved in the program?

- Are we exploring ways of involving all families in the program?

*Reproduced courtesy of Dee Conley

- Are we including the richness of the community in the program?

- Are we making clear the options that are available for families to participate in the program?

- Have we established reciprocity as a core principle in our relationship with families?

RELATIONSHIPS WITH CHILDREN

Many teachers may ask themselves how their relationship with the children in the classroom will change when the teacher's role becomes one of a co-constructor with the children of the learning experiences in the program. Acceptance of the children as competent learners will in itself bring about a style of relating to children that is different from seeing the children as empty vessels that need to be filled with knowledge. When reciprocity is seen as the basis of the relationship between teachers and children, the relationship will be more respectful, more equal, and more interactive.

Opening Channels of Communication

When reciprocity is placed at the core of relationships, it changes the patterns of communication in the classroom. For instance, one of the biggest changes occurs in the teacher's traditional role of controller of all communication in the classroom. The teacher's role is now shared equally among all the participants in the classroom. Teachers who form reciprocal relationships with children find themselves wanting to listen to the children's conversations to find out what they are thinking and what ideas they have on the topics of current interest. They want to consider seriously the children's suggestions for effective ways of solving problems that have arisen in the classroom. They also want to create opportunities to listen to the children's responses to their suggestions. Children have to feel that their ideas are valued and will be listened to. Teachers embracing the Reggio Emilia approach set the stage for productive conversation by making changes in the following areas:

1. the physical space in the classroom

   - creating quiet environments where meaningful conversations can take place

   - making places where small groups can meet undisturbed by activities in the main area of the classroom

2. the daily schedule

- removing all unnecessary interruptions in the daily schedule
- providing for flexible planning, so that if children are discussing a topic, there is enough time to explore it in depth
- adapting group time to enable it to be more interactive than teacher directed

3. the program content

- listening to children, recording their conversations, and following up on their interests
- encouraging children to express their ideas
- enabling children to make their thinking visible
- building on the children's ideas
- allowing for input from the children in planning the content
- accepting different perspectives and conflict as a positive dynamic and using them as a source of energy in the creation of new ideas for program content

4. the teaching team

- collaborating with other adults in the room to observe and record the children's comments and activities
- making time for reflection
- meeting frequently to discuss observations and to plan further directions
- preparing questions beforehand that can be used to stimulate further discussion and possible action
- accepting that conflict is a necessary and dynamic factor in making change effective
- selecting children who work well together to collaborate with teachers in carrying out a project

5. the peer group

- supporting children to work together in a group
- emphasizing the importance of listening to and respecting one another's ideas and opinions

- helping children learn to value the different perspectives that other children hold

- accepting conflict in a positive way so that it can be used as a means of untangling the blockage, and perhaps taking a new direction to solve the problem that caused the initial conflict

6. parent helpers

- maintaining the communication links between home and school

- continuing the conversation at home that begins at school, and vice versa

- encouraging parents to serve as a memory for the child during and after a conversation

- encouraging parents to discuss topics at home and to extend and expand on the children's thoughts

The following excerpts are taken from teachers' responses to the question, "What suggestions do you have for helping teachers listen to and communicate with children?"

Stop talking so much yourself. Observe children's play from the sidelines more often. Find out what they are doing in their own play before it becomes too influenced by your presence, comments, or ideas—then come in with an idea for an extension, a provocation or to assist the children in gathering materials. (Pat Breen, Vancouver Child Study Centre survey, June 1998)*

For me, asking questions is a natural part of developing relationships with each child; therefore, they vary according to which child I'm talking with, as well as the situation. Looking at the example of the conversation [below] with Jack, who was drawing on the sidewalk, I'm sure this wouldn't have worked with any of the others, who would have felt I was sticking my nose into their activity in a most intrusive way. But I know Jack loves to share information and to show what he knows. He enjoyed and was very confident in this exchange.

Jack: I'm going to draw a balloon, a blue one.

Susan** (teacher): And a long string I see?

Jack: Yes, a long string and some bolts.

Susan: What are the bolts for?

Jack: To bolt it to the ground so it doesn't float away. And under it I'm putting a book to weigh it down more.

Susan: It looks very secure now, Jack. What are these things on the side?

Jack: They're snippers to cut the string when it's time to take the balloon home. (Susan Emery, Quadra Island Children's Centre survey, November 1998)

*Reproduced courtesy of Pat Breen
**Reproduced courtesy of Susan Emery

In order to have "real conversations" with the children, a teacher has to really listen. I notice when I ask a question and already have the answer in my head and am waiting to hear that answer, it does not stimulate real conversation. It seems to be useful to paraphrase back to a child the ideas they are expressing. Ask them "tell me more about it." Ask them to express their idea in another language such as drawing or clay. This allows you to understand their thought process better and in turn allows them to further clarify their idea. Developing meaningful relationships between teachers and children, and between the children themselves is a key component to having "real conversation." Everyone has to feel respected and feel that they make worthwhile contributions to the group. Children need to learn how to listen to each other, and see the power of bouncing ideas off one another and how that deepens one's understanding. (Barbara Lee, Quadra Island Children's Centre survey, November 1998)*

The following list drawn up by Donna Mouzard** provides examples of ways that teachers can communicate with children to guide their learning:

1. *Giving words or encouraging children to give words to concepts:* (Adult identifying concept) "Anne Louise, I see that you parked your truck between the red and blue cars." Asking child to give words to a concept: "Goodness, where did that green colour come from? I only gave you yellow and blue paint."

2. *Outlining steps to problem solving:* (Adult modelling) "Christian doesn't want to put on his snowsuit. What should I do? I could get mad or I could try to change his mind. I think it is better to try and change his mind. I could remind him that when he has his snowsuit on he can slide down the playground hill, or I could tell him...." (Asking child to outline) "Carol, I see you did a lot of stamping. How did you get such a nice clear picture with this dinosaur stamp?"

3. *Naming, expanding on knowledge, and encouraging observation:* "Yes, you may have an orange. This is called a navel orange. Another name for your belly button is a navel. Why do you think they call this a navel orange?"

4. *Asking open-ended and figuring-out questions:* An older toddler has just drawn his umpteenth noseless face. "Nicholas, does your person know what is cooking for lunch?" "No." "How could he find out?" (Educator, after giving sufficient time for answers, may touch nose or sniff the air as a clue.) This assisted development will probably never have to be repeated. Faces will generally always have noses after this discovery.

---

*Reproduced courtesy of Barbara Lee
**Donna G. Mouzard. Building Castles. *Canadian Children*. Vol. 22, No. 1. 1997.

5. *Encouraging talking aloud (inner speech):* <u>For self control</u> (child to self): "I will sit down. I will fold my hands. I will wait until everyone is given a snack. Then I can eat." <u>To practise a skill</u> (i.e., scissors): "Open, squeeze, open, squeeze...." <u>For memory skills:</u> "Where did I leave my book, first I went to see Francois. Then I went to the sand table. Then I...." (Mouzard 1997, 38–39)

Susan Emery* summed up a discussion about relationships with the staff of the Quadra Island Children's Centre in July, 2009 as follows:

Relationships are central. If, during, a smooth period, we start to take our relationships with the children or with each other, for granted—when things get rougher, more stressful or frustrating, I'll stop and think, "What is going on?" It is almost always because relationships haven't been maintained—trite but true. At times, the "squeaky wheels" are getting the oil and the children we have a good relationship with begin to drift away from us and form very tight peer-oriented relationships. In effect letting us know that, if we don't have time for them, they don't have time for us. We can find ourselves on the outside trying to manage the behaviour of a group that we are not viewed by them as a part of. Fortunately, when we address it and make a definite commitment to spend time with them, it turns around quite quickly. It's taught me the importance of having an individual relationship with each person, and that it has to be maintained in tangible ways.

Creating a Flexible Curriculum

When teachers consider relationship a fundamental principle and weave it into all aspects of the program, they will approach the more structured times, such as circle time, from a different perspective. The typical format for circle time is still based on the procedure that evolved in the Froebelian kindergartens early in the 20th century. The children sit in a circle, and the teacher reads a story, sings songs, and leads the group in discussing a topic of general interest. Froebel believed that children need to be gathered together under the direction of the teacher at least once a day to create a sense of group cohesiveness. Froebel chose the circle as a symbol of unity with the universe—the children are the stars that circle the teacher, who is the sun. Froebel felt it was important for children to feel spiritually connected to the world around them. The "gifts" and "occupations," that is, the materials and activities he created for children to use in circle time, have long since disappeared, but the ritual of circle time must still hold its meaning and significance to have persisted in early childhood programs.

The idea of unity, or connectedness, that Froebel believed so important for young children becomes the principle of relationship in the Reggio Emilia

---

*Reproduced courtesy of Susan Emery

approach. Circle time in the Reggio Emilia preschools has become, however, a less formal group time, when the children and teacher join together in a discussion on subjects that hold relevance for the group. It is still acknowledged as an important time for creating a sense of belonging, when children and teachers gather together, but the ritualistic aspect has disappeared. The activity during this time has become more informal and more responsive to the interests of the children; thus, it is more spontaneous and interactive. It has become an important time for teachers to listen to children and draw from them ideas and suggestions for the program. As well, during group time much of the co-construction of knowledge between children and teachers takes place. In allowing more flexible use of time and equality in the child–teacher relationship, the Reggio Emilia approach, as Lillian Katz observes, "drives theory, rather than the opposite, and may even be ahead of theory development" (Katz and Cesarone 1994, 9).

In reflecting on how teachers were beginning to reassess past practice when exploring the Reggio Emilia approach, one of the teachers at the Vancouver Child Study Centre wrote the following comments:

> I think we all need to work at being less directive and more sensitive to the children. I would like to reexamine the format of our daily schedule and the benefit of circle time. It does not work for about half the children. Perhaps make circle time shorter—five minutes. This would allow for more small group explorations, which could occur more spontaneously. We need to examine what is developmentally appropriate and provide more able children with opportunities to demonstrate their abilities while allowing younger children the freedom to feel competent and successful at the level they have reached—i.e., Don't make J repeatedly fail with his inability to remain focused during long circle times. Reduce times of "management" challenges, while facilitating times of increased focus for children who are ready for it. (Gloria Rolfsen, Vancouver Child Study Centre survey, June 1998)*

Linking Play and Relationship

For the last one hundred years, since the Froebelian kindergartens were established in North America, play has been given the central position philosophically in most early childhood education programs. The key question for early childhood educators in exploring the Reggio Emilia approach is this: If we are to place *relationship* at the centre of the curriculum, how will this affect our belief in the importance of play? Loris Malaguzzi said, "We should not forget the relevant role of make-believe play. This type of symbolic play is pervasive in young children's experience and has an important role in the social development of intelligence, development of the skills needed for reciprocity among children, the potential for children to persist in activity and conversation

---

*Reproduced courtesy of Gloria Rolfsen

together, and development of the ability to create symbols" (1993, 12). Children in the preschools in Reggio Emilia spend much of their time engaged in play, but the teachers in Reggio Emilia do not focus their attention on the children's play, as do educators in many other programs.

In preschools where play is the central philosophical perspective, teachers spend much of their time and energy on creating environments that foster play. Then, when children become fully engaged in play, the teachers tend to withdraw and observe. Therefore, the teacher is more of a facilitator than a participator with the children in the play. For instance, the teachers at the Sexsmith Multicultural Preschool, described above, observed that the children used the cooking theme most frequently in their play in the dramatic play area. The teachers then used this theme as the foundation for building the content of the program. The children, as they prepared the food for the restaurant, wrote the menu, took orders and served the food to their parents, developed their social and literacy skills, learned new concepts, and developed their vocabulary.

The teachers at the Sexsmith school developed the theme of cooking food from different ethnic groups over six months; in this sense, the project was similar to those carried out in Reggio Emilia because the topic was explored in depth for a long period of time. However, the project differed in the way the teachers used their observations of the children's play, then took the lead in developing the project further. Unlike the teachers in Reggio Emilia, who work collaboratively with the children in developing a project, the teachers at Sexsmith Multicultural Preschool took control of the direction the project would follow. They proceeded to organize the children's cooking activities, decide on the menu, and transform the classroom into a restaurant. If the children had had more say in the project, for instance, the menu may have offered a wider choice of cultural foods than celery sticks stuffed with cream cheese or peanut butter (Fraser 1992). The educators in Reggio Emilia use their observations and conversations with the children as an entry point into the process of developing a project further. They then work *together* with the children throughout this process. The emphasis is on relationship and reciprocity, and the outcome of the project emerges as it unfolds.

Baerbel Jaeckel*, the teacher at the Quadra Island Preschool, describes in a survey in April 1998 how her perspective changed as she began to explore the Reggio Emilia approach and as relationship became more of a guiding principle in the program:

> There is a wish, a desire, an interest to connect, to establish or rather point out webs of connection, of interrelationships—of widening circles, i.e., what a child draws can be related to an earlier event, a book, an experience, etc.—and it becomes more than an individual act. It can be related ... to another child on that particular subject or situation—thus

*Reproduced courtesy of Baerbel Jaeckel

establishing and/or confirming a contact, a relationship, a common interest among the children. Always, or at least often, there is a sense of wanting to bring things—ideas ... and people into context—with previous events, other suggestions, etc.—so that there is a link, a connection not only between ideas, information, etc., but also a connection between people; i.e., a child who usually may not relate to another child on an interpersonal level will find a bridge to that child via a similar thought or by problem solving. Earlier in the year E was often quite solitary; when I related another child's interest and remarks about the rainbows (created by the crystals), this interest became a bridge that linked her to another child. If this is done for and with the child quite frequently, then isolation can be opened up.

I just generally look for more collaboration—the so-called teachership steps into the background; when I feel really connected, I am just part of what is happening. Some parents need a lot of affirming of their qualities as co-creators.

These reflections illustrate the change in perspective as a teacher, inspired by the Reggio Emilia approach, changes from viewing the curriculum as external to the daily experiences in the classroom to viewing it as internal—as an integral part of being and connecting to others. The program content then, is derived from the dynamic interaction of adults and children with one another and with the environment. It emerges spontaneously out of the relationships in the environment, and, thus, it is always fresh and interesting. "Expect the unexpected" is how Loris Malaguzzi described this way of experiencing curriculum.

The educators in Reggio Emilia perceive play as an important medium for fostering relationships, for as children interact in the play group they are given many opportunities to develop their social and cognitive skills. In Reggio Emilia children are given plenty of time to play, but the focus seems to be on the relationship between adults and children as they participate together in the co-construction of knowledge. Reggio Emilia educators also acknowledge play as one of the hundred languages used by children in symbolic development and to make their thinking visible.

Presenting Materials

One of the joys of being an early childhood educator is working with a wide variety of materials, but even more rewarding is sharing the experience with children. There is nothing as satisfying for preschool teachers as arriving in the morning before the children and setting up the classroom with the materials the children will use during the day. The teachers have to consider which materials need to be available in each area of the room. In the art area, for instance, there is the paint to mix and place in the easel, the collage material to arrange attractively on shelves, and special materials that support the children's interests at the moment. The teachers check that pieces of equipment, such as the blocks, are arranged neatly on the shelves and that puzzles and table toys are put out on the tables. In the science area the teacher may want to prepare an area where the children can experiment with water, magnets, or any of the other science materials the children are interested in at the moment. In the Quadra Island Preschool, for instance, the children had planted horsetails, ferns, and moss in the indoor sandbox to create a landscape for the dinosaurs that one of the children had drawn and cut out of paper. Each day, the teacher brought in different books on dinosaurs and placed them beside the sandbox to capture the children's attention. In this way, she hoped to focus their interest on dinosaurs and stimulate further investigation of what they looked like and how they lived.

In preparing the room, the teachers' main concern is in making the materials appealing and easily available. This task involves thoughtful reflection about which materials might stimulate the children's interest. In recent years there has been a change in preschools from a theme-based to an emergent curriculum, which has made the preparation of learning experiences for the children more spontaneous and flexible. In an emergent curriculum, the teachers base their selection of materials on previous observations and discussions about which materials the children will need to further their investigations and representations of their ideas.

The Reggio Emilia approach has made early childhood educators more aware of how relationship deepens the meaning of experiences in the classroom. Teachers in Reggio Emilia classrooms no longer set up materials or experiences in isolation but, rather, think carefully about the interconnection between materials and children and how this relationship deepens the meaning of activities. Before learning about the Reggio Emilia approach, the teacher in the Quadra Island Preschool, when she saw the cut-out pictures of the dinosaurs that one of the children had made, would probably have just displayed them on the walls of the classroom. However, the Reggio Emilia approach made her more aware of the role of relationship. Therefore, she thought about how she could create a context for the dinosaurs in order to extend the children's knowledge of dinosaurs. Other children became interested in the

Sue Fraser

Making dinosaur bones for the museum at Quadra Island Preschool.

CHAPTER 4 Relationships **99**

topic and joined in doing some research and creating a landscape for the dinosaurs. The children then decided to make a museum for the dinosaurs. One child made a sign, and the children created all kinds of bones, which they later identified using a chart of a dinosaur skeleton.

Aesthetics is an aspect of relationship that needs to be considered in presenting the materials in the classroom. To foster aesthetic awareness means to help children appreciate the beauty in the world around them, but it also means to heighten their awareness of the links between things in the environment and the emotional response that the objects evoke. Teachers need to consider how they can bring objects and materials into relationship with other aspects of the environment in the classroom to foster the children's aesthetic sense. The educators in Reggio Emilia have gone further than any other early childhood education program in showing us the value of aesthetics in the education of young children.

One of the teachers in the Vancouver Child Study Centre wrote the following response to this question on the survey: How important are aesthetics, and where do you see yourself incorporating this value in your work?

> I feel that I spend a lot of time focusing on detailed preparation of activity centres to make them look engaging. We avoid cheap, commercial plastic toys and books. We support quality in children's literature. I would like to feel more comfortable with allowing children access to delicate objects. I would like our pretend centre to be supplied with more real dishes, pots, etc. I would like to incorporate the use of more mirrors, light tables, glass bottles and coloured glass. (Gloria Rolfsen, Vancouver Child Study Centre survey, June 1998)*

The Scyther Café

Relationship was most important in all aspects of The Scyther Café. This project was carried out by two teachers, Karen Westphal** and Danica Sparvier***, who teach a group of mainly aboriginal children in the Blue Room at the Early Learning Centre in Regina, Saskatchewan. These two teachers took the children out into the community on a visit to a local art gallery. In doing so they began the chain of relationships that led from the art gallery back to the children's play in their classroom and eventually to the Saskatchewan legislature.

Karen and Danica recounted to Anne Luke, the director of the Centre, in an interview in April 2002, the story of how the project began and the unexpected path it took. "We went originally to the MacKenzie Art Gallery to see the Mi'kmaq basket display. When leaving the gallery we had to go through the Café Guerbois that was set up as part of the Impressionist Masterworks from the National Gallery of Canada exhibit. Each of the tables in the café was created by a different artist who had either collaged them or made some kind

---

*Reproduced courtesy of Gloria Rolfsen
**Reproduced courtesy of Karen Westphal
***Reproduced courtesy of Danica Sparvier

of structure that stuck out from the table. It made them unique and distinct; they were also set out so that the children couldn't just walk by. We had to weave through them. One table in particular caught my interest so I 'weaved' the children across the room to look at that table. We were quite amazed that this table would have this iceberg sticking right out of the centre of it. The children were also interested to see that you could see right through the glass cases where the cakes and juices were. On each table was a little card that mentioned the artist and what they had done. We talked about how each one was done by a separate artist and that is why the tables were all so different."

When they returned to the centre the teachers had set up activities for the children based on the Mi'kmaq baskets they had taken the children to see, but the children's interest seemed to be centred on the café, especially, the teachers thought, the food and the display cases.

The children in the Blue Room asked the teachers, Karen* and Danica**, if they could take the play dough into the playhouse to make food. The teachers made the play dough adding different kinds of drink crystals to give the play dough a fruity smell and bright colour. The children added glitter and sequins to decorate their pies and cookies. The children created many different kinds of food, and the play went on for days. The teachers asked the children, "Who is the food going to be for?" and were told, "For the people who come to our café." The children seemed surprised that the teachers would even ask. That is when the 'big idea' for the Scyther Café was born. Karen told Anne Luke, "I love the café, it's my big interest. I didn't think that the children would really remember or be interested in the tables because it was just something … an offshoot on the way…. Danica and I started talking about how we could build on the children's little restaurant that they were making in the house."

The teachers talked with the children about what they saw at the Café Guerbois. "We made charts with them about what they would need in the café they were creating in their play house. We just brainstormed with them about what they needed to make a café … The main thing they liked, that was even more important than the food, were the tables. They gave us lists of different things they wanted to use (to make their tables). Afterward Danica and I kind of sorted them into different groups … beads and feathers together on one table, seashells and sand together on another one. Then we got the children to draw a picture of what they wanted their table to look like." The teachers made a different station for each table and provided each group with the materials they had listed. At each station the teachers put up the children's sketches of the table they had designed and photographs of each child in the group. Other

*Reproduced courtesy of Karen Westphal
**Reproduced courtesy of Danica Sparvier

children, therefore, were able to see who was working on the table at each station and how it would look when it was finished. "Once the tables became a big thing, all the children (both in the afternoon and in the morning) became interested and they each worked at their tables at different times. Each table was made by four children, some maybe only worked on their table for two days and figured they were finished … some worked every day for weeks until they got their table done to their satisfaction…. As soon as the first table was done it was automatically moved into the café. They each had their little card with the name of who made the table. Any visitors who came, that was the first thing they were shown, 'See this is my table, there is my symbol.'"

The children made the tables from old ashtray stands, three-legged tables, and plant stands, which they decorated with a variety of materials: sand, seashells, beads, feathers, moss, etc. Over the next few weeks, the children printed menus and made many different kinds of food out of the play dough. After a field trip to visit a neighbourhood café, a group of boys built a fireplace similar to one they had seen in the café. The boys solved the problem of how to make the fire look realistic. They decided to place the fireplace near a heating vent so that the draught would make the red and orange tissue paper flicker like a flame. The teachers explained to Anne how relationship was critical in the development of the project. "I think because at the different stages we would

Designs for tables in the Scyther Café

Sue Fraser

Sue Fraser

Decorating a table for the Scyther Café

Sue Fraser

Decorated table for the Scyther Café

brainstorm in a collective group with all the children adding ideas and the children listening to each other's ideas … we all suddenly would go, 'Oh yeah, what a good idea!' The children, I think, set off one another in that way too. They would sit at circle and one boy who didn't volunteer anything at all to the café building, was the one who named the café—Scyther Café—after a Pokémon character."

When the café was complete, it was decided to ask the lieutenant-governor to open it and invite the families of the children, local artists, and people from the local community to the celebration. Unfortunately, on the day of the opening of the cafe, the lieutenant-governor had to attend a funeral, so in her place the director of the MacKenzie Art Gallery cut the ribbon to open the café. The teachers and children, however, were happy to accept an invitation later to display their café in the Legislative Building.

The first and most powerful relationship the children made was not to the Mi'kmaq baskets they had been taken to see at the art gallery (which surprised the teachers considering the cultural background of the children) but to the café, the tables, and the food displayed in the glass cases. It was these objects that the children related to in their play on their return to the classroom. Karen*, in turn, could relate to the children's excitement about the café. It was not surprising, therefore, that the Scyther Café held so much potential for them as a group, because both the teachers and the children were passionate about the idea of a café. The teachers saw themselves as genuine partners in the learning process. Karen said: "If both (teachers and children) are not learning, it's stagnant, not so interesting; the teacher is not fully engaged and the learning is not so deep." It was this shared passion that generated so many of

*Reproduced courtesy of Karen Westphal

the creative ideas for the Scyther Café. Throughout the project, letters were sent updating parents. "Quite a few parents were constantly asking us all about it on our home visits. We would give the whole story and we might tell them about their child, some unique thing that their child had done towards the café in some special way … One Mom was so excited she came along on the trip to the Legislature." (Karen Westphal* and Danica Sparvier**, interview, April 12, 2002).

The success of this project depended on relationships: relationships with materials, with ideas, relationships between children, between children and teachers, between the teachers, between the teachers and the families, between the teachers and the community, and even between the school and the legislature. The learning in the classroom is deepened, and respect and understanding grows and is expanded when teachers involve parents and the community in their experiences in the classroom. Paola Cagliari and Claudia Giudici (2001) write that "… individual participation … takes on further meaning if the school presents itself as a community—in relation to the wider community of the city—which has a broader based project strategy."

Relationship with the Natural World

How can teachers foster in children a lifelong, caring relationship with the natural world? Fewer and fewer children in the busy structured lives they lead, mostly in urban settings, have an opportunity to experience and develop a love for nature. As teachers we have a responsibility to help create a future generation who will care enough about the natural world to become its guardian. Children learn to care for the environment, not through the kind of scientific study offered in schools, but by having someone who can share their enthusiasm for nature with them. How fortunate are children who have a teacher who loves to grow plants, care for animals, or loves to stop and examine little things like a buttercup or dandelion. Who picks a worm off the blacktop and sets it safely on the grass. Teachers who share an attitude of caring and enthusiasm for the natural world are giving children a gift that will last a lifetime.

In an interview with Lella Gandini, Tiziana Filippini describes how children in Reggio Emilia explore a leaf. She says almost everyone in the autumn explores a leaf but in the atelier in the Diana School "…we encourage children to enter into a relationship with the leaf and activate processes of reelaboration and reinvention, metaphoric expression, using analogies and poetic languages to build a personal image of the leaf (Gandini 2005, 68). This activates in the child not just a scientific interest in the leaf but deeper emotional connections to the leaf. The children as they create images of the leaf, both

---

*Reproduced courtesy of Karen Westphal
**Reproduced courtesy of Danica Sparvier

realistic and imaginative, are building an emotional attachment to the leaf and then by extension to the tree and the natural world.

Louv states that in the space of a century, American experience of nature has gone from direct utilitarianism to romantic attachment to electronic detachment (Louv 2005, 16). How can teachers, he asks, find the path that leads to a nature–child reunion? He points out how important it is to give children a sense of place, a grounding in where they live, because this gives them a secure footing to enter the larger world. Teachers can achieve this by connecting children to the natural world around them through the materials, activities, and environment they prepare for them.

At Douglas College one group of students achieved this in the beautiful natural environment they prepared for children in Children Teaching Teachers. They set a stone inukshuk at the door to greet the children as they entered the room and projected a life-sized image of an inukshuk on the wall of the classroom. (An inukshuk is a statue of a man made of very large rocks used as a place marker by the Inuit people of the Arctic. It is the symbol used for the Olympic games in Vancouver (2010) so is visible everywhere.) The children were offered a variety of natural materials such as different sized pebbles and rocks set out attractively on mats on the floor.

> J. began to pile the rocks on top of each other, glancing up at the image projected on the wall.
>
> **D.** (student teacher): Maybe we can find a way to make it more secure so it doesn't fall over.
>
> **J.:** Yeah.
>
> **D.:** What do you think is a good idea?
>
> **J.:** Hmm … like that (looks at the picture).
>
> **D.:** Try to look at this picture—all the rocks are really, really flat.
>
> **J.:** Yeah (he looks in the bucket beside him).
>
> J. and **D.** continue to build with the rocks.
>
> **J.:** Ha, look! Now it is tall.
>
> **D.:** Kinda looks like a person, that one.
>
> **J.:** Yeah!
>
> **D.:** Just like the one—did you see that one by the door when you came…. There's a really cool one, it looks like a person. It's called an inukshuk.
>
> (J. looks at **D.** and nods.)
>
> **D.:** It's when you make a person out of rocks. Pretty cool.
>
> **J.:** Yeah.

Using only natural materials and illustrations of a familiar cultural image, D.'s group, by preparing an environment that reflects the child's world and by scaffolding the child's learning, is connecting a child to his place in the world at a moment in time when the materials and provocation he uses are particularly relevant to a child living in Vancouver as it gears up for the Winter Olympics (October, 2009). If D.'s group had set up a typical preschool environment of commercial toys and unrelated art activities, would Jack's learning have been as meaningful? Would he have had the opportunity to use the materials in an intelligent way and make connections to the culture around him? It is during the process of collaborative critical reflection after each session that the students deconstruct their experiences in Children Teaching Teachers and seek answers to questions like the ones above.

WORKING RELATIONSHIPS

One of the greatest benefits in introducing the principles learned from the Reggio Emilia approach is in the way the need to collaborate improves working relationships. The fundamental principle of relationship ensures that all participants in the program have to collaborate to make the program function successfully. This collaboration, in turn, increases each member's commitment to work toward strengthening the group as a whole. Decisions are no longer made by one person, but in collaboration with others. Team members share their observations and reflections and plan the program as a team. Documentation, in itself, cannot be carried out effectively unless all the participants have shared in its development.

Relationship in the Preparation of Teachers

Children Teaching Teachers, the core curriculum experience in the ECE program at Douglas College, has proved an effective way of preparing students to work collaboratively. Relationship is a fundamental principle in this method of preparing students to work with young children. There have been many changes to Children Teaching Teachers as some of us who began the process retired and new faculty have joined the team. Relationship, however, remains a core principle of the experience as can be seen from the student's evaluations of Children Teaching Teachers in April 2009.

The Children Teaching Teachers has been an integral part of the Early Childhood Education program at Douglas College for over ten years. It continues to be a central part of the students' metamorphosis into fully fledged teachers as can be seen from quotations from two of the students' written evaluations of Children Teaching Teachers in April, 2009:

> From my perspective Children Teaching Teachers has broadened my perspective, showing me what I could learn from children. To see how children express themselves, work together as a group, use their creativity, and interact with the wide range of materials in the environment. The CTT experience has motivated me to learn more and inspired me.

The groups of students who work together in planning and presenting activities to the children discover very soon that for their session with the children to be a success, the members in their group have to learn to work as a team.

The students have been together for one semester at the college before Children Teaching Teachers begins, but it is not until they begin the process that they really understand the importance of team work. They have to get to know one another well and learn about one another's strengths and weaknesses. They have to build trust and learn to communicate effectively individually and as a group. If the members of the group develop a strong relationship, they usually have a positive and enjoyable experience in Children Teaching Teachers. When there are difficulties because of personality conflicts or lack of an equal sharing of responsibility or different levels of understanding or commitment in the group, the experience becomes a challenge for everyone. Often the students themselves are able to resolve their own problems, but sometimes the instructor who is assigned to each group has to step in and help the students overcome their problems to avoid a negative effect on the visiting children. The instructor helps the students to see that conflict can be positive and that the experience they have gained in collaborating and resolving problems with other students will help them develop the skills they need to be a member of a team at work. The following example, taken from a student's reflection paper of April 1998 on her experience in Children Teaching Teachers, describes how members of her group learned to work together as a team.

> I tend to take on the role of leader in many group situations, and in this CTT experience there were two other people who usually take on the same role. We quickly learned that in order to work productively as a group we would have to share the leadership role. Once this transition was made our group functioned smoothly. I found it helpful to share this role with others because it took some of the pressure off each of us who felt we had to take charge. We took turns facilitating productive discussion and keeping the group on topic.

One of the main goals of Children Teaching Teachers is to give students experience in building strong relationships in their work. Students build relationships within each group. The small groups work together in setting up the environment, in deconstructing the experience, and in analyzing the pedagogical documentation they make each week of their session with the children. It is essential that trust has been established between each member of the group before the process of collaborative critical reflection of the pedagogical documentation begins. This occurs both after each session and again later when the students have incorporated feedback from the initial analysis. When respect and trust are present in the group the analysis of the documentation of their sessions with the children can be deconstructed honestly and openly and suggestions for change become more easily accepted. One student wrote the following in her evaluation of Children Teaching Teachers:

> Documentation for me is really a wonderful process to do and be part of because it makes me think deeper and reflect upon the things that happened with the children during CTT.... Documentation also encourages us to make use of our teamwork skills because having different perspectives makes the analysis and reflection of our observation deeper and more meaningful (April, 2009).

Relationships evolve as the students have long and involved discussions within their group and as they engage in deconstruction of their documentation. This process is described in the extract below, taken from a student's reflections in her journal in April 1998.

> During CTT evaluation and debriefing, I shared my opinions and thoughts about that day's CTT. I felt that I was reflective in my comments and shared positive and negative experiences with the other group debriefing with us. I found it helpful to debrief with another CTT group because we shared what was working on a much broader basis than later in the day during video analysis. During video analysis it was again a collaborative effort. I contributed my thoughts as to what portion of the video to use ... I was always eager to not only share my own ideas but to acknowledge others. I feel that I was a positive member of the group and may have helped others feel as though they were too.

The students, thus, began to value collaboration as they saw it at work in practice. They also observed how the instructors collaborated in integrating the course content to make it more relevant for the ECE students.

The value of building relationship in the preparation of teachers can be seen in this student's comments in her reflection paper of April 1998:

> I found Children Teaching Teachers to be very beneficial in building friendships, sharing new ideas and experiences and just getting to know what it will be like out in the field to work with a team as well as a group of children.

SEEING THE RESULTS

The building of strong relationships in every aspect of an early childhood program is the key factor in providing quality care and education for young children. It starts with the first contact, in the process of orientation, when the relationship between the children and parents and the teachers begins to develop. It is important that this introduction of the children to school happens slowly and carefully, so that the children's attachment to their families continues to be nurtured and the children and family are given the time to develop trust in the new environment. It then becomes important to have strategies in place to develop and sustain the relationship with families. Parents need opportunities to get to know one another and the other children in the school so that they feel they are an integral part of the program.

The relationships among the staff also have to be nurtured so that they too feel a sense of belonging to the school community. Staff members need to trust one another so that they can communicate openly and honestly. There has to be enough time set aside for meetings and discussions so that everyone has the opportunity to voice their ideas and concerns. If all the teachers feel that they are valued members of the team, their commitment to the program will grow, and the children will receive the quality program they deserve.

Perhaps the biggest change since introducing the Reggio Emilia approach into the ECE program has been in the teachers' relationships with children. Baerbel Jaeckel, the teacher in the Quadra Island Preschool, said she has had to "unwind her agenda, listen more to children and build a program that evolves from the ideas and interests of the children in the class."

The decision to make relationship central to a program requires teachers to examine the strands in the web of relationships in the school, to test their strength, and to see how they can be extended into every aspect in the program. The principle of relationship extends beyond the human level, as it is woven into every part of the program, including the design of the space, the choice of equipment, and the presentation of materials in the classroom. As the quality of the physical and social environment improves, the people involved feel more satisfaction, there is a sense of joyfulness, and the school becomes an amiable place for the children, teachers, and families it serves.

CONCENTRIC CIRCLES OF ACQUAINTANCE

Alexandra Doherty* describes the role of relationships in her work at Loyalist College:

> An environment for children is a reflection of all the relationships of the individuals who come in contact with each other: the children, the teachers, the families, the classroom, and the school. In this relationship, the individuality of each person should be evident

---

*Reproduced courtesy of Alexandra Doherty

throughout, at the same time as the individual becomes part of a whole. People often ask us how we did what we have done in the child care centre at Loyalist College; to answer that we have to go back and reacquaint ourselves with the developmental process. A metaphor for the development of our schools is that of a pebble in a pond. As the pebble drops into the middle of the pond, concentric circles of relatedness form and begin to ripple in smaller to larger circles, as the ripple makes its impact on the pond.

The first part of any relationship is the acquaintance process. We are constantly in a state of becoming acquainted, but this is heightened in the early stages. The acquaintance process was an enviable position to have, in the beginning—a new school, new faces, new relationships. Meeting all the new staff, all the children, all the parents for the very first time, making their acquaintance and becoming familiar and welcoming them into our new school nine years ago was a position of great perspective. It is difficult, and almost awkward when you meet people for the first time. The foremost perspective, therefore, is to offer a sense of being welcome; the welcoming that begins should never end, in our school or any school. As each teacher or parent comes to our school each day they should feel a sense of belonging, a sense of welcoming and knowing where they belong, where others belong, and the roles and the intricacies. The flow of relationships is clear in every conversation, every moment of meaning, each resonance of the "one" and the "all."

In this time of becoming acquainted, all of the individuals could be perceived as pebbles in ponds and all the concentric circles, because of the vibrations of each, would accept each other but would not necessarily connect. This image highlights again the concept of isolation, the feeling that one is still in the perspective of reaching out and shaking hands and making eye contact and has not quite achieved the level of mutuality that would make one truly feel as though one belonged. From this point people move to become embedded into an environment, embedded into a relationship, embedded into a school.

Although the metaphor of the pebble in the pond fits the idea of how something beautiful yet simple can have an impact on a greater whole, it doesn't go far enough to show that what we all need and want, and what children rightfully deserve, is a feeling of connectedness, a feeling of being embedded.

Cormorant

The Environment as
Third Teacher

Questions to Consider:

- What is the rationale for creating an environment that acts as a third teacher?

- What are the major similarities and differences in the way the environment is planned?

- What are the key principles that need to be considered in creating an environment that acts as a third teacher?

- What are the challenges in creating and working in this kind of environment?

- How does the creation of an environment that acts as a third teacher affect the quality of programming in an early childhood centre?

- Does the creation of an environment as a third teacher presuppose a major rethinking about values?

- How can teachers create environments that encourage children to become future guardians of the natural world?

> The wider the range of possibilities we offer children, the more intense will be their motivations and the richer their experiences.
>
> —Loris Malaguzzi

The space we live in has a powerful influence over us, particularly the space we grew up in. Often we try, without even being aware of it, to recreate in our adult lives the places we remember from our childhood. Long ago, for instance, the immigrants from Europe brought the images of the gardens they had played in as children to their new homeland, where they recreated the rose gardens and flower borders filled with European flowers such as delphiniums and foxgloves.

When teachers plan an environment where children will spend long periods of time, they need to think of the effect this environment may have on their adult lives. Carol Anne Wien, on a study trip to Reggio Emilia in 1997, met some graduates of the Reggio Emilia preschools and noted in her diary that what they remembered about their time there was a particular atmosphere of deep affection, a feeling of family, lasting friendships, images of light and colour, and strong relationships with teachers. Alexis, a student of literature at the University of Parma and head of a theatre group, told Wien, "It gave me a particular sensibility to face the world" (1997). Wien also quotes

Francesco, an atelierista in one of the Reggio Emilia preschools, as saying that "one young man of 23 told her that whenever he feels stressed or upset he takes a walk by his old school and remembers the joy he experienced while there."

The spaces that teachers create for children seem to hold enduring memories for them that have a powerful influence on what they will value later in life. It is important, therefore, that teachers think carefully about their own values and how they affect the decisions they make about the arrangement of space, equipment, and materials in the classroom. Teachers are often unaware of the messages the environment is communicating to children and visitors to the classroom. I remember one year, when psychedelic colours were in fashion, we painted all the children's cubbies in bright, clashing colours. It took us a long time to realize why the children had become so excitable when they were putting on their clothes to go outside.

When I visit a preschool or kindergarten I know immediately upon walking into the classroom and seeing the children's work displayed on the walls a great deal about the philosophy of the school. On one of my visits to the Quadra Island Preschool, I was stunned by the beauty of a multicoloured sheet draped beside the entranceway. Pinned to the sheet were photographs, written comments, and a description of how the parents, children, and teacher had coloured the fabric. They had used eye droppers to squirt food colouring on to the fabric to make a "dragon skin" for the Chinese New Year's parade. I was able to read the "story" of the sheet from the documentation pinned to the fabric. However, I also learned much more, such as how much collaboration among children, parents, and teachers was valued in this preschool. I understood from looking at the beautiful artwork that aesthetics were highly valued. I could see that respect was being shown for children and families from different cultural groups.

One can understand why the educators in Reggio Emilia have termed the environment a third teacher because of the power environments such as these have to inform and shape the kind of learning that will happen in the room. As Lella Gandini wrote,

> The schools in Reggio Emilia could not be just anywhere, and no one of them could serve as an exact model to be copied literally elsewhere. Yet, they have common features that merit consideration in schools everywhere. Each school's particular configuration of the garden, walls, tall windows, and handsome furniture declares: This is a place where adults have thought about the quality of environment. Each school is full of light, variety, and a certain kind of joy. In addition, each school shows how teachers, parents, and children, working and

playing together, have created a unique space that reflects their personal lives, the history of their schools, the many layers of culture and a nexus of well thought out choices. (in Edwards, Gandini, and Forman 1993, 149)

The Quadra Island Preschool, too, began to develop a unique space that reflected the lives of the people involved and the culture of the community it served.

THE ENVIRONMENT AS A REFLECTION OF VALUES

Visitors to the schools in Reggio Emilia are amazed at the care and attention that have been given to the preparation of the environment. It would take a long time, if it were even possible, to become aware of all the details and to comprehend the thinking that has gone into every aspect of the space in the schools in Reggio Emilia. Details have been carefully thought through so that the environment truly reflects the values and beliefs that have evolved in the schools since they were started over 50 years ago.

Respect for the image of the child as rich, strong, and powerful is fundamental in preparing an environment that allows the child to be actively engaged in the process of learning. The importance given to building relationships with children, families, and the community means that learning is viewed as a collaborative process that does not take place in isolation. Spaces, therefore, are designed to welcome families and other visitors. Furniture is placed in the entrance halls to make parents and other visitors feel comfortable and to encourage them to take the time to inform themselves about the school. The documentation displayed on the walls or in portfolios on the shelves in the entranceways provides a record of what has been happening in the program. The space in the classrooms is designed to encourage children to work with others, sometimes in a large group but more often in small groups of four or five children. There are low platforms built above the floor, where a small group of children can work on a project, such as building with blocks, undisturbed by the activity in the rest of the room. Mini-ateliers provide an area adjacent to the main classroom where children can work separately with art and construction materials.

Consideration of aesthetics is evident in every aspect of the program. The thought that goes into creating beautiful spaces for children reflects the belief that children deserve the very best and that their aesthetic sense needs to be nurtured in the early years. As Carol Anne Wien wrote in 1997 in her diary of her visit to Reggio Emilia, "the beauty, serenity and deep affection in the schools stays with the children as a foundation," perhaps throughout their lives. Loris Malaguzzi envisioned Reggio Emilia classrooms as being "transformed into one large space with market stalls, each one with its own children and its own projects and activities" (Edwards, Gandini, and Forman 1993, 84). This layout has similarities with the way many early childhood programs organize their space. In most preschools and child cares in North America, certain areas of the room are designated as places where children can do specific activities, such as creating artwork, building with blocks, and working with puzzles and other table toys. There is an area, usually called a housekeeping or dramatic play area, where children can use props for role play. The traditional curriculum areas, such as music, literature, art, and science, each have their own area of the room where children can use the materials for each aspect of the curriculum. The library corner, for instance, is stocked with books, which may reflect the current topics the children are exploring. On closer inspection, however, a visitor notices that there are subtle differences in the way environments are planned in traditional and Reggio Emilia schools.

Creating an environment that acts as a third teacher supports the perspective that knowledge is constructed not in isolation but within the social group. Teachers embracing the Reggio Emilia approach, therefore, have to think differently about the way they plan the environment. It needs to be designed to provide opportunities for the people involved to interact with one another and with the environment to co-construct knowledge. Lella Gandini quotes Loris Malaguzzi:

> We value space because of its power to organize, promote pleasant relationships between people of different ages, create a handsome environment, provide changes, promote choices and activity, and its potential for sparking all kinds of social, affective and cognitive learning. All of this contributes to a sense of well-being and security in children. We also think that the space has to be a sort of aquarium that mirrors the ideas, values, attitudes, and cultures of the people who live within it. (1994, 149)

Loris Malaguzzi acknowledged the role the environment plays in the education of young children and its power to communicate beyond the classroom walls. In fact, he tells the story of how in the early days when the schools were struggling for their existence, once a week the children and teachers set up their equipment in the centre of town so people could see the school in action. The municipal schools in Reggio Emilia have understood the power of the environment and put it to work in programs involving young children, parents, and the community perhaps more effectively than in any other kind of school. As Gandini describes it, "The environment is seen here as educating the child; in fact it is considered as 'the third educator' along with a team of two teachers" (Edwards, Gandini, and Forman 1993, 148).

Identifying Shared Values

To plan an environment like that of the preschools in Reggio Emilia, which so closely reflects the philosophy and values of the families, teachers, and community involved, is a challenging task. As in all aspects of the approach, teachers have to begin with small steps and then build on these as they feel more confident. The first step, therefore, in planning the environment is to identify the values that are at the core of our work with young children and those of the families and the wider community surrounding the school. This means that teachers, in the early stages of planning, arrange meetings with all the people involved in their programs to clarify the values that are important to the group.

This task sounds easy, but when the abstract values that the group has identified are translated into concrete factors, such as the selection of materials and equipment and the programming of each day, the task gets harder. The team may struggle with such questions as what materials, equipment, and routines are congruent with the identified values. For instance, if authenticity is identified as a core value, this will affect the choice of materials set out for dramatic play. Is it congruent with the stated value to provide the children with plastic models of food and utensils, or should real objects be set out in the play kitchen? In the art area, should play dough be used as a modelling material, or is clay a more authentic artistic material? These are the decisions the group will have to make to ensure their program truly reflects their values. As stated above, one of the distinguishing characteristics of the programs in the preschools in Reggio Emilia is the way practice reflects the beliefs and values of the community. Collaboration, for instance, is highly valued and is seen in operation from the highest level of community-based management of the schools, to the partnership in learning between children and teachers in the classroom.

Teachers wishing to explore the Reggio Emilia approach may find it helps to begin the process of planning an environment that acts as a third teacher by thinking of their own values. Once they have done this individually, they can share their values with the team and members of the community. When the teachers in the child care on Quadra Island decided to reorganize their environment to make it reflect more closely the principles learned from Reggio Emilia, they began by identifying the values that were important to them. The teachers met once a week in the evening and made a list of ideas they valued and felt passionate about. They then reworked the list, until the whole group shared ownership of it. These are some of the values the group listed on a chart: aesthetics, light, coziness, comfort, tidiness, organized space, softness, safety, challenges, open spaces, and clutter-free space. On a separate chart they listed their passions. These included children, music, plants, solitude, travel, food, reading, learning, exploring, nature, animals, laughter, outdoors, arts, dressups, building, and designing landscapes.

The teachers then began to examine the space in their environment to see what needed to be changed to reflect the things that they had identified as important to the group. As they had identified aesthetics as a central value, they looked at every corner of the classroom to see whether it met the criteria for this value. They decided that the heaps of puzzles and games on the shelves in the classroom would have to be stored in a less conspicuous place. These items were replaced with a display of branches and driftwood collected with the children in the forest and arranged attractively in flat dishes on the shelves. An interesting assortment of shells was placed in glass jars and filled with water of different colours. The children were invited to bring in objects that they were excited about to display on the shelves. Very soon, a dull, uninteresting space became a focus of attention in the room.

Quadra Island Children's Centre shelves before introducing the Reggio Emilia principles

Light was also considered an important value, so the group examined the environment to see how it could be used to further advantage. They moved a refrigerator away from a window and replaced it with a painting easel. There was now space and light for a plant to be placed on the windowsill beside the easel. A beautiful, quiet place was created where children could spend long periods of time painting.

Quadra Island Children's Centre shelves after introducing the Reggio Emilia principles

Sue Fraser

The environment demonstrates respect for the children and their ideas in many ways. For instance, the teachers asked the children to help plan the housekeeping corner. A child-sized bed with a soft mattress was built at the children's request. The bed also addressed qualities of softness, comfort, and coziness that the group

Sue Fraser

The staff at the Quadra Island Children's Centre moved a refrigerator away from the window and replaced it with an easel.

CHAPTER 5   The Environment as Third Teacher

felt should be present in their setting. As well, the art area in the classroom was reorganized to form a mini-atelier. Whereas in the past all the art materials had been set out haphazardly on the shelves, they were now carefully selected and displayed aesthetically in attractive containers. Documentation of the children's work was displayed on the walls to celebrate the children's ideas and to make their thinking visible.

The teachers kept asking themselves the following questions as they began to reorganize the classroom space to reflect first their own values and passions, and second the principles they had learned from Reggio Emilia.

- How well does the room reflect the values we have identified as important to us?

- What overall messages will the room convey to children, parents, and other visitors to the classroom?

- How will the environment mirror an image of the child that is rich, powerful, and competent?

- How well does the arrangement of the room reflect our respect for children, families, and the community?

- Does the environment offer experiences that heighten multisensory awareness?

- How can we create a space that invites parents and children to linger and feel welcome?

The search for answers to these questions led the teachers to gradually reevaluate their use of space in the classroom and make profound changes in the physical space, the decoration of the rooms, and the availability of materials. They began to include the parents and the community in their discussions. At one well-attended meeting of parents and community members, the staff asked for specific suggestions about how they could make the space more welcoming to families and other visitors. The parents told the staff how much they valued the documentation in the entrance and how it was "drawing them more into the program." They suggested that a special place be created in the entrance hall where the staff could jot down things that needed to be done (small or big) so parents would know how they could help and volunteer if they had the time and the skill.

EXPLORING REGGIO EMILIA PRINCIPLES

A number of principles, including aesthetics, active learning, collaboration, transparency, "bringing the outdoors in," flexibility, relationship, and reciprocity, need to be addressed to create an environment that acts as a third teacher. Although these principles are discussed separately here, it is important to keep in mind their interconnectedness.

Aesthetics

Louise Cadwell describes the way Amelia Gambetti worked with the teachers in the College School in St. Louis, Missouri, to improve the aesthetics in the environment and how they "transformed our classrooms from dark, dismal places into beautiful, inviting, light-filled, orderly spaces" (1997, 61). She describes Amelia looking at a mural of a tree in the entryway to the school:

> "Let's give this tree more of a reason for being," said Amelia. "What about moving that flight cage of finches that is in the hall in here in front of it. That could solve several problems ... it would give the tree a purpose—a backdrop for the birds; it would make the birds feel closer to the out-of-doors near the colors and image of a tree." (1997, 99–100)

After reading this passage, I summoned the courage to suggest to Baerbel Jaeckel, the teacher at Quadra Island Preschool, that we approach the parents about removing a mural that had been painted some years before on one wall that ran the length of the preschool. This cartoon of an enormous, smiling sun frolicking with small children dominated the room. It smothered the children's "voices" and took up space that we could use for documentation. To my relief, the parents agreed. One parent said, "the mural has outlived its time; it came from another era." Over the holidays they arranged to have the wall painted a warm off-white. It is now an area where the children can see their work displayed and where parents and visitors can read the documentations of the children's experiences in the room. It feels as if the *real* children and their voices are now being heard in the room.

Active Learning

This principle reflects the underlying value of respect for the child, particularly for the image of the child as competent and able to construct her learning either alone or with the support of others. The principle of active learning requires that the classroom have a stimulating environment that offers children many choices, provokes them to engage in many activities, and encourages them to explore a wide variety of materials. These materials need to be open ended to allow the children to act on and transform them in many ways. There also should be many opportunities for children to represent their ideas in different media.

Sue Fraser

The Quadra Island Preschool classroom before the centre introduced Reggio Emilia principles

The classroom at the Vancouver Child Study Centre provides children with a rich and stimulating learning environment. In the fall, the teachers had observed that the children in their group that year were very interested in construction. Over the next few weeks, in addition to the blocks, Lego, and Duplo regularly available in the classroom, the teachers provided the children with many different kinds of blocks to build with: small, brightly coloured wooden blocks of various shapes and sizes, mosaic tiles, and so on. They also brought in carpentry tools and high-quality wood for the children to hammer and nail. The teachers encouraged the children to create many drawings, paintings, collages, and three-dimensional objects representing their ideas about construction. As well, the teachers brought in a selection of books about building.

One group was particularly interested in the story "The Three Little Pigs," so the teachers decided to ask the children if they would like to build houses for the pigs. The children sketched how they imagined the houses might look. They decided to use cardboard boxes as a base for the houses. The children took a walk in the forest behind the school to collect materials to build the houses. A small group of children formed a core group who stayed with the

Godfrey's Wolf

Sue Fraser

Godfrey drew the wolf from "The Three Little Pigs."

project for the whole time, while many of the other children came and went during the three weeks that the project lasted. The children made the first two houses by attaching straw and sticks, which they had collected in the forest, to the wooden boxes with "mortar" they had made with flour and water. The children experimented with food colouring and paint to make the glue they had mixed look more like mortar. Then came the more challenging job of constructing the house made of bricks. The teachers put the cardboard box on the table. One surface of the box had been shaped to form the roof, and they cut a door and a window out of the sides. The teachers showed the children a real brick and discussed how the pigs would have used bricks like this one to build their houses. They set a large block of red clay out on the table and helped the children cut the clay into small, square bricks. The children began to build the bricks up the side of the house to make the walls.

Sally

First Little Pig's House

Sue Fraser

Sally drew the straw house for the first little pig.

Gloria (the teacher): It looks as though it is going to be strong. If it isn't the right size you need to make it yourself. Which size do you need?

William (age 4): Fat and little ones.

Gloria: What is that coming out of the top of the roof?

William: The chimney. We are making a brick house.

Gloria: Look at the heavy, heavy brick here.

William: I have made one [brick]. I need a paintbrush.

Sue Fraser

William announces that he is making a "brick house."

(He begins to use the paintbrush to apply "mortar" to cement the bricks he has made.)

William: I am making a brick house, but it is clay, but when the clay dries it will be brick. The water makes it stick good. It is almost going to be a brick house. How does the door close? How does it stay closed? You can close it if it is almost going to dry. If it is starting to be hard it won't open.

(He cuts some more square bricks. He measures the size of brick he needs and fits the one he made into the space. It doesn't quite fit. He tries cutting the brick with scissors.)

William: A strongman tool. We need a skinny brick for that corner.

Gloria: Godfrey, can you help us on this corner? Which house is the strongest?

William: Look it is strong. I can't blow it down.

Gloria: But what if a wolf came along?

William: That is strong paper. It is called cardboard. Special little bricks. That is a middle-sized brick.

Gloria: It looks pretty strong.

(William calls out to two children who are pounding the clay bricks into a mound: "You *have* to make a brick house!" He goes over and joins them at the clay table.)

This example shows how the experience of constructing a brick house provided the child with many opportunities to actively explore, investigate, and solve problems with the support of Gloria, his teacher. She stayed with him until he put the finishing touches to the house. The transcription gives an insight into how Gloria supported William's thinking process as he estimated the size of the bricks he needed and considered the properties of the clay. He made choices about tools and decided the scissors would be a better tool for cutting the clay than the knife the teacher had suggested. He thought about the strength of the house ("I can't blow it down"). He tried to keep the other children on task, saying, "You *have* to make a brick house." Gloria gave him the freedom to use the material in another way when he decided to join the children exploring the red clay at the next table.

By the time the three little pigs' houses were nearly complete, only William was left working on the house, and he too seemed to be losing interest. Was there any point in bringing out the brick house the next day? The teachers discussed this and decided to bring the project to a close. They put the three houses the children had made for the little pigs on a low shelf below a display board with many drawings, photographs, and written commentaries that documented the experience. The teachers, remembering the way the children had used the clay to make a volcano the day before, wondered if the children were really interested in pursuing this topic further. They had observed that the red clay had made the children think of hot lava. The next day they put out the clay again and observed what the children did with it. The children stated that they wanted the volcano they had made the previous day to explode. The teachers and the children set about figuring how they could make this happen. A small group of children carried on this investigation about volcanic explosions for the next few days.

An environment such as this, which stimulates learning and is responsive to the children's input, is essential to creating an environment that acts as a third teacher. As Lella Gandini states,

> In order to act as an educator for the child, the environment has to be flexible: It must undergo frequent modification by the children and the teachers in order to remain up to date and responsive to their needs to be protagonists in constructing their knowledge. All the things that surround the people in the school and which they use— the objects, the materials, and the structures—are not seen as passive elements but on the contrary are seen as elements that condition and are conditioned by the actions of children and adults who are active in it. (Edwards, Gandini, and Forman 1993, 148)

Collaboration

Collaboration is one of the strongest messages that the environment in its role as the third teacher communicates. An environment planned to act as a third teacher is particularly effective in helping children learn skills for working with others in a group. The approach, for instance, requires that teachers encourage children to contribute their ideas and efforts to group projects. Children learn the value of individual contributions in building the strength of the group. The environment must allow space for working individually or with other children and adults in groups. As Vygotsky says, "With assistance every child can do more than he can by himself— though only within the limits set by the

Sue Fraser

Emma shows us how to use chopsticks.

Sue Fraser

Children paint the skin of the dragon.

state of his development" (1962, 103). The large murals, for instance, that are painted on acetate and hung from the ceilings in the Reggio Emilia schools are created in collaboration with others.

In Quadra Island Preschool, the teacher, parents, and children collaborated in celebrating the Chinese New Year. One of the children in the preschool, Emma, had been adopted as an infant and brought from China to live on Quadra Island. Her parents are determined that she retains her cultural heritage; thus, the celebration of the Chinese New Year became a particularly important celebration for the preschool. Emma's mother shared many of the beautiful objects that she had brought back with her from her trip to China to adopt Emma. A beautiful display was arranged in front of a magnificent wall hanging of a fiery gold dragon. The parents and the teacher discussed how they could construct a dragon for the Chinese New Year's parade. One of the fathers offered to help the children build the dragon's head out of a

Sue Fraser

Des and his mother do calligraphy together.

The dragon dances to celebrate the Chinese New Year.

cardboard box. The teacher helped the children make the dragon's "skin," using a sheet and food colouring. Parents made many contributions—for instance, one mother cooked Chinese food with the children for snack time, and another showed the children how to do calligraphy. The children also made red money envelopes and lanterns to decorate the room.

At last the day of the parade came. When the parents arrived, the preschool was empty; there was not a sound. The children had decided that the dragon should hide very quietly until everyone had arrived. They all huddled in a back room in total silence under the dragon skin, in line behind the child who had volunteered to be under the dragon's head. The parents stood around looking puzzled, until suddenly there was a loud boom from a gong and out tumbled the most magnificent dragon anyone had ever seen. He paraded round and round the room, accompanied by the booming of the gong.

The richness of this experience resulted from the collaboration of everyone in the program. It could not have happened the way it did without the children, teacher, and parents all contributing their ideas and skills. It is essential, therefore, that in creating an environment that acts as a third teacher, children are given the opportunity to work with others in the co-construction of knowledge. The room should also communicate respect for the families and community, as well as for the cultural background of the people involved in the program and in the community served by the school.

Transparency

In the preschools in Reggio Emilia, transparency is evident at many levels in the program. On the surface, transparency is seen in the importance that light plays in the environment of every municipal preschool in Reggio Emilia. Light is everywhere; it not only shines through windows and internal glass walls, but it is used in playful ways. It is captured and changed by coloured, transparent film attached to the windowpanes, it is caught on the shiny mobiles that break up the space between floor and ceilings, it shines through glass objects that reflect it around the room. Light is reflected in mirrors hung from the ceilings and on the classroom walls. Mirrors are found in unexpected places, such as attached to the floor and on the ramps for climbing. Mirrors are formed into pyramid-shaped kaleidoscopes into which children can climb and observe their reflections from many different angles. Light is used as an art medium; for instance, the children paint and arrange collage materials on the glass surface of light tables. The children's artwork is also projected onto walls by overhead projectors. Light shines through the murals that the children have painted on large plastic sheets, which may be hung from the ceilings as room dividers or displayed on the walls of the classrooms. A light source gives an added dimension to the construction area of the classroom. Children can use a light projector to cast shadows of their block constructions on a screen or wall of the classroom.

Transparency is also a metaphor for communication, especially in the documentation that informs parents and visitors of what is happening in the program. This information is made transparent, such as through the documentation of the children's work that is displayed in the entranceways and on the classroom walls. On a deeper level, transparency is seen in the openness of the educators of Reggio Emilia to learning from the ideas of others working in the field of early childhood education and in their willingness to share their approach with visitors from all over the world.

Bringing the Outdoors In

Bringing the outdoors in heightens children's awareness of the natural, physical, and social environments in which they live. This awareness helps to strengthen the children's sense of belonging in their world. This principle, too, has levels of meaning. On the surface, the use of natural materials is seen in the decoration of the room. The teachers in Reggio Emilia added many natural materials to the activities in the room. For instance, there was a snake's skin wound around a piece of driftwood on one of the tables, and rocks, driftwood, and grapevines were available for the children to use with the blocks. On a deeper level, bringing the outdoors in connects children to their roots and gives them a sense of value and respect for their community and culture. The windows in the classroom should be low enough to allow children to watch the passing traffic and changes in the weather and the seasons. If the windows are too high for children to see out of, steps can be built below the

Sue Fraser

The Halloween witch made by the children and parents at Quadra Island Preschool.

window ledge so they can stand and look out.

In the Quadra Island Preschool, the teacher consulted the families of the children about plans for celebrating Halloween. A group decision was made to take a trip to the beach near the school and bring back a large piece of driftwood and materials from the beach, such as stringy seaweed and shells, to create a witch for Halloween. The children made a hat for the witch out of black construction paper and decorated it with grey-green lichen and feathers. They used long strands of seaweed to make her stringy hair. The children gave the witch many faces made out of natural materials, such as shells, bright red Japanese maple leaves, and fir cones. The parents designed a red velvet skirt for the witch to wear. She was the centre of the preschool's celebration of Halloween and developed such a strong personality that her fame spread around the island. Members of the local art gallery put her on display on Halloween night in their gallery, where she stayed in residence until mid-December. How proud the children and their families were to see their work displayed and appreciated by the community.

Flexibility

One of the joys of the Reggio Emilia approach is the spirit of creation that infuses all experiences. Everyone involved in the program is motivated by this extraordinary energy that becomes part of every experience, an example of the "windhorse effect" discussed earlier (Wien 2008). Old, tired practices disappear of their own accord, and everyone, to their surprise, discovers new and more interesting ways of doing things. Being flexible with space, time, and materials and in the way people relate to one another and their work is essential to making beneficial change happen.

Sue Fraser

Driftwood is used to make playground equipment at this child-care centre.

Teachers embracing the Reggio Emilia approach, therefore, have to think differently about the way they plan the environment. In particular, they need to plan for the flexible use of space and materials. Art and science materials, for instance, are no longer segregated in certain areas of the room but, rather, are available for use wherever they are needed, indoors or out. This is one of the reasons the schools in Reggio Emilia adopted the idea of the atelier as a place where children can work with materials from all areas of the curriculum, including art, literature, and science, to produce their ideas in collaboration with the atelierista. Participants in Reggio Emilia programs also have to be flexible and able to change their expectations of the preschool program. For example, the group of children in Quadra Island Preschool did not bring home the traditional jack-o'-lanterns made out of orange and black construction paper, as would have been expected every other year. The teacher and parents had to be flexible about how they planned to celebrate Halloween. The witch that the children, parents, teacher, and members of the community collaborated in making turned out to be a more aesthetically pleasing and meaningful experience than the traditional decorated witches and pumpkins that children made individually in other years.

Flexibility also often involves an unexpected use of materials and equipment. For instance, as the children in La Villetta school worked on the Amusement Park for Birds, they used material and equipment from all areas of the curriculum. They used books to find information about birds, they needed science equipment for building the fountains and windmills, and they employed art materials in decorating the objects created for the birds to enjoy. The children and teachers had many ideas for ways to use space. For instance, they built a bird blind to watch the birds in the playground. This was a completely unexpected object to find in a preschool setting.

Relationship

The emphasis the educators in the schools in Reggio Emilia place on relationship, which was discussed in more detail in Chapter 4, also affects the presentation of materials in the room. Objects are shown in relation to other materials. Lego blocks, for instance, may be laid out with pieces of driftwood on the surface of a mirror. This brings into relationship the artificial and natural worlds. It also gives children a different perspective when they see the construction they are building reflected upside down in the mirror. Clay for the children to work with is attractively laid out on a table with a flower arrangement and examples of finished clay pieces displayed in the centre of the table. Collage materials are kept in clear plastic containers or spread out on trays for use. The abundant jars of brightly coloured paint, the aprons, and the paintbrushes are placed on a trolley beside the easel.

Relationship is also a key principle in the development of documentation. Documentation is designed to help the observer see the relationship between what the children are doing and the underlying theories and philosophical principles that provide the rationale for the experience. Documentation also makes visible the meaning the children are making from their experiences.

Sue Fraser

Paint jars are arranged on a trolley beside the easel at the Vancouver Child Study Centre.

Reciprocity

The notion of the environment acting as a third teacher gives the classroom the qualities of a living being. As such, it must be as open to change and responsive to the children, parents, and community as any good teacher would be. This reciprocal, dynamic environment is a powerful idea. It means that in introducing ideas learned from the Reggio Emilia approach teachers will have to think more critically about what kind of environment they provide for children. They will have to examine each element and think about its purpose and whether it reflects truly their underlying values.

One of the students, Melanie Price*, wrote the following in her reflections on her participation in Children Teaching Teachers:

> From the first CTT to the last, the experience and the knowledge I gained was immeasurable. I have learned that an environment needs to be the third teacher. By following the children's ideas and expanding on them, I was able to help create a curriculum that engaged the children's interests. By doing this it allowed them to expand their knowledge in social interactions, literacy, creativity, and dramatic play ... I also learned how to work in a group and how important it is to have a team that works well together for a common goal. By having this experience, I feel confident in my abilities to express my ideas freely, work as a team, and most importantly plan activities that will develop a child's "selves." Having a curriculum that empowers children will allow them to build self-esteem and confidence, as well as their social, emotional, physical, cognitive, and creative selves.

*Reproduced courtesy of Melanie Price

SUPPORTING REGGIO EMILIA PRINCIPLES IN THE ENVIRONMENT

A strong focus in Children Teaching Teachers is to help students think carefully about the Reggio Emilia principles when they create environments for the children each week. Students are encouraged to think about how space can be designed to foster relationships—to provide gathering places for large groups and small groups and private spaces to retreat from the action. Space needs to be transformable, says Vea Vecchi (2001): "Children are nomads of the imagination and great manipulators of space: they love to construct, move and invent situations" (Vecchi, 2001).

Michelle de Salaberry and Linda Murdoch, teachers in the preschool at Marpole Oakridge Community Centre, returned from Reggio Emilia in 2002 excited by the environments they had seen in the classrooms in Reggio Emilia. They teach in an average-sized room that has large windows and a glass door leading out onto a small balcony that overlooks expansive, grassy playing fields. Eighteen three-year-olds are enrolled in the morning class and 24 four-year-olds in the afternoon class. Each class attends for two-and-a-half hours.

Before their visit to Reggio Emilia, Michelle and Linda had begun to make changes to their environment. They had decided to "get rid of a lot of stuff, clear away the clutter, and create in the classroom a sense of peace and calm." However, it was hard to know what to keep and what to put away. They still wanted their room to reflect the cultures of the children, most of whom came from countries such as India, China, and Japan. Once they had cleared the room, they let Reggio Emilia inspire them in reorganizing the space. Aesthetics were a particularly important consideration in all areas of the classroom. In the dramatic play area, to soften the effect, they had draped transparent material from the ceiling and set a small table lamp on a shelf. They had also replaced the plastic dishes with china crockery and created a space to hang a few really special dress-up clothes. On the shelves lining the corner they arranged samples of the children's art work, indoor plants, a Japanese doll, and other ornaments the families had given the preschool over the years. Considering the importance of creating relational space, they had provided a small table and chairs and a bed large enough for two or three children to use at a time. On their return from Reggio Emilia in 2002, they wanted to add more natural materials to the classroom, so a branch from a tree was set up to mark the entrance to the dramatic play area and more indoor plants were placed on the shelves.

The mini-ateliers they had seen in the classrooms in Reggio Emilia led them to further develop the art area they had earlier created in the far corner of the classroom. A variety of tools and art materials are attractively displayed on shelves that line the wall behind the area. In front of this are tables of different sizes, set up according to the needs of the group. This is where children collaborate to work on projects. Flexibility in the use of this work area is important in a small classroom.

The unexpected construction materials Michelle and Linda had seen on their visit to Reggio Emilia inspired them to make changes to the block area. The light projectors, platforms, etc., they had seen used with construction materials in Reggio Emilia gave them the idea of providing horizontal and vertical planes for children to build on. Earlier they had added a large box platform (63 cm × 127 cm × 76 cm) to the construction area. To enable children to build downwards as well as upwards, they now strung a hoop on a pulley from the ceiling above the platform and provided ropes, clips, tubes, and clothespins for hanging objects above block constructions. They also placed a light projector in the area so the children could throw shadows of their block constructions on the wall.

On the left as one enters the classroom is the group meeting area. On the adjustable shelves lining the wall of this area documentation and props are displayed relating to the current project. This wall provides a focus for the room and is often the first place a visitor is drawn to. The space declares itself the centre of action in the classroom. It is where everyone gathers to discuss important information, where teachers and children negotiate projects, and where children and teachers co-construct the curriculum.

This preschool environment that the teachers have created proclaims it is a place for congenial relationships and for showing respect for each other and the materials. The children respond with behaviour that matches the beautiful space.

Sue Fraser

The display of children's work in the *Castle Project* for Mother's Day at Marpole Oakridge Preschool.

On their return from Reggio Emilia, Linda and Michelle decided that rather than be carried away by a large project with the four-year-olds they would start by taking a more focused approach to the curriculum similar to the investigations of colour, texture, sound, and math that they had observed in Reggio Emilia. The children, however, had a different idea! When they saw the hoop strung from the ceiling with the ropes attached, and the light beaming from the overhead projector, they immediately called it a circus. In the following days, the children added a board to the platform and used toy animals to create circus performances. They added a parking lot and a ticket booth, set up chairs for an audience, sold tickets, and began to practise circus tricks. This was very different from the teachers' plans. They had not, however, counted on the powerful third teacher that was at work in their classroom.

THE PROCESS OF CREATING AN ENVIRONMENT THAT ACTS AS A THIRD TEACHER

The first step for teachers and students planning their classroom space, whether they are starting from scratch or reorganizing existing space, is to decide which values they want their environment to communicate. The next step is to plan the physical layout of the space. The experiences of students in the Children Teaching Teachers program provide examples of how the space in the classroom can be planned to support the values of the participants and the principles of the Reggio Emilia approach.

After reaching a shared understanding of their image of the child (see Chapter 2), the students at Douglas College then begin to think about what kind of learning environment will support the image they have identified. Students consider questions such as the following while planning the environment:

- Does the environment match our image of the child?
- How effective is the environment in acting as a third teacher?
- How are aesthetics addressed in each aspect of our environment?
- What messages are being communicated to children and other visitors to the classroom?

To help them find answers to these questions, the students are given an exercise in which each group is asked to identify the principles they consider important in planning an environment to act as a third teacher. They identify principles such as aesthetics, transparency, relationship, reciprocity, bringing the inside out, and bringing the outside in. Each group then creates a mini-environment to illustrate the principle they have chosen to work with.

Once the students have prepared their environments, they present their ideas to the class and invite students from other groups to experience some of the activities they have planned. For instance, the group that selected transparency as a principle prepared activities using transparent materials, such as cellophane, tissue paper, and sheets of acetate film, as surfaces on which to draw and paint. They used an overhead projector to project images onto the wall, and they set up the light table with translucent paper and ink for painting over a surface of light. They also experimented with mirrors, using them in unexpected ways. Following the presentation to the class, each group created a documentation panel to display in the hall outside the classroom. They used photographs and written documentation to explain what they had learned about the principle they had selected to demonstrate to the class.

Each week during Children Teaching Teachers the tables and chairs are moved out of three classrooms in the college. The students then convert these spaces into environments for children. The "before-and-after" effect is mind boggling—a dull, sterile room is suddenly transformed into a beautiful, rich, and stimulating environment filled with comfortable, child-sized furniture, bright colours, stimulating materials, paintings, collages, natural objects, and musical instruments.

The instructors have observed that each week the environments the students create for the visiting children become increasingly stimulating and reflect more closely the principles learned from the Reggio Emilia approach. In the following weeks, as the students prepare environments for the children, they revisit the documentations to ensure that they include principles such as aesthetics, transparency, reciprocity, relationship, and the use of natural materials in their planning of environments to act as a third teacher. One student describes her experience with this process:

> We learned a variety of things from the children. We learned about the "whole child," including ... open-ended art and literature. Using the environment as the "third teacher" really helped us. Allowing the child choices and time to explore was really beneficial.... We seemed to step back and support the children when it was needed. In using more of the [principles of the] Reggio approach, the children found their own purpose for the cardboard box and seemed to find great enjoyment in doing this also. We learned that aesthetics play an important part in the environment. Because our room is small and has no windows, we felt it needed extra effort in making it [aesthetically pleasing]. To have the children explore and experiment we needed to get their attention first. To do this we focused on making the room bright and colourful. The activity centres were set up to look interesting and inviting, and we tried to use natural materials as much as we could. Most of all, we learned to follow the children's lead, and not to have complicated, structured activities, but rather to simplify and go with the flow. We tried to show the children we respect them as competent human beings. (CTT Journal 1998)

Observations of the children's interests from the previous week are used as a basis for planning for the following week. One group of students, before the first session of Children Teaching Teachers, interviewed Colleen Carpenter, the teacher in the Douglas College* Daycare, and found out that

---

*Reproduced courtesy of Douglas College, Children Teaching Teachers program.

the children who would join them the next week were interested in what was under the ocean. The following extracts from the documentation in the journal that they kept of their experiences illustrate how the Reggio Emilia principles served as a guide in providing the children with a quality program. It is interesting to observe how the theme approach in the first week gradually changed to an emergent curriculum.

21 January 1998

Planning and Preparation: Our focus for CTT#1 was an aesthetically pleasing, theme-based program with the environment being the third teacher.... Our two groups decided to work together to develop our plan and do all the preparation. The initial preparation time was long and involved. We spent many hours making decorations and continuing to plan. We planned for treasure chests, painting on paper on the wall, a quiet area, play dough, sand, and water. Early literacy was incorporated with signs hanging above or near every centre stating what the activity was in clear printing.

The analysis of the first experience shows how the students became aware of a conflict between their theme approach and negotiating curriculum in the Reggio Emilia approach.

Our first CTT went fairly well, all things considered. We all went into CTT with high expectations but no idea of what would happen.... Our entire environment was fairly structured, with treasure chests for an art activity on one large table, play dough on a small table, painting on paper on the wall, a quiet corner with books, and water and sand on the floor. All areas of the room were used throughout the morning and explored by the children but were fairly structured ... there was not a lot of room for creativity in some of the activities that we had set out. Most of the interactions were teacher/child or teacher/teacher with very little child/child interaction. Our small group (of children) could have been a reason for that.

What We Learned: We learned from our first CTT that we need to be flexible and go with the children's interests instead of planning such structured activities. Circle could have been ... more [of] a social activity instead of being so structured. This may hold the children's interest and attention for a longer period of time. We learned to simplify our activities as well as our preparation. We spent far too much time on decorating the room and not enough time concentrating on what the children would enjoy. We definitely learned we need to do planning from now on *from a child's perspective and not a teacher's.* Our group will continue to have sensory experiences for the children because they were successful but will make provisions for a better space for the water and sand. We will carry on with circle, including songs, but will follow the children's lead.... We will allow the children to move freely and expel some energy.

The students, remembering their identification of their image of the child as "competent and resourceful," are now beginning to listen more closely to the children and follow their lead as they plan for the next session.

2 February 1998

Planning and Preparation: We put up large pieces of plain paper on the wall once again [for the children to paint on], we kept the treasure boxes, and brought in beach towels, sun umbrellas, sand, and rocks [as sensory materials]. Everyone from both groups collaborated well, and we helped each other out immensely while planning and setting up the room. We also had the privilege of being the first group to incorporate the brand-new light and water tables to our environment.

What Worked Well and What Didn't: The atmosphere was welcoming and non-threatening, our environment was aesthetically pleasing, and the interactions were generally very good. The materials set out were well used except for the treasure boxes (we found that they were not age-appropriate). We found that a structured circle was not necessary, and the "train" around the room, which was initially a cute idea, did not work for this group of children. The set up of the light and water tables was also questionable as they were set against the wall, which limited the space for the children to play. But overall we were pleased with this session's outcome.

What We Learned from the Children: We learned to be prepared for anything and to be flexible. Keeping in mind the children's interests and individual needs is always important. In addition, clear, positive communication with the other teachers and with the children is very beneficial and helps to prevent misunderstandings.

In the third session the students had returned after six weeks out on practicum in centres in the community. They seemed much more resourceful and confident in their CTT presentations.

18 March 1998

Planning and Preparation: We planned for a Spring theme ... flowers, birds, kites, and brought in a large cardboard box to decorate. We had a free art table with paper, markers, and scissors ... we set out a light table with watercolours enabling the children to explore the combination of light and paint together. In circle, we discussed with the children what they enjoyed about CTT.

What Went Well and What Did Not: The box was the biggest hit; the children decorated and played in it. (They said it was a puppet theatre at one point.) They also enjoyed the umbrella picnic table, which stimulated interesting conversations.

The students are beginning to conceptualize their role less as a teacher controlling the class and more as a partner with the children in the social construction of knowledge. They are also respecting the children's ideas and trusting in the children's resourcefulness and competence. One sees them empowering the children as they allow them to take the lead in transforming the cardboard box, not into something the students had planned, but into a puppet theatre that the children could go in and out of.

25 March 1998

Summary: We changed the cardboard box into a puppet theatre (based on observations from the previous week). The children spent a fair bit of time performing puppet shows and playing in the cardboard box. We also put our documentation on the wall, which interested the children. We changed the format of the session to allow more free play, as we felt it was better to let the children play than pull them away from activities to eat and then return. Our transitions seemed to naturally blend together, and everything ran very smoothly. We worked really well as a team and knew when to step back and not overcrowd the children.

In this session the students are becoming more flexible, not only in their use of space but also in how they use time. They are beginning to be more sensitive to the natural rhythm of the children, following the children's lead in making the transition from free play to snack.

The following extract is taken from the final entry in their journal:

Children Teaching Teachers not only gives students the opportunity to apply their knowledge in practical situations, it allows us to explore the endless possibilities when we allow children to be children. It helps us to understand that we have a special role to play in children's lives. We are not here to "teach," but to guide, scaffold, and facilitate learning. CTT helped us to better understand what roles we play in children's lives. We came to understand the importance of providing children with a consistent environment—one that acted as a third teacher. This consistency allowed the children to feel a sense of trust and familiarity toward CTT. This sense of trust and safety became the foundation for their exploration and discovery.

In terms of planning, we learned that flexibility is key. During CTT we focused on providing open-ended activities that would meet the needs of the "whole child." We followed the children's lead and built on their interests. When the children seemed to enjoy something we carried it into the next CTT, and we learned that when trying to implement an emergent curriculum, it is important to be able to think on your feet and be able to adapt the activities to include all children.

The most important aspect of CTT was what the children taught us. They surpassed any and all of our expectations. They opened up a world of limitless opportunities, and they allowed us to be part of it. CTT and the children helped us to challenge ourselves to try new things and not be afraid to fail! The children made us see what it truly means to be a child.*

*With thanks to Groups 2 and 5 (who shared their journals with me), the children, and the teachers who participated in Children Teaching Teachers in the winter of 1998.

Over the six weeks that the students participated in Children Teaching Teachers, it was obvious how deeply they were thinking about their practice, how they strove to provide the children with more authentic experiences based on the image of the child they had identified earlier, and how the quality of their programming improved as they implemented some of the key principles, such as aesthetics, provision for active learning, collaboration, transparency, flexibility, relationship, and reciprocity, which are at the heart of the Reggio Emilia approach.

HELPING CHILDREN FORM A RELATIONSHIP WITH THE NATURAL ENVIRONMENT

Teachers of young children in the 21st century are aware of how experiences in the natural world are becoming fewer and fewer for children both in rural and urban centres. Children are spending most of their young lives in man-made spaces. Their lives are spent participating in structured activities, watching TV, playing on the computer, and using electronic media. How does the change in the way children are choosing to spend their playtime affect their lives now and in the future? How does it affect all our lives if the present generation is growing up starved of experiences in the natural environment? One young boy told me he liked to learn about snakes, so I suggested a walk to the beach to see if we could find some water snakes sunning themselves on the rocks. After a few moments of clamouring over the piles of seaweed left at high tide, he told me the beach was "yucky" and he would rather learn about snakes on the computer. This is even more distressing when you realize this child is growing up only a few minutes away from a natural beach that stretches for kilometres along the Vancouver waterfront. Why was he so uninterested in his natural surroundings? Had he been discouraged by getting dirty hands from exploring, or was it fear of being in unfamiliar surroundings? Whatever it was it was sad that a young child would find information on the computer more compelling than the real thing. This story makes us realize that as teachers we have to take responsibility for children's knowledge about the natural world. For most children this knowledge is no longer acquired naturally through free outdoor play as it was in the past. It is essential, therefore, when teachers prepare an environment that acts as a third teacher that they include as part of it experiences that connect children to nature and opportunities for children to develop a sense of responsibility for caring for animals and plants.

David Sobel, in his book *Childhood and Nature: Design Principles for Educators* (2008), identifies some principles that he feels teachers can consider in helping children form a relationship with nature. The first principle he lists is creating a sense of adventure when taking children out into the natural world. He states children are at heart natural explorers and if they are sent out in a spirit of adventure, they are much more responsive to an adult's suggestions. Perhaps if I had framed the expedition to find water snakes above as an adventure it would have been more successful. Sobel also stresses the importance of encouraging fantasy and imagination as children engage in nature explorations. The students at Douglas College visited the Japanese gardens and designed in their imaginations ways of crossing the stream (see page 286–289). They suggested a number of fantastic ideas such as riding across on the back of a duck, getting a dragonfly to carry them across, or spinning their own spider webs to cross the stream. He suggests that children be given opportunities "to understand animals from the inside out." For instance, the children at the Vancouver Child Study Centre achieved this by building an aquarium in their classroom big enough for them to become the fish swimming around inside. Sobel notes how children need to explore mysterious paths and special places in the outdoors. There is a universal tendency for children to create their own private places. How many of our playgrounds allow children to do these things? Finally, Sobel believes that for children to become passionate about natural things they need to make their own collections of objects like stones, shells, and feathers. Where can children find these in the man-made environments we create for them? (Sobel 2008)

For children growing up in an increasingly artificial world, teachers have to make opportunities for children to experience nature. For many children nowadays these experiences are not happening at home as they did for previous generations. Teachers have the power in their programs to create environments that teach children to care about nature and spark a passion in them to protect it so that we create a future generation that will see how important it is to become guardians of the natural world.

Heather Fraser

Mei Lin making her special place

EXPLORING NATURE WITH TODDLERS

The toddlers are using natural materials in the environment, i.e., rocks for sorting and leaves to explore colour and shape as well as texture and sound.

Heather Fraser

Mei Lin and Tristan exploring a rope found on the beach

Heather Fraser

Mei Lin and Tristan sorting rocks

The children are exploring how the leaves feel in their fingers as well as the sound they make; Mei Lin has just crunched a leaf and let out a squeal of excitement. She is trying to show Tristan how to squish the leaf between his fingers. When I ask how the leaf feels she tells me that it feels

Heather Fraser

Mei Lin and Tristan exploring a bumpy stump at Lighthouse Park

Heather Fraser

Mei Lin raking leaves

ouchy between her fingers. When I ask what the leaf sounds like she says *ccccrrrruuuussss*. I then ask the children if they would like to go out and see how the leaves feel under their feet.

We find a stream and see how the leaves float down the stream and whether the leaves float or sink, and how far they go.

Mei Lin making leaves into boats

Mei Lin and Tristan exploring how leaves feel and sound

When the children and I go for walks, we talk about what it means to leave nature outside. We talk about how even things that have fallen off the trees and plants will break down and become part of nature. When we collect things to use inside the centre we make sure to return them once we have finished exploring them.

[Toddlers in Heather's Family Child Care, fall, 2009]

Chapter 6

Woodpecker

Documentation

Stand aside for a while and leave room for learning, observe carefully what children do, and then, if you have understood well, perhaps teaching will be different from before.

—Loris Malaguzzi

Questions to Consider:

- What is the purpose of documentation?

- What are the different formats that documentation can take?

- What are the criteria that indicate high-quality documentation?

- What is the rationale for documentation?

- What is involved in the process?

- What are the challenges?

- What might be some of the solutions?

- How can the process of documentation change our pedagogy in early childhood?

THE PURPOSE OF DOCUMENTATION

Documentation is the visible trace of the process that children and teachers engage in during their investigations together. It provides a record of the learning experiences in the classroom, it reveals connections between events, and it provides children, parents, and teachers with an opportunity to review and plan future experiences. "For adults the documentation process furthers our understanding of the concepts children are building, the theories they are constructing and the questions they are posing" (Rinaldi 2001, 134). We have learned from Reggio Emilia to look more thoughtfully at the work children do, to uncover the underlying processes beneath the products they make. In this way teachers discover the paths that children's learning takes.

Educators are now expanding the purpose of documentation to ask questions that challenge the dominant discourses that have shaped our work in early childhood in the past. Pedagogical documentation, as it has come to be known, extends the process of documenting children's and teacher's work in the classroom to providing educators with a forum for engaging in "dialogue and negotiation about pedagogical work" (Dahlberg, Moss, and Pence, 1999, 145). As teachers engage in deconstructive analysis, they ask themselves questions such as: What influences have shaped both the learning child and the learning pedagogue? Through what lenses are the ones who are doing the documentation viewing children? This lens may be one, for instance, that is influenced by child development, cultural expectations, or traditional curriculum practices, such as guidance or policies concerning safety regulations, etc. It is important, therefore, to be aware of how the teacher's own pedagogy is influencing the documentation. Reflections about the documentation often begin as dialogue that leads to teachers making visible the "taken for granted" agendas at work in their centres. When teachers have an image of the child that sees children as capable and competent with interesting ideas that are worth listening to, they become increasingly aware of how traditional curriculum and methods such as theme-prescribed curriculum, planning, and structured art activities fail to match the true potential of children. During the collaborative process of carrying out pedagogical documentation teachers are often able to help each other become aware of the different lenses through which each of them views children. Pedagogical documentation can also provoke teachers to think carefully about the power relationships at work in the centre. Are all children being given the same opportunities to express themselves? Is every child's voice being listened to? Is there someone who takes the time to listen closely to children? Are children free to use materials in such a way as to make *their* thinking and *their* own ideas visible?

The process of pedagogical documentation takes time and reflection and has to be done in collaboration with the others concerned in the process. Multi-perspectives provide deeper insight into many topics under consideration. Whereas documentation helps teachers make visible children's thinking in the process of their learning experiences, pedagogical documentation is proving to be a very powerful means of making changes over the broader spectrum of early childhood education. Lenz Taguchi writes, "...deconstructive processes become part of our professionalism, as we think deeply and critically about how we stage, arrange, do and analyze our pedagogical performances. We do multiple readings, or repeated analysis, to understand the same situation in many ways" (Lenz Taguchi 2006, 1).

Teachers who embrace the Reggio Emilia approach realize very early on that documenting is essential; without it Reggio Emilia cannot be fully experienced. Documentation is the most important way of demonstrating the important principle of transparency in action. It focuses attention on whatever is important and exciting as the learning unfolds, and draws parents and other visitors into the story of what is going on in the classroom. Families are encouraged to participate and contribute more to their children's classroom experiences, building a sense of community. Documentation fosters relationship, allowing everyone to participate at some level in the experi-

Making families feel welcome

ence. This stimulates reciprocity, another fundamental principle of the Reggio Emilia approach. Documentation makes it possible for reciprocal relationships and co-construction of curriculum to occur in the classroom. In creating documentation, teachers learn more about the children they teach and can prepare themselves better to respond to them. Documentation also demonstrates that children's work is respected and valued.

Teachers are amazed at how documentation heightens their level of awareness of what actually happened during the experience. After documenting the children's conversation as they mixed food colouring, Barbara, a teacher in the Quadra Island Children's Centre, said during a teachers' meeting, "When I typed out my notes, I could clearly see the children's *thinking*. I would not have been aware of this or even thought about it before. I got ideas of where I could take the experience next; I felt myself growing as a teacher, becoming a researcher." Barbara describes how documentation enables teachers to be more effective in their work by opening up possibilities and deepening their own and the children's learning experiences.

Teachers use documentation to record the experience of entering the time frame with children and to keep track of the interests that emerge. Documentation is like a system of gears that sets the curriculum in motion. Making visible the children's ideas, thinking, and experiences in some form of documentation provides the teachers with a means of revisiting them with children, discussing them with colleagues and parents, and making hypotheses and flexible plans for further action. The teachers and children can discuss the documentation together, reflect on the experiences, and perhaps get an idea of how to proceed further with the topic. When children and adults review the earlier experiences together through photos and representations such as children's drawings or recorded comments, teachers are able to scaffold the children's learning. The children are moved to a higher level of mental functioning, in which they are encouraged to focus their attention and remember in detail past experiences (Bodrova and Leong 1996).

Parents and other visitors should be able to read from the documentation a story of what has been happening in the classroom and the theory, philosophy, and purpose that underlie the experience. In some cases, when teachers quote children's actual words, they can hear what actually happened during the experience. This is a way for parents to stay connected with what is happening in their children's lives at school at a level that goes deeper than just superficial chitchat with the teachers. Reading the story of their child's experiences at school might suggest to parents ways of contributing to the program or give them topics to discuss at home.

The challenge of documentation is to make explicit in an aesthetically pleasing record both the complexity of the children's experiences and the ever increasing depth of understanding that occurs during the process. Documentation should capture both the depth and breadth of a developmental sequence or learning experience and make the stages in the process visible to others. To produce documentation that is of the high quality achieved by the educators in Reggio Emilia, teachers require skills in observation and collaboration, as well as an understanding of the developmental theories and philosophies of early childhood education. A teacher must be knowledgeable in the areas of the ECE curriculum, including art, music, literature, and science. Teachers also need to have an aesthetic sense and to have the skills (or to recruit others with the skills) to produce graphic designs or recordings that communicate clearly the message of the documentation. They also need to be interested in the world around them, culturally aware, and engaged in events in their local community and culture.

Above all, documentation makes a statement of respect for children and their ideas. It shows the outside community the high level of commitment the teachers have made to the education of the children in their classroom and the seriousness of the role they play in the children's lives.

Loris Malaguzzi told Lella Gandini, "Teachers must learn to interpret ongoing processes rather than wait to evaluate results. In the same way, their role as educators must include understanding children as producers, not as consumers." He went on to say, "They must enter the time frame of the children, whose interests emerge only in the course of activity or negotiations arising from that activity. They must realize how listening to children is both necessary and expedient ... [and] that it is possible to engage in the challenge of longitudinal observations and small research projects concerning the development or experiences of children. Indeed, education without research or innovation is education without interest" (Edwards, Gandini, and Forman 1993, 66, 67).

Embracing the Reggio Emilia approach challenges teachers to change many of their "taken for granted practices." Pedagogical documentation, however, is an effective way to bring about change at a deeper level of pedagogy than documentation would achieve. An issue that demands a major change in values and teaching practices, like the one Malaguzzi refers to above (i.e., viewing children as consumers as opposed to producers of culture), causes teachers to make a major shift in their image of the child and their relationship to the material world around them. The image of a child as a producer of culture is an important value at the heart of the Reggio Emilia approach. Believing children to be producers as opposed to consumers of culture affects many aspects of a teacher's work with children; for instance, how they plan the classroom environment, the materials they provide for the children, and the value they place on the experiences children engage in. It also affects relationship at every level in the program.

The process of pedagogical documentation and deconstructive analysis described in the Collaborative Critical Reflective Protocol offers teachers a collaborative way of dealing with a situation like the one above in which teachers consider the implications of viewing children as producers as opposed to consumers of the culture. To begin the process a videotape documenting the kind of materials and the process in which materials are offered for children to use may be helpful in affecting discussion and reflection on the topic. For instance, viewing a videotape that shows children playing with both commercial toys and natural materials can lead teachers to consider and compare the values and learning potential of both kinds of materials. The resulting discussion may nudge teachers to question any preconceived ideas they may have about consumer toys or bring to the fore fears of health and safety about introducing natural materials into the classroom. Perhaps issues of gender and sexual stereotyping will emerge or perhaps the importance of valuing materials found in the children's own environment as opposed to buying toys from a warehouse might arise from the discussion of the video. Possibly a philosophical or theoretical discussion may result comparing children's learning from a developmentalist or constructivist perspective. Finally, for teachers to have the opportunity of engaging in the process of deconstruction by examining their attitudes towards commercial toys versus natural materials will help teachers see the differences in the depth of thinking each material provokes and how they encourage children to become either consumers or producers.

One of the students at Douglas College wrote in her reflections about Children Teaching Teachers (April, 2009): "For me use of natural materials is so important as it teaches children to respect and appreciate the earth and its beauty. I would much rather surround the children with these types of materials than something store bought that has no real connection to the natural environment." However, she went on to note, "I found myself having conflict with members and having to resolve our issues and differences. I am actually glad this happened because it made me realize that when we are out in the field I will not always agree with my co workers and will have different opinions and beliefs. Having conflict, I think, makes you stronger and you also get to know a little bit more about the other person. Being able to work in a team gives you more opportunities and many different ideas." She had been given many opportunities to experience the process of pedagogical documentation and the debriefing afterwards during the Collaborative Critical Reflective Protocol that follows each session of CTT. As a result she had had the opportunity to experience an effective way of dealing with conflicting perspectives in her group.

It is by engaging in the process of pedagogical documentation that teachers are becoming innovators in their own right. During the process of collaborative critical reflection they have begun to question the traditional indicators of quality in early childhood education that are so embedded in our everyday practice that we never think to question them. When they engage in the process of deconstructive analysis they begin to view the "taken for granted" practices embedded in early childhood programs as "those regimes of truth which attempt to determine for us what is true or false, right or wrong that we may or may not think and do (Dahlberg, Moss, and Pence 1999, 144). As teachers begin to question the validity of these embedded practices, they start to question their own assumptions and cultural biases. In the process questions about social justice and equitable practice emerge. This often leads to feelings among teachers of uncertainty and discomfort. These are, however, a necessary part of the process of change if teachers are to become researchers in their own right and provide children with innovative programs in early childhood education that foster every child's learning potential.

THE MANY FORMS OF DOCUMENTATION

Once teachers realize how important documentation is, they figure out effective ways to do it in their situation. Documentation begins with observation and recording, and teachers are for the most part very flexible in the way they carry it out. Many will keep a running record of the children's behaviour; others might record conversations or focus on interesting moments and events. With experience, teachers become more selective and learn what to record and what details to ignore.

Documentation can be created in many media. It can be a series of photographs and written observations recording the developmental sequences or experiences of the children as they unfold. Depending on the topic, documentation may range from a simple photograph with an explanation and, perhaps, an example of a child's work, to a series of panels that illustrate the process followed in a lengthy project. It may take the form of written observations and photographs collected in a portfolio to give a comprehensive, detailed account of some aspect of the curriculum or child development. If the children are very active, the teachers may choose to videotape the experience. If the children are stationary and the area is quiet, the teachers may decide to audiotape the children's conversation.

Documentation has been a way of understanding child development in the past but recently pedagogical documentation has become the tool enabling teachers to act as researchers and to begin questioning theories of child development as to their validity when applied universally to all children, especially to children who come from different cultural and social backgrounds. Engaging in the process of collaborative deconstructive analysis, teachers begin to apply multiple perspectives to their views on children's abilities, competencies, and potentials. In the observations and collaborative deconstruction of toddlers' exploration of clay (described on pages 165–172) many preconceived notions of what toddlers were capable of came into question. The teachers saw how their language, expectations, and the method they chose in presenting the clay to the toddlers was in fact shaping and in some ways controlling how the children responded to the medium of clay.

Documenting children's language is important. The teachers in the Quadra Island Children's Centre spent a long time trying to decide how they could record the stories the children were telling one another as they swung back and forth on the swings in the playground. In this case they decided that the only way would be to have an additional staff member write the conversations down. Baerbel Jaeckel, the teacher in the Quadra Island Preschool, placed an exercise book next to a fish tank filled with tadpoles that one of the children had collected. Anyone who was near the fish tank wrote down questions the children asked or comments they made as they watched the tadpoles changing into frogs. The teacher and helpers encouraged the children to draw their predictions and their observations as the process unfolded. Baerbel added these drawings to the written comments in the book, together with the photographs taken of the children as they examined the tadpoles in the tank of water. The teacher and helpers then discussed information in the notebook throughout the experience to gauge the children's level of interest in the topic and to get ideas for possible directions to follow the next day.

DOCUMENTATION AS A CYCLE OF INQUIRY

Lella Gandini and Jeanne Goldhaber visualize the documentation process as a cycle of inquiry which begins with framing a list of questions. The questions guide the teacher in selecting the topic to be investigated and in making decisions about what to observe and record and what artifacts need to be collected. The observations and artifacts (children's drawings, paintings, and three-dimensional work) are then organized. As part of a work in progress, they may be sorted into files, clear plastic envelopes, or placed on a holding panel on the wall. Later the material is organized into a more permanent form, perhaps in a portfolio or on a wall panel. Teachers must make visible the theories the children are building about the topic and show how these change and grow during the process. From time to time the observations and artifacts are analyzed and interpreted, and the results included in the final documentation. Documentation material should be available at all times so that teachers and children can use it to reflect on previous experiences and ideas. The cycle of documentation, therefore, begins with framing questions, continues on to analysis and interpretation, and leads to planning new directions in the development of the project. The documentation cycle is repeated many times during the project, as shown in Figure 6.1 (Gandini and Goldhaber, 132).

The final documentation, whether it is displayed in a portfolio, in a book or an album, or on wall panels, should convey clearly the following:

- a title stating the topic of the documentation

- an overall theoretical or philosophical statement; for instance, the activity with tadpoles described above could be related to Vygotsky's theory by explaining how it moved children to a higher level of mental functioning (i.e., to representing their ideas symbolically)

FIGURE 6.1   The Documentation Process as a Cycle of Inquiry*

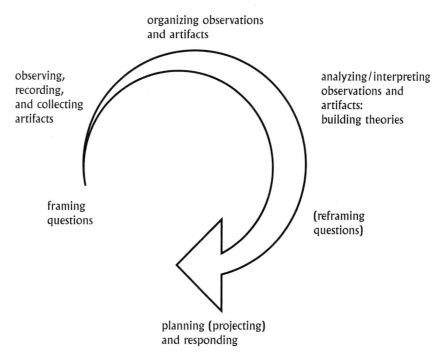

organizing observations
and artifacts

observing,
recording,
and collecting
artifacts

analyzing/interpreting
observations and
artifacts:
building theories

framing
questions

(reframing
questions)

planning (projecting)
and responding

- an indication of the purpose or rationale of the activity or topic being documented

- an illustration of the experiences covered, such as in photographs or written commentaries

- a description of the process of development or learning that has been observed and recorded

- a record of the experiences and voices of the children and teachers

- a display of the children's work

- an analysis of the experience in light of theory and philosophy

- a statement of implications for future work

- a concluding statement

THE DOCUMENTATION PROCESS

Observation

Documentation begins with observation. Children are observed in many different situations and for many different reasons. For instance, they may be observed as they engage in solitary activities, as they collaborate in a group on a project, or as they participate with other children in play. They may be observed as they separate from their parents on arrival at school and enter the group or as they work on activities during the day. Selecting the best tool for observing children depends on the kind of information that the teacher is seeking. The decision to carry out observations is usually the result of a question that has arisen about a child or a group of children and their behaviour or activities in the centre. The decision to carry out documentation also can arise from the teacher's interest in following the path of a learning experience. In making the decision about which method to follow, however, it is essential that teachers collaborate to ensure that the documentation has input from all the people involved.

Teachers, with practice, learn to be objective in their observations of the children's behaviour. They learn not to make assumptions that might bias the recorded information. For instance, they avoid using phrases in their recording such as "she likes to play" or "he is happy when...." Phrases such as these may be inaccurate statements of the child's real feelings. Teachers learn to be selective, but truthful, in what they record, so that the information captures the essential qualities they are looking for in their observations. The use of descriptive language also helps teachers describe in detail the behaviour they are recording. The following observation, which I recorded in February 1998, of a child looking up at sand spattered on a fence provides a rich source of information about the child's intellectual abilities—his awareness, his curiosity, and his thoughtful, reflective

Sue Fraser

Illustrating the Reggio Emilia principles in documentation

Frazer examines the sand on the fence.

Sue Fraser

style of investigation. It also provides the teacher with clues for a follow-up discussion.

Frazer stood in front of the fence bordering the large sand area in the playground. He stood gazing up at patches of sand stuck to the boards of the fence. He had a puzzled expression on his face. Picking up a small shovel, he reached high up above his head to trace with the tip of the shovel the pattern made by the sand on the boards of the fence. He touched the pattern carefully without destroying it and then stood examining it for a few more minutes.

The educators from Reggio Emilia have taught us to be alert for opportunities such as this to see whether children might be interested in pursuing topics further. The observer who recorded this incident might want to see if Frazer could put his thoughts about the sand into words. Did he have any questions that might lead to further investigation? Could any other children be drawn into the conversation? Would there be any interest in doing more experiments with the properties of sand and observing transformations when sand is combined with water? Where else do we see examples of sand stuck on surfaces? Would the children be interested in sketching their ideas about sand? How many different media could be used to make visual representations? Perhaps it was the pattern that the sand made on the wooden planks that captured the child's interest. Where else do we see patterns? What patterns can we make and in how many different languages? These are the sorts of questions that an observer would list and share later with the other teachers to decide how or whether they should proceed further.

The fundamental skill in all documentation is the ability to observe and record the children's behaviour. Teachers who follow the Reggio Emilia approach perceive the child as "rich in resources, strong, and competent" (Rinaldi 1998, 114). This image of the child has a profound effect on observation. The image becomes a lens through which observers view children as active participants in the co-construction of knowledge in the classroom. If the children are appreciated for their contributions and perceived as imaginative thinkers who ask interesting questions and who can provide unexpected solutions to problems, teachers will be motivated to observe children closely to find out what they are thinking and to listen to and record their conversations to try to capture their ideas. As collaboration is an important principle in the Reggio Emilia approach, these observations will need to be discussed later with colleagues to gain deeper insights into the children's behaviour or thinking. Teachers, as a group, can also revisit the experiences they have recorded to discuss different approaches or to make predictions about how the topics that seemed to interest the children in the observations could be further developed. Pedagogical documentation deepens the observation process, for as teachers deconstruct an observation collaboratively "taken for granted" ideas, values, and teaching practices are revealed and this often changes pedagogy.

Teachers use a number of different methods to observe children. The tools for observation range from simple ones, such as pencils and notepads, to more sophisticated electronic equipment, such as digital cameras, audio recorders, and video recorders. Recently, many teachers have begun to use laptop computers to capture interesting moments. The choice of method depends on the situation and on the focus for the observations.

Tape Recordings

A tape recording of children's conversation is useful because it provides the observer with a detailed account of exactly what the children say. When an observer matches a taped conversation with a written record of a conversation, it is surprising to see how much detail is missing in the written version. On the other hand, a tape recorder is nonselective, so the observer often has to listen to a lot of unnecessary data before getting to a segment of conversation that is useful. It is also a challenge for a teacher to make an audiotape of children in conversation that is clear and easily understandable. There is often too much background noise, and the children move out of hearing range too quickly to catch what they are saying clearly. Frequently, the speech on the tape is meaningless when it is heard out of context. To tape children's conversations successfully, the teacher may find it helpful to review the following set of questions:

- What is the purpose of the observation?
- What will be the focus of the observation?
- Whose conversations will need to be recorded?
- Where might the conversations be taking place?
- When and for how long will they take place?
- What questions, objects, or materials will provoke discussion?
- What factors need to be considered to tape clear, on-topic conversation?

For instance, if the teachers described previously who observed Frazer examining the sand on the fence thought that his curiosity about the pattern of sand could be further investigated, they would need to make a plan to test their hypothesis. Answers to the above questions would give the teachers some direction for putting their plan into action. Taping a conversation with Frazer and a small group of children who are also interested in the topic might be their first step in this process. The teachers could move a small table out of the main classroom to a quiet area where there are few distractions so that they could tape a conversation between Frazer and the other children. On the table, the teachers could display a photograph of Frazer examining the pattern of sand on the fence and materials such as sandpaper and objects with raised decorative motifs to provoke discussion. A later analysis of the transcription of the taped conversation would indicate whether Frazer or any other children showed enough interest or enthusiasm to pursue the topic of sand and/or patterning further. It is important that all the teachers involved collaborate in analyzing the transcription of the tape so that discussion is as rich as possible and everyone has a shared understanding of the process if it proceeds further.

Photographs

Once teachers have developed an idea for creating a documentation, they need to choose between a number of photographic techniques: black-and-white, colour, and slide photographs, as well as computer printouts from a digital camera. The documentation, if it is to tell the complete story of the experience, should record the process from the beginning to the end. The first step is to decide what kind of photographs would most clearly communicate the ideas being conveyed by the documentation. Because direction can change in the middle of a project, planning must be flexible. The group of teachers at the Vancouver Child Study Centre who were working with the children on the "Three Little Pigs" project (described in Chapter 5) realized, while it was still in progress, that parents would be interested in seeing how the project was being developed. They decided to take slides to show at a parents' meeting in addition to the photographs that were already being taken for the wall panels.

Videotapes

If the topic involves a lot of activity and high energy, a videotape might be the best form of documentation. For instance, a group of ECE students at Douglas College observed that the children who visit their classroom once a week to participate in Children Teaching Teachers were acting out a camping theme in their play. The following documentation, taken from extracts in their journal, illustrates how the children and students developed the topic of going camping into a project on volcanoes over a period of six weeks. Interest in volcanoes is often high among children who live on the West Coast of Canada, perhaps because many volcanoes, such as Mount Baker, are close to where they live*.

A tent was set up with authentic materials such as a Coleman lantern, cooler, branches of trees, sleeping bags, fishing rod, and food items like beans, juice, and pots and pans. Children used the camping equipment and materials to pretend that they were up in the mountain camping by a cave. The children began to discuss the types of animals that lived in caves, such as bats and bears. They then used their imaginations to pretend to be the bears and bats that live in the cave. This play developed further into a camping trip. The children began to use the flashlights to explore the cave; later they sat around the rock fire pit, and used the pots, pans, and canned food to pretend to cook over a camp fire. We asked the children: "What else can we do on a mountain?" This led into a conversation about how we could build a pretend mountain, and together with the children we decided to build a large papier-mâché mountain. We built the frame with chicken wire and masking tape to seal off the edges. We laid out papier-mâché made out of flour, water, and white glue. Children started to explore the papier-mâché through sensory exploration. Some of the children were more interested in touching the mâché than putting paper on the mountain. The next time we will build on ideas developed by the children.

We decided to decorate the mountain using paint and different sorts of media such as toothbrushes, rollers, and sponges. The children explored different ways of getting the sand onto the mountain. Pouring glue and then pressing handfuls of sand seemed to work the best; other exploratory ways were to dip the paintbrush into glue and then into the sand and rub it on the mountain.

The children's sensory exploration of the natural materials with the glue and paint resulted in lots of conversation and language. The language focused on the texture created by mixing the paint and glue with the sand and the way it made the mountain look. One child mixed the sand with red paint and glue, and while applying it to the mountain using a paintbrush, told us that this was the hot lava flowing out of the volcano.

From now on the artwork the children did began to express the notion of the mountain being a volcano erupting. The children made many sketches and clay representations of their ideas of volcanoes and volcanic eruptions. (Group 4 students' journal, Douglas College, November 1997)

From observations and recordings of the children's conversations, the students realized that the children had converted the papier-mâché mountain into a volcano. This sent the students on a search for information about volcanoes to share with the group. The children soon decided they wanted to

---

*Reproduced courtesy of Douglas College, Children Teaching Teachers program.

make the mountain they had built out of papier-mâché explode like a volcano. The students carried out a series of experiments with the children to figure out how they could simulate a volcanic eruption. They investigated things that would safely explode in the classroom that they could use to make a volcanic eruption. This led to making popcorn and watching it "explode."

The papier-mâché volcano

Sue Fraser

Eventually, the students and children decided that the best way to simulate a volcanic explosion in the classroom was by mixing vinegar and baking soda together in a container placed in the hole at the top of the papier-mâché volcano and pretending that the foam it made was lava pouring down the sides of the mountain.

The students videotaped the experiences each week and analyzed each segment. They then used this analysis to plan for the following sessions. The students compiled in a portfolio written commentary and photographs of the key experiences. They then shared the portfolio with the children's teachers and parents. Eventually, the students made an edited videotape of the project and showed it on many occasions to groups in the community.

Students, during this project, learned about the value of listening to children and helping them realize their ideas. They had experience in collaborating with one another and with the children. They gained a sense of accomplishment from staying with the same topic over a long period of time and exploring it in depth. The documentation of the experience on the videotape, photographs, and written observations at each stage of the process helped them analyze and revisit episodes to discover different approaches or new directions and discuss where they could have gone deeper into their investigation with the children.

In their concluding comments in the portfolio, the students wrote:

If we had more time with the children we would discuss what happens when a real volcano erupts. We would talk about things like what would happen to the trees, wildlife, and even the people who live near the volcano. As well, we would discuss the effects a volcano has on environments, such as all the smoke, ash, and pollution that travels through the air and where it lands. Then we would follow the children's leads by taking their ideas to move on to a new provocation.

Over a period of six weeks, the students and the children created an exciting and a meaningful learning experience that was carefully documented with photographs, written observations, and videotapes. At each stage in the process the students were able to use the documentation either to go forward or to "change gears" and explore a different direction, as they did when the mountain became a volcano.

Interpretation of Observations

An analysis of the data that has been collected from the observations is an important step in the process of documentation. The more data that are available, the more valid will be the interpretation of the information. All the data collected during an experience, including written observations, tapes, artifacts, and photographs, need to be shared with colleagues throughout the learning experience. During the analysis, which is also done in collaboration with the teachers involved in the project, any philosophical points and relationships to theory should be noted. At intervals and on completion of the project, the points drawn from the analysis and interpretation will be organized and added to the other material compiled for the documentation.

At any stage, documentation may cause a shift in focus so that the whole project may go off in a different direction or be the starting point for the group to begin working on a new idea. In the "Three Little Pigs" project, for example, the children decided to build a house that the wolf could not blow down—a brick house made of clay. Some of the children worked on building the walls and the roof, while others experimented with the remaining clay on the table. An observer recorded the conversation of one child as he began to shape the clay on the table.

William: I am making a volcano.

I am making a bigger volcano.

Mine is up.

This is a volcano. Fire is coming out of it.

Now this is the ... what is that called ... the fire hole ... lava comes out.

How does it get down?

Gloria (the teacher): What is lava like?

William: Hot and sticky and you can't get it off.

This is the lava coming down....

It is red it has to be a volcano.

The volcano has to be erupting.

It is water lava because all the volcanoes have holes so they could erupt.

Later, the observer shared the above transcription with the child's teachers. This discussion showed the teachers that the project that had started off as building a house with clay bricks "that the wolf could not blow down" had now taken a different direction. The children, and William in particular, now seemed more interested in building a clay volcano with a crater and lava pouring down the sides. The teachers discussed this new direction and decided to bring in some books about volcanoes to see if the children were really interested in exploring the topic further. They could see that interest in building houses for the three little pigs had waned (the brick house was nearly finished), and it was now time to follow the children's lead to pursue a new topic. This decision would have been harder to make if the children had lost interest partway through the project. This is why it is so important to be sure when embarking on a project with children that it is truly derived from the children's ideas, rather than imposed on them by the teachers. It is also important that the project is open ended, so that if children lose interest, the project can be brought to a satisfactory conclusion at any point during the process. The termination of a project, however, should never be done lightly, because once embarked upon it is important for everyone involved that the project reach a satisfactory conclusion.

On discussing the "Three Little Pigs" project later with the teachers, we realized that although initial interest in the topic was very high, and enthusiasm for building the houses was maintained until just before the end, to reach a satisfactory conclusion, all three houses had to be completed. This was a long and involved process, which might have resulted in the children giving up before the end. Fortunately, this did not happen, but we all learned something about the careful thought that needs to go into selecting a topic to follow and into evaluating the predictions the teachers make at the outset. The abrupt termination of the children's interest at the end of the project also made us realize that we had a lot to learn from the teachers in Reggio Emilia. We needed to find out more about the process they follow in carrying out the large projects, or *progettazione,* such as the Amusement Park for Birds, which last for many months. Perhaps a celebration could have been planned, as is sometimes done in Reggio Emilia, to which the parents would be invited to celebrate with the children and teachers the conclusion of the "Three Little Pigs" project.

Analysis of the Documentation

The process of documenting the path of learning in the classroom requires adults to collaborate, share and interpret observations, articulate their understanding of theory and research, and analyze the data they have collected. This means that teachers can no longer work in isolation, for it is impossible to capture the complexity of an experience unless teachers work as a team in planning the form and function of the documentation, in reflecting on the learning as it unfolds, and in working together to develop the panels, portfolios, or other kinds of documentation. This transforms the teacher's role into what Brenda Fyfe terms a *collaborative action researcher.* She states that documentation is an essential component in the process of moving toward a co-constructed, negotiated curriculum. She states that this is not a linear but a cyclical process of action research that moves from observation to reflection, analysis, planning, and action, then back again to observation (1998, 23).

Collaboration with children, colleagues, families, and, at times, people in the community is essential in producing documentation that reflects a broad range of ideas and experiences. Brenda Fyfe states that "consideration of multiple perspectives will contribute to its [the documentation's] ultimate power to communicate. Since children and parents make up a large part of the audience that will read the documentation, it can be important to ask for their consultation in the process of organizing a panel or other form of public presentation of learning" (1998, 20). Documentation that communicates the entirety of an experience needs input from all the participants. Everyone involved will have experienced the project in a slightly different way, and by sharing the individual experiences with the whole group, a more complete picture of the project will emerge.

The key points of the experience, the ones that will need to be shown in the documentation, become clearer as the group analyzes and synthesizes the material that the participants have accumulated. The group then needs to review previous decisions to decide whether the format for documentation is still appropriate. The next step is to delegate the work in producing the documentation. There are a number of different tasks, such as printing the commentaries that explain the photographs, transcribing the children's conversations onto cards to be attached to the panels, labelling the children's work, and mounting the photographs. Individuals can carry out these tasks on their own once the group has made decisions about format, graphic design, and so on. Once the displays, portfolios, or videotaped documentation are complete, the group as a whole has a sense of ownership of the project. Whereas documentation can be said to be the gears that allow the learning experiences to move in new directions, collaboration is the fuel that drives the process.

Brenda Fyfe* has developed four sets of questions for each stage of documentation to help teachers produce documentation that captures the depth and breadth of an experience. The first set of questions is asked during the initial phase of documentation. These questions address practical, philosophical, and organizational issues. At this stage, teachers collaboratively answer the following questions:

- What should we document?

- When and for how long should we document the experience?

- Who will do the documentation?

- Where will we do the documentation?

- What are the focus and rationale for the observation?

- How will the documentation be used?

- What tools and techniques will meet the purpose?

Once they have decided what, when, who, where, and why to document, teachers can move to the next phase, called the *discourse phase*. At this stage, the following questions require reflection and interpretation:

- What does the documentation reveal about children's ideas, interests, feelings, opinions, assumptions, and theories?

- What does it show about environmental conditions and how they affect behaviour, interactions, and relationships?

- What does it tell about connections with home and community?

In the next phase, called the *design phase*, teachers draw conclusions from interpretations and reflections, and they design future observations and make projections. The questions addressed in this phase are as follows:

- What are the implications based on the interpretation of the data collected?

- What has surfaced that needs to be studied in more detail?

- What further ideas need to be explored?

- How can we make children's ideas visible?

- How might parents become involved?

*Fyfe, Brenda. 1994. Images from the United States: Using ideas from the Reggio Emilia experience with American educators. *Reflections on the Reggio Emilia Approach*, edited by Lillian Katz and Bernard Cesarone. University of Illinois, Urbana: ERIC/EECC.

During the *documentation phase,* teachers think about how they can continue observation and documentation. They might ask the following questions:

- What tools and techniques will be needed to document the next set of observations and experiences?

- How will these be organized?

- How will the parents and community be involved?

Design, discourse, and documentation form a cyclical process in which teachers collaboratively revisit, reflect, and then reframe data in the process of negotiating the curriculum. Brenda Fyfe states that "documentation goes beyond telling a story to presenting a study" (1998, 23).

CREATING DOCUMENTATION

The final form documentation takes may vary. Sometimes teachers decide that the information and artifacts they have collected will be best displayed on panels or organized in a portfolio. Following are two examples, one of documentation organized on panels and one of documentation organized in a portfolio.

Sue Fraser

Poster display case for documentation panels, Quadra Island Children's Centre

The Circus Project— Documentation on a Panel

A documentation panel consists of a large sheet of cardboard displayed prominently, usually made up of text, photographs, and examples of children's work. Recall from Chapter 5 how changes to the environment inspired by Reggio Emilia suggested a circus to the children at the Marpole Oakridge Community Centre preschool. When teachers Michelle de Salaberry and Linda Murdoch noticed that the children were using the blocks and the hoop to build a circus environment and putting on spontaneous circus performances, they framed some questions:

- What aspects of the circus are the children most interested in learning about?

- What experiences could we provide for the children to support and expand their interest in a circus?

The teachers began the cycle of documentation by recording the children's conversation.

We are making a circus, it has ropes and pointy things.

Here's the animals for the circus.

The school bus and cars park underneath.

The teachers also observed that two children, Jeffrey and Gurshabad, decided to draw on the chalkboard the circus they had created. Gurshabad's drawing included the ramp, ropes, lights, and a light switch. The teachers recorded in the documentation that this was "the first time anyone on their own had decided to represent their work in another way." They noted on the documentation panel the important moment when two children made their theory about the circus visible.

Drawing a design for the circus tent

In the following months, observations, recordings of the children's conversations, drawings, and photographs of their work were collected and eventually organized on display panels. The documentation panels showed that the lights continued to be an important consideration in many of the children's drawings and constructions. It was this documentation of the children's interest in the lights that helped the teachers decide what direction the project should take.

In a group meeting at the beginning of the project, the teachers were surprised at how much the children knew about a circus. Some of the ideas the children had were listed on the documentation panel:

- Animals go in a circus.

- Elephants swing people.

- The walkers walk on the high wire.

- The lions jump over the hoop.

- You have to have a ticket.

- There are clowns.

- Sometimes the clowns juggle.

- There is a trapeze.

- There are lights.

- The circus is a tent.

- You eat popcorn and candy.

The observations and photographs on the panels show that in the weeks following, the children recreated many of the above ideas using different materials and languages to represent various aspects of a circus in the classroom. The teachers discussed the list of ideas and decided that the children might be interested in studying clowns. As a provocation, they invited a real clown to visit the classroom and put out materials for the children to draw clown faces, to make clown faces using play dough, and "to go shopping for clothes from an assortment of colourful collage materials for their clowns so they could make bodies for the clown." In the meantime, the circus play continued in the classroom. The documentation reads:

> The first circus is cleared up so the children are able to start over. The two tall tubes are set up with a wooden high wire. We put the overhead projector on so the shadow of the high wire is projected on the wall. Terrence wants to build a ticket booth. He soon has a small structure built with all the people lined up in front for tickets. We look in a book to see how the seats look in a circus. He then builds a set of seats from blocks for each little person to sit on. The next thing he thinks of is to put the animals in front of all the people. The next day we ask the children to draw Terrence's circus. The children included lights in many of their pictures, "dots along the top, those are the lights." This was an important observation in guiding the teachers in what to investigate next, because the children then had to think about what they would need to string the lights on. This discussion led to the idea of building a circus tent in the classroom.

> At the start of the project, the children had decided that to be a real circus tent we would have to have a roof with a point, it needed to be colourful, and have a flag and lights.

The photographs, text, and drawings on the documentation panels show how the teachers and children designed and then constructed the circus tent. The documentation material is organized into the following sections:

- designing the circus roof

- choosing the design

- copying and painting

- making the point

- the final touches

- raising the tent

The project ended by the children putting on a wonderful circus performance with the help of teachers and parents. The final documentation of the project was a videotape of the performance.

Sea Life—Documentation in a Portfolio

A portfolio is a folder or flat case with pages or pockets where observational materials, photographs, and examples of children's work can be organized and displayed. A single child's work is often compiled in a portfolio, but a portfolio can also be a collection of materials describing a class project.

Shannon McGregor*, a student in the Early Childhood Education Program at Capilano College in North Vancouver, created a portfolio to document a series of investigations of sea life she and the children carried out in her practicum. The organization of the information in the portfolio was simple, but the underlying structure made it easy to read and understand. The portfolio was organized into sections: first there was an introduction, followed by a description of each separate investigation. Each of these sections included a statement of the teacher's intentions, a description of the activity or activities, a list of materials used, the procedure the children followed, and a list of the questions the teacher used to guide each exploration. At the end of each exploration and activity, there was a written reflection and a statement headed "What next?"

Introduction: Shannon began her documentation of the project by explaining why she had decided to investigate sea life. She had observed that the children in her class showed interest in sea life throughout their play and conversations and frequently chose books at reading time about "the most dangerous and largest predators of the sea." At group meeting time she asked the children what they knew about sea life and what they would be interested in studying. She made a web of the children's responses, which indicated that they were interested in investigating creatures like whales, great white and hammerhead sharks, sting rays, crabs, and starfish. She also listed some of the questions the children asked her. "What was inside the shark's body?" and "How do fish make bubbles?" It is important to record these initial questions, because children often ask really interesting questions that can send a project off in unexpected directions.

*Reproduced courtesy of Shannon McGregor

Example of a page from the portfolio

Activity: Shannon began by giving the children an opportunity "to draw from observation" to help the children look carefully at the sea creatures they had chosen to investigate. She listed the materials she had set out for the children's initial exploration of sea life: mirrors, plastic sea mammals and fish, magnifying glasses, paper, black pens, and charcoal. She also included a number of questions to ask the children when they were using the materials, for example, "I wonder what sharks eat and where do they live?"

The following pages of the portfolio described separately each investigation, such as the dissection of the fish, the fish printing, and the painting of the sea mural.

Reflection: Each section ended with a reflection about what had occurred to her as she observed the children engaged in the investigation. For instance, in her reflections on the first activity, she noted that children seemed particularly interested in the hammerhead shark: "Because it has two parts to its head and it goes like this (child moves head back and forth sideways). Because it has hammers sticking out of his head. I want to draw a hammerhead."; "Sharks eat ham and people." She realized from her conversation with the children that only a couple of children had ever seen a real fish or sea mammal and there were gaps in their knowledge and false assumptions. Her reflections guided her decisions about where to go next with the investigation.

What Next: At the end of each investigation, Shannon wrote her thoughts about what she could do as a follow-up to the previous activity. For the first activity of the project described above, for instance, she noted that she would bring in a specimen of a real fish the following day so that "the children can build a relationship with the object and have a concrete understanding and a hands-on experience."

Conclusion: In this section at the end of the portfolio, Shannon included an overall summary of the project and her analysis of the significant learning that had occurred. She found it most significant that in investigating sea life, the children had constructed their own learning and knowledge. "The materials, teachers, and learning environment all supported children in being a community of learners."

PEDAGOGICAL DOCUMENTATION

The following is an example, taken from a documentation panel, of how pedagogical documentation and the process of deconstructive analysis enabled teachers to gain a new understanding of how their assumptions and "taken for granted" notions had influenced and in some ways limited the children's exploration of clay.

Documentation of the Toddler's Exploration of Clay

The following is a step by step account of the thinking behind the construction of a documentation panel of two toddlers' exploration of clay in Heather's Family Child Care Centre. It was carried out by Heather, the teacher, and I (the author) took the role of recorder. Our investigation was inspired by two books, *Poking, Pinching and Pretending: Documenting Toddlers' Explorations with Clay* (Smith and Goldhaber 2004), and *Bambini: The Italian Approach to Infant/Toddler Care* (Gandini and Pope Edwards 2001). We decided to frame our documentation of the toddler's exploration of clay using the questions from Bambini (2001, 135).

1. How will young children's exploration of clay become more intentional?

2. How will it evolve into more symbolic efforts?

3. What are the roles of the physical and social environments?

We engaged in deconstructive analysis after each session to examine our assumptions and teaching strategies; i.e., to question the way we believed the clay should be presented to the children and to examine the language we used to see how it shaped the children's responses to the clay.

DAY ONE

Heather introduced the clay to the two toddlers, Tristan aged 1 ¾ years and Mei Lin aged 2 years. It was the first time they had been exposed to clay. The two toddlers were seated at a small table in the child-care centre. I began the written recording. We also tape-recorded the session.

Heather set out four small balls of clay on the table. She gave each child a ball of clay.

H: How does it feel in your hands?

ML: Pokes her finger into the ball of clay.

T: No, no, no. (He holds a ball of clay in each hand.)

H: Do you want to make a ball?

They reach for each other's clay balls and then go back to using their own balls of clay.

ML: Ball

Silence

H: What else can we do to make a ball? Do you want that one in a ball?

(I make two flattened balls with the lumps of clay on the table.)

ML: Takes a slab in each hand and smiles as she bounces the clay balls up and down in each hand. Tristan copies her actions with his two balls of clay. *Are they both exploring the weight of the two clay balls in their hands?*

H: One for each hand.

ML: In a ball.

Tristan is banging his clay on the lid of the bucket lying on the table.

He appears to be losing focus so I try rolling a snake for each of them. Tristan pretends to eat the snake.

H: What are you eating?

The clay now becomes a source for dramatic play around the idea of food.

…..

T: Cook.

Heather Fraser

Toddler's initial experience with clay

H: What are you cooking?

T: Something for Mummy and Daddy.

Tristan takes the clay pieces over to the oven. While Tristan continues on with his "food" play, Mei Lin returns to the table and begins to pinch little clay pieces off her ball of clay.

H: Are you squishing, Mei Lin?

Heather made a circle for both toddlers out of a coil of clay lying on the table.

M: Mei Mei's bobble.

They both run round the room holding the clay circles on their heads pretending they are hair elastics.

We invite them to return to the table by giving them water in two little plastic containers. They dip their clay in the water. The clay soon becomes messy and they begin to lose interest.

Heather Fraser

Making bobbles for hair

Deconstruction:

We were both surprised at the behaviours the children brought so early to their exploration of the clay. Throughout the observation we noted how the children made use of previously learned schemas (e.g., thinking strategies and play behaviours) in their exploration of the clay. Their immediate use of prelogical math thinking and symbolic play was interesting. The two toddlers moved so quickly, from sensory exploration to weighing the clay balls in each hand, then into symbolic play even though the clay was an unfamiliar material for them. The children copied each other in their choice of symbolic play themes. First, Tristan initiated the idea of using the clay for cooking, then he followed Mei Lin's lead by making the coils of clay lying on the table into bobbles for their hair. It was interesting to see how the toddlers "scaffolded" each other's responses to the clay through symbolic play, a schema that was familiar to them. When reviewing the documentation, we wondered if by making the coil circles of clay for them, we had not given the children enough time to discover the physical properties of the clay for themselves. On reviewing the documentation, particularly the language we used, we questioned if we had inadvertently pushed the two toddlers into using the clay symbolically and interrupted the time they might have spent exploring the "affordances" inherent in the clay itself. The dilemma we had was that one of our questions was how to get toddlers to use the clay in more symbolic ways and yet when they did we worried that their responses were distracting them from really learning about the true properties of the clay as a malleable material.

DAY TWO

On day two we decided to set out slabs of clay instead of balls hoping that the slabs would offer the toddlers more open-ended ways of responding to the clay than the balls and coils we had given them to use on the first day. The toddlers did respond more freely by pounding, pinching, and tearing small pieces off the clay slabs. We hoped that this would give the children more opportunities to learn about the possibilities inherent in using clay. For instance, Mei Lin began to embellish her slab of clay with little pieces she had torn off and Tristan copied her. However, once again we resorted to rolling balls and coils to keep the toddlers' interest in using the clay.

H: Is that the snake?

Mei Lin picks up the coils and pokes them into the flat slab.

Tristan tears small pieces off the clay slab. He pretends to eat the pieces.

T: We roll balls. I make a pinch pot and we drop balls into it.

H: Did you put your balls in the hole?

Tristan makes a blowing sound. Heather explains to me that he is pretending his coil is an elephant trunk.

We poke a hole in the clay slab and play "peekaboo." They poke their fingers through the hole in the slab.

Heather Fraser

Playing peekaboo with clay slab

Deconstruction:

We again felt we had shaped the children's behaviour by rolling balls, snakes, and pinch pots and by playing a game of "peekaboo" with the toddlers. However, the children had brought their own strategies to the clay exploration in that they had initiated pinching small pieces off the clay themselves and used them to decorate their slabs. We noted that the toddlers continued to use the clay symbolically by inventing little games, for instance by pretending the clay was an elephant's trunk and by making blowing noises with it and by pretending to eat the clay.

DAY THREE

On day three Mei Lin again began the session by pinching small pieces of clay off the slab and then pressing them back onto the slab of clay. Tristan on the other hand needed some help to stay at the clay table as the following documentation shows.

Tristan takes a small piece of clay and pretends to eat it. He tells us it is for Mummy and Daddy. Then he appears to lose interest. I roll a coil and give it to him, hoping to refocus his attention on the clay.

T: Worm, worm.

He puts the clay coil on his lip. Tristan kisses the "worm" and then leaves to go over to the car track.

Again hoping to capture his interest, I bring two cars to the table. I make a flattened strip of clay and suggest they drive the cars on the clay "road." I am hoping to encourage Tristan to return to the clay table. Mei Lin picks up on the idea and drives the car back and forth. Tristan joins us briefly and we talk about the tracks the cars are making in the clay. Tristan leaves to play with the cars on the car track and it is not until Heather puts two small containers of water on the table that he returns and begins to make puddles with the wet clay until it becomes so mushy we decide to pack it away.

Deconstruction:

Mei Lin was involved for about 20 minutes on her own manipulating the clay. She did not need any props or teacher intervention. She just kept busy pinching, poking, and pressing the clay and decorating the large clay slab. We were pleased as this uninterrupted time, we felt, gave her the opportunity for learning about the "affordances" that clay offered. It was what we had been hoping to see happen. Later she joined Tristan making tracks with the trucks in the clay and then adding water to make the clay mushy.

DAY FOUR

On day four we observed that the toddlers began to use many new strategies in exploring the clay. They were much more confident and began to use a much wider variety of strategies in their exploration of the clay. For instance, they began to use water strategically to moisten the clay so they could smooth surfaces and make marks in the clay.

ML: Water?

She smoothed the clay surface and then scratched it with her finger.

They seemed to be recalling previous experiences and integrating them into new schemas for exploring the clay.

ML: Choo choo? (She is asking for the train to make tracks on the slab.)

They poke their fingers into the clay slab and then fill each hole with small pieces of clay. *Is this an example of prelogical math, i.e., one-to-one correspondence?* They experimented with the weight and volume of the clay slabs, flipping them over and examining the smooth side that had been lying flat on the table. They experimented with size:

ML: Two balls, Yeh! Small ball. Huge ball.

Tristan does a little dance holding a clay ball in each hand.

DAY FIVE

On day five we decided to give the toddlers some small wooden clay tools: a spoon, a fork, a knife, a spatula, and a bobbin to use with the clay. They both immediately wanted the wooden bobbin that has sharp edges and a sharp point at one end. This made us realize that they had learned a lot about the "affordances" of clay and knew exactly which tool would be the most effective one to use with the clay. They both spent 40 minutes using the tools to poke, chop, scoop, and cut the clay. The bobbin was much in demand, but they shared it back and forth between them, surprising us with their social skills.

In conclusion we revisited the three questions we had asked ourselves at the beginning of day one.

1. *How will young children's exploration of clay become more intentional?*

The children's exploration of the clay over the five sessions, we felt, had become more intentional and purposeful. In the last two sessions, they demonstrated that they had begun to explore the properties of clay as a material. In the beginning they used familiar, previously developed schemas, like symbolic play and adding water to explore the clay, but then gradually they expanded these strategies and developed new ones. By session four and five they were beginning to use the clay more as an art medium. They spent longer and became more engrossed as they learned more about the clay itself and how to use it. For instance, they used water to smooth it, and then made marks on the surface. Why was the addition of water such an instantaneous draw for both toddlers? They began to try joining chunks of clay by pressing them together. Our reflections on the documentation after each session gave us, the teacher and the recorder, insights into how our language and teaching strategies had on occasion shaped and sometimes limited the children in their own explorations.

2. *How will it evolve into more symbolic efforts?*

We were surprised at how quickly (day one) the children used the clay symbolically to make pretend food and "bobbles" for their hair! We came to realize that they were bringing previously learned schemas to their clay explorations. We

Heather Fraser

Weighing the clay balls?

observed that by making balls and coils for them (that they quickly turned into snakes or worms) only served to focus their attention on the symbolic possibilities of the clay instead of giving them the opportunity to really explore for themselves the "affordances" inherent in the medium of clay itself. Making realistic objects too quickly with the clay, we felt, interfered with sensory motor exploration and the development of a deeper understanding of clay and its possibilities. Had the way we presented the clay, i.e., by offering the toddlers coils of clay as opposed to a slab of clay, shaped their responses to it?

We were surprised by how many mathematical strategies the toddlers used to make meaning of the clay. They poked their fingers into the clay, perhaps exploring object permanence. They counted balls of clay, "one, two." They fit pieces of clay into holes they had poked in the slabs of clay, perhaps exploring one-to-one correspondence? They were often observed balancing or weighing a ball of clay in each hand. Were they comparing perhaps the size and the weight of the lumps of clay?

3. *What are the roles of the physical and social environment?*

We felt it was important that we understood how to present clay to young children so that they could acquire a deep understanding of it as an art medium. We began by putting out on the table smallish balls of clay. We realized quickly that this predetermined how the children used the clay. We decided to give the children fairly large slabs of clay which proved to invite more open-ended responses. We did not provide tools until the last session although we did give the children toy vehicles in session three to make tracks in the clay. This linked the clay experience with a previously familiar, popular experience of driving the trucks on a track. It did prove to be an effective strategy for keeping the toddlers' attention focussed on the clay. Did the truck we gave Tristan interfere with his own ideas about exploring clay?

We found that having a small table prepared for clay work is important as this limits the number of children who can participate at a time to a small group. We found by offering the clay to a small group at a time, the toddlers were able to share materials, experiences, and ideas more readily with each other. In fact, we were surprised how often they shared back and forth and copied each other in their exploration strategies.

Our supplementary readings, Poking, Pinching and Pretending: Documenting Toddlers' Explorations with Clay (Smith and Goldhaber 2004) and *Bambini: The Italian Approach to Infant/Toddler Care* (Gandini and Edwards 2001) guided our thinking and surprised us in how similar our toddlers' responses to the clay were to theirs. We were amazed at how our toddlers like theirs used so many prelogical math skills in their investigations and how well they scaffolded each other's learning. When we saw how competent and collaborative toddlers can be as they go about making meaning of their world, we realized how easy it is to underestimate their abilities!

Finally, we realized how important pedagogical documentation was and how deconstruction after each episode helped us think critically about our language and teaching strategies so that we could make adjustments in the following sessions. Having questions to guide us focussed our thinking and deepened our awareness of how we at times were unintentionally shaping the children's responses. Without engaging in the process of pedagogical documentation, particularly deconstructive analysis, we felt we would not have achieved the level of understanding we did about how our assumptions, teaching strategies, and language affected toddlers and their exploration of clay. This experience has given us a deeper understanding of how toddlers strive to make meaning of their world and taught us a great deal about ourselves as teachers, and about toddlers and their relationship to an art medium such as clay.

Documentation in Progress

The Holding Wall

It is important to have a system in place that can be used to store documentation materials temporarily while a project is still in progress. There are many ways of organizing material, but one way that works well is to fasten labelled envelopes or clear plastic pockets to a board on a wall in the classroom or hallway. Teachers and even children can file documentation material as it is generated in the classroom. This saves time later on when creating the final documentation.

Vignettes

Creating small vignettes during a project helps teachers and children revisit helpful ideas and plan new directions. This helps children and teachers sustain a project and invites children and parents into the narrative. For instance, a teacher can take one or two photographs of an interesting event or a child's or group's contribution. The photos are mounted, with a brief explanation, and shared during group meeting time. For instance, during the Castle and Knight project Linda Murdoch showed the children a photograph of a child designing and making the drawbridge (see p. 43). "Look what Ian did yesterday; he figured out how to get inside the castle!" These vignettes can be displayed in the classroom to show work in progress, and they can also be sent home to be shared with parents. When compiled in the final documentation, they illustrate the important steps in the project's development.

CHALLENGES OF DOCUMENTATION

Making Time for Documentation

When teachers undertake documentation, they need time to plan the focus for the proposed documentation, then to reflect, analyze, and interpret once the documentation gets underway. Consideration of theoretical implications also takes time, as does the interpretation of the observations. Collection of the visual material, such as photographs and videotapes, is also time consuming. It then takes time to design and produce the documentation panels. Therefore, documentation works best when the work is shared by a group of people. When the group collaborates, the work does not become too overwhelming for any one person, and the final documentation reflects the energy and enthusiasm of all the people involved.

Sometimes, however, teachers who work alone have no option but to carry out documentation on their own. A teacher in the public school system in Alberta, Kathleen Laycock, describes in a letter to the author dated 5 November 1998 the method she uses for documentation in a large kindergarten class*:

> Last year I taught a total of fifty-nine children in kindergarten. Thirty-four of these children were in one class. I was anxious to start documenting their conversations using a tape recorder, as is done in Reggio schools. This soon proved frustrating for me because of the background noise, the actual technicalities of setting up a tape recorder in various spots of the classroom, and the way children would be distracted once I set up a tape recorder in their midst.
>
> One day I heard a conversation I wanted to document. I grabbed a paper and pencil and started to write. I was able to document the entire conversation. I then took a picture of the children at play to include with the written documentation. This worked so well for me that I started doing several a day. I would simply sit down with a group of children at play and document for a few minutes. Sometimes the conversations seemed insignificant, but I soon found that a great deal could be learned about the children from each and every conversation. The conversations were typed, matched with the corresponding photo, and placed in a binder for further study. Extra copies were made for the children's scrapbooks.
>
> Each photograph and the accompanying dialogue was like a snapshot of that child's life at one particular moment in time. When I shared these documentation sheets with the parents at a parent–teacher conference, I was interested in the fact that parents were far more interested in the documentation than in how the children were doing academically.
>
> One parent was concerned that her daughter was monopolizing conversations and directing the play of the other children. As we studied all the documentation sheets that included her daughter, it was evident that her child was a team player as she worked with other children. In some cases it became apparent why their child had been experiencing difficulties with other children, or in other cases they were delighted to see their children sharing, helping, and playing cooperatively. Each of the documentations gave us very specific information to help us work with that child. Some parents were so excited about this glimpse into their child's life that they decided to start documenting their children's conversations at home.
>
> The school speech therapist took a special interest in the documentations. As she studied conversations of specific children over a long period of time, she was able to see their development in the area of language usage. This became an important tool for her.

*Reproduced courtesy of Kathleen Laycock

This type of documentation came to be known as *drop-in documentation*. It was an excellent description, because I would literally drop in on a conversation. The children became used to me doing this and would carry on their play without seeing me as an intruder. I would not contribute to their conversations unless invited to do so. I would merely document what I heard. These conversations became powerful tools in helping me understand the children in my class and in preparing lessons and activities that would be meaningful to them. The following is an example of one of my sample sheets:

Adventure Under the Sea

The children in my class took me on a surprise adventure. Let me explain how they did that. One day, I heard three boys playing at the water centre. Rather than interrupting their conversation with a series of questions (which teachers are prone to do), I simply sat down beside them and wrote down their conversation and took a photograph of them playing. Their conversation posed some interesting questions about sharks and some creative answers.

The next day, the same three boys checked some books about sharks out of our school library. More questions were posed about sharks, sharks' tongues, and sharks' jaws. Once again, I noted their dialogue without any attempt to direct it.

As these children sought answers to their questions, more and more children became enthralled with sharks or other sea creatures. A project was born.

I learned that a child's conversation has the power to lead you and your class to the tops of the mountains or to the depths of the sea. Listening to the children just may be the beginning of a new adventure.

Corey, Connor, and Mark playing at the water table:

Corey: Pretend you saw a baby shark and then a crab came.

Mark: The submarine catches the shark. Get the submarine out before it kills the shark. The shark is going crazy, it's hungry and wants to eat octopus.

Corey: The shark ate the food in the clam.

Mark: I see blood on the shark's tongue.

Connor: Do sharks have tongues?

Mark: Yes, but I think they are different than ours.

Corey: Why are they different?

Mark: They are different because sharks don't talk.

Corey: Well let's make this tank a special tank for baby sharks.

Heather Fraser

Corey, Connor, and Mark have an adventure under the sea at the water table.

Finding Space

Teachers need space for meeting with one another and parents to collaborate on the planning, design, and development of the documentation. They need wide, flat surfaces to work on the large panels that are the major form of documentation. Storage space is essential, both for work in progress and for storing the documentations that have been completed. It is interesting to note that in the schools in Reggio Emilia, the documentation stays on display in the classrooms for years, even after the children involved have left the school. This gives newcomers to the room a sense of the history that has gone on before. It may give suggestions to newly enrolled children about activities they can do in the classroom. Sometimes teachers will need to revisit documentation from previous years, so a system for storing material is essential. Classrooms also need shelves or cabinets for filing photographs, children's drawings and paintings, and the large documentation panels developed in the course of a project. A visitor to Reggio Emilia commented on a portrait she had seen a child drawing of her teacher on a previous visit. She was astounded when the atelierista was able to go to the file and give her a photocopy of the portrait she had seen the child drawing two years before. This demonstrates the value of having a system in place for filing material so that it can be quickly and easily accessed.

Finding Funds

Documentation can be expensive in the time it takes to produce and in the materials it requires. When budgets are prepared for early childhood programs, the people responsible need to be sure that teachers are given the resources they require to produce documentation of the highest quality. Documentation is worth the cost because it makes the program, especially the children's experiences, visible to the families and the wider community. It allows parents to be part of their children's experiences at school. It shows the teacher's commitment to providing an educational program that matches the learning potential of the children in the group. It also demonstrates that preschool education is both a serious and an enjoyable experience.

In November 1997 and again in June 1998, I issued a questionnaire to the teachers in the Quadra Island Children's Centre, the Vancouver Child Study Centre, and the Quadra Island Preschool asking them how they viewed the Reggio Emilia approach and how they had applied it in their schools. When

I asked about their experiences in doing documentation, the teachers in the Quadra Island Children's Centre said,

> We have seen how important documentation is as a means of capturing the essence of children's ideas and activities. But it is a difficult aspect of the Reggio approach, as we simply do not have the time built in for documentation and collaboration as they do in Reggio Emilia. This may become easier, something that needs to be constantly worked at as we evolve toward the Reggio philosophy. Many things that were initially difficult or confusing have become part of our centre now, and this will hopefully be the case with documentation—it will fit in better as we change, and the place for it during our day will grow.

> It is challenging! It works for me in keeping genuine, respectful (attention) to the children's ideas. It keeps me informed and it draws adults to the children's work in a more authentic and reciprocal (form of) communication.

> I think, if we as teachers have an openness, a sense of excitement about what we all are presented with in a day and about what we all contribute, and if we observe closely and listen, there will be many "hinges" we can use to delve deeper and to start progettazione.

Nine months later I asked the same group of teachers the following questions:

How have staff found time to document and share ideas?

> We have weekly staff meetings for two hours. The first hour we discuss specific children and other items on the agenda. The second hour is dedicated to discussing documentation [and] children's interests and sharing our ideas. We use our communication book extensively throughout the week to share our thoughts and insights with each other. We struggle with the lack of time to document and share ideas due to lack of money to bring in replacement staff. However, we will not let this obstacle stop us. A key component to documentation is clear communication on the floor. When staff observe children's conversations, listen to their ideas, and decide what seems worthwhile documenting, then they need to ask one of the other staff to support them by taking over their share of the duties at that time. It is important that other staff members know they will also have to guide other children who are not actively participating away from the process. When a provocation is set up in advance, it is helpful to discuss beforehand who will document, who will facilitate the experience following the provocation, and how each staff member can support the process. We still feel we are in the process of learning how to document; however, the more we do documentation the more we learn through trial and error what is effective and useful. (Dee Conley*, Quadra Island Children's Centre, November 1998)

> Time is set aside at meetings to do documentation, and sometimes a large part of the meeting will be spent organizing photos and deciding on text together. We read through each other's observations and comments and make suggestions on how we can use them. We sort through all transcriptions and make separate files of topics that have generated interest over several sessions. We keep a file we call "other" in which we collect transcriptions of conversations or experiences that seemed more than usually meaningful (i.e., insights into a child's thought processes or developing understanding). These were ones that did not lead to extended activity.

---

*Reproduced courtesy of Dee Conley

Spontaneous experiences, such as watching the insect digging in the garden, happened so fast, I only had time to grab a piece of paper and pencil and write just enough to enable me to recall the rest later. Since I can't write everything, I focus on the children's words, as they tell us which parts of the experience mean the most to the children. The description of what we were doing is not likely to be irretrievably forgotten. At the first possible opportunity, which is usually a break, I will fill in the gaps while it is still all there in my mind. Sometimes, if another staff member can cover, you can take time right then. Some of the children enjoy helping to remember while others find this too boring or irrelevant, having moved on to something else. (Susan Emery, Quadra Island Children's Centre, November 1998)

What is worth documenting, and how do you decide?

This is not an easy question to answer. First, you have to listen very carefully to the children and know what truly interests them. We have found that offering a provocation around a previously expressed interest and then documenting that process seems to be worthwhile. Also, documenting on the spot, when a child is expressing their ideas in building a theory on some topic can be helpful. The documentations are then discussed later with the other teachers at the next staff meeting to see if the ideas are worth pursuing. (Dee Conley, Quadra Island Children's Centre, November 1998)

This is very subjective. I tend to want to record times when I hear children voice a theory, such as what they think bugs do underground or how they can get corks out that are stuck in a bottle, but I often miss out on opportunities to record imaginative play. We hope, as a staff, to balance each other out, but gaps do occur. Sometimes we all decide at a staff meeting what we want to make into a display, and sometimes we just go ahead and do it independently. We all wish there was more time for documentation and discussion so that we can shorten the time-lag between an experience and getting it back to the children to revisit and perhaps extend the experience. Often, I think opportunities are missed because the children are just not interested by the time we get it done. (Susan Emery, Quadra Island Children's Centre, November 1998)

Who pays for the film?

The society [that runs the day care]. We make double prints and set out the second set for parents to purchase for 50 cents a picture. This helps cover the costs for film and processing. (Dee Conley, Quadra Island Children's Centre, November 1998)*

It is interesting in comparing the teachers' earlier and later comments to note how much more detailed and specific were the comments made in November than those made nine months earlier. During the nine months the teachers in the Quadra Island Children's Centre had begun to realize the complexities of doing documentation. They had begun to solve some problems, including how to meet the cost of materials such as film and of having the photographs developed. They had begun to build in the time to meet and discuss their observations, but they were still having difficulty finding the time to

*Reproduced courtesy of Dee Conley

create the panels to display the documentation. They were also struggling to achieve documentation that communicated a deeper level of understanding of what the children were doing in the classroom. The teachers realized, however, that to implement the Reggio Emilia approach successfully, documentation is essential. Four years later, the teachers were still refining their documentation skills. They commented that it was worthwhile "being part of the experience and then working away and thinking about it and figuring out what happened, both from the head and the heart, even if not every parent reads it." They said, however, that the final documentation had to be "distilled down to what is important"; otherwise it is irritating. They noted that collaboration had enabled them to edit each other's work and freely express their opinions (interview, June 2004). Documentation addresses many levels of the program. For the children it acts as a memory device, enabling them to revisit previous experiences and make connections to past, present, and future events and experiences. It gives teachers opportunities to help children move from unassisted to assisted learning and achieve a higher level within the zone of proximal development (Vygotsky 1951, 103). It enables children to use higher mental functions, such as focused attention, deliberate memory, and symbolic thought, as opposed to the lower functions of reactive attention, associative memory, and sensorimotor thought (Bodrova and Leong 1996).

Documentation also expands the role of the teacher and provides a tool that enables the teachers to be more effective in their work with children. It requires them to become critical thinkers and researchers in the classroom. Pedagogical documentation, especially during the collaborative process of deconstructive analysis, helps teachers to become aware of any assumptions and "taken for granted ideas" they may hold that will impact their work with young children. The discussions that are a necessary part of the process give teachers different perspectives to consider which broaden their understanding and introduce them to new ideas that may change their pedagogy. Documentation displayed in the classrooms and entranceways gives the teachers more credibility in the outside community. As parents and visitors to the centre read the information and see the work the children are doing in the program, they can understand how much serious consideration teachers give to all aspects of the program, especially to the task of learning. Documentation serves as a communication channel from the centre to the outside world. It is, therefore, an important tool in building relationships among the teachers, the parents, and the outside community. Above all, documentation makes apparent the teachers' commitment to high-quality preschool education for children.

THE RELATIONSHIP BETWEEN DOCUMENTATION AND ASSESSMENT

Assessment/evaluation is a tool frequently used to measure an individual's abilities or school achievement or to assess the effectiveness of an educational program or curriculum. These tools were developed during the scientific era and are reflective of our faith in the scientific method and certainty that the results are objective and fair. But as Hillevi Lenz Taguchi writes, "The more complex things become, the more we seem to desire processes of reduction and thus increase control—but such reduction strategies simultaneously make us risk shutting out the inclusion and social justice we say we want to achieve" (Lenz Taguchi 2007, 1).

Documentation, on the other hand, takes the form of a narrative, to quote Carlina Rinaldi, "Its force of attraction lies in the wealth of questions, doubts, and reflections that underlie the collection of data and with which it is offered to others—colleagues and children" (Rinaldi 2006, 71). Whereas, assessment/evaluation takes a narrow view of children, documentation looks at children using a wide lens as it endeavours to capture the richness and depth of their learning. Conventional assessment most often takes place out of context and measures not the depth of a child's learning but the ability to respond quickly to factual questions. This type of assessment requires professional judgements and comparisons concerning a child. Documentation on the other hand, expects that teachers are part of the process, partners with children in the learning experience and that learning does not occur in isolation. Children are studied as part of a group so that the individual's participation within the group becomes apparent and adds to the richness of the narrative.

Whereas, assessment will focus only on a limited range of a child's forms of expression, e.g., logico/mathematical or linguistic responses, documentation captures the full range of a child's use of multiple languages and intelligences; verbal, visual, graphic, musical, symbolic, metaphoric, etc. Documentation reveals a child's theories about the world, their social interactions, the role they play within the group. It uncovers the path of learning and makes it visible to the outside world. With this information, teachers are able to reflect on how the learning is proceeding, they can sense what resources or materials might further the children's investigations. Through reflective deconstruction of the documentation throughout the project, they identify their own subjectivities and biases that might be having an impact on the children's learning. The result is that documentation is a fairer, more truthful, and more comprehensive record of a child's behaviour.

Woodpecker

Negotiating the
Curriculum

Questions to Consider:

- What are the differences in theme, emergent, and negotiated learning approaches to planning curriculum?

- How do teachers negotiate learning in the preschool curriculum?

- What is a provocation, and how is it used?

- What communication strategies are needed to set the process of negotiated learning in motion?

- How do teachers collaborate with children in making predictions?

- What does it mean to "expect the unexpected"?

- What are the challenges in using this approach to curriculum?

- How can the process of deconstructive analysis heighten awareness of how biases and preconceived notions affect curriculum?

The educational institution is, in fact, a system of communication and interaction among the three protagonists [children, educators, and families] integrated into the larger system. Given this system in its complexity, it can be understood why the potential of children is stunted when the endpoint of their learning is formulated in advance.

—Carlina Rinaldi

THE TEACHER-DIRECTED CURRICULUM

There have been a number of changes in the way early childhood educators have approached the planning of curriculum over the last 20 years. During this time the focus of the curriculum has changed from being teacher directed to becoming first child centred and then emergent. Now, as teachers, inspired by the Reggio Emilia approach, have woven the principles of reciprocity and collaboration into the planning process, meaning that the approach to curriculum has changed yet again to become "child originated and teacher framed" (Forman and Fyfe 1998, 240).

When the curriculum was solely teacher directed, educators often wrote their teaching plans in advance for the week or month, and sometimes even for the whole year. Teachers knew what the theme was for each week, what they would be doing each day, what supplies they would need, and what preparation they needed to do. Teachers would plan the activities for fall and Thanksgiving, followed by Halloween, when they set out all those pumpkins for carving, and then the winter festivals. Soon it was spring, time for planting seeds in styrofoam cups. Finally, the teachers would plan a summer picnic, before packing up the curriculum boxes for another year. The problem with this approach was the children often had different ideas; for instance, they were more interested in the new funnels in the sandbox than in discussing why leaves change colour in the fall. The teacher's dilemma was how to reconcile the two ideas about curriculum—in this case, completing the teacher-planned activities related to the theme of fall or allowing the children to pursue their own interests and investigate what happens to the volume of water when it trickles out of a funnel.

In the 1960s and 1970s, when governments invested money in early childhood education, such as in the Head Start programs in the United States, accountability became increasingly important. Early childhood programs were required to demonstrate that they were well organized, able to set clear goals, and able to evaluate the program. This procedure was felt to be essential in justifying the expenditure of taxpayers' money on programs for children before school age. Early childhood educators needed to show that preschool education was a serious endeavour and that it had not only short-term but also long-term benefits for children.

Accountability became even more important in the 1980s, when, owing to a recession in the economy, funding became increasingly scarce. One way to demonstrate accountability was to show that the program was well organized and to make the organizational structure clearly visible. Many early childhood programs attempted to demonstrate accountability by selecting a theme for each week or month of the year, setting goals and objectives, identifying the concepts that children needed to learn, deciding on appropriate activities, and evaluating the outcome to ensure that the goals and objectives had been achieved. This was the preferred method of program planning taught in ECE programs in the past two or three decades.

The teachers often mapped out the themes they chose on a chart, which they displayed in the classroom or printed in the newsletter sent home to parents. Many teachers based their themes on the belief that it is important to encourage children to develop a positive self-concept and heighten their awareness of themselves and the world around them. In many early childhood programs, the year often still begins with a theme of self and others. Included in this theme will be activities to do with body image, awareness of the senses, and expression of feelings. This theme may then be expanded to include activities that encourage children to get to know the other children in the class, their families, and the wider community. Often teachers will arrange field trips so children can learn about the neighbourhood; for instance, children may visit the firehall or the grocery store. Seasonal change and holidays throughout the year are also popular themes in preschool programs.

Although many preschool programs still base their planning on a theme approach, teachers often find that the experiences that actually happen in the classroom have little relationship to the written plan on the chart. They find, for instance, that children sometimes come up with more interesting ideas than the teachers had thought of. Teachers find themselves caught in the dilemma of sticking with the theme or abandoning it and following the children's interests. Many teachers have found that theme planning is too rigid and that more flexibility is needed to provide children with experiences that are responsive to their ideas. "Everyone acknowledges that curriculum becomes intriguing, alive and compelling when something out of the blue captures the imagination of a group of children" (Sobel 2008, 96).

THE EMERGENT CURRICULUM

In recent years theme planning has begun to give way to a view of the curriculum as emergent—as arising out of the children's interests. "Curriculum is what happens," write Jones and Nimmo. "In early childhood education, curriculum isn't the focus, children are. It's easy for teachers to get hooked on curriculum because it's so much more manageable than children. But curriculum is *what happens* in an educational environment—not what is rationally planned to happen, but what actually takes place" (1995, 12).

An emergent curriculum begins with observation of the children and their interests. Teachers observe the children in the classroom, listen, and record their ideas, and then they select from these observations one or more topics that seem to interest the children. Teachers then, either individually or as a group, create a web on a large sheet of paper. They write the topic in which the children are interested in large letters at the centre of the web. Next, they brainstorm the possible directions that they and the children might take in pursuing the topic further. They then write these subtopics on lines that branch off in different directions (see Figure 7.1). The words in dotted-line squares represent the children's ideas, and the words in solid-line squares are the adults' suggestions. Teachers add new ideas and suggestions to the web as they emerge during the experience. A thick coloured line traces the path on the web that the experience actually follows as it unfolds. Teachers find that the advantage to this kind of planning, as opposed to theme planning, is that it is more responsive to the children's interests, and it enables teachers to be more flexible and creative in the planning process. The experiences mapped out on the chart can change direction at any time in

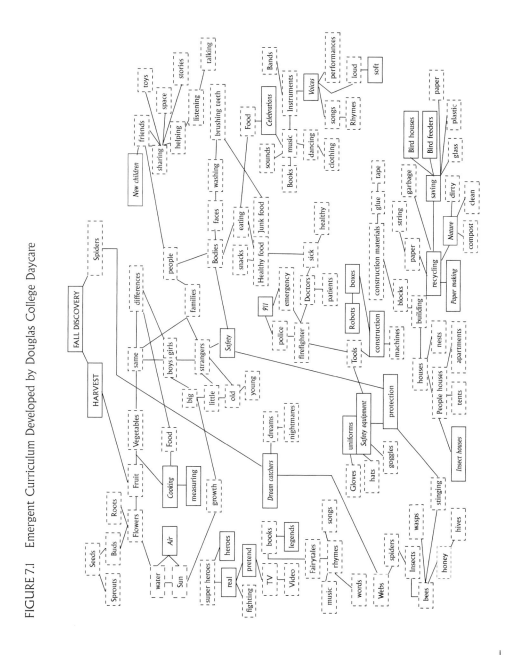

FIGURE 7.1   Emergent Curriculum Developed by Douglas College Daycare

CHAPTER 7   Negotiating the Curriculum

response to new ideas and suggestions; therefore, the project remains fresh and exciting for the teachers and children (Jones and Nimmo 1995).

THE NEGOTIATED CURRICULUM

Negotiated curriculum is in many ways similar to emergent curriculum as teachers inspired by the Reggio Emilia approach perceive the curriculum as emerging from the interests and ideas of the children, but they also believe that there should be negotiation between all those involved in the development of the curriculum—in the planning and in the projects as they unfold. This perspective of curriculum is based on the theory that children co-construct knowledge within their social group. George Forman and Brenda Fyfe state that "this theory holds that knowledge is gradually constructed by people becoming each other's student, by taking a reflective stance toward each other's constructs, and by honouring the power of each other's initial perspective for negotiating a better understanding of subject matter" (1998, 239). Negotiated learning, therefore, begins with observations of the children and by listening closely to their conversations; however, it goes beyond observation "to uncover the children's beliefs about the topics to be investigated.... [The teacher's] analysis reveals the reasons behind the children's interests, the source of their current knowledge, and the level of articulation about its detail" (Forman and Fyfe 1998, 240). Teachers then share this information with other adults. Perhaps the teachers will see in this discussion that there is the germ of an idea that might become the topic for a future progettazione. All those who will be involved in the project then discuss the possibilities and the many ways in which the project could evolve. They write down their hypotheses and predictions for future directions the topic may follow. They discuss the possible choices the children will make and where these choices might lead. The team then will need to decide whether the idea for the topic will sustain the children's interest for a long period of time. If they agree that the topic has long-term possibilities, they begin to prepare for subsequent stages of the project (Rinaldi 1998).

In taking a negotiated learning approach to curriculum, teachers move beyond simply providing children with experiences. They probe further, either by asking questions or by engaging the child in discussion to discover why children are deeply absorbed in exploring a material, or they try to figure out what children are thinking as they touch, taste, examine, or explore the texture of interesting objects.

George Forman and Brenda Fyfe have identified three components, *design, documentation,* and *discourse,* which define negotiated learning (see Chapter 6).

Design Phase

The design stage begins when the teachers and other adults, from observations and transcriptions of the children's conversations, have decided on a subject that they believe will be of long-term interest to the children. Teachers use various methods of planning curriculum, but one that works well for many teachers is similar to the method for planning an emergent curriculum, described above. On a large sheet of paper, teachers make a web, with the main topic at the centre. They then brainstorm as a group to identify possible directions the project may follow and write their predictions on the chart, drawing lines from the topic to the subtopics that may possibly evolve from the main subject as the project unfolds. The chart also includes a list of ideas for provoking the children to think more deeply or broadly about the topic. These provocations might be questions that a teacher plans to ask the children to find out how well they understand a topic and to provoke them to further investigation, or they might be plans for arranging equipment and materials in the classroom to encourage children to see relationships and develop deeper understanding of a subject.

Children are also involved in the design phase of the project. Teachers select a small group of children who have shown real interest in pursuing the topic. At each stage they encourage the children to discuss and symbolically represent their ideas about the subject so that the teachers can assess their level of understanding of the topic. Teachers also encourage children to make their theories about the topic visible by representing their thinking using a variety of appropriate materials. "*Design* refers to any activity in which children make records of their plans or intended solutions. A drawing can be a design if it is drawn with an intent to guide the construction of the items drawn, or to guide a sequence of steps" (Forman and Fyfe 1998, 241). Teachers share and discuss these representations with the other children and adults in the group; with input from others, the representations tend to become more detailed and elaborate as the investigation proceeds. They also become part of the core material for the documentation that is developed as the project unfolds.

Documentation Phase

Documentation is a central component of negotiated learning. In the early stages, the teachers will have met to decide on the possible forms the documentation will take, such as written observations, transcriptions of audiotape, slides, photographs displayed on panels or in portfolios, and videotapes. Whatever media the teachers choose, the documentation will be used to describe the process the teachers and children followed as they negotiated the learning that took place during the project. Forman and Fyfe state that "when teachers document children's work and use this documentation as part of their instruction with the children, the net result is a change in the image of their role as teacher, a change from teaching children to studying children, and by studying children, learning with children" (1998, 240). Documentation also provides the group with a means of revisiting previous experiences and discussing future directions the project may take.

Discourse Phase

When communication is conceptualized as *discourse,* interaction goes beyond just listening and talking to children. It includes the added dimension of reflecting on and analyzing what is being heard and said. Discourse requires teachers to pay careful attention to the language they hear and speak, to ask questions to uncover the meaning behind the words, and to try to figure out the reasons for the child's comments. Transcribing the children's conversations and then examining and analyzing them with the other adults is essential in developing a project. "Treating talk as discourse causes teachers to look for theories, assumptions, false premises, misapplications, clever analogies, ambiguities, and differences in communicative intent, all of which are pieces to be negotiated into shared meaning by the group" (Forman and Fyfe 1998, 247).

Educators also use transcriptions of the children's talk to remind children of thoughts and ideas they expressed in earlier conversations and to help children extend their understanding of a subject. The photographs, drawings, and text in documentation can act as cues in helping children remember what happened previously in the project. Revisiting past experiences helps the children focus on the topic and perhaps come up with new or related ideas. Using cued responses is an effective way to move a project forward or find a new direction (Gabarino, in Phillips 2000). For instance, a teacher might observe a child's continuing interest in the movements of the snails in the tank. Reflections on the transcriptions of the child's talk the previous day might lead her to provoke the child to think further about the subject. "Yesterday, you said the snails reminded you of an elastic band because their bodies stretched and contracted. Look at this snail upside down on the lid of the tank. How does he stay up there? Could an elastic band do that?" Used as a provocation, this question might lead, as it did at the Vancouver Child Study Centre, to a short project investigating snails and their habitat. In the early spring, the children collected snails in the forest and constructed an environment for the snails in the classroom, planting moss and ferns to make it look like the place where they had found the snails in the forest. The children fed the snails fresh fruit and vegetables every day. Many of the children sketched and made three-dimensional representations of the snails. One morning, the children were delighted to find that the snails had laid a mass of eggs at the bottom of the tank. Before the children left for the summer holidays, they carried the snails back to the forest and placed them where they knew they would be safe. The children and teachers were concerned that the children who attended the class in the afternoon would wonder what had happened to the snails. They decided that they would draw a map to show the afternoon group where they had set the snails free in the forest. On their return to the classroom, Vivian Urquhart, one of the teachers, noticed Neilson sitting at a table with another child and drawing shapes and long lines on his sheet of paper*.

> **Neilson:** I am going to do the Salish trail after I have done the Spanish trail.
>
> **Vivian:** Would you like to write the word? It starts with an *S*. Are you drawing the map so the afternoon children will know where the snails are?
>
> **Neilson:** I did! *X*—that is where they [the snails] are.
>
> **Vivian** (pointing to the shapes on the paper): I like the way you drew the horsetails—now they will know where to look for them.
>
> (Earlier on the walk, the children had placed the snails near a patch of coarse, green plants that Neilson had told us were horsetails. "But," he had said, "there is a problem. Horses can't eat them for food. I don't know why they are called horsetails.")

From the observation and recording of the child's talk above, the teacher inferred that Neilson was making a map that included a drawing of the plants that grew near where the snails had been released in the forest. His question about why the plants were called horsetails when horses, in fact, did not like to eat them is an example of what Loris Malaguzzi called expecting the unexpected. If there had been enough time left in the school year, this child's comment might have been an interesting idea to follow up. Horsetails are a fascinating plant in themselves, but they were also the dominant plant species during the dinosaurs' time on earth. Many of the children in the group, like most children, are fascinated by everything to do with dinosaurs, so the teachers could have considered investigating horsetails with the children, which, in turn, might have led to a project on dinosaurs and their environment.

Listening attentively to what children are saying and being able to follow up with questions that uncover the child's level of understanding are essential skills in implementing a negotiated learning approach to curriculum. Both skills take practice. An image of the child who is competent and full of ideas is central to listening attentively to what children say. When teachers

---

*Reproduced courtesy of Vivian Urquhart

expect children to say interesting things and to contribute ideas, they will be much more likely to pay attention to what children have to say. When children know that their ideas are appreciated, they will be more willing to share them. Slowing down and taking the time to really hear what the child is saying and then trying to see it from the child's perspective is important. Reflecting on the child's responses to questions also helps a teacher learn what kind of questions are most effective. For instance, if the kind of questions the teacher poses elicit one word or no response, the questions the teacher is asking may be too direct. A question that is more reflective may encourage a more elaborate response. A question phrased as, "I wonder what is happening here?" encourages the child to think about what he is doing and to make a response that provides a teacher with unexpected insight into what he is thinking. Reflecting what is understood from the child's comments is also helpful, as in, "I think I am hearing you say … Is that right?" This response may also help clarify the child's thinking. Rejoicing in the child's competence with comments and questions such as, "That is amazing! How did you do that?", will probably encourage the child to further effort and may even generate some explanation of the child's thinking. Sometimes a teacher may need to encourage children to clarify or go deeper; for instance, they may say, "I don't quite understand what you mean by saying that.... "

Giving the child many opportunities to engage in authentic conversations is important. An authentic conversation is one in which the participants engage in a dialogue that has a purpose and is of genuine interest. This kind of talk is more likely to happen when teachers respect children, view them as competent, and are genuinely interested in hearing what they are thinking about. Sometimes children have ideas, but they have not developed enough vocabulary to express them clearly. This is why it is important that teachers have established close relationships with the children. When a teacher knows a child well, she is more likely to be able to infer what the child is trying to say and provide the child with the missing words. Margaret Mead tells the story of taking her grandchild for a walk, when they passed a display of pussy willows in a florist shop. Margaret Mead heard her granddaughter say "pussycat," and she knew immediately that the child had connected the branches of pussy willows to a poem she had taught the child's mother years ago:

I'm a little pussy

But I'll never be a cat

'Cause I'm a pussy willow

And that is that!

From the one word the child uttered, Margaret Mead was able to access the child's meaning, and the two of them went on down the street reciting the poem together. To be able to engage in meaningful dialogue with children, therefore, teachers need to do the following:

- establish an environment that values communication in all its different forms—verbal, gestural, symbolic, and so on

- establish a close and trusting relationship with the child

- hold the image of the child as competent and filled with ideas that are worth listening to

- be genuinely interested in what the child is saying

- listen attentively

- slow down the pace of the talk and reflect before responding

- provide a variety of materials to enable children to use their preferred material to represent their ideas (e.g., clay to create three-dimensional forms or pens and pencils for drawing)

- probe to uncover meaning

- scaffold the child's ability to express ideas by supplying the missing words or offer materials to the children that will help them to make their thinking visible

- encourage the child to think about thinking (metalinguistic knowledge)

- encourage the child to use a wide range of language techniques, such as metaphors, analogies, and hypotheses

- accept the inevitability of conflict and view it as a positive dynamic in moving ideas forward

In the following transcript of a conversation, Susan Emery*, a teacher at the Quadra Island Children's Centre, shows how she used some of the above suggestions in a conversation with Grant to help him come up with a mutually satisfying solution to their problem.

There are many silver strips hanging down from the skylight, reflecting light on the floor and walls. I am holding a strip that has fallen down. Grant comes over.

Grant: What are you doing with that?

Susan: It fell down and I'm wondering how to put it back without going and getting a ladder.

---

*Reproduced courtesy of Susan Emery

Grant: Stand on a chair.

Susan: I'll try that. (I'm a long way from reaching the skylight.)

Grant: Now JUMP off the chair and REACH UP and stick it on!

Susan: I'm worried I might hurt myself if I do that.

Grant: You won't. Go on. Jump!

Susan: Well, Grant, I'm thinking of how I could reach it up there without breaking my ankle.

Grant: A big stick.

Whatever he'd said—within reason—I would have tried, but he saved me the trouble by coming up with a workable solution himself. I got a broom and stuck the silver strip back on the skylight with the handle.

Susan: Your idea worked fine, Grant.

At Douglas College, the students are encouraged to put such techniques into practice as they work with children in Children Teaching Teachers. The students observe and record one another communicating with the children. They then analyze the transcripts to see what kind of responses the children made to their questions and comments. They learn to avoid using what we call "dumb questions," such as, "What colour is that stop sign?" and questions with a hidden agenda, such as, "How many chickens can you see?" They learn that judgmental comments, such as, "What a beautiful painting" or "I like the man you drew," are comments that close down rather than open up the conversation. They discover that questions that arise out of the teacher's agenda, such as, "Tell me about your picture," are one-sided comments that do not foster a negotiated learning approach. They begin to understand that teachers ask questions only when they are genuinely interested in the answers. With practice, they begin to realize the value of listening to children. They learn that when they *really* hear what children have to say, a meaningful dialogue develops. Conversation becomes discourse when teachers begin to use dialogue to collaborate with children in co-constructing theories about subjects they and the children are interested in discovering more about.

Design, documentation, and discourse are essential components in planning and implementing a negotiated learning approach to curriculum. These three components do not necessarily occur in a linear fashion, but rather are interwoven throughout the process as the project evolves. Each one affects the others. Documentation, for instance, informs the discourse, and discourse the documentation. Design forms the structure on which the project grows.

THE BRIDGE-BUILDING PROJECT

In the spring of 1998, the teachers, Chava Rubenson* and Pat Breen**, and children at the Vancouver Child Study Centre began an investigation about the building of bridges, which carried on until school closed for the summer holidays at the end of June. Since the beginning of school in September, the teachers had observed that both the morning and afternoon groups of children seemed particularly interested in the construction materials in the classroom. Many of the children spent much of their free-play time building in the block area or using the small blocks set out on tables in the room. Earlier in the year, the morning group had built the houses for "The Three Little Pigs" project (described in Chapter 5). The afternoon group had also shown a strong interest in construction. They had previously built swimming pools, the first one out of Styrofoam and other recycled material and the other out of clay bricks. In both groups the children's interest in construction continued to grow as the year progressed. One day, a teacher read the story "The Three Billy Goats Gruff"during

circle time. Later, the teachers observed the children building bridges in the block corner. The teachers decided to see whether the children would be interested in an in-depth investigation of building bridges.

The first bridges the children made using the blocks

*Reproduced courtesy of Chava Rubenson
**Reproduced courtesy of Pat Breen

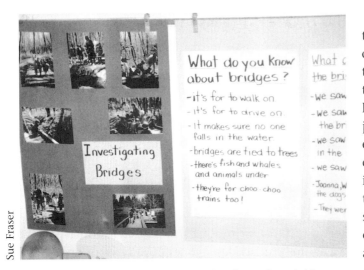

The first step in the process (the design phase) was to find out what the children already knew about the subject. The teachers encouraged the children to draw their ideas and make pictures of bridges with shapes cut out of construction paper and popsicle sticks of various sizes and widths. From these

The initial exploration of what the children knew about bridges

representations, the teachers were able to see the children's present level of understanding of bridges and how they were built. From their initial explorations with the children, they found the following misconceptions:

- Some children thought that bridges are built along the side of a river.

- There was misunderstanding of how traffic gets up onto the bridge deck. Some of the children, for instance, had not realized the significance of having a ramp leading onto the bridge.

- None of the children had much understanding about the different supports a bridge needs to span a wide expanse of river.

Once they identified these misconceptions and gaps in knowledge, the teachers planned activities that would enable the children to further their understanding of bridges. The teachers decided that they would use written observations or running records, anecdotal records, and photographs to document the learning experiences as they unfolded. Once the preliminary work was complete and the teachers had discussed the possibilities of doing a project on building bridges, they and the children embarked on a journey of investigation together.

The teachers encouraged the children's interest in building bridges in the block corner by setting out the animal characters on the carpet in front of the blocks. The carpet on which the children played had a pattern on it of roads and a river. The teachers placed a truck loaded with small blocks on the carpet as a provocation. A few children began to build bridges across the river on the carpet and hop the toy animals over them, saying "Trip trap, trip trap," as they had heard the teacher say when she read the story "The Three Billy Goats Gruff."

The teachers decided to take the children on a walk through the forest that surrounds the school to look for bridges. One child, upon coming to a small bridge across a stream, shouted, "Look, Gloria, a bridge!" The children used a variety of materials, such as felt pens, construction paper, and popsicle sticks, to represent their understanding of bridges. The teachers arranged a field trip to Van Dusen Gardens to show the children the many different kinds of bridges that had been built there. A newsletter went out to the parents asking them to take their children to visit a local bridge and to draw the children's attention to bridges when they crossed them while out driving or walking. Vancouver has many bridges, as it is situated at the mouth of the Fraser River. Many of the children crossed at least one big bridge every day as they travelled with their parents about the city. The teachers visited the library and brought back a selection of books about bridges, which they displayed prominently in the classroom. At circle time a few days later, the teachers, wanting to discover how much knowledge the children had acquired of bridges, asked them to tell the group what they had learned about bridges.

May 4, 1998

Noah: Bridges have railings because we don't want to fall off in the water.

Aaron: Some bridges wiggle like floating bridges; they are broken.

Julie: A car is sometimes like a bridge.

Sally: Some bridges are made of stones and bricks.

Douglas: Some bridges are strong and some are not strong. You don't want to go in the water— that is why we need a bridge.

Teacher: What do people who build bridges do before they start building the bridge?

Aaron: They need to think.

Patrick: They need a barge.

Teacher: Yes, you need a barge to take out the supplies.

The children in the afternoon group seemed particularly interested in the topic,

Sue Fraser

Bridges have railings.

so the teachers gave them glue, pieces of wood, rocks, and clay and encouraged them to build bridges. The children began by building arches. The documentation of this stage showed that the children were struggling with the problem of getting the supports for the arches of the bridge to stay upright. Note how Pat, one of the teachers in the afternoon group, was able to scaffold the children's efforts:

> Pat: Is it sticking? Maybe you could count to ten. Now what about the other side? We don't want it to fall over on the other side.

At this stage the children did not think about creating ramps at either side of the bridge.

The teachers met to discuss which materials would help the children develop their notions of bridge construction further. They decided to paint a blue river with narrow and wide sections on a large sheet of plywood and to challenge the children to build a bridge across the river (discourse phase).

> May 19, 1998
>
> They introduced the river to the group during circle and asked the children to suggest how to build a bridge across the river.
>
> Pat: What have we here?
>
> Children: A river. Yes, let's call it the Beautiful Blue River.
>
> Aaron: I know, we are going to build bridges.
>
> Pat: Yes, let's pretend we are bridge builders and we must decide where we should build a bridge across a river.
>
> Many children scramble to point out a place where they could build a bridge.
>
> Pat: Just a minute. Let's cut a piece of ribbon to cross the river. Gillian, show us where you would build a bridge.
>
> Gillian: Across here. (She points out the spot.)
>
> Pat: Think carefully about where would be the best place to cross the river. (Aaron points out a narrow place in the river.)
>
> Pat: Why did you choose that spot, Aaron?
>
> Aaron: Because it wouldn't take as much.
>
> Pat: You mean it wouldn't take as many materials. Why?

Sue Fraser

Designing a river crossing

Aaron: Because it is smaller.

Pat: Yes, it is a smaller distance. See, the river is narrower here and broad over here.

The teachers handed out pieces of string of various lengths and asked the children to estimate the width of the river and then choose a piece of string that would be long enough to cross the river. The teachers put out small coloured blocks and Kapla blocks beside the painted river, and six children remained after circle time to construct bridges with the blocks across the river.

May 20, 1998

The next day at circle time, Pat and Chava again placed the plywood sheet in the centre of the circle.

Pat: I remember yesterday that many of you used blocks to build across the river.

Chava: What do real engineers use to build a bridge?

Aaron: Stone. Only stone is strong enough.

Chava: Yes, bricks and metal too.

Pat: We also have to make mortar. Now we are going to take our beautiful blue river and experiment to make bridges—a footbridge ...

Chava, adding to the list: A truck bridge, a man bridge, or a bicycle bridge.

Chava and Pat placed the painted river on the plywood sheet on the floor and set out wood, string, toilet rolls, rocks, tongue depressors, and clay nearby. Many of the children began by constructing an arch out of three pieces of wood. They had trouble stabilizing the structure, as on being set upright the arch swayed back and forth. Douglas sang "London Bridge Is Falling Down" as he watched Sally's arch collapse.

Chava: This is not an easy task. You will have to make your bridge so it doesn't fall down. Sometimes bridges have a support in the middle of the river and boats can go on either side. Is this the only material we have, or are there other things we could use?

Sally then began to build a pillar to support the bridge in the middle of the river.

Pat, emphasizing the need for collaboration, encouraged the children to help one another: Work together. Real bridge builders work together.

Douglas, after watching the children's difficulties with the swaying arches, solved the problem by making balls of clay, placing them on top of each other to form two towers on either side of the river, and strengthening them by driving short sticks downward to hold the balls of clay together. He used two tongue depressors as extensions to provide a wider foot for the ball of clay at the bottom of each pillar. He then placed a strip of cardboard between the two towers, pressing the surface down hard onto the clay to make a bridge of the right size to span the width of the river.

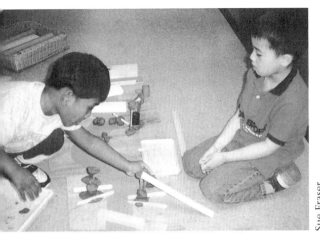

Solving structural problems

Chava, to the children sitting round the plywood sheet: How would you get over this bridge?

Sonja: Maybe an elevator.

Liselotte: Jump. Everyone has to jump.

Douglas: I have an idea.

Douglas tried different materials to form the ramp on each side of the bridge deck, eventually deciding to use two thin strips of wood at either end. Aaron also made the pillars for his bridge out of balls of clay, but he used two tongue depressors as braces to support them. Julie began by looking at the picture of a suspension bridge in a book propped open on the table. She selected a long, narrow piece of cardboard for the bridge deck and then returned to examine the picture.

Pat: Have you seen a bridge like that?

Julie: You know, the animal bridge.

Pat: You mean animals go over the bridge?

Julie (laughing): No, no, the one with the lion.

Pat: Oh, do you mean the Lions Gate Bridge?

Julie: Yes, yes.

Pat: I see you have a bridge deck. What else do you need for the Lions Gate Bridge?

Julie pointed to the cables in the book.

Pat: Yes, you will need cables. I could get you some string.

She left and returned with string and scissors and cut off some lengths of string.

Julie placed the deck over the river and contemplated how to tie the string. She returned to look at the book.

Pat: Do you see that the cables are attached to big supports? Let's see what you could use for supports.

Pat looked in a tray of materials and found pieces of wood, rocks, popsicle sticks, and

Julie investigating how a suspension bridge is made

Julie figuring out how to stabilize the structure

tongue depressors. Julie selected popsicle sticks and began. When she spotted coloured popsicle sticks, she exchanged hers for matching pairs. She attempted unsuccessfully to stand popsicle sticks at the end of the bridge.

Pat: Perhaps you could use something to support it, to hold it up. We have rocks, clay, and wood.

Julie selected a ball of clay to hold up the popsicle sticks. In the process she discovered that she had to provide support on both sides. When she finished installing supports at both ends of the bridge, she began to tie string to each end. She examined the results and looked puzzled. She returned to the book to look at the cables. When she returned she pressed the string down in the middle of the span.

Pat: I wonder how you could hold it down. Perhaps you could try a piece of clay.

Julie: I know.

She cut a piece of string and anchored both string cables in the middle by tying a piece of string around the deck. She smiled at her accomplishment. Pat reminded Julie that the Lions Gate Bridge has two stone statues of lions at one end of the bridge. Julie spent the remaining time making two lions out of clay and installing them at one end of the bridge.

On discussing all the methods the children had used to make a bridge to cross the painted river, the teachers decided that the next day they would encourage the children to work collaboratively in extending Julie's idea of constructing the Lions Gate Bridge. Earlier, the children and teachers had seen an idea for building a suspension bridge in one of the books on bridges they had borrowed from the library. The teachers worked with the group of children to build a suspension bridge in the classroom by using chairs and sheets of cardboard as in the illustration they had seen in the library book. The group placed two adult-sized chairs back to back and a cardboard deck between the chairs. They tied two ropes to join the backs of the chairs.

May 21, 1998

Gillian tested the strength of the construction by pulling on the rope. The chairs tipped.

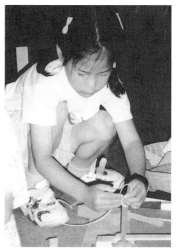

Julie building a suspension bridge

Sue Fraser

Documentation of the bridge construction

Sally (shouting): Put a brick on the chair!

The chair tipped again.

Aaron: Try two bricks.

The chairs still tipped.

Chava: Here is some more rope.

She tied the rope and pulled it taut. Gillian tested it again, the chair did not tip.

Chava: I would have to sit here and hold it all the time.

Julie: How about putting the brick on it?

Chava: Let's tie it (the brick) to the rope.

They tied another rope at the end of the bridge, and several children went to the other end of the bridge to tie two more ropes to the top of the chair and then anchored the ropes to bricks. The children had difficulty pulling the ropes taut, owing to space restrictions.

Chava: Tell me, is this bridge finished?

Noah: We need to fasten this down. (He points to the bridge deck.)

Douglas: How will the people get up?

Chava: That is a good question.

Cole: You could climb the ropes.

Aaron: But you would FALL OFF!

Noah (returning to his concern about the unstable bridge deck): You need more rope.

Chava: What if you put a rope here? (between the cable and bridge deck)

Sue Fraser

Noah and Gillian helping to build a suspension bridge in the classroom

Building a ramp for the bridge

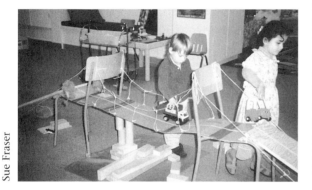

Driving across the bridge

Noah: You need a drill to make a hole.

Aaron (wondering how the cars would get up on to the bridge deck): We need some long blocks.

He ran off to fetch them.

When the children drove a car up the ramp and over the bridge deck, the deck sagged in the middle.

Chava: How can we solve this problem?

The children suggested many ways to anchor the bridge deck. For instance, the children built a tower of blocks up from the floor to provide support underneath the bridge deck. They also tried putting blocks on the cardboard, blocking one end of the bridge deck.

Chava: How will cars drive through?

Chava reminded the children of Noah's earlier suggestion of using more rope. Some children tied ropes from the cables joining the backs of the chairs to the bridge deck.

The idea evolved that this was indeed the Lions Gate Bridge, and the children ran to find lions to decorate the bridge. The discussions about the real Lions Gate Bridge prompted the children to drive many vehicles across their bridge. When the bridge became busy with traffic, Pat asked the children to suggest how to avoid collisions. They discussed traffic lanes and directions, and a teacher helped the children to make arrows and centre lines with tape. Pat reminded the children of the signs used to control traffic on the Lions Gate Bridge. She offered to write a sign for the children to copy. Four children made signs. For some, this was their first attempt at writing words other than their names! The teachers taped their signs to the bridge, and the children made many other signs and taped them to the bridge. (Observations and transcriptions by Pat Breen, Vancouver Child Study Centre, May 19–21, 1998)

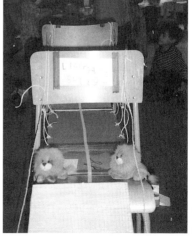

The Lions Gate Bridge

Making traffic signs

Exuberant play followed for many days with the suspension bridge the children had built in the classroom. The children continued to take walks to visit the bridges that cross the stream that flows through the forest surrounding their school. As spring turned into summer, the weather improved, and the teachers set out construction materials in the large sand area in the playground. The teachers helped the children dig a river, which they filled with water. For many days the children spontaneously built bridges, complete with ramps and reinforced pillars, over their river in the sand.

This project was an attempt by the teachers at the Vancouver Child Study Centre to implement a negotiated learning approach to curriculum and to carry out a project that was sustained over a long period of time. The teachers tried to incorporate many of the principles they had learned from the educators in Reggio Emilia. They documented the process and displayed panels of photographs and observation materials throughout the classroom. The children, teachers, parents, and community collaborated in the project. The children worked as a group in constructing the suspension bridge in the classroom. Parents became involved by taking their children to visit bridges and discussing with them how they were built. An expert from the community brought in interesting materials for the children to use in building bridges over the river they had dug in the sand area of the playground. The teachers encouraged the children at all stages to make symbolic representations of their ideas. It was interesting to see how their drawings developed from simple representations of a square arch at the beginning to more complex drawings, showing their understanding of ramps, buttresses, and supports for the bridge deck of central pillars or cables suspended from tall towers at either end of the bridge (documentation phase).

On completion of the bridge-building project, the teachers reviewed the observation data. Chava Rubenson and Pat Breen discussed the project in January 1999 and reached the following conclusions:

Documentation of the bridge project

Deconstruction:

I think we will repeat this project again because it was so successful; however, with more experience [of the Reggio Emilia approach] there are things we would do differently next time. Perhaps holding discussions with smaller groups would ease the facilitation and documentation of the discussion since the larger the group, the harder it is to honour each child's contributions, comments, and queries. It would be easier if we had a homogenous age group, as they do in Reggio Emilia. Many of our children also do not speak English as a first language, and this makes it difficult for them to be part of a long discussion. The above documentation does not capture all of the discussion, nor does it represent the totality of the discussion, as "bridges" was a spontaneous topic of conversation throughout the days and weeks of our investigation. It would be better on selected occasions to videotape or audiotape the discussion to complement the written transcription in an effort to be more accurate. We can see, however, that there were times we missed opportunities to encourage the children to expand or extend their thinking. For instance, on May 19th, when Pat asked Gillian to show us where she would build a bridge. Gillian pointed and said, "Across here." We missed the opportunity to ask her why she chose that spot. The next day, on May 20th, Chava asked, "What do real engineers use to build a bridge?" Aaron answered, "Stone. Only stone is strong enough." Perhaps at this point we should also have asked for other opinions from the children. The reality is you always lose opportunities in an attempt to keep on track when trying to manage 16 or 18 children. One of the difficulties of large group discussions is if you wait too long for an individual child you lose the attention of many of the other children. This reminds us of the need to help children stay focused and get used to discussions. In some instances a teacher may elect to forgo an opportunity to continue discussion with several dominant discussion participants in favour of drawing in a younger or more reluctant contributor, even if this means missing the chance to advance the depth of discussion. We are still learning. The bridge project was undertaken early on in our exploration of the Reggio Emilia approach.

In the Spring of 1999, the teachers thought the children might be interested in building bridges again. However, the children and teachers discovered a mutual interest in mountains, which led to a project exploring avalanches and cable cars, among other things.

CHAPTER 7 Negotiating the Curriculum

THE CIRCUS PROJECT

Let's reexamine the Circus project at Marpole Oakridge Preschool, discussed in Chapters 5 and 6. The germ of the project started when changes to the block corner proved to be a powerful provocation for the children. The platform suggested a stage, and the hoop and ropes above the platform suggested a circus ring or tent. The beam of light from the overhead projector suggested stage lighting and performance. The children added components of their own to the circus structure growing in their imaginations, such as a parking lot, seating for the audience, and a ticket booth. The teachers, entering into "the irony," as Giovanni Piazza calls it, gave the children cheerios and popcorn to "sell" for snack food during the performance. The children created roles for everyone in the group: audience, builders, and performers.

In the following weeks, the children continued to show a very strong interest in the circus, and after a while the teachers wondered where they could take it next. They brought in many books, showed the children a video about a circus, and observed them to see if their play took off in any new directions. The children seemed particularly interested in the circus tent, especially in the strings of lights around the roof.

The teachers went back to the web they had drawn up earlier to help them decide where to take the Circus project next. Documentation of the children's conversations showed that they "liked the balancing, juggling, and doing silly things like clowns do," and they were incorporating clown acts into their own circus performances. Linda and Michelle decided to start by exploring clowns because they could provide a concrete experience by inviting a clown to visit. The teachers and the children began by researching clowns. They discovered that there are different kinds of clowns—sad, funny, white-faced— and they all have different styles and behaviours. Linda showed the children how some clowns move, and they began to practise walking, rolling, and somersaulting like clowns. Michelle invited Peetee, a 75-year-old white-faced clown. Some of the children were frightened of him at first, until he took off one of his white gloves. "He is real!" they shouted. "Of course I am real," said Peetee, and then the children relaxed and began to enjoy his visit, especially when he made each of them a creature out of balloons.

After Peetee's visit, Linda set out a variety of art materials for the children to represent their ideas of clowns. The children drew clown faces and made clown faces from play dough. They then used collage material to create bodies and clothes. A natural lull in the children's explorations followed. The teachers revisited the documentation to see what path they should take next and decided to bring up the tent idea again.

Somewhere along the way, the children talked about needing circus lights when they did their performances. Linda brought in the lights, but the children said they were Christmas lights, not circus lights. Michelle found some little round lights, which the children preferred. They then discussed how they would need a roof to put the lights on, which led to the idea of creating a "circus tent" over the circus area. The teachers asked what the tent roof could be made from. After choosing a big sheet, the children said, "We are going to try and draw what it will look like." They looked through a number of books to find pictures of circus tents, and then Linda took five children into a separate room to design the tent. Working either individually or in pairs, the children drew designs with coloured felt pens for a roof for the circus tent. It was surprising how the children could manipulate the image of the tent in their heads from seeing it laterally to visualizing how it would look from below. This was a more advanced perceptual skill than the teachers had thought four-year-olds were capable of. Two designs for building the circus tent were voted on. Each was placed on a table and the children were asked to go to the table with the design on it that they liked best. Shea's design with the carefully drawn, colourful lines, a point at the peak of the roof, and lights around the edge was chosen. "They chose mine, it's the best," she whispered.

The teachers and children decided to use the second one, Jeffrey's design, for the flag. Shea's design was put on an overhead and projected on to the white sheet hung up on the wall that the children had chosen earlier to use for the tent roof. The children carefully traced the lines projected onto the sheet, transferring the grid in Shea's design on to the sheet. When the children could not reach the top part of the sheet, the teachers built scaffolding out of planks, a saw horse, and the janitor's tall ladder. Instead of painting intersecting lines, the children completed the grid design, square by square. They very carefully copied the same colours Shea had used in her design. The children formed themselves into a line to take turns painting the sheet. Every child took responsibility for completing a section of the design. No one painted out of the lines. The children showed amazing self-control and coordination for four-year-olds. They manipulated their bodies to reach every square outlined on the sheet, sometimes facing forwards and painting backwards. On finishing a section of the design, each child carefully placed a coloured dot in the centre of the square just painted.

When the children had finished painting the sheet, Michelle asked Shea, "Does it look like you thought it would?" She said, "The dots aren't black and it needs loops on the bottom." Shea had observed carefully the children reproducing the elements of her original design and she was aware of the ones they had missed. She put the finishing touches on the tent, making sure that

Allen painting the circus tent

Shea putting the finishing touches on the tent

Rachel and Shea putting the dot in the centre of each square

the colours of the scallops at the bottom matched the ones in her design. Shea showed an amazing ability to observe details, make comparisons, and then fill in the missing pieces accurately.

Now came the job of raising the tent. Linda said, "I had an image how they could put up the tent but I wanted the children to figure it out." Lots of ideas arose as to how to raise it. The children suggested using poles, ropes, or wind to blow up the tent. One child thought Linda could stand underneath the tent and hold the pole, but Linda asked her if she knew how long she would need to stand there. The children then suggested using tape to hold the pole upright. The children soon realized the pole wouldn't work because you couldn't tape it to the floor. Everyone stood around trying to come up with an answer. Kadin, who earlier had spent a lot of time examining the circus books, said that they needed elephants to raise the tent. Finally someone thought of putting a rope through rings fixed to each corner of the sheet and hooks to attach them to the ceiling. In the next few days the children and teachers experimented with ropes and pulleys and eventually figured out how they could use them to raise the tent. Once all four corners were up, the children were surprised that the roof didn't have a point. The sheet hung down in the middle and didn't have a peak like a real circus tent. Vanessa stuck a pole up into the centre of the sheet. "There's the point," she said, but Linda asked again if she knew how long she would have to stand there holding the pole. "We need a string to tie it in the middle and tape it to the floor." She seemed crushed when the point still hung downwards, "It has to go up!" Vanessa said. "We need to tie it to the top," Shea told her. Eventually they solved the problem by attaching a rope to the sheet and tying it to a hook on the ceiling. At last the children had a structure for the lights to be attached to, which is what they had wanted from the beginning of the project. Finally, Jeffrey transferred his design onto fabric for his flag. He had very definite ideas about how and where he wanted it put on the circus roof. It had to be above the roof, but that was another problem they had to solve, as the sheet was already attached at its point to the ceiling.

During group meeting time, the children planned the circus performance. They decided to have five acts: ponies, lions, strongmen, clowns, and tightrope walkers. Vanessa suggested making a poster to advertise the circus, and a top hat for a magician. Later, the children decided that Vanessa, who had made a top hat earlier, should be the ringmaster, and Maddie decided she needed a hat too so she could help. The children worked hard and fast making props for the roles they had chosen. Michelle took pictures of the clown figures the children had made earlier out of collage materials to create a poster to advertise the circus. Vanessa, for the grand finale, pulled a ribbon out of her top hat that grew longer and longer until it circled the whole room.

The teachers were amazed at how different the Circus project turned out to be from the idea they had had for curriculum on their return from Reggio Emilia. At the beginning of the year they had thought the children would be interested in exploring elements such as sound, light, or colour, similar to the investigations Linda and Michelle had seen in Reggio Emilia. The children, however, had led them to develop a much larger project, encompassing construction of a tent, costume-making, a performance including music, dancing, magic, and animal tricks, and posters that involved the whole community.

Educators sometimes wonder if co-constructing curriculum can work with children from different cultural backgrounds who are just learning English. An analysis of the Circus project documentation showed that it can, provided the following factors are present:

- *Teachers hold an image of the child that views the children as competent contributors of ideas to the curriculum.* The teachers observed the children's play and listened closely to their conversation to pick up on their ideas and interests. They believed in the children's ability to construct a circus tent in the classroom. They trusted the children to be responsible and considerate of each other, for instance, when they lined up on their own and later stood beside each other on the scaffolding to paint the design on the sheet.

- *Teachers know that by listening to children they will get ideas and direction in the development of projects.* The teachers thought the children were interested in clowns, but when they really listened, they realized that what the children really wanted to do was build a circus tent and put on a performance.

- *Teachers understand the power of creating an environment to act as a third teacher.* The new arrangement in the block corner acted as a powerful provocation in initiating the children's interest in creating a circus.

- *The group (including the teachers) has had time to form a "circle of we" and develop a strong sense of trust in each other.* The children, especially once the construction of the circus tent began, took responsibility for the project, organizing themselves in taking turns to paint the sheet, deciding on the roles each person would take for the performance, and supporting each other as a group so that it would be a success. For example, one child volunteered to support a rather shy child in the challenging role of ringmaster by offering to be her partner. This demonstrated a level of empathy and awareness above what was previously thought possible in preschool children.

- *A hundred languages are available.* When other means of self-expression are available, proficiency in English becomes less critical. The teachers provided a wide variety of materials. There were also many opportunities for children to use one or more multiple intelligences: linguistic, logical, spatial, kinesthetic, musical, interpersonal, and intrapersonal (Gardner 1983).

- *Teachers encourage the children to make their thinking visible.* Two children drew the tent they wanted to build on the chalkboard, and later others, individually or in pairs, drew designs for the tent roof.

- *Teachers have strategies to enable the group to function effectively.* The teachers designated a comfortable space for the group to meet each day. Children paid attention because they knew they were respected and expected to be participants in a discussion of importance. They learned to respect and listen to different points of view and ideas, knowing they would have an opportunity to be listened to and their contribution to the group would be valued. The teachers fostered collaboration, without which the project would not have succeeded.

- *There is a big idea fuelling the children's passion and interest in the topic.* Carol Anne Wien terms this "the windhorse effect" (see page 42). What engaged the children so profoundly in this topic that they maintained their interest for five months? Was it the fact that they could leave the real world and live in an imaginative world they had created? Was it the fascination of trying out roles of performer and audience? Was it that many of the children in the class came from Asia, where acrobatics and magic are popular entertainments? In revisiting the documentation, the teachers realized that the children were most interested in the magic and acrobatic aspects of the performance.

- *Teachers know how to sustain and develop the topic by asking questions such as, How? With what? What could we use?* When Linda said, "I can't stay here and hold this pole, so what are we going to do about it?" the question led the children to problem-solve. They began an investigation of how to use ropes and pulleys to raise the circus tent and then how to make the tent have a peak in the middle.

- *Teachers value aesthetics.* In this case the teachers valued and promoted the dramatic aspects of the project; for instance, they heightened the children's awareness of performance and what it entailed. They made posters and costumes for the performance. They also encouraged the children to think carefully about a design for the tent roof and then provided the materials for the children first to draw a design and then to build the tent.

- *The project is documented, and the documentation used for reflection.* The documentation informed the children and parents about the project. Revisiting the documentation enabled the teachers to see that if they were truly going to follow the interests of the children, they needed to change the direction of the project. Therefore, they changed their direction from learning about "clowns" to following the children's idea of building a "circus tent."

- *Documentation is used as research.* The documentation showed that children felt safe in the classroom because the teachers had built a secure environment and a "community of we." It highlighted how the children showed empathy for each other and observed the teachers demonstrating they were learners too. These children were confident and competent enough to scaffold the teachers and try to let the teachers allow them to produce their own cultural version of a circus, one that probably came from their own heritage.

CHALLENGES IN NEGOTIATING THE CURRICULUM

There are many challenges in moving to a negotiated learning approach in all early childhood education programs. One of the most important factors is the image of the child held by the teachers. If teachers see children as competent, inventive, and full of ideas, then it follows that they will value the children's ideas, see the importance of listening to children, and provide them with the opportunities and materials they need to represent their ideas. Another crucial factor is the establishment of trusting relationships among teachers, children, and their families. Good relationships are essential in a curriculum that is co-constructed; as the outcome of a project is unknown initially, it will become apparent only through negotiation between children and teachers along the way. The third important factor is communication. For negotiation to be successful, children and teachers need to be able to carry on discussions and to understand the importance of listening to one another. They need to know how to sustain conversation through turn taking and asking and answering questions that enable them to probe deeper into a topic. A negotiated curriculum depends on "offering contexts that facilitate learning, creating enriching situations and helping the children to be the direct agents and constructors of their own learning processes" (Spaggiari 1997, 10). Finally, by engaging in the process of deconstructive analysis, teachers view the curriculum they offer children through multiple lenses. This collaborative process helps the group become aware of biases and preconceived notions that might affect the final outcome of the negotiation.

Chapter 8

Blue Bird

Questions to Consider:

- What are the underlying values in an art program based on Reggio Emilia principles?

- How does consideration of aesthetics influence the presentation of art materials in the classroom?

- How does the principle of relationship affect the art program?

- How important is technique in the creation of art?

- What are the inherent qualities of each material?

- What is meant by "intelligent" materials?

- What is the role of the teacher in the art program?

- How can the community be effectively involved in a preschool art program?

- What is needed to incorporate an atelier and atelierista into a preschool or child care?

Aesthetics in the
Program

There are many remarkable things about the municipal preschools of Reggio Emilia, Italy. What seems most remarkable to me, however, is the educators' deep understanding of the power of materials and of words to shape experience. Alongside this is a respect for the complexity and beauty of the natural world, and for the intelligence and creativity of young children and the adults who work with them.

—Louise Cadwell

A WALK THROUGH THE CLASSROOM

Walking through any preschool classroom, the visitor can see from the art displayed on the walls the kinds of experiences that are provided for children in that environment. The children's artwork indicates whose head and hands have been busy in the room. If there are a dozen or so identical pictures on the wall, the visitor knows immediately that the teacher's or parent helpers' hands have probably cut out the shapes and they have told the children how to use the cut-outs. When this kind of structured art is on display, there is no indication that the "intelligence and creativity" that Louise Cadwell refers to above is valued or encouraged in the classroom.

On the other hand, there may be on display drawings and paintings that show the developmental stages children pass through in art. In this case a visitor may note that the teacher is viewing children's art through a developmental lens. These pictures will perhaps be scribbles with random marks zigzagging or circling on the page, illustrating children's work at the earliest stage of development. There may be on display examples of children's drawings at a later stage of development, with well-formed ovals, circles, and lines that become suns and people, the typical shapes found in the drawings of three- and four-year-old children. Some of the children will have probably begun to use symbols to represent objects that the visitor can recognize. Art that shows samples of children's work at different stages of development indicates that the teachers believe in providing children with an unstructured, developmentally appropriate art program, one that allows the children's art development to unfold naturally. A visitor to this classroom will probably see from the art displayed that the children also have had many opportunities to finger paint, manipulate play dough and clay, and use paper, paste, and a wide assortment of collage materials. Children in a classroom with teachers who believe in fostering development will have spent much of their time using their senses to explore and learning about colours, shapes, and textures of materials. They will not be expected to create representational art until they are about five or six years old.

The art on display in the classrooms in the municipal preschools in Reggio Emilia is very different from that in either structured or nonstructured art programs in traditional preschools in other parts of the world. Visitors to Reggio Emilia are amazed at the overwhelming beauty of the work the children have created and also perplexed at the complexity and high level of maturity apparent in their art. Children in Reggio Emilia, for instance, produce very detailed representational work, as in the mural the children painted on large sheets of clear plastic of the poppies and insects they had seen in a field on a visit to the country. Visitors are also amazed at the level of skill needed to create much of the art, such as the large clay pieces of the fountains that the children in La Villetta school made for their Amusement Park for Birds. They learn, however, that children are introduced to materials like paint and clay at a very young age in the infant–toddler centres.

The skill and complexity of work such as documented in the Amusement Park for Birds led educators from other parts of the world to think about the artwork children produce in their own schools and, perhaps, to question whether preschool children should be allowed to be entirely free and creative in their art. Teachers wonder whether they are doing the right thing by standing back and letting the children's art development unfold without adult interference, or whether they should expect children to use skills and art techniques at such a young age.

Those of us who are inspired by the Reggio Emilia approach become aware of some fundamental differences in the approach to the role of art between traditional and Reggio Emilia programs. In Reggio Emilia, for instance, art is more than just a curriculum subject—it is one of the essential tools, one of the hundred languages, that children use to affect their learning. In the preschool years children are continually learning to use language to make sense of the world. Children, when encouraged to use art as a tool for communication, become much more practised in using it as a means of communication, in much the same way as children become increasingly expert in using language during the preschool years.

George Forman makes an important distinction when he notes that the children in Reggio Emilia "draw to learn as opposed to learn to draw" (Edwards, Gandini, and Forman 1998, 1–7). In his description of "the intelligence of a puddle," he explains how the children in Diana School put their skills in drawing representational figures to work to learn about the difference between shadows and reflections. The teachers noted that one day after a rainstorm, the children observed that only the upper torso of their bodies was reflected in the water as they approached a puddle in the playground. When children in the preschools in Reggio Emilia notice something that puzzles them, the teachers encourage them to draw their theories about it. In this case, a teacher placed a mirror on the ground and encouraged the children to experiment with their reflections in the mirror. The children began to compare the reflections they had seen earlier in the puddle of water and the images they saw of themselves in the mirror on the ground. The teacher then encouraged the children to draw and cut out figures to place on and around the mirror. The children noted what happened to the image in the mirror when they placed the cut-out figures in different positions and viewed them from different angles. The investigation was carried further by giving the children a flashlight so they could discover the difference between the reflection and the shadow of an object. This project reveals that the educators in Reggio Emilia take a different perspective of the role of art in the program. In Reggio Emilia art has a broader purpose that goes beyond sensory exploration and self-expression and becomes a tool for learning, a means of communicating ideas, and one of the hundred languages children use in representing their ideas.

Early exposure to art media also enables children to create the high-quality art seen in the preschools in Reggio Emilia. Children, for instance, who have attended the infant–toddler centres will have been given paint, clay, and other art materials to explore before entering preschool. They will have learned a great deal about the possibilities inherent in the many art materials available for use even before they are three years old. Many children will, therefore, have passed through the stage of needing to explore the materials in a sensory manner and be ready by the time they enter preschool to learn the skills and techniques for producing more elaborate artwork.

The high value placed on aesthetic awareness in the preschools in Reggio Emilia also fosters children's artistic abilities. This emphasis reflects the value placed on aesthetics in the Italian culture as a whole. Italian children, for instance, absorb the beauty of the culture around them when they are out in the community, whether they are walking with their families and looking at the goods so beautifully displayed in the shop windows or experiencing the stone carvings in the streets and piazzas. In the Reggio Emilia preschools, beautiful objects, potted plants, and bowls of flowers are displayed on shelves and tables, and light is everywhere, shining through coloured strips of plastic or reflected in the many mirrors in the room. The beauty so apparent in the classrooms is designed to inspire children to become more visually aware and to motivate them to create beautiful artwork themselves. In turn, the teachers show their appreciation for the quality of the children's work by mounting and displaying their art on the documentation panels on the walls of the classrooms and entrance halls. The children and the parents can see that children's art is valued and respected. All this makes a strong statement about the value of aesthetics in the preschools in Reggio Emilia.

Lella Gandini in an interview with Tiziana Filipinni describes an exchange Tiziana had with the children in the Diana School in Reggio Emilia, which, I believe, captures the essence of fostering aesthetic awareness in young children. Tiziana notes that "[m]ore or less everyone explores leaves in autumn. Pedagogy suggests working with the children on how to represent the leaf and on the leaf's relationship with the tree through observing the leaf in the natural world. In fact, pedagogy suggests working with the children on how to represent the leaf and on the leaf's relationship in the natural world. In fact, pedagogy supports an idea of knowledge as a reproduction of an event or object." In the atelier in the Diana School, however, as the children explore leaves in the fall, they encourage the children to form a relationship with the leaf, to play with ideas about the leaf by transforming it into the shape of a tree or a leaping figure, to create a design inspired by the shape of the leaf. She writes that by activating processes of "reelaboration and reinvention, metaphoric expression, using analogies and poetic languages" children come to know the leaf at a deep emotional level and engage in an "...expressive experience that is not separate from the cognitive one." Gandini goes on to note that the above process is the same one individuals use in the construction of knowledge and understanding" (Gandini 2005, 69). As Mara Krechevsky said, "Beauty and pleasure are strongly integrated into the knowledge building processes" (2001, 51).

The educators of Reggio Emilia have made it a priority, as well, to provide the space and resources necessary for children to engage in a wide variety of aesthetic experiences. In each school an area is set aside as an atelier, which is filled with art materials and equipment. There are cupboards, ample storage space, and shelves on which materials are attractively displayed and accessible to the children. Large surfaces on tables and easels provide sufficient space for children to work comfortably. Sinks are located nearby for easy cleanup. Children are given many different tools to use in creating their artwork, such as high-quality paintbrushes of various widths, lead and coloured pencils, felt-tipped pens, chalk, pastels, charcoal pencils, and tools for modelling clay. Many different coloured paints are mixed in glass jars, which are set out on trays or trolleys beside the easels. Paper is available, including transparent papers to use on the light tables, coloured tissue, and cellophane paper. The children are also provided with many less common materials, such as wire, plaster of Paris, and recycled materials. Clay is provided in abundance, and children work with it using a variety of techniques.

All of these materials are available in the atelier, which Loris Malaguzzi described as a "place where children's different languages could be explored by them and studied by us in a favorable and peaceful atmosphere. We and they could experiment with alternative modalities, techniques, instruments, and materials; explore themes chosen by children or suggested by us; perhaps work on a large fresco in a group; perhaps prepare a poster where one makes a concise statement through words or illustrations.... What was important was to help children find their own styles of exchanging with friends both their talents and their discoveries" (1993, 68–69). The success of the atelier encouraged the educators in Reggio Emilia to provide mini-ateliers adjacent to each classroom. The mini-atelier provides a space where a smaller group of children can work with a wide assortment of art materials on projects that are less complex than those carried out in the main atelier. Some of the schools also have an outdoor atelier, which is used in good weather. In the Reggio Emilia preschools, therefore, children are given the time and space that allow for careful, uninterrupted work and the support of an atelierista, who has specific training and can help the children interpret their ideas in a variety of art media.

Selecting Materials for Children to Use

Teachers embracing the Reggio Emilia approach select what the educators of Reggio Emilia call "intelligent materials": those "that invite questions, curiosity, and experimentation" (Krechevsky 2001, 252). Materials should offer lots of possibilities; children should be challenged to use materials in a way that respects the *affordances* inherent in the materials themselves: that is, the materials' intrinsic qualities and expressive potential. For instance, when children wanted to create windows in the Windows and Landscape project (discussed in Chapter 1), Giovanni Piazza explained that he selected clay because of its three-dimensional quality. The different properties inherent in a material can be thought of as a vocabulary. What, for instance, is the vocabulary for paper compared to wire? Both can be used for making two-dimensional representations, but paper has different qualities than wire. Children can fold and tear paper but they have to bend and snip wire. Before choosing the material for a project, it is helpful to identify its vocabulary.

Adding a tool like an overhead projector gives children a different perspective, and they begin to use materials in surprising ways. The children at Marpole Oakridge Preschool, for instance, found that they could use cellophane paper on the overhead projector to throw coloured shapes on the wall. Then they discovered that the cellophane paper could also be made to stick to the wall because of its static electricity.

AN APPROACH TO ART INSPIRED BY REGGIO EMILIA

Principles fundamental to the Reggio Emilia approach, such as respect, relationship, collaboration, transparency, reciprocity, and documentation, are also apparent in a Reggio Emilia inspired ECE program.

Respect

The respect that the Reggio Emilia educators show for children and the image that they hold of the child as rich, strong, and powerful seem to encourage the children to create art beyond what we had in the past believed them capable of. Educators also show respect for children's abilities by giving them authentic materials of the same quality as those an artist would use and by presenting them in a way that makes them appealing and accessible. Teachers in talking to children about their art and the appropriate use of the art materials encourage children to learn to respect the materials and their inherent qualities. The children's artwork is richly documented in panels that describe in great detail the process the children followed.

Laurie Kocher, in a discussion with the students at Douglas College about the use of intelligent materials in early childhood settings, stated:

> A sensory approach would list the physical attributes that the child experiences as wet, cold, etc. The constructivist approach would look at what the child understands, what is the child's theory of how the materials behave and work, how do the actions that the child makes with the materials behave? The child is always thinking about what might happen, what happened that I did not expect, what causes this to happen? We must think in terms of what problem or question might the child be working through. When we begin to approach the child's work in this way, it shifts our mindset into thinking about how the child constructs their knowledge and how or what theories they hold and are working through, as teachers we then shift into that deeper level in our work in formulating the 'what next.'
>
> [Kocher, written communication, 16th Jan, 2010].

Relationship

Teachers inspired by Reggio Emilia have made relationship a basic principle in their approach to art. Art, for instance, is not considered in isolation but is integrated into the program as one of the hundred languages children use to investigate and represent their world. In many preschool programs, collage materials, play dough, and sometimes clay are available for the children to use each day, but teachers seldom encourage the children to use the materials other than for sensory exploration and self-expression. In the preschools in Reggio Emilia, however, the children use the materials, often in collaboration with other children and teachers, to achieve a purpose. In the project of the Amusement Park for Birds, for example, the children and the atelierista, Giovanni Piazza, worked together with clay to create the prototypes for building a waterwheel and fountains for the birds. Teachers also provide support, or scaffolding, for children in helping them explore in greater detail the objects they are representing. In the above project, the teachers projected a slide of the angel fountain onto a light panel to enable two children working together to trace the outline of the fountain and then make a schematic drawing of the fountain's inner workings.

The principle of relationship is also evident in the way art materials are presented in the classroom. For instance, teachers set out clay on a table on which they have attractively arranged other natural materials, such as wood, rocks, shells, and dried grass. The unexpected arrangement of different materials captures the children's interest and focuses their attention on the aesthetic qualities of texture, form, and colour inherent in the objects themselves. When the Canadian delegation visited Diana School, they saw the children working with clay on a table on which feathers and a bird's nest with a tiny toy bird peeking out of the nest were displayed. The teachers placed these materials together perhaps to provoke the children to think about how birds use mud in building their nests and also to suggest how the children could use the clay themselves.

Collaboration

Collaboration, which is essential in Reggio inspired programs, is also evident in their approach to art. Teachers and children collaborate in developing many of the projects. The teachers discuss ideas for the projects and decide which art media will be appropriate for representing their ideas. Children often work in a group on an art project, as they did in creating the large murals of the poppy field mentioned earlier. The space in the classrooms is designed to encourage small groups of children to work together. Easels are wide enough, for instance, to allow three or four children to paint at the same time on one large sheet of paper.

Transparency

The use of light as an art medium is an example of the principle of transparency that is woven into many aspects of the program. Overhead projectors, light tables, and mirrors allow children to experiment with light, shadow, and reflection. The children often use cellophane and tissue paper in their artwork. The Canadian delegation observed the children in Diana School pressing bunches of different coloured tissue paper into wire mesh that had been shaped into balls, which were later hung from the ceiling to make a display of the planets and the sun. In La Villetta school, the children arranged objects on an overhead projector within a checkered pattern they had previously drawn on a sheet of acetate. The children experimented with various sizes of objects by placing them on the grid and then observing the pattern they projected onto the wall. One child placed a fern on the grid and then arranged the objects around the fern so that it looked like a Christmas tree when projected. Louise Cadwell relates how Vea Vecchi, the atelierista at Diana School, projected pieces of blue acetate onto the walls to simulate the sky and then made a cloud which the children "blew out of the window" (1997, 28). In the video *The Creative Spirit*, a slide projected onto the classroom wall shows the children dancing in the brilliant red poppies photographed during their visit to the poppy field.

Reciprocity

The relationship that develops between the children and teachers during the three years the children remain with the same teachers in the preschools in Reggio Emilia also helps children create art of such high quality. The trust and respect that develop from this long-term relationship enable the children and teachers to learn from one another and to share their ideas and skills as they collaborate in creating artwork.

Documentation

The documentation of the process the children follow in doing their artwork enables teachers, children, and visitors to see each step in the development. The teachers and children can revisit each stage of the experience and think about what equipment, materials, and skills they needed to express their ideas, what they could do differently next time, and what they learned from the experience. This process enables the children and teachers to refine their skills and techniques and to gradually build expertise in creating art.

PUTTING THE PRINCIPLES OF AESTHETICS INTO PRACTICE

The teachers in the child care and preschool on Quadra Island and in the Vancouver Child Study Centre were inspired, each in their own way, to implement the principles they learned from the educators in Reggio Emilia in their approach to art. Each program adapted the principles in a unique way and focused on different aspects of art. Although the teachers felt satisfied that they had made some progress in implementing the principles, the teachers in all three programs realized that they still had much to learn before being able to provide children with a program that would foster the high standard of artwork seen in the preschools in Reggio Emilia.

Building a Puppet Theatre

Early in the fall, the teachers in the Quadra Island Children's Centre focused on the principle of collaboration. They collaborated not only within the children's centre, but also with a local artist. The teachers were interested in exploring ways in which an artist could share her skills and scaffold the children's art experiences, and they hoped that this experience would make up in a small way for the lack of an atelierista in their program. They invited Lesley

Learning how to make papier-mâché at Quadra Island Children's Centre

Mathews, a local artist who they knew was comfortable working with children, to the centre. She had volunteered a few years before, when her own children were enrolled in the child care. Lesley was enthusiastic about sharing her skills with the children and agreed to come once a week to participate as she had before.

On her first visit Lesley brought along a collection of papier-mâché figures and masks she had made. Displayed in the entrance hall at that time was the documentation of a visit the children had made to the Campbell River Museum to see the work of First Nations artists. Lesley also knew that many of the children would have visited the museum on Quadra Island to see the ceremonial regalia, especially the famous transformational masks, made by artists of the Kwakiutl nation who live on the island. She thought, therefore, that the children might be interested in making masks themselves. Lesley met the children at group time and, as a provocation, passed around some masks she had made for the children to try on. After the children examined the masks, she explained how she had made them out of papier-mâché. The children were interested in the masks, but from the teachers' observations it became apparent that they were more interested in how the masks had been made out of papier-mâché than in the masks themselves. The teachers noted that many of the children connected the papier-mâché with piñatas, and, of course, piñatas with parties and candy. "Expect the unexpected," Loris Malaguzzi said, so Lesley and the teachers decided to change their plan of making masks and instead make a piñata out of papier-mâché with the children. In this way the children became familiar with the medium and learned techniques, such as how to cut the paper into thin strips, what consistency to make the glue so it could be applied smoothly, how to dip the paper into saucers of glue to get the right amount, and how to press the glued paper strips down firmly and smooth them out on the form for the piñata, made from a blown-up balloon.

On a later visit Lesley, the teachers, and the children discussed what else they could make out of papier-mâché. The children suggested making puppets and a puppet theatre. The teachers brought out paper and pencils, and the children began to draw their ideas on a large sheet of paper. It was interesting to note how they used the rounded form that they had experienced in making the piñata as the base of their design for the puppet's head. Children are indeed amazingly competent, as the educators in Reggio Emilia have shown us.

Once the children had made representational drawings of how they wanted their puppets to turn out, they began to work on making a structure on which to build the puppet's head. Lesley, the teachers, and the children discussed how they might make a shape on which to build the rounded heads the children had drawn in their sketches. As the heads

The forms for the puppet heads

needed to be smaller than the piñata they had made earlier, they decided to use a tightly rolled ball of newspaper as a base. They crumpled up half a page of newspaper into a tight ball, twisted the free end to fit into a toilet paper roll, and then kept it in place with masking tape. Not all the children used this method to make puppet heads; one child made a snake puppet by using

Children's drawings of their ideas for making puppets

a long, tightly rolled sheet of newspaper as a base for the papier-mâché. The children were then able to apply their skill in using papier-mâché, which they had learned in making the piñata. They layered the strips of paper over the base and shaped it to create the features of the puppet they had designed earlier. Then they placed the puppet heads upright in cottage cheese cartons to dry. The cartons also held the puppets upright so the children could paint them

Sue Fraser

Designing the puppet theatre

later and add hair, fur, and even, in one case, an elephant's trunk.

In the meantime, Lesley began to work with a small group of children who were interested in designing and building the puppet theatre. Together, they discussed what they needed to construct it and decided on the dimensions, and Lesley drew a pattern based on their ideas on a piece of paper. She then helped the children follow the pattern in marking the correct measurements on large sheets of Styrofoam.

She used a sharp knife to cut out three rectangles, one with an arch on one of the long sides of the rectangle. She also cut out a half circle from one of the Styrofoam sheets for the front apron of the puppet theatre. This piece also served as a base for the three upright walls of the theatre. She cut out a large, square window below the semicircle on the piece of Styrofoam that was to be the front wall. Then the children, again with Lesley's help, began to assemble the structure, using duct tape to join the upright walls to the base. They discovered that the two side walls were a bit wobbly, so they decided to place paper towel rolls between the cir-

Sue Fraser

Building the puppet theatre

cular apron and walls at an angle to brace the structure. When the construction of the puppet theatre was complete, the children worked with Lesley to cover the Styrofoam sheets with papier-mâché. The children carefully placed strips of newspaper in the bowls of glue and then spread them flat on the boards.

Eventually, when the whole structure was covered and the papier-mâché was dry, the children began to paint the puppet theatre. They had a long discussion about how they would paint the walls and decided to use blue, yellow, pink, and green paint. The children painted a large pink crown covered with jewel-like dots in the arch above the window. They covered a section of one wall in a pattern of horizontal pink and yellow stripes that looked like a ladder going up one side of the building. The predominant features were a large star outlined in pink with a solid

Sue Fraser

Plastering the walls

The finished puppet theatre

blue circle in the centre and a bright yellow sun that Lesley painted on the wall opposite the star the children had made. The children then surrounded her sun with dots similar to those on the crown above the window. When the children had finished painting the puppet theatre, the bright colours and folk art images resembled paintings on circus structures. It was amazing how the children had spontaneously created images and chosen colours that matched a style of decoration traditionally used for entertainment.

The puppet theatre was placed on a table, and a curtain was draped across the front to hide the legs. The collaboration with a local artist, which lasted many months—from October to March—had created a beautiful piece of equipment that they and future generations of children attending the child care would use for many years. At the end of the project, the teachers reviewed the photographs that they had taken to document the project and felt satisfied that they had successfully implemented at least two of the principles learned from Reggio Emilia. First, they collaborated successfully with an artist in the community who understood how to support children in making art without taking over too much of the control herself. Lesley demonstrated many of the qualities of an atelierista in Reggio Emilia, knowing intuitively when to follow the children's lead and when to take the lead herself. She was particularly skilled in listening to children and then helping them figure out how to carry out their ideas successfully. She was able to share her skills without imposing expectations on the children that were too high. Second, she and the children had created a beautiful object that demonstrated the value of aesthetic experiences in the education of young children.

Weaving Experiences

Baerbel Jaeckel, the teacher at Quadra Island Preschool, began to implement Reggio Emilia principles in her approach to art almost immediately after school started in the fall. Early in September, the children became interested in the spider webs that are seen everywhere in autumn. Baerbel wondered if the children would make a connection between spider webs and weaving looms. She hoped that encouraging the children to become aware of this connection would help her to introduce the principle of relationship into her approach to art.

The children drew their theories of how spiders spin their webs on large sheets of paper. Many of them had drawn circular shapes with criss-crossing lines, but when they examined the web closely they were interested in how the spider uses two branches as a frame to attach the silk thread, first making a *y* and then weaving strands of silk in a spiral to form a web. Baerbel discussed with the children how they could build a loom in a window in the classroom, like the spider, by using two branches and strings between them. The children helped her lay out the string on the floor, making about 30 loops measuring about 1.5 metres in length. She then cut the string at either end and helped the children tie the strands to the branch they had hung from the top of the window frame.

Constructing the loom at Quadra Island Preschool

Sue Fraser

They then tied the ends to the second branch, which hung just above the ledge at the bottom of the window. Once they had made the loom, the children worked singly or in small groups to weave strands of different coloured wool back and forth between the strings of the loom. Baerbel or one of the parents who regularly assists in the preschool would often sit with the children as they worked on the loom, giving them help if necessary. The loom stayed in the window throughout the time the children were in preschool, and by the time school ended in June the children had woven about 25 cm of cloth on the loom.

In reviewing the project, Baerbel felt that although she still had more to learn, she had been successful in implementing some of the Reggio Emilia principles in the art program. She had tried introducing the principle of relationship in presenting the art materials, such as in the way she helped children make connections between the spider's web and a loom for weaving. She had encouraged a great deal of collaboration between children and adults in many of the art projects they had done throughout the year. She ensured that there were opportunities for discussion between her, the parents, and the children and that the adults

Tying the string on the branches

provided support if the children needed help in mastering a skill, such as learning how to weave. Overall, Baerbel's greatest strength was her skill in making aesthetics a strong value in all aspects of the art program: in the arrangement of the room, in the presentation of materials, and in the beautiful artwork that the children created.

The following interview with a parent of a child enrolled in the Quadra Island Preschool, which I conducted in August 1998, reveals how parents perceive the benefits of the Reggio Emilia approach to art*.

Emma weaving

Susan Fraser: Baerbel, as you know, has been trying to implement the principles learned from Reggio Emilia in her approach to art in the preschool. Tell me your impressions of the art your child has done this year.

Joanna Annett: After I had seen the slides [of the artwork created by the children in Reggio Emilia] I thought that the work that the children do in Reggio Emilia is unbelievable, but later I appreciated it as I saw it played out in what the group of children did as they painted together. I did notice the children getting really inspired and proud of their group work. There was a feeling of belonging and cohesiveness that grew during the year. I

*Reproduced courtesy of Joanna Annett

The weaving near completion

thought the children did some interesting things, some beautiful things really, like the artwork they did using the eye droppers on tissue paper and on the fabric [to make the dragon skin for the Chinese New Year]. I think Baerbel was really skilled at finding simple activities with aesthetically beautiful results. Now I notice my child is very free in her art. She does wildly different things—perhaps it is just her—she doesn't place limitations on herself. This week on her own she went out and picked grass ... then she made loops with the grass and turned one loop into a sun, but it looked more like a ghost than a sun. She then painted over it all to make a beautiful textured painting she herself was proud of. She seems very comfortable about what she does. Sometimes she is pleased with the product, but other times she puts it aside and moves on and tries something else. It doesn't seem to frustrate her like my other child, who gets frustrated because she tries to make a product and the end product doesn't please her.

I thought the group dynamics in the preschool moved slowly at the beginning of the year because Baerbel waited for all the children in the group to be drawn in before moving on. Later in the year she allowed children who wanted to go off and do something different to do it. This worked better once she had gotten to know the children and could prepare materials that met their individual interests.

Painting Lupines

The teachers and children at the Vancouver Child Study Centre carried out many projects that were inspired by the Reggio Emilia approach to art. One project in particular, the lupine painting, was clearly inspired by a video the teachers had seen, *The Creative Spirit* (1992), which showed the children's paintings in Reggio Emilia of poppies. In early summer, on one of the field trips to find out more about bridges, the teachers and children discovered fields of lupines growing wild in the grass on the way to the park. The children were thrilled by the lupines, squealing with delight as they danced in the grass, losing one another in the brilliant mass of purple and mauve flowers. The teachers took photographs of the children holding hands and running through the field of lupines. Bridges were forgotten as the children hid and chased each other in the lupines, some of which were taller than the children's heads. They decided to collect a few bunches of flowers to bring back with them to school. The next day Pat and Chava, the teachers, mixed paint

A child paints his impression of lupines at the Vancouver Child Study Centre.

Sue Fraser

in shades of purple. They poured the paint into glass jars and placed them next to a jar of green paint on a tray on the table so that children could see the different shades of colour, from deep purple to pale mauve, available for them to use. They also placed the photographs of the field trip and a large bowl of lupines on the table to trigger the children's memory of their experience in the park. All through the afternoon a steady stream of children came to paint at the table. All of them produced paintings of the lupines with tall green stems that filled the page and small purple and mauve oval shapes running down each stem. They frequently stopped to examine the photographs and look at the lupines in the jar. The children seemed totally absorbed in their painting and said very little. The experience seemed to reach to the roots of aesthetic awareness in the children, helping them to bring their keen sense of colour, shape, and texture to the surface as they expressed symbolically their delight in the lupines.

The Ecology of a Kindergarten Curriculum

Katherine McLean, the kindergarten teacher at Edgehill Elementary School in Powell River, B.C., became interested in the Reggio Emilia approach after seeing the video, *The Creative Spirit* (1992) on PBS in the early nineties. Today she is the kindergarten teacher in a classroom that reflects the aesthetics and the respect for children and their environment that is so evident in the municipal preschools in Reggio Emilia. I visited Katherine's kindergarten classroom in the early spring and the following account explains her philosophy of teaching and goes on to describe how beautiful her classroom environment is*.

> **Katherine:** Every summer I find myself thinking about what kind of lived curriculum my students will bring with them in the fall. It is this authentic curriculum that I am interested in understanding and becoming familiar with in the classroom. I wonder how my special interests in the environment, in developing the aesthetics of the classroom, and in seeing the world through an artist's eyes will compliment or create tension with the children's learning and understandings. How will we co-share our space and learning together? What will it look like? What will be important? What will we explore together?

*Reproduced courtesy of Katherine McLean

What tensions will be apparent in our learning? What projects will they want to develop? What will their passions be? What transformations will take place? What learning path will we follow? What will the process look like? What learning will emerge from our collective presence?

The unfolding of curriculum in a classroom is like the "budding of a plant." Its structure is dynamic and organic. It is ever-changing; waxing and waning in the seasons. Sometimes the plant dies immaturely; sometimes it lives a long fruitful life. Sometimes it emerges in its own seedpod the next spring—in spite of all odds, bursting through the early spring snow. Metaphorically, this is the ecology of the lived curriculum in the classroom. This is how I have come to understand curriculum and how I work with it in my classroom.

What is my authentic curriculum? What do I bring to the classroom learning space? Knowing what a teacher brings is as important as understanding the children's authentic curriculum. Perhaps this is the missing piece for many teachers? "Know oneself," Emerson stated. In sharing essential aspects of myself with my students I am establishing who I am. I am creating space for establishing honest and truthful relationships with the children.

I begin by sharing what is important to me. I value how nature can shape our learning together. Every year I walk with my children at least one afternoon a week through the forest that surrounds the school. The environment becomes a third teacher. Every year more natural materials enter my classroom space. All plastic containers have been replaced with wicker baskets. Natural materials such as pine cones, stones, branches, sea shells, different kinds of leaves, wasp nests, bird nests, and driftwood replace man-made plastics, commercial toys and posters, and anything metal. Most of these materials live in transparent large glass jars. Everything is visible to the eye. I value the honesty of the materials, their simplicity, their beauty and their integrity. I like to keep open spaces where the eye can pause and rest. There is space on the shelves for student projects and their displays. I value their work. I want to create an atmosphere that is aesthetically pleasing and calming. I want the children to see I value these qualities.

Art is a child's first literacy. I value this way of being in the world. Children have taught me to look at art as a way of understanding, of being and of seeing. As a learner, as a teacher, and as an artist, I see representational art is not as important, as learning how a child experiences a tree using colour and line, and clay, branches and wool. They seem to create a "language" using these materials to explore the trees very essence. They create their own 'grammar." If I can co-exist with the children in this learning space, I believe I can begin to understand this grammar; these languages of children and with this understanding begin to navigate the more formal traditional ministry guidelines and curriculum.

This is what I like to call the actual "lived curriculum" in the classroom. It is a marriage of the authentic curriculum the children bring and the actual living curriculum that emerges in the classroom, as all co-players inhabit the space.

On a visit to Katherine's classroom I was greeted in the passage outside her classroom by a flutter of butterflies the children have made from twigs, seeds, and rose petals that are displayed on a bulletin board outside her classroom door. Inside, the room is filled with many more wonderful examples of children using their imaginations to make beautiful things with natural materials. These have been gathered from her own garden and from the beaches and forest surrounding the school. The natural materials including some recycled materials are also replenished by the children and their families, so everyone is involved in the creative process. This collection of materials is displayed attractively on tables and shelves around the classroom ready for the children to use in creating beautiful works of art. On one shelf there is a little grove of trees the children had made from twigs and shimmering strips of materials. Katherine told me the children have expanded this display by using branches, poppy heads and lichen, moss and wool to make a magic forest of trees in the classroom. There was a flock of birds made from rose hips, fir cones, and feathers on a branch against one wall.

On another wall was a collection of faces made from the oval shape of dried rubber plant leaves decorated with dried flowers, chrysanthemum petals, and seeds. One whole panel was covered with strips of fabric the children had decorated with dye from flowers and leaves pounded into the fabric to make interesting patterns. The children discovered that they could make an exact image of the veins and shape of a nasturtium leaf by pounding it with their rock crushers onto the fabric. My favourite panel was covered in fairies the children had created from twigs and leaves dressed with petals and seeds.

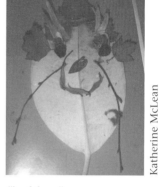

"Leaf faces"

There were many examples of early literacy displayed on the walls; for instance, one child had written a story and drawn a diagram of how to make a trap for a bear who had been sighted on the playground. Katherine explains how the children develop early literacy by using the materials to explore colour, texture, size, shape, pattern, sequencing, classification and to learn about numbers and the alphabet. The children have created from their own environment the letters of the alphabet and the numbers out of twigs, leaves,

Fairy

seeds, and petals. A circle of bright red arbutus berries was a clever way to write a circle for the letter "d." They are literally using nature in learning to read and write. These numbers and letters the children have made themselves out of natural materials are displayed on the walls of their classroom, replacing in a much more aesthetically pleasing way the commercial alphabet and number charts seen in most elementary schools.

Katherine McLean

Numbers

The children in Katherine's classroom are creating their own learning tools from their own environment. They are being producers and not consumers of the culture, which is exactly what Loris Malaguzzi said children should be. In the process they are learning to think about nature in a respectful way, to love and appreciate it. As they investigate and examine the beautiful materials in the classroom and think about what to use to represent their ideas, they are learning to look closely, to pay attention to details, to discover patterns and textures, to think about possibilities, to make transformations: all essential to the creative process. In the process they are developing their aesthetic sense because for these children as mentioned earlier, "beauty and pleasure are strongly integrated in the knowledge-building processes" (Krechevsky 2001, 51). What a joy it is to walk into Katherine's classroom. It is so full of the unexpected, so different from most classrooms because it reflects Katherine's belief that "If art is a child's first literacy, then nature is their classroom."

THE ROLE OF MATERIALS IN THE CLASSROOM

The classrooms in Reggio Emilia are filled with a wide variety of materials that children use to explore and represent their ideas. The development of the recycling centre, REMIDA, offers the children and teachers opportunities to work with many different and unexpected materials. Teachers visit REMIDA regularly, sometimes taking the children with them, to collect materials. Cathy Weisman Topal and Lella Gandini in their book *Beautiful Stuff* (1999) outline a process of introducing children to recycled materials.

First they suggest giving children a small bag to take home to collect recycled materials. Included is a letter to parents with a list of suggested materials. The bag is small to limit the size and quantity of items sent back to school. When all the bags have been returned, the items the children have collected are emptied out on the floor. Teachers encourage the children to examine and talk about any items that appeal to them. The children as a group decide on categories for sorting the materials. Perhaps they will suggest sorting items by shape, size, or texture; or they may choose unexpected categories like "see-through" and "non-see-through." Once the items have been sorted, they are arranged in clear containers and displayed attractively on shelves, providing the foundation for an atelier in the classroom.

Weisman Topal and Gandini (1999) suggest that teachers slow down the process of introducing children to recycled materials. Before storing the materials, they recommend giving children lots of time to explore and reflect on the inherent qualities of the materials, and encouraging them to share their observations. The authors also point out that documentation of the process gives teachers insight into the children's level of understanding and conceptual development. Documentation also communicates to parents the importance of learning with materials.

At Marpole Oakridge Preschool, Michelle de Salaberry and Linda Murdoch have applied these suggestions. In the three-year-old class, they take time to introduce the children to the materials in the classroom slowly, so that by the time the children are in the four-year-old class they are able to select and use materials to represent their ideas with fluency and confidence. The majority of children in the class do not speak English as a first language, so materials provide them with another means of expression. Their literacy with materials shone through when they decided to construct and furnish a castle and build a larger-than-life-size knight (Castle and Knight Project, see below).

The Castle and Knight Project

This project (discussed in Chapter 2) began early in the school year and ended with a wonderful celebration at the end of June. In September, Linda Murdoch decided to begin the year by initiating an in-depth exploration of clay with the four-year-olds. Many of them had experienced clay the year before, and Linda wanted to expand and broaden their experience. She put out on the table a large block of clay and then stood back and observed how the children responded. The first group of children poked and prodded the clay. Three girls built a castle, and the boys scoffed at it. "Castles have points," they said. So the next day the boys were invited to build one themselves. Linda was surprised that the children used the clay representationally so quickly. She tried to slow them down by sitting with them every day over the next few weeks to help them learn the necessary skills for working with clay. However, after they had practised rolling and building with slabs, the children returned again and again to their initial idea of building a castle. They either built individual castles or added pieces, like turrets, a ladder, and a king with a crown, to the castle the group had begun building on the first day. The children tried various ways of making turrets. A group of girls looped coils of clay along the top of the walls. The boys made sticks of clay until Nikki, one of the boys, discovered that if you roll a coil of clay more at one end it forms a point, which creates a spire for the turrets on the castle.

The children continued to show a strong interest in castles throughout the winter. Every day, one would see children building castles in the block corner, fighting with pretend swords, or pretending to be princesses in the dress-up corner. The teachers decided that they would try and expand the children's knowledge about medieval times by inviting members of the Society for Creative Anachronism to visit the classroom. Actors dressed as a lord and lady arrived to tell the children how life was lived in a medieval castle. They brought props which included armour and tapestries. The children were particularly interested in how food was cooked, how babies were looked after, how the animals lived right in the castle with the people, and how waste was thrown into the moat around the castle walls. They wanted to know if alligators lived in the moat. They were fascinated with castle toilets and learned that castles had a "garderobe," a passageway leading to a toilet on the outside of the walls, which emptied into the moat below.

Sue Fraser

Wesley's castle made of clay

It was at this point in the project that Nicole brought in a castle she had built with her family at home. Soon other children started bringing in home-made castles, books, and other related props from home.

The children and teachers decided to build their own castle in the classroom and furnish it with all the things they had learned could be found in a medieval castle. In group meeting time the teachers and children drew a plan for the castle, and wrote a list of supplies they would need. The teachers brought in wood, and Sarah had the idea of contributing rocks to build the castle walls. Over the next few weeks teachers and children built the walls and towers using small pieces of wood and rocks. A drawbridge, attached with pulleys to the wall, could be lowered over the moat that surrounded the castle walls. The children added details based on the information they had learned from the visitors, such as a garderobe and outside toilet. A group of girls decided on their own to provide the castle with a garden. Every day groups of children worked with a wide variety of materials to create furnishings for the castle. For instance, they built four-poster beds, tables, chairs, and a throne for the king out of wood. They used clay to construct a well for the courtyard and a whole herd of horses for the knights. The children wanted to make tapestries, like the ones the medieval lady had shown them, so the teachers suggested that the children embroider cloth panels for the walls. The variety of materials used was extensive. At the end of the project the children had worked with felt pens, paint, wood, recycled materials, clay, rocks, fabric, wire, and beads.

A group of boys continued to show a passionate interest in everything to do with knights. They made shields and swords and practised fencing movements

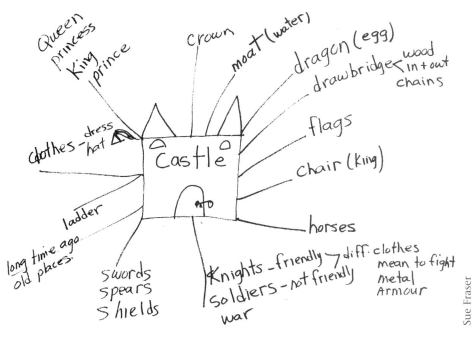

Web for the castle

The castle and the garderobe leading to the toilet above the moat

Horses and well for the garden of the castle

like the ones the medieval lord had shown them. Michelle decided to ask the children, as a provocation, if they would like to build a knight to surprise their fathers when they came to school for Father's Day. The children were thrilled, especially when Michelle told them they could build the knight as tall as the ceiling and keep it a secret. Michelle had gathered some interesting recycled metal materials, like very large tin cans, an old wire frame for a lampshade, tin trays, and aluminum plumbing fixtures. She emptied these out on the mat so the children could lay the materials out. Over the next few weeks groups of three children worked with Michelle in a room across the hall from the classroom, wiring the metal pieces together to form the knight's body. The head was covered with the wire

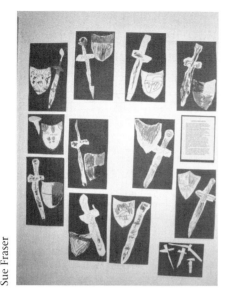

Sue Fraser

Swords and shields

lampshade to look like a visor; smaller cans were wired together in a chain to form the arms and legs; and the plumbing fixtures were used for the hands and feet. The knight held a large tin tray as a shield and a sword made from curtain runners. On the night of the party, the knight was stood up against one wall in the classroom. He was impressive, shining silver and towering from floor to ceiling. No child had given the secret away, so it was a complete surprise for the fathers.

In the days following the excitement of Father's Day, Linda and Michelle discussed doing something equally exciting for the Mothers' Day tea. Building on the interest in princesses the girls in the class had shown throughout the year, the teachers suggested using recycled materials to create princess dolls. They wondered if this would lead to making a life-sized princess with the children. Most children made a princess, but the passion that had driven the children during the Knight project never resurfaced. When the mothers visited the school, the princesses were set out on the shelves. The room looked beautiful, and each mother was given a present of a piece of embroidery the children had made mounted on a wooden board. The mothers were thrilled, and took as much pleasure in the children's work as the fathers had.

To bring the project to a close, teachers arranged a visit to Fantasy Gardens to see the castle in the grounds. Michelle asked a parent if he could find a dragon and hide it as a surprise for the children. When the teachers and children arrived and gathered on the lawn, out of

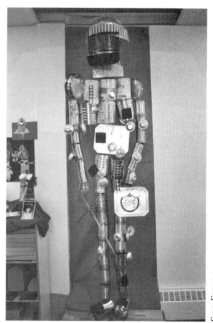

Sue Fraser

The knight made by the children at Marpole Oakridge Preschool

Sue Fraser

Nicole's embroidery inspired by the medieval tapestries

the bushes came an enormous Chinese dragon! He came across the lawn and did a dance for the children. The children squealed with excitement and began to chase the dragon across the lawn. After a while, the parents revealed themselves and then gave the children a turn to hold up the dragon and dance across the grass. It was a wonderful ending for a project that had lasted since October.

The Castle and Knight project went far beyond the initial exploration of clay to include other three-dimensional materials like wire, embroidery, and a wide variety of recycled materials. The project had provided the children with a very rich experience in exploring a wide variety of materials. In following the children's interest, the teachers had again embarked on a big topic, similar to the Circus project of the previous year. The

Sue Fraser

A Chinese dragon surprised the children in the park

Castle and Knight project provided the children with many opportunities to work collaboratively, learn and share knowledge, represent their ideas, and create really beautiful art work. Both boys and girls had many opportunities to contribute their ideas and demonstrate their skills, especially their fine motor skills. The children seemed to know instinctively when to hang back and let the teachers lead the project and when to step in and take the lead themselves. Michelle commented that there seemed to be natural lulls in the progression of a project, and then either the children or the teachers would do something to start the momentum again. For instance, Nicole sparked the group castle by bringing in her homemade one. Michelle noted, "On reflection you see that all the children had a part in the project; they seemed to choose activities for themselves that suited them. In the end, the whole project had seemed to flow together." Families also contributed by sending in materials and by providing the surprise dragon.

EXAMINING ART MEDIA

Reggio Emilia has inspired teachers all over the world to reexamine their approach to art for young children. Teachers have come to view art as one of the hundred languages that children use in representing their ideas, investigating the world, and making their thinking visible. They have also deepened their appreciation of the value of providing art experiences that encourage children to develop aesthetic awareness and learn, with the sensitive support of adults, some of the skills and techniques of working with art materials. Teachers have tried to understand the complex process that enables the children to create the art on display in the preschools in Reggio Emilia and in the exhibit *One Hundred Languages of Children.* In particular, they have come to realize that they need to have a deep understanding of how children create art, especially in the media of drawing, painting, modelling with clay, and using light, wire, and recycled materials.

Drawing

Teachers recognize that children spontaneously use drawing as a language to represent their ideas and to express their emotions. The educators in Reggio Emilia have helped us understand, in addition, how important drawing is in communicating the thinking of young children, who have not yet developed an adequate vocabulary to convey the same information through words. The images children draw either from reality or from their imaginations make the meaning visible. The marks they make on the paper become the invented symbols that hold

Drawing a kingfisher and a hooded merganser duck after visiting the Reiffel Bird Sanctuary

meaning for them and act as markers on the page to help them keep in mind the ideas or the series of events they are drawing. This process is known as *schematic drawing.*

We have learned from Reggio Emilia the importance of encouraging children to also make representational drawings. Teachers encourage the children to look carefully at the objects they are drawing, to take time to study the details, and to think how best to represent the information. Children often collaborate in this process so that they can share ideas and learn from one another. For the teachers, the children's drawings are a reflection of what the children are thinking. In examining the drawings and discussing them with the children, the teachers can discover any disequilibrium in the children's thinking or any gaps in understanding that they need to address. The teachers can then use this information to decide on possible directions they might follow in furthering the children's learning.

In the project on bridges, described in Chapter 7, the teachers at the Vancouver Child Study Centre realized that the children had not included ramps on the bridges in the pictures they

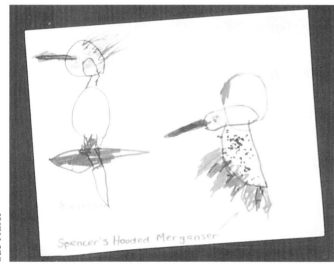

Spencer's Hooded Merganser

Spencer's final drawing of the kingfisher and the hooded merganser made. The teachers discussed with the children their theory of how people and traffic get up onto the deck of the bridges in their pictures. They realized that the children needed to observe more closely how bridges are constructed, so they took the children to see bridges, and together they discussed their observations. Representational drawing led to further investigations in other media.

Painting

When first introduced to paint, children use it primarily to explore its physical properties. They are fascinated by the way it drips down the page and by how it can be applied to the paper with smooth sweeps or short, stabbing movements of the brush. They discover the way colours change when they overlap on the paper. Paint gives children many opportunities to explore elements such as line, colour, and texture. They discover the many ways they can use paint to make lines that are thick and thin, straight and curved, and looping and zigzagging all over the page. Many children also spend long periods of time in sensory exploration of the colour and texture of the paint. They may make patch paintings, in which they lay circular patches of solid colour side by side or in horizontal or vertical stripes to see the effect. Then they may experiment with texture by making brush marks on the surface of the wet or dry paint. Later, they make schematic or representational paintings, just as they do in drawing.

Before introducing paint to children, teachers should experience for themselves the different combinations of paint, paper, and tools for applying paint.

Paper: Provide children with a wide variety of inexpensive paper such as newsprint and construction paper, as well as more expensive paper for special projects, such as cartridge paper and hot- and cold-pressed watercolour paper. Other materials such as clear plastic sheets (a plain shower curtain works well) or three-dimensional forms such as cardboard boxes also provide interesting surfaces for painting.

Paint brushes: Always make a variety of good quality brushes available for the children to use: thick and thin, wide and narrow, flat and pointed, with long and short handles.

Paint: When choosing paints it is always important to check that they are water-soluble and safe for children to use. A variety of paints should always be available, such as liquid and solid tempera, acrylic, watercolour, and ink. Most often children will be free to select their own colour paint, but at times teachers may select only the primary colours, analogous colours, or complementary colours to heighten the children's aesthetic awareness of colour. White and black paint should also be available so children can create light tints and dark shades. It is helpful to have a colour wheel available. Paint should be displayed attractively in transparent containers with lids for storage.

Surfaces for painting: In preparing the environment, carefully consider where and on what surface children will paint. Sometimes it is best to use the floor, a table, or an easel. Children enjoy painting on vertical surfaces such as the sides of small and large cardboard boxes. Textured surfaces such as corrugated cardboard are also appealing.

Painting Skills

Encourage children to

- hold the brush with the fingers (not the fist)

- vary their brush strokes by sometimes using the tip and sometimes the side of the brush

- select flat or round, thick or thin brushes depending on the purpose the brush is being used for

- wash brushes between applications of paint

- control the paint flow by limiting the amount of paint on the brush

- wait for paint to dry before adding more details

- explore colour by mixing the three primary colours, red, blue, and yellow, to create a wide range of secondary and tertiary colours

- mix a little of the colour's complementary colour to form greys and browns (Heberholz and Hansen 1995, 175)

- experiment with colour value creating darker and lighter colours for painting

Louise Cadwell, on her return from Reggio Emilia, describes how she selected specific colours of paint at the College School in St. Louis, Missouri, to heighten the children's aesthetic awareness of fall colours:

During our investigation of leaves, we mixed colors we had noticed outside from quarts of a wide range of tempera colours. Many children had the opportunity to paint at the easel and to use these colours. I wanted to offer the children the chance to make stronger connections with their experience in the midst of this brilliant season through autumn hues in painting. (1997, 73)

In this project, children were not only given the opportunity to respond aesthetically to the autumn colours, but were also encouraged to use paint as a means of investigation. Louise Cadwell describes how her experiences in learning to be an atelierista in Reggio Emilia changed the way she presented paints to children:

> When I saw even very young children in Reggio Emilia painting with three or four gradations of yellows, pinks, blues and greens, on easels outside in the spring air, or 4-year-olds investigating and then painting the variations of violets and greens in the wisteria blooming on the trellis outside their school, I felt that surely even those of us with much experience and background could learn a great deal from this way of introducing young children to paint. (1997, 78)

The educators of Reggio Emilia have increased our understanding of what preschool children can learn with a great deal of exposure to various kinds of paint and with the appropriate scaffolding from adults. We have learned that children, with the sensitive support of adults, can develop more advanced skills in painting. The large murals the children created in Reggio Emilia are an example of the advanced work children can create with this kind of support. Further, we have learned from the educators and atelieristi in Reggio Emilia to respect art materials such as paint and to expect children to use them, as would an artist, with thought, care, and attention.

Clay

As with paint, teachers encourage children first to explore the clay and to discover for themselves the many possibilities inherent in the material. The children discover how clay becomes more malleable as they add water and how when it dries it becomes difficult to manipulate. Spontaneously, they discover that they can use their hands to control the shape the clay takes, they pinch it to form little pots, roll it into coils, and flatten it with their hands to form a slab. They discover that they can make imprints in the clay with objects or embellish the clay by adding small pieces of clay to the surface.

Later, the teacher can build on these early experiences to help children learn techniques such as coiling and building forms with slabs of clay. Children learn how to join two pieces of clay by using a stick to roughen the edges and then applying slip, which is a mixture of clay and water, before pressing the edges together and smoothing the seam. If the children decide to build clay forms that need support, the teacher can show them how to use wire as an armature, or if the children want to make the clay into rounded forms for heads or pots, how to crunch up newspaper into tight balls to act as a support for the clay as they mould it into rounded shapes. The children can, if they wish, embellish the clay forms they have made either by adding small pieces to form features (using the method described above for joining clay) or by using textured objects to indent the surface of the clay.

When the piece is finished, it needs to be dried slowly to prevent the clay from forming cracks, either by covering the clay with a wet towel for a few days or by wrapping it in plastic and letting it dry for a couple of weeks. If children want to keep working on their clay at a later time, it can be wrapped in plastic; however, it will need to be sprayed with water occasionally.

Often children view their work with clay as a process and are willing to roll up their clay into a ball when they are finished working with it, but sometimes they want to keep their work. In Reggio Emilia the large clay forms that the children made were covered in shellac to preserve them. It is preferable, however, to fire the clay if the children want to keep the clay pieces they have made. The dried clay pieces can be fired either in an electric kiln or in a pit fire if no kiln is available.

A pit fire should be built in a backyard where an outdoor fire in the ground can be safely lit and allowed to burn for two or three days. First, a hole in the ground needs to be dug deep enough to cover a galvanized iron garbage can (see Figure 8.1). The top of the garbage can should be at least 10 cm below the surface of the ground, and the soil should be packed closely around the can to keep heat from escaping from the sides. The ground around the can should be free of dried grass and foliage to prevent the fire from spreading. Next, an estimate is needed of how many layers of pots will fill the garbage can in order to decide how wide to make the sawdust layer between each layer of pots. The bottom of the can is filled with sawdust up to the level previously decided on, and some of the clay pieces are placed on top of the sawdust. Dried horse manure may be added to the sawdust, so that the carbon from the manure will give the pots a deep black colour. Sawdust is packed tightly around each piece, and the next layer of sawdust is spread over the clay pieces. The process is repeated until the last layer of pots is about 15 cm from the brim of the can. Then the garbage can is filled with sawdust to within about 8 cm of the rim. It is now ready for firing. A layer of hot burning coals is placed on the top of the sawdust, three bricks are positioned around the outside edge of the garbage can, and the lid of the can is placed on the bricks. A large sheet of metal covers the pit in case of rain. After about 24 hours, with time allowed for the pit to cool, the pieces are ready for unpacking. The sawdust will have burnt away, leaving the blackened pots at the bottom of the can. The pots can be cleaned by brushing off the soot with a toothbrush and then scrubbing them with a brillo pad.

FIGURE 8.1   Garbage Can Pit Kiln

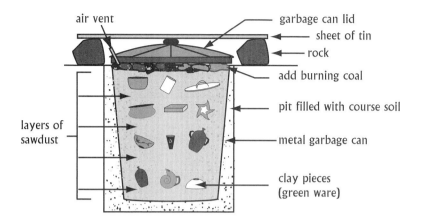

air vent

garbage can lid

sheet of tin

rock

add burning coal

pit filled with course soil

metal garbage can

layers of sawdust

clay pieces (green ware)

Sue Fraser

Wire

Wire is an ancient material and was used in the past to make a wide range of household materials that are now for the most part made with plastic. Recently there has been a revival of wire craft, and many fine works of art are now made using wire as a medium. Wire has also been used by children for centuries to make homemade toys. The wire toys made by children in Africa are famous and are exhibited in many museums all over the world. In Reggio Emilia, children use wire to create forms and figures, and also as armatures for their clay work. Often they will use wire together with other materials such as paper and clay. We saw children in Reggio Emilia using wire to form grids for the math games they were inventing. Another group were weaving materials into cages or tunnels made out of chicken wire set on a mirrored surface. We also saw many mobiles the children had made out of wire and other materials.

We tend to think wire is not appropriate for preschool children, perhaps because most children have not had

Sue Fraser

Nikkie and Kathryn make a wire crown

enough opportunity to explore this material or because of our own unfamiliarity. Wire is, however, inexpensive, very versatile, and engaging for children. We just need to learn a few basic techniques and have the right tools and wire available.

Tools

- a pair of round-nosed pliers
- a pair of straight-nosed pliers
- a pair of wire cutters
- an overhead projector pen
- safety goggles (It is very important to use these at all times.)

Materials

Have three or four of the following available:

- Aluminum wire (soft and easy to work with—aluminum wire as thick as 6 mm can be bent by adult hands)
- brass wire (harder to bend)
- copper wire (the most versatile and malleable, is used for beadwork)
- telephone wire (as above, but needs separating)
- galvanized wire (strong wire used for fencing)
- black annealed wire
- wire mesh
- square woven mesh
- expanded aluminum mesh
- galvanized chicken wire
- garden ties
- acrylic spray (optional)

Note: Wire is measured either in millimetres or by the standard wire gauge (SWG), from 8 to 50. In this system, 8 is the thickest wire, and 50.025 is the thinnest.

Basic Techniques

- *Bending wire.* Hold the strand of wire to be bent with the pliers and then keep the pliers still and pull the end of the wire around with your hand to bend it.

- *Binding.* The simplest way to join two pieces of wire is to bind them with a thinner wire. The wires to be fastened can be temporarily held together with garden ties. Make a series of light indentations on the surface of the wire to be joined so that the binding wire does not slip.

- *Linking loops.* This is a useful technique for making circles or any other closed shape. Make a loop at each end of the wire. Link the loops together and crimp them closed with a pair of pliers.

- *Twisting wire.* To make a two-ply twist, cut a length of wire and bend it back on itself in the middle to make a loop. Allow more wire than you think you need as the wire will become shorter during the twisting process.

Presenting Wire to Children

An adult needs to be present to help children learn how to manipulate wire. Children should be encouraged to explore the wire using many different techniques. When they have discovered all the possibilities, they will begin to create shapes and three-dimensional forms. They will begin to add wire to other art materials such as paper, beads, or clay and to work with others to create interesting structures. For instance, the children at Marpole Oakridge Preschool used wire and beads to make crowns in the Castle and Knight project.

Light as an Art Medium

Perhaps one of the most powerful memories that visitors to the preschools in Reggio Emilia bring away with them is of the use of light as a medium in art. In the preschools in Reggio Emilia there are many different ways for children to explore the possibilities of light. Overhead projectors have been added to the blocks in many classrooms to throw shadows of the children's block constructions on the walls. Children manipulate light by arranging transparent objects and pieces of coloured tissue or cellophane paper on the surface of the light tables or overhead projectors. A light table consists of a wooden box with two strips of cool fluorescent light tubes fastened to the bottom and a

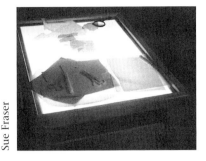

The light table set up for Children Teaching Teachers

sheet of opaque plexiglass covering the top (see Figure 8.2). The inside of the box is painted white. Besides arranging transparent objects and paper on the surface, children can use coloured inks to paint and felt-tipped pens to draw on tissue or transparent paper on the surface of the light table. Sunlight shines through the murals the children have painted on clear plastic sheets that were hanging in some of the classrooms we visited. The principle of transparency is evident in the creative use of light in the classroom and especially in the many different ways that children use it in their artwork as one of the hundred languages to investigate their world and represent their ideas.

FIGURE 8.2   Light Table

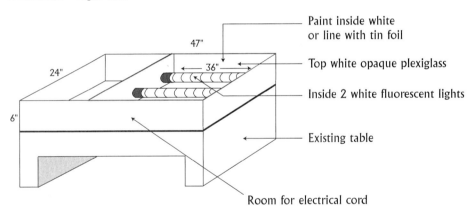

Note: inside of light table must be large enough for a 36" fluorescent light fixture

Multimedia

Children gain a deeper understanding when they are encouraged to use more than one art medium to represent an idea. For instance the children in Reggio Emilia created the fountains in the Amusement Park for Birds project using a variety of media. They drew sketches for fountains with coloured pens and ink, traced the drawings on a light panel, and created three-dimensional models in clay. In this way, children are encouraged to think about different aspects of a problem or idea. The teachers in Reggio Emilia are more likely to supply the techniques children need to represent their ideas, such as by helping the children build wire armatures to support their clay structures. Carol Seefeldt (1995) describes observing the teachers in Reggio Emilia modelling how to construct vertical clay structures by cutting strips from the base of the slab and pulling them up. Art experiences are cumulative, unlike the one-shot art activities so often provided for children in other parts of the world.

Teachers need to encourage children to find the best medium for expressing an idea. It is always a thrill to see a child select a material and transform it in an unexpected fashion. In the Castle and Knight project, one child used triangular pieces of wood to create alligators for the moat around the castle. He then used beads to make eyes for the alligators.

Children should also be encouraged to repeat ideas using different media; for instance, the children in the project above drew the shape of a knight, built knights out of paper tubes, made collages out of small recycled metal pieces for knights, and eventually built a giant knight out of various metal objects. Each of the previous experiences consolidated their understanding of the structure needed to build the large metal knight.

Using different materials in the creation of the same subject gives children different problems to solve as they explore the properties inherent in each material. The feedback from each material the children use adds information to their knowledge base as they create for themselves an "alphabetic" vocabulary for each material they use. For instance, drawing a castle, making it out of a lump of clay, and then actually building a castle out of recycled materials provided children with different challenges. The drawing required children to think about representing a three-dimensional form on a flat surface. The clay posed challenges of how to make a soft material rigid enough to stand upright. Working on a large structure made of recycled materials introduced structural problems like balance. Dealing with the unique possibilities and challenges of different materials encourages children to be flexible thinkers and change their perspective as they work with different materials.

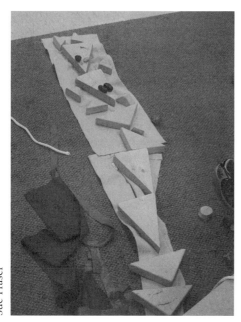

Sue Fraser

Alligators for the castle moat

George Forman stresses the importance of not imposing adult standards of construction on children. The circus tent that the children built in the Circus project did not have sides, but the roof they constructed satisfied the children because it met their goal of supporting the circus lights around the edge of the tent.

RESPONDING TO ART

The first introduction to the world of art for many young children is the illustrations they see in picture books, but with encouragement from parents and teachers, children can also become very enthusiastic and responsive to the work of famous artists. Helping young children respond to art needs some thought, but it can be a very rewarding process. Each group of children is different but some general strategies can be helpful:

- Read stories about real artists to children. This helps them realize that art is a form of expression that one can pursue for a lifetime. It is as important as any other of the hundred languages of childhood.

- Provide children with a variety of art reproductions in the classroom. Take time to point these out to the children and engage them in discussions, perhaps by asking them to search for colours, shapes, textures, and lines. Then help them make comparisons of how artists vary their use of each of these elements. In this way children will begin to build a vocabulary they can use in talking about art.

- Discuss the feelings that each piece of art evokes. Children will need time and a lot of practice to heighten their awareness and develop a vocabulary that matches feelings to visual images.

- Ask questions that heighten awareness. For example, "How would it feel to be inside the picture? What would it smell like? Sound like? What could you touch and how would it feel?" With more experience, children can also be asked more abstract questions, such as "How do artists change the way we look at things?"

- Invite artists to visit the classroom, maybe just to paint in a corner and talk to the children about their artwork, or even perhaps to work on a project with the children.

- Help children to understand that art is a personal thing with the potential for communicating and conveying their feelings and thoughts. Art can become a means of expression just as profound as using words. However, the artist needs time and practice using different brushes and painting implements, different papers, paints, and representational materials to develop the skill and technique needed in working with a variety of art materials.

- Arrange a visit to an art gallery. This can be a very rewarding experience, especially when children are given the opportunity to respond to the art they have seen on display by talking about it and, more importantly, by creating their own art. The art gallery experience is enhanced when the children have been well prepared for the visit.

PREPARING TEACHERS

ECE students need to experience firsthand in their classes the approach to art learned from Reggio Emilia. The most difficult barrier to break through in exploring the principles learned from Reggio Emilia in teacher education is probably integrating art into all other aspects of the curriculum. Courses may need to be rescheduled so that the curriculum subjects can be taught together. This, in turn, requires instructors in the different curriculum areas to collaborate and teach subjects such as art, music, literature, science, and social studies as a team.

At Douglas College, we have found that by making Children Teaching Teachers the core curriculum course, content for all the other subject areas can be drawn from instructors' observations of the students and children. In one session, for instance, the students had put out balls of clay for the children to use with water in a cottage cheese carton on the table. One of the first children to show interest in using the clay was a three-year-old boy. He sat down at the table and immediately poured the water over his ball of clay, flooding the table and turning the clay into liquid mud. The students made a quick decision to clean up and pack the clay away. I could see, as the instructor observing the session, that in our next class, I would have to give the students more information about how to use clay as an art medium. I also saw that we needed to discuss how the experience with the clay might have been used as an opportunity to help the child, if he were interested, discover more about the properties of clay and how it is transformed as water is added. We would also need to discuss broader issues, such as development, and review the typical behaviour of a three-year-old on encountering a new material. We would have to revisit Vygotsky's theory and discuss how the zone of proximal development can be nudged upward when the adult scaffolds the child's learning. It becomes impossible, therefore, to teach art as a separate curriculum subject. At Douglas College we have found that it makes more sense to integrate all curriculum areas, but this means that instructors have to work, like the students, as a team.

THE ROLE OF THE TEACHER IN THE ART PROGRAM

Teachers, as they gain more understanding of the Reggio Emilia approach, come to view art as one of the hundred languages of children. Teacher's goals expand from merely seeing the importance of providing children with developmentally appropriate art activities that foster sensory exploration and creativity to making art a part of the total experience, a means of expression, a tool for investigation, a medium of communication, and above all a way of making thinking visible. The relationship of teachers to children's art changes when they view art as another language children use in making sense of their world. To help them explore the Reggio Emilia principles, the teachers in the programs described earlier in the chapter asked themselves questions such as the following:

- Are aesthetics considered at every stage of the process, from preparation of the art materials to presentation of the materials to the children?

- Is respect shown in the way the materials are used in the classroom?

- Is relationship evident in every aspect of the program, for instance, in the way in which materials are presented and in how the children's work is documented by the teachers?

- Are there opportunities for the children to use the materials on their own and in collaboration with other children and adults?

- Are children encouraged to use a wide variety of media to represent and communicate their ideas?

- Are children encouraged to make both schematic drawings of their ideas and representational drawings of real objects?

- Are children encouraged to use drawing as a means of making their thinking visible to teachers?

Sue Fraser

Drawing a map of the Reiffel Bird Sanctuary

- Are there opportunities for adults to share their skills in creating art with children?

- Are there opportunities for children to share their ideas with adults?

- Are the materials selected for children to use "intelligent materials," i.e., materials "that do not impose a direction but that pose questions and elicit hypotheses" (Krechevsky 2001, 67)? Are the materials ones that encourage experimentation as opposed to materials that merely entertain children?

- How is the principle of transparency woven into the art program, for instance, in the visibility of materials provided for the children to use, in the use of light as both a tool and a medium of expression, and in the documentation of the children's work?

- Have natural materials been used in the preparation of the environment and also made available for the children to explore and use in their artwork?

- Have the teachers established links with the community by inviting people to share their art or skills with the children?

Giovanni Piazza in an interview with Lella Gandini says, "It is only when the children have a sufficient level of familiarity that they discover how each material has internal alphabetic qualities. Later they discover that this internal alphabet shares qualities with other materials and it is contaminated by them." He goes on to say that it is important that teachers "observe the child's journey of understanding with each material (Gandini 2005, 134). When we documented the toddlers' exploration of clay described in Chapter 6 we became aware of how the toddlers brought previously learned schemas to explore the clay. For instance, they used their previously learned experiences playing with water to pour, moisten, and splash the clay as they tried to figure out what to do with it (see page 169).

In the descriptions below, Arolynn Kitson*, a kindergarten teacher in Alberta, explains the changes she made, after being inspired by the schools of Reggio Emilia, to the physical and interpersonal environments in the classroom.

One Teacher's Journey

The environment is referred to as "the third teacher" in the schools of Reggio Emilia. It is with this concept in mind that I began to look at my surroundings in a different light.

*Reproduced courtesy of Arolynn Kitson

I made three specific environmental changes in my classroom. The changes included the physical environment, the interpersonal environment, and activities to stimulate development in the environment.

The Physical Environment

The first environmental change I made was to set up a more appealing art studio. As the first picture indicates, my initial art studio was full of materials placed in a semi-organized manner.

My first attempt at a more appealing art studio was a simple one. It involved coordinating the drawing tools by colour and presenting them in clear jars. Although this was a simple idea prevalent in the schools of Reggio Emilia, I began to see how the children and I began to look at the materials in different ways. I also began to introduce the children to higher-quality materials, including various drawing pencils, fine line markers, charcoal, and watercolour pencil crayons. We talked about how they were responsible for choosing the right tool for their work. Comments overheard in the art studio included: "I need a big black felt because I need a big line" and "You shouldn't use the charcoal in your Life book because it will smear."

This organizational change promoted decision making, as the children were not only given the opportunity to choose their own tools but were expected to do so.

A surprising outcome of this organization was that the children began to show more respect for their tools. We talked about how artists cared for their tools. The children always put their tools back properly. I was not to see another dried-out glue stick.

Sue Fraser

Sue Fraser

The organization of art materials in Arolynn Kitson's kindergarten

Parents as Partners

I have always valued and respected the important role the parent has as an advocate and participant in their child's education. Although I appreciated and was grateful for the help that the parents gave in the classroom, by working with children and helping to make materials, I was uncomfortable at the same time. I felt the parents should have a more pronounced influence on their child's program, but at the same time I did not want the parents to feel that my role as the teacher was compromised by asking for their input. Inspired by the invaluable partnership that is honoured in the schools of Reggio Emilia, I decided to take a somewhat intrepid step into forging a better relationship between the parents and myself. I asked the question: Are there any artists out there? To my delight, one parent stepped forward, and we slowly began to talk about how she could share her skills with the children.

A most magical thing happened when the parents simply painted with the children. The children worked on one painting for a complete hour. One child in particular chose to continue his painting at snack time. It was his words that I will always remember: "See I'm a little bit of an artist." This was the same child who never chose any activities that required him to hold a drawing or painting tool. Another comment that was equally important to me was the parent who commented, "It was really fun! I hadn't painted for a long time."

Activities to Stimulate Development

The children and I talked a lot about taking our time and really looking at things, whether it was observing our crabs, worms, and plants or photographs of real objects. In my previous kindergarten class I had never given the children the opportunity to draw from either real objects or photographs. I was delighted to see how the children responded to using these materials. The children were observed paying close attention to their models and spending increased time periods drawing. Amy spent an hour drawing her grasshopper. She shared with myself and her peers many things she learned while closely observing and drawing this grasshopper.

When we as teachers create aesthetic environments for children, we invite them into a different world of experience, one that provides rich sensory experiences and unexpected pleasures. This heightens the children's awareness and appreciation of beautiful things. Learning becomes an especially enjoyable experience. The children in a classroom where the value of aesthetics is evident thrive because they feel connected at a deep level to the beauty in their environment, and they respond by creating beautiful work themselves, Relationships become increasingly congenial and the tone of the classroom is one of joy and productivity.

Chapter 9

Blue-footed Booby

The Investigating
Classroom

We see the child as strong, capable, full of resources: how serious the child is in wanting to grow, how strong a researcher, a semioticist, asking "Why am I here?"

—Carlina Rinaldi

Questions to Consider:

- What are the ingredients necessary to promote investigation in a preschool classroom?

- What theoretical information do teachers need to help them in their understanding of how young children learn?

- How do children construct theories to interpret reality?

- How much emphasis should teachers place on fantasy and reality in the child's investigations?

- What is the role of the environment as a third teacher in the child's search for knowledge?

- What is the role of play in promoting learning?

- How have the educators in Reggio Emilia contributed to our understanding of how children learn?

- Through what lens do teachers view "investigation?"

DISCOVERING THE INVESTIGATING CLASSROOM

Most of us can discern immediately on entering a classroom whether or not it promotes investigation. There are a number of clues, some obvious and some more subtle, that tell a visitor whether children in the room are encouraged to be active agents or passive recipients in their learning. The classroom, in the way the environment is planned, in the materials selected for children to use, and in the work on display, makes a strong statement about what kind of activity is valued in that space. If the visitor sees that there are areas in the classroom that are designed to encourage small groups of children to work together, that there is a wide variety of materials that are easily accessible, and that the materials are of the kind that allow children to transform them, then she knows that she is in an environment where children are encouraged to be active participants in their learning. Environments that encourage investigation are orderly without being rigid and are free of strict rules forbidding children to take materials from one area and use them somewhere else. In a classroom that encourages investigation, for instance, children can carry sand from the sandbox over to the art area and use it with the glue if they have a specific purpose or maybe a question about whether sand can add texture to their designs.

Besides having the usual materials of paint, clay, and drawing tools for art, the investigative classroom also has equipment for sand and water exploration and science equipment, including balance scales, magnifying glasses, and tools for measurement. In a classroom that fosters curiosity, many different materials are arranged to provoke an element of surprise. In the preschools in Reggio Emilia, visitors see children using many unusual materials and equipment; for example, the children may use antique brass scales to weigh an assortment of nuts and real fruit. The classroom environment should have about it a quality of expecting the unexpected. This kind of environment draws children and adults in, intrigues them, and sets them off on a journey of investigation.

In a classroom that promotes investigation, the children have many opportunities to engage in the sensory exploration of materials and to learn about the properties of the materials. Later, they can move beyond sensory experience and use the materials more purposefully as a means of investigation or as a medium to represent their ideas. Carol Anne Wien describes an incident during her visit to Reggio Emilia in which she observed a child's attempts to solve a structural problem in trying to create an insect out of clay. The child struggled "to get his rather large knobbed antennae to stand up in the air, attached." The teacher, noticing his difficulty, scaffolded the child's learning by first providing him with a piece of curved bark to act as a support for the insect's body, and then later helped him find a photograph in a reference book, which he used as a guide in positioning accurately the insect's antennae (Wien 1997, 36). In this example, the child, with assistance from the teacher, achieved two things. He discovered that wet clay has limitations and that unlike a more rigid medium, a thin, cylindrical piece of clay, when placed in an upright position, does not have the strength to support a heavy knob of clay. He also learned, with scaffolding from the teacher, about the body parts of an insect and how they are connected.

The teacher's interactions with the children in the classroom also indicate whether investigation is encouraged. Does the teacher, for instance, encourage the children to ask questions and to embark on a search for answers? Does she model curiosity and excitement in response to the children's ideas and suggestions? Is she resourceful in helping children find ways of furthering their knowledge? Does she encourage children to use a wide variety of materials to represent their ideas and to make visible their thinking? If the answer to all these questions is yes, then it is probably true that the children in the classroom are encouraged to be active agents in their construction of knowledge.

THE THEORIES BEHIND THE INVESTIGATIVE ENVIRONMENT

Teachers who view investigation through a developmental lens usually take a cognitive developmental approach to learning. They follow Piaget's belief that children construct knowledge through actively exploring the environment. Children between three and six years old, who are still in the preoperational stage of development, will bestow magical qualities on phenomena in their environment. Their thinking is transductive, meaning that they draw conclusions based on disconnected observations. They may state, for instance, that there is snow in their garden but not in their neighbour's because the fence surrounding their yard keeps it in.

A teacher who views children from a developmental constructivist lens will theorize that they have moved into the concrete operational stage in kindergarten and are able to pursue a more logical train of thought. Their thinking will be less influenced by immediate perceptions based on sensory information, and they will be able to take other perspectives into account. At this stage they are believed to have a more accurate understanding of concepts such as volume, size, and area. Children in the concrete operational stage of development, for instance, are able to consider a number of reasons why snow remains in their yard and not in the neighbour's. They may think about factors such as sun and shade or exposure and sheltered spaces in thinking through the problem. At this stage they are able to consider more than just one aspect of a situation. They are able to perform simple mental operations, such as reversing their thinking in order to reach a more logical conclusion. This development in the thinking of children at the concrete operational stage also enables them to make more accurate, detailed, and realistic representations of their ideas.

In more recent years, teachers have begun to take the theories of Vygotsky into account. They have come to understand how knowledge, in addition to being self-constructed, is also co-constructed with others in a group. Teachers have learned from studying Vygotsky that when children collaborate with others, especially with a more knowledgeable or skilled partner, they can increase their level of ability. Vygotsky terms the range of ability between what a child can achieve on his own and what he can achieve when assisted by others the *zone of proximal development.* The understanding that children can achieve a higher level of functioning when given support has heightened awareness of the importance of teacher–child and child–child interaction in the classroom. William E. Doll notes that as we have become more aware of how intelligence is co-constructed, "a sense of community is placed in a new light. More than being merely a pleasant frame in which to work or in keeping with our democratic beliefs, community—with its sense of both cooperation and critical judgement—may be essential to meaningful deep learning" (1993, 105). He also notes that when people share their ideas, conflicting opinions often arise in the group, but that instead of acting like a road block, the conflict can become a source of energy that enables the group to change direction or find creative solutions to problems. He writes that "we need to realize that much of human learning comes from this interaction—via the conflicts that create the dilemmas which generate growth" (1993, 120).

Howard Gardner defines intelligence as "the ability to solve problems or fashion products that are valued in at least one cultural setting" (1983). He has broadened our view of intelligence by identifying the different kinds of intelligences children may possess. Gardner's list of types of intelligence serves "to help us change our sense of what an intelligence is and to help us to recognize the diverse skills that are valued in societies all over the world" (Krechevsky 1993, 8).

The first intelligence Gardner identifies, which he calls *linguistic intelligence,* is an awareness of both the structure of language, including sounds, grammar, and syntax, and the functions of language, including semantics, or meaning making, and pragmatics. We find this intelligence in very verbal children who enjoy reading and writing, playing with words, and inventing imaginative stories. The second intelligence Gardner calls *logico-mathematical intelligence*, which is demonstrated by people who have the ability to use logic in their reasoning and who excel in science and mathematics. Young children who are interested in discovering patterns and noticing the relationships between numbers are probably demonstrating this kind of intelligence. *Musical intelligence,* a heightened sensitivity to rhythm, sound, tone, and so on, in music, develops very early and is often apparent by the age of two or three. *Spatial intelligence* involves "the ability to match patterns, to perceive similarity in rotated forms, and to conceptualize spatial relationships" (Krechevsky 1993, 8). This kind of intelligence is often seen in children who produce complex constructions with three-dimensional materials, such as with blocks or Lego in preschool. *Bodily-kinesthetic intelligence,* the fifth in Gardner's theory, is the ability to use one's body in effective and creative ways. Children who are observed using their athletic ability to make the fullest use of the playground equipment or who move expressively and rhythmically to music are demonstrating bodily-kinesthetic intelligence. The sixth and seventh intelligences are two personal or social intelligences. *Interpersonal intelligence* involves an understanding of others, and *intrapersonal intelligence* involves an understanding of oneself. The child who demonstrates interpersonal intelligence is particularly sensitive to emotional cues and to the dynamics of the social environment. Children who demonstrate intrapersonal intelligence are in tune with themselves; they know their likes and dislikes and their strengths and weaknesses. In the preschool environment these are the children who make choices easily and who seem to know instinctively exactly what activities they will enjoy doing. The eighth intelligence added to the list more recently is termed *naturalist* which recognizes an ability to understand the natural world, to be able to classify individuals, species, and ecological relationships, and to be able to interact effectively with living creatures.

Krechevsky notes that "everybody who is normal has significant proportions of all of them [the eight intelligences described above]. But people differ in their particular configurations of intelligences. Furthermore, one never finds an intelligence in isolation. Most roles, tasks and products involve a combination of intelligences." She goes on to say that "the interesting challenge in education is to understand different intellectual profiles and to figure out how to build on them" (1993, 8). Gardner continues to expand the number of intelligences listed above, for instance, he has in recent years began to consider a ninth intelligence *pedagogical/teaching intelligence* (Gardner in Shearer 2009, 107).

PROMOTING INVESTIGATION IN THE CLASSROOM

Teachers who create classrooms that promote investigation have a broad vision of how children learn, accept a wide range of abilities, value the many dimensions of intelligence in children, and provide them with many languages with which to express their ideas. By having a sound understanding of the kind of environment that promotes learning in young children, teachers help them to grow intellectually. They understand, for instance, that children need many opportunities for acting on materials and transforming them in order to grow intellectually. These teachers know the importance of giving children access to materials so that they can use a variety of media to represent their ideas. They understand how to scaffold children's learning and how to create an environment that encourages children to work with others in the co-construction of knowledge. They ensure that there is enough flexibility in the organization of the room so that children are free to use materials and equipment in creative ways. Most important, they know how to listen to children and to recognize and support the big ideas or overarching concepts that emerge from the children's thoughts about a topic. They then know how to open up an experience by asking questions, helping the children see relationships, expanding on their ideas, extending their thinking, and scaling down the elements to make the project manageable. They understand how to negotiate with children and are sensitive to when it is appropriate to take the lead and when to follow the children's ideas.

Children are able to build theories about subjects that are of interest to them when teachers encourage them to be active learners, to use a variety of media to represent their thoughts and ideas, and to participate in the co-construction of knowledge with teachers and other children in the classroom. The following example describes the process in which the children, with the support of the teachers at the Vancouver Child Study Centre, co-constructed their knowledge of how snails reproduce.

One day in the spring, the teachers and children returned from a walk in the forest with some snails, which they kept in a terrarium in the classroom for the next few weeks and examined each day. Eventually, the children discovered the snails had laid eggs under the leaves at the bottom of the tank. They examined the mass of little white eggs with magnifying glasses and discussed the differences between these and chicken eggs. The following documentation, compiled by the teachers in the Vancouver Child Study Centre on May 12, 1998, reveals how the children co-constructed a theory about how snails hatch from eggs.

> At meeting time we had a chance to talk some more and reflect about releasing the snails. All of the children knew now that the snail eggs had been discovered in the fish tank. We had put out four different kinds of magnifiers to look at the snails, the eggs, and the cottonwood tree catkins. (The children may have thought the catkins were seedlings.) I wrote out two questions: "What are these?" (next to the catkins) and "The snails have laid eggs. What will happen next?" Some children offered answers during their investigations with me, and others offered answers at meeting time.
>
> **Stewart:** They will hatch.
>
> **Godfrey** (who speaks English as a second language): Like a chicken.
>
> **George:** Baby snails will come out.
>
> **Paige:** When they crack open, they won't crack open because they don't have beaks. (Paige was recalling a story, *Bluebird Seven*, which we had read earlier in class.)
>
> **George:** They will use their antennas to hatch out.

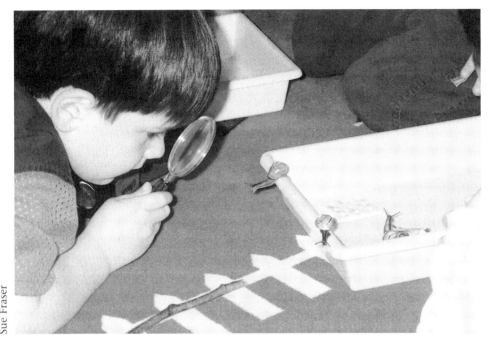

Sue Fraser

Spencer investigating the snails

Spencer: When they hatch out, we'll have a birthday party to help them grow.

Rachael: Their mother will sit on them to help them hatch.

Neilson: When they have their birthday party, they can go bowling with their eggs.

The teachers realized from this documentation that some of the children were getting confused between how snails and chickens hatched from eggs and that there were many gaps in the children's knowledge.

Through a similar process of group discussion and investigation of a topic, the same children at the Vancouver Child Study Centre began to build a theory about how bridges are constructed (see Chapter 7). At the beginning of the project the children thought bridges stood upright because they were tied to trees and that to get up to the bridge deck the cars would need to take an elevator—one child said, they could jump "one, two, three!" The children, through group discussions, opportunities to represent ideas in a wide variety of media, ongoing documentation, and field trips in the community, learned that there are many kinds of bridges and many ways in which they are constructed. Throughout the bridge-building project, the children demonstrated their increasing knowledge of bridges by making more detailed and accurate pictures of bridges, including foot bridges, floating bridges, and suspension bridges. During their investigations, they corrected some misunderstandings about how bridges are constructed.

Howard Gardner writes that "a human intellectual competence must entail a set of skills of problem solving—enabling individuals to *resolve genuine problems or difficulties* that he or she encounters when appropriate, to create an effective product—and must entail the potential for *finding or creating problems,* thereby laying the groundwork for the acquisition of new knowledge" (1983, 60–61).

The following account relates how a student, in setting up an apparatus for the children to investigate the flow of water from ceiling to floor in their classroom, enabled them to solve problems and acquire new knowledge. In the deconstruction of the project she examined the different lenses through which a teacher can view children's investigations.

Exploration of Water

Juliana Gali, a practicum student at Marpole Oakridge Preschool, set up an intriguing apparatus for the children to investigate water. She strung a clear plastic tube from the ceiling of the classroom into the water table below. Marcus found that when he filled the tube with water it did not flow through to the water table, so Linda suggested attaching a pulley so that the children could raise the level of the tube so the water would flow out at the other end. Later, Juliana added a tub below the water table as an extension of the play so the flow of the water could be observed from different heights. At one point Marcus attached a baster tightly to the end of the coil and then pumped out the water. The children enjoyed emptying the coil again and again until all the water was finished. The teachers wondered what it was that intrigued the children so much. The children seemed fascinated by the water whirling around the funnel as it entered the container. But why were they so determined to

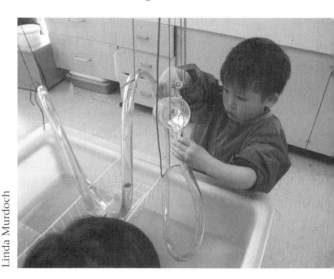

Linda Murdoch

Pouring experiments

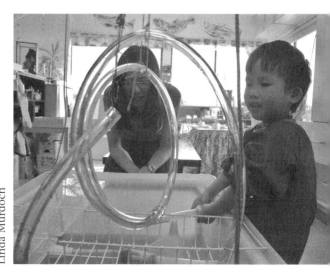

Linda Murdoch

Setting up apparatus

completely empty the water table each time?

"Hurrah, we did it!" shouted the children as they emptied the water table.

Keiran: Look it is going down in a circle.

Juliana: Does water have shape?

Marcus: No.

Juliana: It looks like a rectangle shape to me.

Marcus: If you pour it down it goes everywhere.

Marcus began pumping the baster which he had fixed into the tube.

Marcus: It sounds like a drum.

Kieran: It sounds like a chicken.

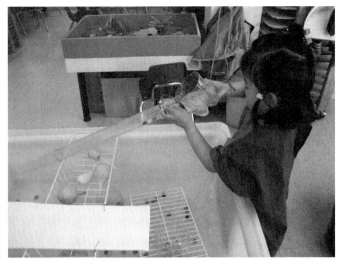

Linda Murdoch

Investigating water flow

Deconstruction:

Looking at the experience from a developmentalist point of view, the children were working on their fine motor skills, learning to share tools, taking turns, etc. Taking a cognitive constructivist perspective, the children could be said to be engaged in sensory exploration that led to conceptual knowledge. For instance, Marcus experimented with the visual and sound effects he made with the baster as he pumped the water out of the tube. The children explored spatial concepts as they labelled and drew the shape the water made as it came out of the tube, e.g., circle and rectangle. Perhaps they were investigating concepts about cause and effect, full/empty, and object permanence. Inspired by Reggio Emilia, Juliana asked the children to draw their theories about the path and shape of the water. In this way she thought the teachers might discover the overarching "big ideas" that had engaged the children with the apparatus so completely for so long. If Juliana had had a longer time to spend on the project, this might have opened new paths for her and the children to investigate.

FANTASY AND REALITY IN THE CURRICULUM

The question arises during a systematic investigation of a topic such as water exploration and bridges described earlier is whether children are being given enough time and encouragement to use their imaginations and engage in the fantasy play typical of preschool children. The importance of play has been the foundation of early childhood education philosophy since Froebel wrote *The Education of Man*. In this book he stated that,

> Play is the purest most spiritual activity of man at this stage, at the same time typical of human life as a whole—of the inner hidden natural life in man and all things. It gives, therefore, joy, freedom, contentment, inner and outer rest, peace with the world. It holds the source of all that is good. A child until physical fatigue forbids will surely be a thorough, determined man, capable of self sacrifice for the promotion of the welfare of himself and others. Is it not the most beautiful expression of child life at this time a playing child, a child wholly absorbed in his play? ([1887] 1974, 55)

Some educators, such as Gretchen Reynolds, have wondered what degree of importance the teachers in Reggio Emilia place on the role of play. On a study tour in Reggio Emilia, she asked whether the teachers document the children's play. Antonia, the pedagogista in Neruda School replied, "We believe observation is an attitude. That attitude does not regard only projects. It's a way of listening that takes in the whole day. This morning in the playground some things were happening. I make ongoing observations of how the children move in the playground outside." Antonia then described an episode in which a group of children tried to include another child who was having a hard day. She went on to say, "I believe the role of the adult is to make sure children listen to themselves but also listen to others. Because what you observe are children who have been together a short time and need to learn to do this" (Reynolds 1998, 7).

Reynolds inferred from this answer to her question that the educators value "relationship, dialogue, exchange, and communication" in play. She went on to say that Antonia "watches play carefully, she reflects on its meaning so that she can understand the children's motivation and she tells stories to explain it to others. As the children's teacher, Antonia is in a relationship with them. Over the year a shared understanding has developed among them. From this particular place of understanding, Antonia knows her role as teacher—to observe, give comfort and coach when necessary, and to remain in the background of the play. As they learn to understand and support each other, solidarity and a strong sense of community develops among the children" (1998, 7).

As we think about Froebel's belief in the value of play and his view that a child in play is "capable of self sacrifice for the promotion of the welfare of himself and others," we can match these ideas to those of the educators in Reggio Emilia, especially in the importance they place on reciprocity and relationship in the play of young children and in the role of the teacher in children's play. Whereas educators in other parts of the world stress the principle of learning through play, the educators in Reggio Emilia emphasize learning through the *relationships* that are promoted through play. The teachers in Reggio Emilia do not worry so much about finding a balance between fantasy and systematic investigation in preschool programs; rather, they concentrate on fostering and valuing the relationships that children have with teachers and other children as they play and as they investigate their world. The relationship between children and teachers, therefore, becomes more equal as teachers become partners in both the play and the children's investigations. When a partnership develops between children and teachers, the teacher's agenda disappears, and the children are free to follow a more natural path that may alternate between systematic investigation and imaginative play. Children are then able to use their imaginations, express their ideas, and move through periods in which their thoughts are more influenced by "magic" than by logic. Gradually, with the scaffolding of adults and other children, they begin to refine their theories and ground their ideas in reality as they try to figure out how the world works. Rinaldi states that "The dimension of play (with words, pretending, and so on) is thus an essential element of the human being. If we take this dimension away from children and adults, we remove a possibility for learning" (Rinaldi 2005, 171).

The children in the Quadra Island Children's Centre experienced this process after visiting the local veterinarian's office. In the days that followed, the teachers set up an animal hospital in the classroom, with a desk, laboratory equipment, toy animals, and cages. The following documentation of the children's play and conversation indicated to the teachers the children's level of understanding, as well as gaps in their knowledge, of what happens to animals at the vet's office.

Dee (the teacher): Do you know what is wrong with that puppy? We have an injured puppy.

Grant: It is bleeding everywhere.

Des: O.K. I have an idea. There are things you take pictures. I am just trying to put it ...

(He puts the animal in a box that he was pretending was an X-ray machine.) I think his heart wasn't working very well ... special thing

Sue Fraser

Des, the veterinarian

stuck on here and water will make it go down. We have got special medicine. (Des brings medicine over and injects it into the toy animal.) A small piece of dirt that got in his mouth. See you next time.

(Des sits at the desk, looking at a magazine about animals. He asks the teacher to put a mask on his mouth.)

Barb (teacher): What would a vet use a mask for?

Des: To stop germs getting in mouth. (He takes off the mask.) ... I will check his blood. (He presses a syringe against the dog's body and pretends to put blood in a bottle, which he places on a tray.) I'm checking for germs.... We have to get that kitty into the dishwasher. I guess you can lift her up.

Barb: How will she like that?

Des: We have to put her asleep for a long time because we have to do things that hurt a lot. We have to put blankets on her so she stays asleep.

(Susan Fraser, Quadra Island Children's Centre, November 27, 1998)

The teachers read through the documentation later and were surprised at how much Des had learned from his visit to the vet. They discovered that he had learned many details about the procedure a vet follows in the course of his day's work. Des showed from his conversation that he understood why the vet followed certain procedures, such as taking an X-ray, putting a mask over his mouth, and taking a blood sample. The teachers also analyzed their interactions. They noted the initial provocation the teacher made when she entered the play by asking the children, "Do you know what is wrong with that puppy?" They noted that she was successful in engaging the children with the materials. They discussed whether the questions they asked were open ended and furthered the children's understanding. They pondered whether the question about the mask was appropriate, wondering whether it furthered the children's play or interrupted their thinking. They noted how Des demonstrated his concern for the animals and how the teachers supported his empathetic responses with questions that helped the children reflect on their actions, such as, "How will she like that?" The play continued for over three weeks. A documentation panel at the entrance to the child care kept the parents informed about the children's growing understanding and co-construction of knowledge of a veterinarian's role in caring for animals.

A classroom that fosters investigation, therefore, provides children with materials to explore the physical, social, and natural world and helps them build theories on topics of interest to them. It is an environment in which teachers view the child as competent, inventive, and full of ideas. It is a classroom in which teachers focus on the children's strengths, rather than their needs, and use the kind of language that fosters investigation.

Barb Gerst*, a kindergarten teacher in Alberta, describes how she has found the Reggio Emilia approach "a wonderful inspiration." She notes that as she became increasingly familiar with the approach, she made fundamental changes in her program:

> I started to work with children as a collaborator. I knew that I had to let go of my previously held view of myself as a director in my environment. I became interested in helping the children deepen their understanding of whales and dolphins, our chosen area of study that fall. My new role as a collaborator allowed me to take on a variety of roles in my classroom that I had not valued before. Sometimes I was a nurturer supporting the children's growth. Other times, I became their partner in learning as we discovered a new fact about dolphins. I became a provocateur, challenging and probing the children to expand their abilities to think critically. (1998, 43)

Gerst also began to view her aide and parent volunteers as collaborators, who helped her, in particular, reflect on the children's conversations she had begun to record in the classroom. For instance, she recorded the words a child imagined the mother whale would call out to prevent her baby from getting lost.

Pamela: They would actually say to each other, "Where are you?" He would answer, "I am in a group!"

Colleen: "I love my baby!"

Tanner: "Come here because I want to show you something!"

Colleen: "See my new calf!"

When Gerst played back the tape of this imaginary conversation, she observed how much greater the level of the children's interest and involvement in the whale project was, and "how much richer and detailed children's large group discussions" became. She concludes by stating that,

> The richness and depth of many conversations that took place during this Reggio-inspired project [on whales and dolphins] will inspire me to consider several ideas when having conversations with young children next year. Most importantly, I will continue to place a high value upon children's thoughts and convey interest in their words through my enthusiasm. I have become aware that meaningful conversations take place in quiet environments away from distractions. Additionally, I have discovered that placing an emphasis upon good listening skills and respect for others' ideas is crucial. I believe that reflections with parents and teachers about types of questions that

---

*Reproduced courtesy of Barbara Gerst

may stimulate discussion is valuable. Involving a parent during a conversation is important. A quick summary of the main points in a conversation helps children stay focused and interested in a topic. I have learned that tape recording conversations allows children's ideas to become alive in a classroom. (1998, 47–48)

Gerst discovered that as she began to use ideas learned from the Reggio Emilia approach, the human relationships in the classroom became more equal and collaborative. In particular, the teacher's role changed from that of a director to a partner in the co-construction of knowledge. Communication skills such as listening became critical, but of most interest was the role that imagination played in taking the experience to a deeper level of meaning for the children in the class. Following the lead of the teachers in Reggio Emilia, she saw the value of the coexistence of both fantasy and reality in the children's experience with the whales and dolphins. She did not demonstrate a need to replace fantasy with scientific knowledge, as so often happens in classrooms. In the whale and dolphin project, Gerst saw how imagination deepened the level of investigation.

EMBARKING ON AN INVESTIGATION OF PLANTS

Early in the spring, when the first daffodils are blooming in local gardens, the students at Douglas College began an investigation of plants. We took our inspiration for this investigation from a segment in the video *The Creative Spirit,* which documented the children in Reggio Emilia visiting a poppy field and then expressing in a mural the joy and excitement the poppies evoked in them. In the investigation of plants workshop, we tried to give the students an experience that evoked similar feelings of joy and excitement. We also wanted to expose the students to specific aspects of the Reggio Emilia approach, such as experiencing an authentic artistic experience. We wanted to help them appreciate that art should not be viewed as an isolated activity, but rather as part of a broader experience that includes aesthetic awareness, scientific investigation, and schematic representation. In the video *The Creative Spirit,* the children were encouraged to observe the poppies very closely and then to do a series of detailed drawings before they began to paint the mural of the poppies. The children, therefore, were not learning to draw but *drawing to learn.* We wanted the students to experience a similar process. Further, we wanted to enable the students to follow an experience from the initial provocation

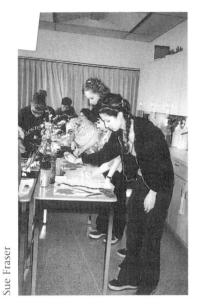

Sue Fraser

Douglas College students painting spring flowers

through to collaborating in the final task, as the children in Reggio Emilia did in expressing their collective ideas in a mural they painted on large sheets of plastic.

A few weeks before the investigation of plants workshop, to prepare for the class, I soaked red runner bean seeds overnight and put the seeds on the inside surface of a large glass jar, pressing them firmly in place with layers of wet paper towel. Later, at intervals in the two weeks prior to the first class, I germinated more seeds by covering them with wet paper towel on pie plates. I wanted the seeds to be at different stages of germination when we were ready to use them. By the time we began our investigation of plants, some of the seeds in the glass jar had grown into vines and had begun to form bright red flowers. I also picked a few branches of forsythia, and quince, cherry, and plum blossoms, which I brought indoors for a few days to force them to be in full bloom for the class. On the day we began our investigation of plants, I arranged bunches of spring flowers—crocus, grape hyacinth, daffodils, and the flowering branches—in vases on each table in the classroom. When the students arrived the room was filled with the scent of the spring flowers and ablaze with colour. The unexpected transformation of the classroom into a spring garden acted as a powerful provocation for the students to engage in exploring the plants. After they had time to enjoy the blossoms, I handed out paper and pencils and suggested that they fold and staple the pages together to make a small book. This book would become the documentation of their investigation of plants.

Once the students had constructed their books, I gave each student two beans: a dried bean from an unopened packet of scarlet runner seeds and one of the beans that had begun to germinate. I asked them to compare the seeds and to sketch the beans at different stages in their growth. At this point, I introduced a provocation by asking the students, before they opened up their beans, to draw a sketch of how they thought the inside of the bean would look after it was opened. I suggested that they begin to work together in small groups to share their ideas and keep a documentation of how these ideas changed as they examined one another's sketches and shared information.

Finally, they opened up their bean seeds, all of which were at different stages of germination, and compared what they saw to their previous sketches. I then asked the students to tell the class what they learned from this part of the investigation. Many of them were intrigued by the different patterns they discovered on the outside skin of their beans, others by the difference in size between the dried bean and the germinated seed. Most students were amazed at the complete little bean plant they found growing between the two cotyledons when they opened up the seed. The students then had time to complete their books. They became quite excited by their investigation and were inspired to write imaginative stories or to draw realistic or imaginative pictures of a bean plant, using the bean vines I grew earlier as a model for their sketches. Others wanted to find out more information on the plants in the classroom from the reference books. The students' books, when complete, were put on display in the classroom so we could all enjoy them.

In the second class, I taped large sheets of white paper onto the tables in the classroom. I poured acrylic paint (for painting on plastic surfaces) into glass jars with white paint added to some jars to make the pastel shades of spring blossoms. I also cut sheets of plastic to the same size as the paper on the tables and set them aside for use later. On each table, I provided a bowl of flowers, soft pencils, erasers, a tray of paint in clear glass jars, and brushes of various widths. There were also the vines growing in the glass jars and some dried vines and pods laid out in baskets.

We began the class by watching the section in the video *The Creative Spirit* in which the children in Reggio Emilia visited the poppy field and then made murals of the poppies and insects they saw in the field. The students, inspired by the children's murals of the poppy field, began in groups of three or four to design their own murals. They drew their motifs from their earlier investigation of bean seeds and from the spring flowers decorating the room. Once each group was satisfied with their basic outline for the mural, they laid the plastic sheets over the paper and used the design they drew on the paper under the plastic as a guide in painting the mural on the plastic sheet. Once the murals were finished, we hung them in the windows in the classroom. The effect of the spring sun shining through the transparent murals was breathtaking. We created a video and photographic documentation of the experience so that the class could revisit and reflect on the experience. The following examples are from the transcription of the students' discussion in the debriefing that followed the second class.

Melanie: The fresh flowers [were a provocation]. I felt it put me in the mood to draw flowers and so did having the smell of flowers too!

Chelsea: Colours [were a provocation] ... the variety of colours; we could mix the colours. No stipulation of what you had to do with the colours.

Marsha: I get really involved in the picture I am doing. And I like to pay close attention to details. It was really nice after not having painted for a long time to get kind of sucked into what you are doing and being able to express that in detail.

Kim: I also think too ... the approach where everyone works as a group—it doesn't put pressure on you to actually have to create something of your own. When you work together, like they say [in Reggio Emilia], you create one big picture, and it is better than one individual's art. So the whole creation of all of us working together makes for such a beautiful result instead of each being individualized.

This experience is an example of how the principles learned from Reggio Emilia have inspired the ECE program at Douglas College. The principles that were most in evidence in the investigation of plants were aesthetics, collaboration, reciprocity, and the use of natural materials. Aesthetics were also important in how the classroom was prepared and in the choice and presentation of the materials. At all stages of the experience, we tried to ensure that students were aware of the underlying value of aesthetics. Students experienced the principles of collaboration and reciprocity throughout their investigation of the bean seed and in their creation of the spring murals. Reciprocity was evident in the way students shared their knowledge of seeds and plants and in the way they worked collaboratively in designing and painting the murals. Natural materials were used thoughout the experience, especially as a provocation to capture the students' interest and to motivate them to investigate and represent their ideas about plants. This provocation was particularly effective in the spring after a long Canadian winter.

Baerbel Jaeckel*, the teacher from the Quadra Island Preschool, came to Douglas College to take part in the investigation of plants workshop. She wanted to try out some of the things we were doing at Douglas College with the children in the preschool. In a documentation panel, she said about the workshop, "I could sense the energy from over there—there was this calmness and this concentration and I could not believe what I saw—how everyone was so involved and the paintings that came out of it were really beautiful—and see how the sun makes the red [shine through the plastic up on the window]." She returned to Quadra Island inspired to try out an investigation of plants with the children in the preschool.

On her return, she provided the children with sunflower seeds to plant in small plastic cups so they could observe the growth of the plant through the clear plastic of the cup. In the next few weeks, each time the children came to school, they examined the plastic cups and noted how the roots were beginning

*Reproduced courtesy of Baerbel Jaeckel

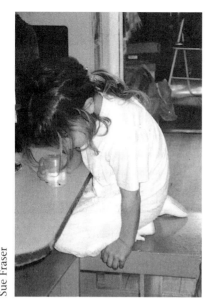

Observing the germination of sunflower seeds

to fill the lower part of the cups with "squiggly white lines." She encouraged the children to represent their ideas verbally and in drawings and paintings of the seeds as they grew. In group time the children moved their bodies, stretching their arms and wriggling their fingers to show how their seed was growing into a sunflower. The parents helped the children make a garden by digging and adding compost to a flower bed in the playground so that they could plant some sunflowers outside, as well.

When the seeds in the plant pots had grown to be about 10 cm tall, the children gathered around the table to shake one of the plants out onto a pie plate. They carefully examined the roots, discussed how they were connected to the stem, and speculated on when the flower would appear. Baerbel suggested that the children use the Plasticine she had put out on the table to make three-dimensional pictures of their sunflowers in bloom. The pictures that the children made captured many of the details they had observed as the seed grew into a sunflower. They used thin strips of Plasticine for the stem, and a few children amazed us when they captured the fragility of the stem by making curves in the Plasticine. They placed the leaves carefully two by two up the stem, exactly as they had seen them on their own plants. Some children rolled fine threads of Plasticine and joined them to the end of the stem for roots and placed a cluster of leaves at the tip of the stem to represent the stage of growth their plant had reached. Other children went further and made a flower with a round centre and petals radiating outward, just like the sunflower they had seen on the seed packet and like the one that would appear on the plant in a few weeks.

Symbolic representation of sunflowers

Examining the roots of the sunflowers

The children's ability to render their ideas in a three-dimensional medium to represent realistically what they had observed and what they predicted would happen to the flower was remarkable. Their achievement reinforced for me how, in following the Reggio Emilia approach as best as we can without the assistance of an atelierista, we have encouraged children to produce detailed representational art at a much younger age than we had previously believed possible.

In the fall, when the children returned to school, Baerbel took them outside to examine the sunflowers they had planted in the garden in the spring. She helped the children pick a sunflower head and brought it over to a rug on the grass, where they examined the flower.

Baerbel: How do you get started? You poke your finger inside.

Emma: I just want to get a seed out ... nothing inside.

Baerbel: I wonder why there are no seeds inside?

John: We could shake them all out.

Kelsey (discovering an insect): Bug! Bug!

Baerbel: That bug needs to live—there is lots of room....

Jamie: We could put seed heads on the blanket and shake it.

Amanda: Mine has one little one and one big one.

Baerbel had brought out a book called *Backyard Sunflower,* by Elizabeth King (1993), which she looked at with the children. They recalled how they had planted the sunflower seeds in the spring. Looking at the pictures in the book, they began to compare them with their own experiences with sunflowers.

Watering the sunflowers

Emma: It needs earth to grow. It has to have roots, the roots make it stand up, they attach it to the ground. The water goes into the roots and makes it grow. The plant needs water to grow just like people.

Amanda: I took my seeds and my plant home. It grew up 'til it was so big we couldn't touch the seeds. It was growing slow. It had lots of time to grow tall. We were giving it water.

Kelsey (picking out the seeds from the sunflower head): I know! I can plant these then next year I will have lots of seeds.

(Baerbel Jaeckel, Observation, October 8, 1998, Quadra Island Preschool)

Baerbel compiled photographs and transcriptions of the conversations in an album to create a documentation of the project, from planting the seeds in the spring to harvesting the heads in the fall. The documentation demonstrated the depth of understanding that children had developed over the seven months. From the conversation among Emma, Amanda, and Kelsey, it can be seen that in a classroom that supported investigation, the children had built a fairly accurate theory of how a plant goes through the cycle of growth, from seed to plant and back to seed again, from their observations, from their actions on real materials, and from the books they had read.

EMBARKING ON AN INVESTIGATION OF EAGLES

In the following documentation of the "Observation of a Baby Eagle" carried out at Marpole Oakridge Preschool in Vancouver, the children and teachers investigate eagle behaviour and share with us their discoveries*.

Linda Murdoch

Drawing of eagle

After a stormy night, the children were excited by all the branches that had been blown down by the wind in their playground. They ran around picking up sticks and chasing each other around the playground. The teachers Natsuko Motegi and Linda Murdoch were worried that someone was going to get hurt so they called the children and (to quote from the documentation) Linda writes "…after casually mentioning that birds used these kinds of

*Reproduced courtesy of Linda Murdoch

sticks to build nests. Much to my surprise, Aaron, Ethan and Caden started to build a nest! After collecting and placing many sticks in a found hollow in the sand they sat on it, first just one at a time, and then they wiggled around and made room for all three of them. This play continued for a couple of days and we saw them fly off from their nest flapping their wings to find more sticks, bringing them back to make it bigger.

We decided to show them a website we had heard about. It is a live web camera of an eagle on a nest in Sidney, B.C. The baby eagle had just hatched from its egg and the children were able to see it, watch the parent feed it, and gently sit down on top of it to keep it warm."

The children in this preschool have had a great deal of experience drawing their ideas and theories. It was no surprise that as they checked the video every day they chose to draw the nest and the eagles and carried on lengthy discussions around the topic.

The Daddy brought food.

The Mommy sits on the eggs so they can be nice and warm.

It's her turn to eat because she was hungry from feeding the baby.

We decided to talk about some factual information at group time. We discussed using books from the library to help us find answers—what they ate, how they caught their food. We drew their attention to the shape of the beak and the "talons" on their feet. We found that they have four toes, three in the front and one in the back. The children found this all very interesting and had so much to talk about.

They eat food with their feet because they don't have hands, they have wings.

Linda Murdoch

More detailed drawing of eagle

The beak is down.

When he pecks on a tree he has to go like this. (He tilts his head way back so the curved beak will peck on the tree.)

Later, as the children drew and made three-dimensional representations of the eagles, it was clear how carefully they had observed and remembered details from the illustrations in the books they had examined.

The feathers are brown, like chocolate.

The head it's like white chocolate.

After deciding that we would make an eagle's nest we went on a walk to collect sticks. There was discussion on how the eagles got the sticks to stay together and they listened, at group time, to each other's theories. Some thought they had glue, but others realized that eagles can't carry glue. Someone, drawing on their knowledge of trees, suggested the "glue" was the sap inside the sticks. There was also the idea that: "They don't use anything, they just pile them up."

Many of the children described how the eagles used their mouths and feet to carry and place the sticks. There was no shortage of ideas and everyone was so eager to share their thoughts.

Sometimes they use their mouth and hold with feet, but they let go.

Perhaps they put them with their wings.

While looking at the nest on the computer the children could see all the centre of the nest filled with grass and soft things We invited them to bring something soft to place in the centre of our nest. The next day many of the children arrived with leaves, flowers, grass, feathers, soft pipe cleaner (for a perch), and even a sock. They carefully placed them inside the nest. Once it was finished we turned our thoughts to making an eagle to sit on it.

Linda Murdoch

Building an eagle nest

The teachers decided on papier-mâché as the best kind of material for the children to create their eagle. They had a discussion about what would be the best shape to make the eagle's body. After drawing circles and ovals they decided to form the chicken wire into an oval shape as a base for the papier-mâché for the eagle's body. As a group they tore paper strips and then took turns applying the strips and glue to the wire form. When the body was dry, the children painted it and one child cut a circle and painted it green. He commented that he had seen a picture in a book of an eagle with a green eye! Later he made a second eye for the eagle on the other side of the head.

Unfortunately the eagles had by this time decided to poop on the camera lens, which brought viewing the eagles to a close. For the children, however, the project had reached a successful conclusion. The eagle they had made sat majestically in the nest keeping the little babies they had made earlier warm and safe.

Linda Murdoch

The nesting eagle

Deconstruction:

What made this investigation of eagles so successful? First, it grew out of the children's excitement about the sticks they found in the playground that later were used to build the nest the children used for dramatic play. The teachers by listening closely to the children realized that this could be a topic the children would be interested in finding more about. Very important too was the time some of the children spent pretending to be birds flying to and fro from the nest. It seems that through their own dramatic play the children themselves took ownership of the project. The teachers' interest in the world around gave them the idea to access the TV channel that furthered the children's knowledge about eagles rearing their babies in the wild. The teachers were able to support the children with suggestions and materials to give them the tools and encouragement to represent their thinking. Ongoing documentation of the project informed the parents, who could then join their children in observing the eagles, discuss what they saw on TV, and contribute to the building of the nest.

FACTORS THAT PROMOTE INVESTIGATION IN THE PRESCHOOL CLASSROOM

Teachers

- see themselves as equal partners in the learning process

- pay attention to the child's thinking rather than feeling responsible for teaching facts or concepts

- encourage children to make their thinking visible, either verbally or by drawing, painting, or using three-dimensional material such as Plasticine or clay

- provide a wide variety of materials that can be used in representing ideas and thoughts

- discover the child's intent and provide help (scaffolding) in realizing these intentions

- keep a trace of the children's experiences in the classroom through documentation

- welcome and learn to expect the unexpected

- slow down and give children the opportunity to explore topics in depth

- extend topics into all curriculum areas: art, science, math, social studies, and literature

- identify interesting questions ahead of time to provoke children's thinking
- question, rather than give answers
- model a sense of inquiry and curiosity
- encourage the use of imagination
- encourage children to work together as a group

Materials

- are of good quality, there is a wide variety, and are easily accessible
- can be used flexibly and in many creative ways
- are shown respect and used in a responsible way
- are arranged in unusual configurations in the classroom so they capture attention and provoke thinking
- are presented and used to reflect the principle of relationship
- are stored and presented to evoke the principle of transparency
- can be transformed by children
- reflect the principle of aesthetics in their presentation
- promote math and logical thinking skills
- promote early literacy

Environment as a Third Teacher

- invites investigation
- provokes investigation through the arrangement of materials and equipment
- reflects the principle of aesthetics in the planning of the space
- reflects transparency at many levels
- provides documentation for the purpose of information and as a means of revisiting previous experiences
- provides support for children to make their thinking visible
- offers children opportunities to learn and to respect and care for the natural environment

Chapter 10

Hummingbird

The Hundred Languages
of Children

Questions to Consider:

- What ingredients are necessary to foster the child's imagination in a preschool classroom?

- How do children make meaning of their world?

- What role does the environment as a third teacher play in the child's search for meaning?

- What is the role of play in promoting early literacy and math skills?

- How can we increase children's awareness of the community and culture in which they live?

- How does the Reggio Emilia approach contribute to our understanding of how children make meaning of their experiences in the preschool years?

- How do we help children develop environmental literacy?

The child has a hundred languages
(and a hundred hundred hundred more)

—Loris Malaguzzi

Children learn language because it is all around them; they absorb their mother tongue like a sponge. But to master language they have to not only hear but also use it in meaningful contexts. The educators of Reggio Emilia have made us aware that the same process applies to more than just spoken and written language.

One of the most important contributions Loris Malaguzzi and the educators in Reggio Emilia have made to preschool education in other parts of the world is in extending our awareness of how many languages children can use to express themselves and represent their world. Just as Howard Gardner has broadened our view of intelligence beyond valuing only the logical-mathematical and linguistic aspects of intelligence, so have the educators in Reggio Emilia increased our understanding of how children use graphic, verbal, literate, mathematical, symbolic, and imaginative play "and a hundred hundred hundred more" languages in making meaning of the world.

One of the greatest joys for a preschool teacher is being a part of the early experiences of young children as they make meaning of their world. What could compare to sharing in the discovery that the marks the children make in their early attempts to communicate in drawing and writing hold meaning for other people, or to being one of the first people to read or tell stories to children, which, as Bruno Bettelheim says, scatter seeds.

> Some of these will be working in his conscious mind right away; others will stimulate processes in his unconscious. Still others will need to rest for a long time until the child's mind has reached a state suitable for their germination, and many will never take root at all. But those seeds which have fallen on the right soil will grow into beautiful flowers and sturdy trees—that is, give validity to important feelings, promote insights, nourish hopes, reduce anxieties—and in doing so enrich the child's life at the moment and forever after (Bettelheim 1977, 154).

What a privilege it is for a parent and a teacher to realize that through choosing and reading stories to young children, they can sow small seeds that may grow and help them make meaning of their lives. By sharing books and encouraging early literacy in the preschool years, adults also have the ability to foster in children a lifelong love of reading and writing. "Stories told and stories heard: all develop individual 'pools of knowledge' as unique as fingerprints" (Goodman 1998).

For all of us, making meaning of our world is a lifelong endeavour. How we do this depends on our social context and on the tools we bring to the task. For Piaget, knowledge is primarily constructed through active interaction with the physical environment. According to Vygotsky, however, "cognitive construction is always socially mediated; it is influenced by present and past social interactions" (Bodrova and Leong 1996). The social context, therefore, profoundly influences how and what we think. Both Piaget and Vygotsky stress the value of play in the child's growing ability to make sense of the world. They both emphasize the value it holds for symbolic representation and symbolic action. For Vygotsky, however, there is the added value in the opportunities play provides for children to develop self-regularization through their social interaction in the group. From the educators in Reggio Emilia we have expanded our awareness of the many languages children use to make meaning of their world, and as teachers, we have learned from them the importance of our role as mediators of both the physical and social environment in the lives of children.

THE LANGUAGE OF IMAGINATION

Herbert Kohl, in his foreword to Gianni Rodari's book *The Grammar of Fantasy*, notes that Rodari envisions the teacher as "an adult who is with the children to express the best in himself or herself, to develop his or her own creative inclination, imagination, and constructive commitment" (1996). Rodari, a friend of Loris Malaguzzi, was influential in making the imagination a strong ingredient in the education of young children in Reggio Emilia. Rodari, an exceptionally creative children's author and teacher, had a great deal to say about imagination and creativity in school. "We have many intelligent theories about play, but we still do not have a phenomenology of the imagination, which gives life to play" (1996). Rodari states that when there is something wrong with society and it needs to be changed, "to change it, creative human beings are needed, people who know how to use their imaginations" (1996, 110–13). We can see the power of these ideas in the kind of early childhood education provided in Reggio Emilia. When imagination is valued and encouraged in all aspects of the curriculum, the classroom comes alive with the creative input of children and teachers. The result is rich and stimulating early childhood education.

There are many ways in which teachers can encourage imagination in their classrooms. For instance, they can make an assortment of fairy tales, folk tales, and picture books available to children. There are so many wonderful children's authors to choose from such as the Canadian author Warabe Aska, who takes children on a magical walk through Stanley Park in Vancouver in his book *Who Hides in the Park?* and through High Park in Toronto in *Who Goes to the Park?* There should be an assortment of materials for dressing up and playing out themes that are important in the children's lives. The old favourites are the housekeeping materials and the equipment for playing doctors, nurses, and firefighters. Then there are the dress-up clothes—the crowns and capes that the children use in dramatizing the characters they are introduced to in fairy stories.

The teachers in the Quadra Island Children's Centre transcribed the songs and stories the children made up as they swung on the swings in the playground. These transcriptions, which I recorded on February 3, 1998, gave the teachers insight into what the children were thinking about, which would allow them to plan the props they would set up later for the children's play.

Chloe: I am a princess. How about my name is Sunflower Rose and my big sister and the witch go in my car.

Serena: Sister! I am at McDonald's. We are almost at the ferry; turn off the car.

At a meeting that evening, the teachers and I noted how there were all the ingredients for a fairy tale in this dialogue. With the addition of props, including a crown and cape for the princess, a hat for the witch, and a large box for the car, and perhaps even the materials for the restaurant scene from McDonald's, the children's conversation could be developed further in their play. We also discussed whether there might be enough interest in the topic of fairy tales to make puppets of witches and princesses so that the children could create their own puppet show of a fairy tale. One of the teachers suggested putting out the fairy tale characters and the felt board to see if the children were interested in using the felt characters to tell or create their own fairy stories. We made the following recording as three girls, on one of many occasions in the next few weeks, used the felt board to tell one another imaginative fairy tales.

> The three girls were sitting in front of the felt board, and Serena told a fairy story.
>
> **Serena:** How about the prince be sleeping beauty? She growed and growed. She [the witch] got burnt by the candles.
>
> Serena made the felt figure of the prince, who had now become the sleeping beauty, chase the witch onto the candelabra above.
>
> **Serena:** She [the witch] got burned by the candles. The end.

The children had listened to many fairy stories that the teachers had read. It was interesting to see how the children were able to use the elements of a fairy tale in creating their own characters, a plot, a surprising transformation, and then, as in many fairy tales, with a victory of good over evil.

It was about this time, in the spring, that the teachers in the child care were joined by a practicum student, Barb, who is married to a local carver, Max Chickite, from the Kwakiutl Nation. She brought in many books of native legends from the West Coast and read them to the children. It was a wonderful extension from listening to fairy stories that originated in a land far away to hearing legends that had been created by the people

Sue Fraser

Max Chickite, a carver, visits the Quadra Island Children's Centre.

in the place where the children lived. One day, the practicum student invited her husband to visit the child care and bring in some of the drums, shakers, and masks he had carved to show the children. The following are excerpts from Susan Emery's* documentation of the visit, recorded in April 1998. (Each of the comments in the documentation of the experience is illustrated with photographs, all of which are compiled and attractively displayed in a folder.)

> Max told us that the button blanket represents the Big House and when "you dance in one for 20 minutes wearing a 30-pound blanket, it gets heavy."

> **Martyn:** We got to try on this stuff [the button cape, apron, white fur hat, and masks].

> **Kevin:** I like the sound of the shells rattling on the apron.

> Max showed us how the rattle is used by the first dancer, checking out the space before the other dancers begin. The rattle is for protection. He showed us his drum. Max told us that the drum represents the mother's heartbeat (or mother earth). It is sometimes calm, sometimes anxious. When it goes from a regular beat, a change or transformation is coming. All the children had a turn to play the drum.

> **Serena:** If you wipe the drum, it makes the sound of a killer whale.

> Max performed a dance for the children, demonstrating how the rattles and drum were used in traditional native dances. He then offered to stay and show the children how he made a carving. Everyone was thrilled.

> We all watched as Max took his chainsaw and began to cut the piece of wood he had found on the beach. As he carved, the wood began to take on the shape of an octopus. He told us that the octopus means change. It can change to the colour of the rocks if something is after it. He asked us if we had ever seen one in the water.

> **Barbara:** No, but I know they are real!

> **Max:** What do you guys think I should do with this?

> **Martyn:** Paint it!

> **Max:** If I leave it here would you all keep care of it for me?

> **Frazer:** Yeah!

The carving of the octopus, painted with traditional Kwakiutl designs, is now on the shelves with the other treasured objects that the teachers and children have collected over the year. It has become part of the beautiful display that the teachers were inspired to make after seeing slides of the environment in the preschools in Reggio Emilia which Lella Gandini and Carolyn Edwards showed at the symposium in North Vancouver.

The ingredients, therefore, necessary for fostering imagination in a preschool classroom are (1) an understanding of the value of rich fantasy play

---

*Reproduced courtesy of Susan Emery

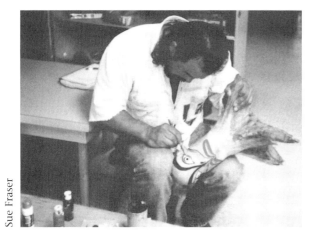
Carving the octopus

The finished carving on display

in a child's life, (2) the provision of a wide variety of materials in all aspects of the program, including literature, music, art, science, and dramatic play, and (3) a stimulating program that broadens children's horizons, that gives children opportunities to experience creativity and imagination through art, music, and literature. But perhaps what is even more powerful is for children to see for themselves someone, like Max the carver, using imagination and creativity in his own work.

CHILDREN'S PARTICIPATION IN THE NATURAL WORLD

Nature is imperfectly perfect, filled with loose parts and possibilities, with mud and dust, nettles and sky, transcendent hands-on moments and skinned knees. What happens when all the parts of childhood are soldered down, when the young no longer have the time or space to play in their family's garden, cycle home in the dark with the stars and moon illuminating their route, walk down through the woods to the river, lie on their backs on hot July days in the long grass, or watch cockleburs, lit by the morning sun, like bumblebees quivering on harp wires? What then? ...nature may inspire different kinds of creativity and different art than the built environment (Louv 2005, 96/7).

The children in the Quadra Island Children's Centre spend large parts of their day playing in the garden and often take walks in the forest surrounding their school. The teachers note that "....the children share a love and fascination for the garden; watching as the seeds sprout, the plants grow and various creatures come to visit or make their homes there. This all provides limitless opportunities for learning and imagination. Every year brings a new experience as we follow not a set "spring curriculum" but the interests of the children who are here now." The Invitation to the Garden Project, as can be seen from the following documentation, grew from a few simple questions in the initial stages to a complex all-encompassing exploration that helped develop in the children a sense of caring for living things in their environment. It also gave them the opportunity to use their imaginations and creativity to make their garden a welcoming place for birds.

Invitation to the Garden

The project began when one of the teachers noted:

"We have a scientist in our group, she can't go outside without looking for bugs, but she wants to bring them inside and then they end up dying!" This dilemma was shared first with the teachers and then with the children in the group. We decided that the next time anyone brought in a creature or found one outside, instead of putting it in a jar—or worse—we would ask them:

"Where did you find it?"

"Why is it there?"

"How would we feel if a giant hand plucked us out of our bed?"

The next time Maeve brought in a ladybug she had found in the garden, the children remembered to ask the above questions. She agreed to take the ladybug back outside so she could show them where she found it.

Teacher: Why do you think the ladybug chose to live there?

Maeve: Because it was shady and sunny. It wouldn't want to get hot. It's a good hiding place because of the flowers and leaves.

The teachers encouraged the children to draw pictures of where the ladybug lived. Then the teachers suggested that the children find other places that animals lived in their environment. They were given cameras to record their findings. The children photographed among other things snails, spider webs, and worm tunnels in the compost. The children by sharing their explorations with each other became interested in all aspects of the garden. Over the next few weeks, they made compost, planted seeds, designed and built arches out of driftwood for the honeysuckle to climb, and built a bean tepee. The children were also encouraged to draw their observations, dramatize the bird's nesting behaviours, and paint a mural of their garden. The teachers observed that the children had become particularly interested in the birds. The teachers and children began to think of ways they could entice more birds into their garden.

Ella drew a picture of a family of birds each on a separate piece of paper to put outside to invite other birds to visit the garden. She asked us to Mactac them so they wouldn't get ruined if it rained. The teachers asked the children what else would birds like to have in the garden?

Sophie: Get some food for them. Birds like to take baths. We can put water in a basket that has no holes in the bottom.

Several children became interested in following up on Sophie's idea of a birdbath, using clay rather than a basket. We started off with a large lump of clay. Emma and Hannah took small pieces from it and went to work at another table individually, while the other four worked together on a large one. Right away the children experienced the difficulty of making a hollow in the lump but were determined to work at it. When they at last formed a bowl for the birdbath out of a large lump of clay, they began to make suggestions. They discussed the colours they would paint the birdbath, and added many other parts and decorations. Emma returned with a tap she had made at the other table. They all discussed it before allowing her to attach it to the side. Maeve made a bridge for the birds that did not want to get wet and added some worms to go over the bridge. She called it a "worm bridge." Emma made bath toys which started several others making toys and couches for the birds to sit on to get dry.

After the clay pieces had been fired, the children had many ideas about where to place them in the garden. They decided to put the couches and toys on the posts around the fence. The birdbath itself ended up in the long garden where the children agreed it would get the most sunshine and privacy. The teachers asked the children how they would know if the birds had used the baths when they weren't looking.

Ella: There will be footprints.

Dynah: Little wet dots around it would mean that the birds have been there.

Deconstruction:

"The Invitation to the Garden Project" described above grew out of the teacher's concern for the bugs that died when Maeve brought them into the classroom. The teachers shared their concern with the class as a whole. From the discussions that followed, the children set off on an investigation of the animals living in their garden. This led to the idea of creating the beautiful birdbaths out of clay to invite more birds to visit their garden.

The teachers in the Children's Centre, as can be seen in the above project, have an image that views a child "…as active and who along with us [their teachers], searches every day to understand something, to draw out a meaning, to grasp a piece of life" (Rinaldi 2006, 112). The teachers believe children to be natural scientists who do many things real scientists do. For instance, the children in their investigations in the garden observed that "Maeve's bug needed both shade and sun, flowers and leaves and a good hiding place to protect it from 'frogs and bugs that might eat it'." During the project the children were seen to be observing, inferring, making predictions, hypothesizing, and communicating their findings just like real scientists. The teachers were partners with the children, asking questions to provoke thinking, listening carefully to their questions and concerns, and following their lead in what direction the investigation should take. The teachers also ensured that there were materials and tools available for the children to investigate and make their thinking visible. The children, for instance, were given cameras to record their discoveries of animal habitats in the playground and draw their observations. They were encouraged to dramatize the bird's nesting behaviours, for as Sobel states "…children need to become animals before they can learn about them or save them" (Sobel 2008, 75). The children were given opportunities to make graphic representations of their ideas, for instance, by drawing designs for the birdbath and painting a mural of their garden. They were given materials such as clay to create a bath and toys to encourage the birds to visit the garden. From this project it can be seen how important it is for children to have experiences that develop a sense of caring and responsibility for the natural world. The children's investigations of what the animals in their environment needed fostered their imaginations and creativity as they worked together drawing, painting, and making the birdbath for their garden.

The Maple Tree

The children not only play in the garden, they often go with their teachers on walks into the forest around the school. On one occasion the children were taken to visit an ancient maple tree growing in a grove of elephant ears in the forest. They took the children to the tree to look at it more closely to help them with the building of the tree inside the classroom. The teachers had thought the children would be interested in finding out more about the characteristics of trees. They intended to ask the children questions such as: What holds it down? Are the branches all the same size? If we could go into the tree how would we get in? The children, however, on their walk back to the centre had a lengthy conversation about fairies, especially forest fairies and their world.

When the children were asked what they would like to do with materials from the imagination box, it became apparent they wanted to build a tree with a small space for two children to fit inside. A letter was sent home asking the parents if they had any tubes to use for the project. First, they gave the children paper towel rolls to experiment with building a tree on a small scale and then began work on building a floor to ceiling tree.

The children worked cooperatively assembling the cones in a like manner (to the paper towel rolls). They left a large crack in the middle for the door.

Kazu: The door is too high, you can't get in.

Boden: We'll use a ladder.

They explored the tube inside and out. On another day, a different group of children tried solving the problem in a different way. They also crawled in and around the tube;

however, this time before drawing the tree they all drew two friends and then drew the tree around them. The teachers noticed that the tree in all their drawings was fatter at the bottom. The children were then given two toy people and a paper towel roll to experiment with on a smaller scale. They discovered that only one toy would fit in at a time. A bigger tube was found and the teachers asked the children to redraw their ideas, after seeing the new tube, and show in their drawings how they could add a space (inside the tree trunk) with a door to the tree to solve the problem of fitting two people in at the same time. Boden showed us his idea and Kazu noticed the door in the middle of the tree trunk.

Kieran: The door could be a circle. The shape could be like this with branches all over the top and bark.

The two boys see if they can both fit into the tree

The children complete the project by making a door they can open and close

Eventually the maple tree was built by slicing the tubes and joining them together to make a wider circumference. A circular door was cut into the trunk so the children could climb right inside the tree. The whole exterior of the tree was covered with papier-mâché and painted. The children returned to their idea of having fairies come to live in the classroom by building them a fairy playground in the sand table.

Deconstruction:

The teachers took the children out into the natural environment to visit an ancient maple tree in the forest. The children responded to the tree, not in the way the teachers expected, but by using their imaginations and creativity. They came up with the idea of building a tree big enough for themselves to climb into in their classroom.

The teachers encouraged the children to work as a group, sharing ideas and materials. First they were helped to build small prototypes of the tree to solve spatial problems, etc. Then they transferred their ideas into building a floor to ceiling model of the tree. Parents were involved in supplying tubes to form the skeleton for the trunk. Making a door presented a challenge that the children as a group were able to overcome. Eventually with a great deal of cooperation the tree was complete and a playground created in the sandbox for the fairies who the children thought visited the classroom at night!

Bringing Imagination to the Classroom

Inspired by the work of Gianni Rodari and by the imaginative approach to early childhood education in Reggio Emilia, the instructors in the ECE program at Douglas College have tried to ensure that we emphasize in the preparation of teachers of young children the power of the imagination. Herbert Kohl, in his foreword to Gianni Rodari's *The Grammar of Fantasy*, writes, "There is no imagination curriculum or pedagogy of the imagination in our schools. Yet, if as the poet Wallace Stevens wrote, 'the imagination is the power of the mind over possibilities of things,' then to neglect the imagination is also to impoverish children's worlds and to narrow their hopes" (1996, ix). When we neglect the imagination in early childhood education we not only impoverish children, we also impoverish the students who will become teachers of young children in the future.

We have, therefore, especially in the art, literature, music, science, and social studies classes and in the core curriculum course, Children Teaching Teachers, tried to encourage students to become aware of how valuable it is to use their own imaginations in planning curricula for young children. As a result, the instructors have tried to model for the students the value of using imagination in our own approach to teaching the courses at the college.

Just before the students begin their first session of Children Teaching Teachers and when the weather is still good in the fall, we took the students to a small park called the Friendship Gardens two blocks away from the college in New Westminster. These gardens are part of a small park that a particularly imaginative landscape architect designed in recognition of New Westminster's sister city, Moriguchi, Japan. The park has many unexpected features, such as a bridge that seems to end in the middle of the stream but then takes a sharp right turn to reach the far bank and a miniature mountain that provides a secret lookout over the stream that flows through the gardens. The relationship between Canada and Japan has not always been as amicable as it is now. The architect has placed, therefore, at the entry to the park a pole on which is written in English, French, Japanese, and Spanish the words "Let Peace Prevail on Earth." Here, we begin our walk through the park with the students. We follow a small stream that flows down the hill and tumbles over small water-falls into tranquil pools of water, where mallard ducks swim amongst the lily pads and dragonflies skim the surface of the water. The banks of the stream are bordered with unusual trees, such as weeping mulberries and flowering fruit trees. There are no blossoms at this time of year, but many of the branches of the trees hanging over the banks of the stream are adorned with spider webs.

In preparation for our visit to the park we read in class the children's book *Who Hides in the Park?,* by the Japanese author Warabe Aska, to the students. The story, which takes the reader on a magical journey through Stanley Park in Vancouver, is a wonderful way to provoke the students to use their imaginations as they explore the park. We give each group of students two tasks to carry out, which are written on a sheet in the form of a provocation and are handed out to the groups as they set off on their walk through the park.

Provocation 1: Walk downhill along the bank of the stream and stop at one of the duck ponds. Your challenge is to think of ways you might cross the stream without wading across. Be as imaginative as a child might be in thinking up solutions. Appoint a recorder to keep a trace of your ideas, and then sketch the ones you find most interesting.

Provocation 2: Discover at least two unexpected things about the park. (The landscape architect, for instance, has designed some unusual ways of crossing the stream himself.)

Douglas College ECE students considering Provocation 1

Sue Fraser

Predictions: Draw up a flow chart, similar to the one the teachers in Reggio Emilia created of the adult predictions for the Amusement Park for Birds, and predict how you may use some of these ideas with children as you plan your next session of Children Teaching Teachers.

Responses to Provocation 1

The students suggested many imaginative ways of crossing the stream. They thought they might be able to ride across on a duck's back or perhaps stuff a cushion with the duck feathers lying on the banks of the pond and float across. They were inspired by the way the spider webs stretched over the surface of the water to spin their own webs to cross the stream. Some groups thought of using the branches of the weeping mulberry tree to weave a rope ladder and make a swinging bridge across the stream. Someone suggested weaving a small basket and asking a dragonfly to carry them across in the basket.

Predictions

Each group drew up a flow chart listing their predictions of topics they thought the children might be interested in pursuing when they visited the college to participate in Children Teaching Teachers (see Figure 10.1). The experience in the park stimulated the students to think of activities they could prepare to promote the children's learning about topics of possible interest, such as water, air, plants, insects, and birds. The students were also inspired by the aesthetics in the design of the park. This increased their own awareness of the importance of aesthetics in planning the environment and art materials for the children.

Documentation

The students returned to the college with the sketches they had made of their imaginative ideas for crossing the stream. Each group developed documentation that incorporated their sketches, the written transcriptions of their discussions of their ideas with the other students in the group, the web they had drawn up, showing their predictions of how they could use the ideas with children, the activities they developed in their sessions with the children, and the photographs taken at each stage in the process. The documentation panels were displayed outside the classrooms so all the people involved in Children Teaching Teachers could see the process the students had followed in their planning and presentation of experiences for the children.

FIGURE 10.1   Flow Chart Developed by Group 4 for Children Teaching Teachers:

Adult Predictions in Their Initial Meeting Together

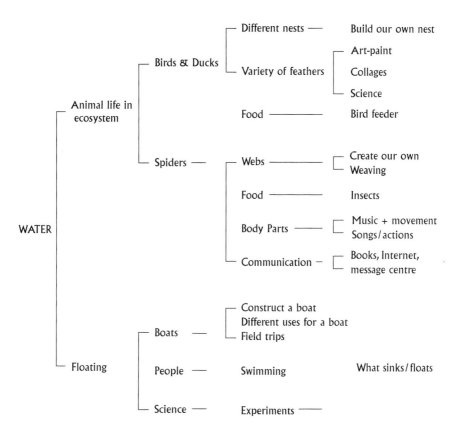

ADULT PREDICTIONS
From discovering and observing the environment we found a variety of ways we could
cross the pond. It was through our observations that we found the interests that led to animal life
and floating devices.

We believe that Gianni Rodari would have been happy to know how his suggestions for "thinking outside the box," described in his book *The Grammar of Fantasy*, had inspired us to encourage the use of imagination in the preparation of teachers.

LEARNING THE LANGUAGE OF ART

Talking about art is another language, one that children can learn if they hear it and are encouraged to use it. Art has its own vocabulary, like other subjects, and children can learn to communicate as artists if teachers expose them to the vocabulary artists use to think and talk about their art. Children need to hear words that artists use to describe texture, line, shape, pattern, and design in their art work. In talking to children about their art, for example, the teacher can use language that focuses on the elements like line and colour. "Look at the swirling lines, and how the wet paint sparkles. When it is dry how will it look, will the colours look any different?" "You used lots of round, yellow shapes for making your sunflowers." Or, "I feel happy when I look at the pointy lines in your painting; they make me want to laugh!" If the art-work is three-dimensional, and the child has used clay or collage materials, the teacher can talk about form or texture. "Your clay piece is made of rounded shapes. Look how the pattern you have made in the clay with the end of the stick matches the round form of your clay."

Teachers can ask questions about the children's art work that will urge children to think more deeply about what they have seen. For instance, as the teacher and child examine a collage using shells, the teacher might say, "Do you remember how the mallard duck's feathers reminded us of the inside of a sea shell?" It is also important for children to build skills in self-evaluation. "Are you happy with the way the paint dripped down the paper here? Does it look like you want it to look?" Children also need to learn vocabulary to respond to art. "Look at how the artist used droopy lines in his painting. How do they make us feel?"

THE RICHNESS OF CHILDREN'S WORDS

Children, in the early years, work hard to make meaning of the world around them. It is often in the preschool years that they first show an interest in encoding and decoding the written word. One of the first indications of an emerging interest in learning how to read and write is children's recognition of environmental print, in letters such as the *M* for McDonald's restaurants and words such as STOP on traffic signs. At about the same time they begin to assign meaning to their scribbles and may even expect adults to be able to read their "writing." These early attempts at writing usually emerge spontaneously from the child's drawings. Bob Steele* outlines the connection between a child's drawing and writing and notes how adults can support this process. He writes,

> Drawing evolves from single configurations into elaborate pictures.
> Human subjects are depicted in action and placed in environments.
> At this point pictures now become the pathfinder for using single

*Reproduced courtesy of Bob Steele

Sue Fraser

Drawing evolves into elaborate pictures

words to describe complex situations.... 'This is Mom holding my hand. We are crossing the street.' Drawing is a rewarding language activity in its own right, but its value to literacy is heightened when children and parents (and teachers) talk and write (print) single words and short sentences about the drawing's content. This can happen only when adults take the time to be involved. (Steele 1996)

Note, however, that the principle of respect rules out actually writing on children's art without their permission, or requiring a child to write on a drawing. Instead, teachers can write on a separate sheet or encourage children to attempt writing in whatever format they prefer.

As children become more aware of the need to use conventional symbols for writing, their drawings become dotted with shapes and approximations of the letters of the alphabet. The most recognizable letters are often those they have learned to print in writing their own names. Gradually, children begin to grasp the concept of sign—that written symbols can convey meaning. They combine mock letters and later more conventional print to form words. The children, at first, use invented spelling to express their ideas; it is only later that they become aware of the need to use conventional spelling in their attempts at writing (Clay 1975).

The attitude of adults is a critical factor in fostering young children's literacy. Children whose parents have read to them since they were infants will probably develop a strong interest in learning to read books themselves. As well, children who have received an enthusiastic response to their initial attempts to communicate in writing will probably be motivated to try harder to learn how to use conventional print in expressing themselves. Parents and teachers also help children in their progression toward becoming fully fledged readers and writers by providing them with many authentic literary experiences. They can encourage the child to "write" letters, perhaps to other family members who they know will appreciate the child's attempts at beginning writing. Children can be encouraged to write lists and messages for their family or the teacher at school (Harste, Woodward, and Burke in Asseline

The communication centre in the Children Teaching Teachers program

1997). In preschool, teachers can enrich the children's play environment with literacy materials. They can provide note pads beside the toy telephone, recipe cards by the stove, and a receipt book by the cash register. At the University of British Columbia Child Study Centre a few years ago, the teachers set up the writing area as a newspaper office and encouraged the children to pretend to be reporters and interview one another and the teachers. The next morning, one of the families woke up to find their young son missing. They found him out on the sidewalk, notebook in hand, interviewing the workmen who were repairing their street!

There are many opportunities for including early literacy experiences in projects such as the bridge-building project at the Vancouver Child Study Centre. The children, in this case, had many opportunities to practise their writing skills as they made signs for controlling the traffic on the bridges they built in the classroom and outside in the playground. Roskos and Vukelich state that teachers should "encourage 'littering' the play environment with print. If print 'flows through' the play world of young children, then there is greater likelihood that children will become familiar with it in ways that are not only informing but also pleasurable and motivating" (Roskos and Vukelich 1991, 33).

Setting up message centres like those the teachers have created in the preschools in Reggio Emilia is another way of encouraging early literacy in young children. When the Canadian delegation visited Reggio Emilia in 1993, we noticed how much careful thought had gone into designing the space and materials in the message centres in the classrooms. The space allowed a small group of children to work together. The children all had their own mailboxes, which were labelled with a graphic symbol and their name. On shelves nearby were good-quality paper and writing tools for the children to use in writing their messages. There were photocopies of pictures of animals and other objects and copies of the children's photographs in a variety of sizes, so even children who were not yet readers and writers could send messages to one

Sue Fraser

The thank-you letter to the Daycare fairy, Quadra Island Children's Centre

another using pictures. On a display board above the desk the children had pinned a random selection of their written messages to one another. In addition, a computer and a typewriter were set on low shelves for the children to use.

The message centre provides children with the incentive to read and write in an authentic way. As children write notes to one another and receive messages from their friends, they become increasingly aware of the need to use conventional symbols as a means of communication. The message centre enables children to co-construct knowledge as children with assistance or scaffolding from teachers and more knowledgeable peers produce representational work ahead of their independent level of performance, that is, they achieve more with assistance than on their own (Vygotsky 1962). The message centre enables children to perform higher-level mental functions; for instance, they move from reactive attention to more focused attention, and they begin to use deliberate memory for learning the conventional symbols in writing letters, words, and, eventually, sentences.

> Written speech is not just oral speech on paper but represents a higher level of thinking. It has a profound influence on development because
>
> 1. It makes thinking more explicit
>
> 2. It makes thinking and the use of symbols more deliberate
>
> 3. It makes the child aware of the elements of language (Bodrova and Leong 1996, 102).

The teachers in the Quadra Island Children's Centre created a communication centre in the classroom by setting a cupboard with slots for mailboxes beside a desk with a drawer full of assorted writing materials. Carrying on with the interest that the children had shown in fairy stories, the teachers, who hoped to provoke the children's interest in literacy, wrote a note to each child from the Daycare fairy. The children found these notes in their mailboxes the next day when they came to school. They decided to write their own replies as well as write a group thank-you note to the fairy on a large sheet of paper.

CREATING A MESSAGE CENTRE

The students at Douglas College are encouraged to set up message centres as part of their presentations for the children during Children Teaching Teachers. This is especially important in the third semester, when some of the children who participate in Children Teaching Teachers come from the grade one class in the local elementary school. The instructors ask each group of students to generate a list of materials and equipment they think they will need to create a message centre, such as the following:

- a small table and chairs or desks that can be placed against the wall

- shelves on which to set up small boxes so each child will have their own mailbox. Transparent boxes with a slit in the lid are best but are difficult to find, so students may use shoe boxes with windows cut out of the front and covered with acetate. One group of students used clear plastic pop bottles with the tops cut off and set horizontally, attached to each other with duct tape.

- labels for each mailbox—stickers with a symbol chosen by each child, a photograph, or a self-portrait labelled with the child's name

- shelving units

- a typewriter or a computer with a printer (optional)

- a wide assortment of pens, pencils, paper, cards, and small pads

- envelopes and stamps

- an alphabet or ABC books

The instructors encourage the students to consider principles such as aesthetics, reciprocity, and collaboration in setting up the centres.

Aesthetics

In planning the physical layout for the message centres, the students put considerable thought into how they can make them visually appealing and inviting for the children. They often define the space by draping a length of fabric from the ceiling to the wall above the tables and chairs. One group of students, taking their inspiration from the slides they had seen of the environments in

Reggio Emilia, hung a clear plastic sheet from the ceiling to the floor to separate the message centre from the rest of the room. The students often include items such as a small bowl of flowers or an attractive lamp on the writing table. They provide good-quality paper, attractive cards, and writing tools in glass or pottery jars set out attractively on a shelf for the children.

Reciprocity

The principle of reciprocity is evident in the way the students establish a process that children can follow in sending messages and writing responses. One group of students helped the children draw a symbol to identify each child's mailbox. They then photocopied these symbols and put them into a small container labelled with each child's name. The children can then use these symbols as stamps. If a child decides to send a message to a friend, for instance, she can find the symbol for the friend's name, paste it on the envelope or on the message, and then match it with the one on the mailbox of the child to whom the message is to be delivered.

Collaboration

The message centre provides many children with opportunities to share their literacy skills as they assist one another in writing names and words on their messages. The principle of collaboration is much in evidence as the students practise their skills in scaffolding the children's emergent writing abilities and help them to read the messages they receive in their mailboxes.

The instructors, in debriefing the experience with the students, discuss what the benefits are to providing a message centre for the children. The students have often observed how the centre encourages positive social behaviours, such as sharing and taking turns. They often comment on how it gives the children a means of relating to one another and the teacher in a small group. They find that, especially during the first session, one of the students needs to stay in the centre while the children are using it in order to demonstrate the procedure. For instance, at first they may have to help the children to select paper and writing tools suitable for their purpose, for example, pencils and paper for messages and coloured felt pens for invitations or birthday cards. The students find that the children often ask them for help in writing words and sentences for their messages. Sometimes they need to remind the children to sign their names and then help them to find the recipient's box. The students find that as they work with the children in the centre they learn a great deal about emergent literacy. They learn how to identify the different stages of emergent writing, and they practise helping children write letters, words, and even sentences. Some of the younger preschool children sometimes need help in writing their own or their friends' names on their letters. The message centre seems to encourage a sense of belonging in the group. It provides children and teachers with a natural way to form relationships with one another. Later, the children themselves begin to suggest ideas for the message centre. One group of children suggested writing messages in bottles and then floating them across the water-play table.

In later sessions, if the children's interest seems to flag, the students discuss ways they can vary materials to make the message centre more inviting for the children. One group of students solved this problem in a creative way. They designed and built a double-sided telephone booth so that a person on each side of the booth could use a telephone, made out of two tin cans connected by a string, to speak to the person in the booth on the opposite side. The telephone booth had a number of additional features that encouraged the children to develop their communication skills as they played with the telephones. Inside the booth the students had pasted on the wall a telephone directory listing the emergency numbers for the police, ambulance, and fire station. The students made a number grid for the children to use as a dial to punch in telephone numbers. On a shelf beside the phone the students also provided note pads and pencils so the children could take down messages. The following extracts are taken from observations in the students' journal of the children using the phone booth.

> To extend and expand on the children's interactions and language development and early literacy skills, we introduced a phone booth to the dramatic play area. The children used problem-solving skills, expressive and receptive language, sharing, and turn taking and practised social skills in learning how to conduct conversations. The children, in writing messages, were given the opportunity to develop emergent writing.

J: I'm J. You can call me J.

I: What are you doing?

J: Nothing. I don't know.

I: What are you doing?

J: I'm going to a friend's house.

B: Hi.

J: Who's that?

B: It's B.

J: I'm J.

B: I'm busy. I have to go.

By adding the telephone we wanted to explore other forms of communication. We hoped to provide opportunities for the children to develop relationships and build their social and communicative skills. (Groups 1 and 4 students' journal, Douglas College, February 1998)

ENVIRONMENTAL LITERACY

It is our responsibility as early childhood educators to help young children develop love and care for the natural environment. As the world becomes increasingly urbanized, children are having less and less opportunity to have joyful experiences in the natural world. The result is they grow up feeling alienated, ignorant, and perhaps even fearful of nature. Are we rearing a new generation with negative attitudes towards the natural environment, when more than ever we need people in the future who will nurture and care for all living things on the earth?

Environmental literacy should be as important a part of children's education as are the other literacies in math, language arts, and the visual arts, etc. As teachers, one of our major priorities should be to ensure that children develop a close personal relationship with nature. We need to provide them with many enjoyable, stimulating experiences exploring and learning about the natural world so they grow to love it and care about it. Sobel states that children need safe, free time in nature "...not just a concept to learn or a problem to solve, but to become friends with trees and animals" (Sobel 2008). As a result we hope they will grow up comfortable in the natural world, curious to find out more about it and above all wanting to protect and live in harmony with it.

As teachers of young children, we have the power to achieve this. We can provide them with a multitude of experiences: planting seeds, harvesting vegetables, composting leftover snacks, and taking field trips to learn first hand more about the natural environment in their corner of the world. But there is more we can do, we need to help children learn environmental literacy. Children need a vocabulary to build and express their knowledge about math, science, etc., but they also need a vocabulary to talk and write about their experiences in the natural world. We also need to think carefully about the kind of language and metaphors we use when we discuss environmental topics with children. Kelly Young writes that we must become aware of the language we use around nature and avoid commodifying it. She notes that much of the language we use to talk about nature unconsciously makes us see it as a resource there for humans to exploit. For instance, we will talk about "woodlots" instead of "woodland." We also use mechanistic metaphors to explain natural phenomena, such as words like pump and valve to describe how the blood flows through a living organism (Young 2010). This vocabulary has the effect of desensitizing us to the natural world.

As teachers, we need to help children "grow" their knowledge about the natural world, but we also need to enable them to be fluent in their use of environmental language so that they have both the skills and the tools to become enthusiastic guardians of the natural world.

THE LANGUAGE OF NUMBERS

In one school we visited in Reggio Emilia, we noted that the communication centre was being used more as a centre for mathematics. On the wall were hung large graphs made of small, colourful pictures of fruit pasted in horizontal lines which showed how many children liked each fruit. A number of tape measures hung down from a shelf. Two children were busy weighing real fruit and nuts in a beautiful, antique brass balance scale and recording the weight on a sheet of paper.

The teachers at the Vancouver Child Study Centre were also interested in expanding children's early attempts at using conventional symbols in writing to using numerical symbols for expressing simple math concepts. They also wished to find out more about how well the children understood concepts of time. They decided that although many of the children knew the purpose of a calendar, they were unsure whether the children understood the measurement of time on a calendar.

At the end of 1997, the teachers in the Vancouver Child Study Centre brought in a number of old calendars and left them in the library corner as a provocation. Many of the children were fascinated by the calendars, and during the next two or three weeks, the calendars were often the most frequently chosen item from the bookshelves. For many days the library corner had calendars strewn all over the floor as the children examined each page and discussed the pictures, the printed numbers, and the letters for the days and months with their friends. Often they asked the teachers to help them find their birthdays on the calendar. The teachers decided to see if the children would be interested in using their early literacy and math skills to make their own calendars. They began by asking the children in group time what they knew about calendars and listed their responses on a chart as follows:

Calendars:

- have pictures
- have numbers
- have pages

- have letters
- have a hole to hang them
- have twelve pages

The teachers put out a variety of materials in the writing area: construction paper, white paper on which to draw pictures with fine-tipped felt pens, and small squares of paper cut from an old calendar, with the date on each square. The teachers also added small, blank squares of paper on which the children could write their own dates. On the table they placed a card with 1998 printed on it for the children to copy, if they wished. The children drew many interesting pictures for their calendars, some of which seemed to have been inspired by the pictures of scenery they had seen on the old calendars. There were pictures of mountains and trees, and one child drew a snow scene, with a perky snowman perched on the side of a steep hill and people skiing down the ski slopes. Once the children had pasted their pictures on the large sheets of construction paper, they began to paste the small squares of paper with the dates. Some of the children chose to write their own numbers, using either conventional or invented symbols, on the squares and if they could not find the printed number they were looking for, they sometimes wrote their own and placed it on the calendar. Most children pasted their squares in random order all over the construction paper, but a few of them put the dates in order. Only one child got as far as pasting the numbers in correct order from 1 to 11, but he placed the dates vertically moving up the page, instead of in a line across or down the page. Most children copied the year 1998 from the card on the table and placed it in a prominent position on their calendars.

The calendar project, as could be seen by the children's enthusiastic response, was a successful experience. The teachers were surprised at the deep level of interest the children showed in the topic of dates and calendars. The teachers were also amazed at how much information the children already had about calendars and how much they understood about the concept of measuring time with a calendar. Many of the children, for instance, could find the date of their own birthday and other special dates among the numbers printed on small squares of paper. The interest in calendars lasted for nearly a month, from the time the children discovered the calendars in the library corner to the time when they had made their own calendars to display in the classroom. The teachers learned from this project how important it is to follow the children's interest. They realized that if they were to repeat the experience, they would need to slow down more and explore the topic in more depth. In this way they might also give the children who were slow to show an interest more time to get involved.

THE LANGUAGE OF MAP MAKING

Children are full of surprises and much more competent and capable than we ever believed possible, as the following account of children's mapping skills and representational abilities demonstrates when they with their teachers celebrated the 2010 Olympics in Vancouver.

One evening in 1993, when the Canadian delegation was visiting the municipal preschools in Reggio Emilia, we were astonished to see the piazzas in the city suddenly fill with crowds of people singing and cheering and cars and Vespas tearing through the streets honking, waving flags, and trailing long streamers behind them. What was happening? We learned later that it was all about the soccer team winning the national championship. We wondered if the people in a city like Vancouver would ever show the same spirit of community celebration. Then came the Winter Olympics held in Vancouver in February 2010. Suddenly huge crowds were pouring into the centre of Vancouver, singing and shouting "Go Canada Go" and waving their maple leaf flags. The children in Marpole Oakridge Preschool picked up on all the excitement and started to draw, paint, and create with 3-D materials their own impressions of the Olympics.

The teachers, Linda and Natsuko, invited me to see how their preschool children had responded to the Olympics. The majority of children in the preschool are learning to speak English as their second language. Their families are either new or second generation immigrants. They told me that even before the Olympics the children were enthusiastic about playing ice hockey. When the Olympics began, however, the children wanted a maple leaf flag on the goal posts and

Linda Murdoch

Building the Olympic flame

shouted "Go Canada Go" as they whacked the hockey puck across the gym floor.

The following account is taken from a discussion with the teachers and their documentation of the project.

> Evan was the first to mention the Olympics in our classroom. One day he built a small structure out of blocks and with a big smile announced "Inukshuk, Olympics." (The Inukshuk, a rock structure used by the Inuit as a direction marker, was chosen as the 2010 Winter Olympic emblem.) Over the next few days Evan drew, painted, and used clay and the paper squares he had cut out, to represent his idea of an Inukshuk.

> The other children noticed what he was doing and so we provided them with some real rocks they could use to build an Inukshuk. In discussing what an Inukshuk was with the children, they told us:

> > The Inukshuk is to make it look Olympicky.

> > An Inukshuk is a pretend man.

> > He doesn't walk.

> > He is made of clay and rocks.

> > We have them for everybody to look at.

> About this time the Olympic Torch Run passed near our school and a couple of parents took their children to see it. From then on images inspired by the Olympics began to appear in many of the children's drawings and paintings. The teachers decided as a provocation to leave photographs from the newspaper of the Olympics out on the table to see how interested the children would be. This resulted in great discussions and from then on, especially, after most of the children had watched the opening celebration on TV, the Olympics became their major topic of interest. The children decided to build Olympic cauldrons like the one they had seen lit at the opening ceremonies. The teachers decided to offer newspaper wands decorated with silver and brightly coloured tin foil to make the triangular form used to hold the Olympic flame. The teachers asked the children why we have an Olympic flame.

> > It's too cold.

> > So TV can show the Olympics.

> After that the children came up with many images and ideas to represent their own experiences of the Olympics. Natsuko brought in the medals she had received on

Linda Murdoch

Ice skating body positions

completion of marathon runs and the children tried wearing them and making their own versions of silver, gold, and bronze medals. They created a miniature ski hill and curling, speed, and ice skating rinks to act out symbolically in the classroom what they had observed the competitors doing in the Olympics. The teachers were amazed at how accurately the children copied the movements of the competitors they had been watching on TV. They pretended to speed skate down the hall, for instance, holding one hand behind their backs just like they had seen on TV. The figure skating seemed to make a huge impression on the children. Many spoke of the skaters' movements, body positions, and their fancy costumes. The teachers decided to see if the children would be interested in making representations using collage material of the figure skaters they had been watching perform.

We decided to use a small wooden mannequin to help the children visualize and explore the movements they were trying to express. "We had precut shapes to be used that represented the shapes that made up the wooden figure. Using these the children then recreated the position they had imagined. The next day we presented them again to the group and asked each child who had made one if they could show us with their body what they had created. They all could remember precisely what they had intended and were very keen to show us their pose."

The children often had to struggle with how to depict bent knees and arms. Once these basic shapes were glued onto the paper, the children selected fabric to dress their skater's bodies. "They all seemed to agree that they needed sparkly materials." The children's finished portraits of the skaters showed many accurate details of the costumes and the body positions taken in the routines the children had seen the skaters perform.

After it was all over, the children did not want to let go of their enthusiasm for the Olympics. One day, an Olympic tourist guide to Vancouver came to the classroom. After examining the map the children started recalling places they had visited during the

Linda Murdoch

Collage figure

Linda Murdoch

Collage figure

Olympics. There was so much excitement over this map, the teachers wondered if making a big map would allow the children to continue to recall and share their personal experiences. The teachers asked the parents to bring in photographic memories of their Olympic experiences. By the time these arrived the map was nearly completed and the children started to make connections between their photos and specific locations on the map. They started to lay their photos on the map telling us this is where I did this, or this is where I saw that. The children wanted to make drawings to put on the map to show themselves at the sites. As the children had already done a lot of drawing to represent their Olympic experience the teachers decided to offer the challenge of making a 3-D map of Vancouver.

Throughout the Olympic exploration the children often used drawing as a method to communicate what they saw and knew to us, so we wanted to provide them with a challenge to represent the Olympic events and sites in three dimensions by presenting boxes and plain paper. The children showed their eagerness and started to tackle the job of covering the boxes with plain paper. They learned to measure the height of each box, use a ruler to draw a straight line on a sheet of paper, cut along the line, and wrap the box with paper. It was not an easy task for many children, but with their enthusiasm all the boxes got covered with plain paper quickly.

One child made the fourteen-storey tall building covered with the Canadian flag; another child constructed the Art Gallery with its floor to ceiling exterior paintings of Taiwanese decorative fabrics. The children remembered how they had travelled about the city and created a miniature sky train and the zip line that crossed Robson Square.

After two weeks of making this map and revisiting our experiences looking at family photos, the children were satisfied. The project seemed to be completed. The children had turned their separate Olympic experiences into the collective group experiences through sharing stories and photos and working together on the map.

Deconstruction:

The teachers are still pondering what they learned from this project. They were amazed at how media influences children as early as the preschool years and noted how closely the children must pay attention to it to represent in such graphic detail what they had viewed. They found out how powerful a shared experience was in motivating the children's learning and how these shared memories provoked complex, collaborative group work. For

Linda Murdoch

Olympic map

instance, the reproduction of the tourist map of the Olympics in 3-D resulted in the children demonstrating they could perform abstract, representational work at a very high level. The children and teachers experienced again and again the power of being caught up in the emotional experience that carried the project forward and enabled the children to perform at a level beyond what was thought possible of children in their age group. This is an example of the "windhorse effect" described earlier by Carol Anne Wien, page 42. The project demonstrated how important it is to have available a wide variety of materials for the children to use and how these, especially when the children do not share a common language, enable them to communicate across language and cultural barriers. The teachers noted how helpful it had been to introduce cues such as photographs and newspaper articles to support the children in re-creating experiences. The powerful effect of collaboration between teachers, children, and families— especially the sharing of their memories—was evident throughout the project. Documentation captured the experience of the project as a whole and enabled the teachers to debrief and think together about what happened and why. The project seems to demonstrate how strongly children strive to be part of the culture surrounding them, how closely they are observing and then trying to replicate what they see happening out there in their world so they can feel a sense of belonging.

THE LANGUAGE OF RELATIONSHIPS

The deepest language of all, and the hardest to articulate, is the language of relationships. It goes much deeper than the more easily measured skills like logical thinking and problem solving. Learning is about making relationships, and this is the language that enables us to absorb information and process it at a deep level. It is the language that enables us to make connections between our thoughts and our values, to recognize patterns that link ideas, objects, and events. It is the language that helps us develop our aesthetic sense so that we can say, "This idea can be expressed in clay but it can be better expressed with wire" or "This room arrangement pleases me because it expresses respect for who we are and what we value in our culture." It is the language that connects us to the deep expressive force at the core of our beings—the force that enables us to respond to the world around us with our hearts as well as our heads. It allows us "to tune in to the pulse of life"; it "is constructed through watchful and intense relationships"(Vecchi, 212). The educators of Reggio Emilia maintain that teachers need to learn the language of relationships "in order to listen to it, to understand and assess it" (Vecchi, 212).

SCHOOL READINESS

There has been a powerful drive in the last few years to get children "ready for school" by introducing academic subjects into early childhood programs;

preschool and kindergarten children are expected to learn to read, write, and do arithmetic. Teachers are increasingly required to demonstrate the children's level of knowledge through assessments and checklists.

This is a very narrow view of school readiness. Early learning is multidimensional. Language, literacy, and numeracy cannot be isolated as separate subjects; they are all a part of a child's foundation of learning. Would it not make more sense, instead of focusing on just three languages, to expand children's languages to a hundred and "a hundred, hundred more"? We have learned from the research at Harvard (Project Zero) that there are more than just two intelligences, linguistic and logicomathematical; there are multiple intelligences. If we encouraged children to use the language that matched their style of learning, whether it was musical, kinesthetic, spatial, interpersonal, or naturalist, would we not give children an opportunity to be competent, successful learners? Children cannot forge ahead and later meet academic demands in school if they are not ready in all domains, physical, emotional, social, and intellectual. To focus so much attention on just a few aspects of learning upsets the balance of a child's whole development and weakens the foundation for learning in later life. It can also seriously damage children's enthusiasm, motivation to learn, and confidence in themselves as learners. Instead, the image of the child as capable, competent, resourceful, and inventive must endure.

The child has

A hundred languages

(and a hundred hundred more)

and they steal ninety nine.

(No way. The hundred is there.)

Loris Malaguzzi

Epilogue

Making Reggio Our Own

I have been fortunate in the last few years to travel across Canada, Taiwan, China, the United States, and Abu Dhabi visiting preschool and kindergarten classrooms and working with teachers who are interested in using the ideas learned from the municipal preschools in Reggio Emilia in their programs. The challenge for all of us who have become inspired by Reggio Emilia and want to make changes in our own programs is that the Reggio Emilia approach grew in a very different culture and context from our own. Teachers continually ask questions such as these:

- How much of our own programs do we have to give up to integrate ideas learned from Reggio Emilia in our programs?
- How do we do this without the support the preschools in Reggio Emilia have, such as a pedagogista and atelierista available for every school?

Then there are more practical questions such as:

- How do we change our environments to make them as beautiful and inspiring as the classrooms in Reggio Emilia are?
- Is documentation an acceptable replacement for assessment and evaluation?
- How do we reorganize our schedules to give children and teachers more time to work on projects and do documentation?

Loris Malaguzzi said, "We follow the children, not the curriculum." How do we do this and yet fulfill the expectations of administrators and supervisors who have a set curriculum they want to see transmitted?

Teachers working with the Reggio Emilia approach are continually struggling with such questions. However, as I have travelled across the world I have been heartened to find that people are finding solutions, and making Reggio their own. When I observe teachers working with the ideas learned from Reggio Emilia in their classrooms, I have been heartened to see that their programs become more joyful, their environments more beautiful, and the children more involved in learning in an authentic way. Behavioural challenges diminish, and families seem to participate and support the program much more enthusiastically.

It is important to remember that Reggio Emilia is accessible to us because we share the same theoretical foundation. When you visit the preschools in Reggio Emilia, for instance, you see classrooms arranged in recognizable ways: the dramatic play corner with dress-up clothes, tea sets, and cooking utensils; an area for blocks; and a science corner. I saw a store set up in one school and a doctor's office in another. This way of planning our classroom space goes back to John Dewey, who said that kindergarten children should experience life as it is lived in the real world. He recommended giving children real materials and tools to work with. Dewey believed it was essential that children experience the processes of democracy and practise skills such as cooperation and critical thinking. Group time, he stressed, should be designed to help children participate in discussions, listen to other points of view, and make decisions based on the wishes of the majority of children and teachers present. We also share with the educators of Reggio Emilia a Piagetian perspective in which children construct knowledge by acting on the environment, first through sensory exploration and later by transforming materials (e.g., making ice turn into water and then to steam). In this way children are building conceptual knowledge, which becomes increasingly more abstract with experience and skill development. Vygotsky expanded our understanding of conceptual development, helping us to become aware of the importance of social interaction and how information sharing is a critical component of the learning process. Howard Gardner was a very early visitor to Reggio Emilia, and his theory of multiple intelligences has been instrumental in expanding our focus on logical intelligence alone to valuing other forms of intelligences. His work has encouraged teachers to consider children's different learning styles and provide them with a much wider variety of experiences and materials ("the hundred languages" of children) to express their ideas and make their thinking visible.

One of the big differences between most North American programs and Reggio Emilia is that whereas we begin with theories and try to fit the children's behaviour into them, they began with very close observation of children. From much reflection on these observations they have created an image of the child that is competent, resourceful, inventive, and full of ideas. When teachers think of children in this way they give them and their ideas respect. They realize that children are worth listening to. An image of the child as having something important to say is absolutely essential for teachers who want to make Reggio Emilia their own. Such teachers understand that children can make a major contribution to curriculum; they pick up on children's ideas and help them to develop these ideas further. A dialogue develops between teachers and children as together they co-construct the curriculum. A true partnership is created between the teachers and the children as they work together. The program becomes much more spontaneous, imaginative, and full of surprises because children have ideas that are much more interesting than those of adults.

Teachers who are trying to make Reggio Emilia their own need to familiarize themselves with the founding principles of the approach: respect, relationship, reciprocity, and transparency. Respect is evident between children, teachers, families, and community. Respect is shown for the environment and for the materials and equipment in the classroom. George Forman said, "You can always tell the children are being respected when they talk like professors!" Relationship also permeates every level, from including the families in the program to planning the space so that every object in the room is seen not in isolation but in the context of the children's learning. Reciprocity means that teachers talk to children; they are genuinely interested in the children's ideas, and give them the materials to make their thinking visible. "Draw what you think" is a phrase often heard in one of these classrooms. Finally, transparency is evident in the room arrangement. Light sets the mood; perhaps it is used to provide a calm, peaceful space or played with and made to dance and sparkle about the room. Transparent materials, such as cellophane paper, are used on equipment such as light tables and overhead projectors. Transparency is also seen in the design of classrooms where walls are replaced by windows. Most important, transparency is evident in the documentation that makes the program visible to everyone involved: the children, the teachers, the families, and the community. I have seen documentation, for instance, displayed in the local library so that people can find out what is happening in their neighbourhood child-care centre.

Finally, for teachers to make Reggio their own successfully, they have to have at least two qualities. The first is an ability to enter into children's thinking or as Giovanni Piazza puts it, to "enter into the irony with children." What it means is that teachers can recognize the big ideas children are grappling to understand and can join them in bringing these ideas to the surface. It is this process that is responsible for the creation of projects like the Amusement Park for Birds. The second quality is a passion for materials; for all the myriad art materials, natural materials, children's books, and props for dramatic play. Some teachers just have an eye for finding unexpected materials that intrigue children and fire their imaginations. This is why collaboration is such an important part of a Reggio Emilia classroom: Teachers can share their strengths and work together to provide children with a classroom rich in resources.

We *can* make Reggio Emilia our own. It has a different feel to it in each different community where it is practised. Some things, however, that are essential: teachers who have an image of children as powerful contributors of ideas; teachers who see their role more as partners with than as controllers of the children; an environment that acts as a third teacher; and documentation that draws everyone into the learning experiences. With these elements, a classroom can be "Reggio inspired."

The group of children who were in the Preschool and Children's Centre on Quadra Island in the late nineties are now graduating from high school. At a recent gathering of their parents, the parents commented on what a remarkable group the Quadra graduates were because they were able to go ahead and do amazing things, "nothing seems to daunt them." For instance, Emma's mother told the group how Emma, who had arrived from China before entering preschool on Quadra Island, had built her own sailing boat as a teenager. The parents agreed this confidence to take on challenging projects came from her experiences in the Quadra Island Preschool and the Children's Centre. They felt that much of their teenager's abilities and confidence came from the Reggio Emilia approach that the teachers had began to explore during the years their children were in preschool and child care.

In the years since then many of the early childhood education training programs, child-care centres, and preschools have continued to make the Reggio Emilia approach their own in their own way as can be seen from the following "Afterword" by Pamela Wallberg.

Afterword

The Classroom through a Relationship Lens

Pamela Wallberg*

Pamela Wallberg is the founder and current peda-gogista of Alderwood House School, a school for one-to five-year-olds in Richmond, British Columbia. Pamela shares her thoughts about how, at Alderwood House, they have been inspired by Reggio Emilia, particularly in making "relationship" the heart of their program. In the following account she shares her thoughts about Reggio Emilia and the influence it has had on her work with young children.

In various conversations I have about Reggio Emilia preschools, I regularly hear the objection "You can't do Reggio outside of Italy."

True. The municipal infant–toddler centres and preschools of Reggio Emilia have not, and will not, provide a manual or certification process so that educators across the world can "do" Reggio. How could they? On each of my trips to Reggio Emilia, it has struck me that the energy of dialogue, participation, and community is woven throughout the entire city— it is not something that begins when one walks through the doors of a preschool.

Reggio Emilia offers educators "an understanding of the school as first and foremost a public space and as a site for ethical and political practice—a place of encounter, interactions and connections among citizens in a community, a place where relationships combine a profound respect for otherness and a difference

*Reproduced courtesy of Pamela Wallberg

with a deep sense of responsibility for the other, a place of profound interdependency" (Dahlberg & Moss 2006, 10). This understanding of the role early learning centres can play is different from the understanding usually embraced by educators in North America. In a system in which young children are increasingly assessed on individual outcomes and development, there is all too often no room left for relationship and community. While attention to social and emotional learning is growing—causing some educators to introduce social or emotional based experiences in the classroom—this has been situated as learning that will contribute to stronger academic outcomes. The long stretches of time required to experience interconnectedness and to develop relationships through playful interactions continue to be sacrificed to make way for increased attention to early academic curriculum.

The image of the child which has been provocatively offered by Reggio Emilia positions the child "as an active citizen" (Dahlberg & Moss 2006, 10). I urge educators who tell me "you can't do Reggio" to think about school not as a physical space or reflection of a particular teaching style, but as a place in which children are considered active citizens, as opposed to not-yet citizens (France 1998), in deficit of adulthood; a place where children are capable and competent in their roles as active citizens, as opposed to children who need to be taught how to be citizens. From birth, children are a social, contributing force to the unfolding cultural and political ways of being. This is not an idea that is fenced into the municipal boundaries of the city of Reggio Emilia; it is not an idea that can only be lived in Italy. Indeed, educators the world over are considering what the image of the child in their community context is, and how they can shift this image towards the image offered by Reggio Emilia.

What does this mean to me, in practice?

It means tossing out ideas of early childhood education such as carbon copy crafts; pre-planned teacher-run circle times of one-song, one-book, one-felt-story, one-motor-activity; or teacher-imposed problem solving such as "we share our trikes at school." It means surrendering the self-image of teacher-as-authority, or teacher-as-expert. Instead, the image of teacher-as-researcher or teacher-as-co-learner must be embraced. It means answering questions with "it depends" or "I don't know." It means being comfortable with uncertainty and not knowing. It means having more questions than answers and—and this is the hard part—being OK with that.

When Alderwood House School opened as a "Reggio-inspired" school, teachers began with an image of the child as *competent and powerful, an active citizen who is a part of the world from birth.* However, it wasn't until teachers at Alderwood realized the conflict between our Image of the Child as a philosophical statement and our Image of the Child in practice that we truly began to experience what "doing Reggio" meant. All the digital cameras and beautiful art materials in the world couldn't help us "make Reggio our own"; it was only by becoming aware of and acknowledging the conflicts between our stated philosophy and our day-to-day practice and admitting "I don't know," that educators actually began to take on the role of learning with the children, rather than teaching them.

Reggio-inspired practice, to me, no longer means a beautiful environment or documentation on the walls (although that inevitably emerges out of the classroom). Rather, Reggio-inspired practice is a willingness to observe and bring attention to the tensions and conflicts within relationships, and use the tensions to understand and, ultimately, make visible the ways in which children construct meaning and engage in the community around them.

My own understanding of children as active citizens was first confronted one sunny afternoon in late August. Two young girls—Maria, aged 2 and Sarah, aged 3—were playing happily outside. Maria noticed that Sarah was carrying a sparkly and fuzzy pink backpack and decided to grab it out of Sarah's arms. Sarah screamed—a sound that doubtlessly sent all nearby wildlife scurrying for cover. Sarah grabbed for the backpack, which was now firmly around Maria's shoulder. Maria's body was yanked towards Sarah. I was six metres away and was about to run to intervene, when another teacher stopped me. "Wait," she said.

I had visions of blood and broken bones, and did not want to wait. Young children were in danger! Small, fragile children needed me! But the teacher physically stood beside me, holding me back. "Wait," she repeated, "give them a minute."

Maria grabbed Sarah's hair. Sarah yanked the backpack, kicking and slapping Maria. Yells of "Mine! It's mine!" threatened to break eardrums. I was angry that I was being held back. I was a *teacher*. This was my *job*.

Then, as quickly as it began, it was over. Maria handed the bag to Sarah and said "Sorry." Sarah held the bag, looking it over, and then handed it back to Maria. "You can use it for a minute," she generously offered. The two girls returned to their play.

I was astonished by the problem-solving skills evidenced in this incident. The girls recognized that the first strategy was not going to realize their goals, and they moved on to using other tools. I suddenly realized that in controlling the classroom by providing solutions to conflict, by providing answers and a pre-set path that should be followed, I was stealing from children. I was stealing their ability to live as competent citizens; I was stealing moments in which they could learn to sit with, and navigate uncertainty; I was stealing the opportunities for situated learning.

Reflecting on my experiences working in child-care settings, both as a manager and teacher, I am ashamed at the amount I have stolen from children by simply operating under an image of the child as "not-yet citizen." Too often educators, through the environment, the temporal structure and their own need for control in the classroom, position the child not as a capable person who is living his or her potential everyday, but rather as a person in deficit of something.

When an educator views the child as an active citizen, the entire classroom changes. It is a necessary change. Children are no longer being prepared for kindergarten, or being given skills to help them in the world. Children are suddenly already *in* the world, contributing to the world as powerful and insightful community members.

Some time ago, I had the good luck to work with a 5-year-old girl with high behavioural needs. She struggled in working with peers, often resorting to kicking, biting, and screaming. On one particularly difficult day, after I had been pinched and punched, I called a colleague for advice. Funding cutbacks meant a long waitlist for support workers, and I didn't know what to do. My colleague listened as I struggled to explain the problem. "I don't know how to help her," I summarized.

"Have you asked her?" she queried.

I had again fallen into the role of "teacher" and had forgotten that I should, instead, operate in the role of co-learner. I hadn't asked the child why she was behaving the way she was, and what she needed. I had participated in Individual Education Planning with parents, support workers, and doctors; I had theorized with teachers about how specific peers or environmental influences might be causing difficulties, but I had forgotten to ask the child. We all had.

Developmental theories view the child in terms of progress toward becoming an adult: development is a linear progression in which "adulthood" becomes the goal. Considering the classroom through a developmental lens, materials are tools to develop emotional, social, physical, and cognitive areas that are considered developmental areas for people in deficit of adulthood. Blocks are for teaching fine motor skills; dance is to teach gross motor control; teaching the alphabet is so that children can read; circle time is to teach new ideas and explain what will happen in the day. The focus is on the result, on the product that will be produced, not on what already is.

What would happen if instead, the classroom was considered through a relationship lens? If, instead of identifying what children needed to be taught, educators—together with the children—asked "How can I actively contribute to this relationship?" Snack becomes a routine in which all children contribute and participate as active community members; writing becomes a means to communicate ideas and thoughts with others; blocks are for creating beautiful designs with others and for problem solving design issues in a real way; circle time is an opportunity to pose questions and gather possible hypotheses and diverse perspectives. As children negotiate how to remain true to their own perspectives while giving space to other children to maintain their own perspectives, they begin to deepen understandings about self-identity, self in relation to other, collaboration, cooperation, and interdependence. Relationships become the curriculum and the teacher's mandate then changes to nurturing relationships between children and the environment, children and teachers, and between the children themselves. The focus moves from result to process, the day-to-day lived experience.

"Relationship" can be the true curriculum of an early learning centre. Language, artistic expression, geography, mathematics—all emerge out of a need to participate within a social context. If educators treat children as active citizens, academic outcomes will inevitably follow as children immerse themselves in a social community. Needs for new forms of communication, for commerce and assessing value, for expressing opinions and understanding opinions of others will lead children to seek out these "academic" skills. Educators who view the child as an active citizen and focus on relationships in the classroom will inevitably create an environment that supports not only academic learning but also a strong community.

The schools of Reggio Emilia have challenged early childhood educators internationally to consider the child as an active citizen within a web of relationships. It is now up to individual educators to bring this image into their practice, and create environments that focus on relationships. As relationships deepen and classroom communities develop, conflict will emerge. Every relationship is full of conflict, and it is in this conflict where children "bring their beginnings into a world of plurality and difference in such a way that their beginnings do not obstruct the opportunities for others to bring their beginnings into this world as well." (Biesta 2007, 760) Children regularly experience the world as a place of inequality, a place of unresolved conflict, and a place of questions and the unknown. It isn't out of concern for the child that adults cast children in the role of "not-yet"; I propose it is out of fear for ourselves. To view children as capable and competent, as active citizens, it requires shifting the image of the educator from that of expert, power, or authority to one much more similar to that of the child: a capable, competent, active citizen. This loss of power is disconcerting and uncomfortable but I would suggest, necessary.

Embracing the Reggio-inspired image of the child means embracing a new self-image and a new way of being that is full of uncertainty. I first made this connection when I was viewing the Wonder of Learning/100 Languages of Children exhibit: delighting in the rich questioning and curiosity documented in the exhibit, and the rambling, energetic, and vibrant paths taken by children to understand the world, I was struck with the fact that this uncertainty wasn't something to "get through" once I was more experienced, once I had learned enough. Uncertainty wasn't part of the journey to get somewhere, uncertainty was the somewhere.

By focusing on relationships as a context for learning, classrooms can become communities in which children can experience authentic belonging. You can't do Reggio? "Doing Reggio" is absolutely impossible outside of Italy. It simply depends on what you consider Reggio to be. To me, Reggio Emilia, while a wonderful city with inspiring schools and brilliant educators, isn't a secret to be learned. Every municipal school in Reggio Emilia looks different from one another because educators focus on the relationships within their own school and ensure that the voice of each individual is heard and valued, and the group that is this collection of voices is unique and unable to be replicated. To me, "making Reggio our own" in North America is no different than how each of the Reggio Emilia schools make Reggio their own: through a daily, lived practice of active citizenry in the classroom.

The Educators

QUADRA ISLAND CHILDREN'S CENTRE

Dee Conley

Dee completed her early childhood education diploma at North Island College in Campbell River. She began working at the Quadra Island Children's Centre in 1989 and became the administrative director in 1994. She is currently working toward a bachelor's degree in child and youth care. In her spare time, she enjoys working with clay and would dearly love to have the opportunity to train as an atelierista.

Sherrie Fudikuf

Sherrie has a bachelor of general studies from Simon Fraser University, with a major in education. She transferred to Simon Fraser from the Faculty of Education at the University of Calgary.

Barb Lee

Barb was born and raised in England, where she completed the Nursery Nurse Examination (NNEB). She transferred the qualification to an ECE certificate in British Columbia by adding 500 hours of practice.

Susan Emery

Susan trained in Montessori and worked as a director in a Montessori School. She worked in the Quadra Children's Centre when it first opened and returned a year ago, after hearing they were implementing the Reggio Emilia approach.

Lise Burnett

Lise was born and raised in Quebec. She took two years in special education (for children with special needs) in college. She moved to British Columbia and completed an ECE certificate at North Island College. On completion of one practicum at Quadra Children's Centre, she was hired to join the staff.

QUADRA ISLAND PRESCHOOL

Baerbel Jaeckel

Baerbel was born in Munich, Germany, where she completed elementary school training. She immigrated to Canada in 1971 and completed her teaching certificate in 1974. She worked as a substitute teacher, then she moved to Quadra Island and taught German and crafts at the Quadra Waldorf School. She completed her ECE certificate in 1989. She taught at the Quadra Island Children's Centre from 1987 to 1997 and became the preschool teacher in the Quadra Island Preschool in 1997. She has a wonderful daughter, Katie.

VANCOUVER CHILD STUDY CENTRE

Patricia Breen

Following the completion of a bachelor of education degree at the University of Calgary, Patricia's teaching career began in the elementary schools of Alberta, but her interests quickly shifted to early childhood education as she became involved in her own children's preschool. She subsequently enrolled at the University of British Columbia to further her education in this area. After many years as a teacher at a parent participation preschool in Vancouver, she returned to UBC to undertake a master's degree in ECE. As a graduate, she was employed at the UBC Child Study Centre in the programs for two-year-olds and three-/four-year-olds. This setting provided ample opportunities to question and reflect on the theoretical underpinnings of accepted teaching practice. Her interest in the teacher's role in preschool play became the basis for a master's thesis, entitled, "The Role of the Teacher during Free Play in Preschool." After graduation she continued to work at the Child Study Centre until it closed in 1997. She is presently employed by its successor, the Vancouver Child Study Centre.

Gloria Rolfsen

Gloria trained as a registered nurse and worked for seven years in the field of acute care psychiatry in Comox, B.C., and Arizona. While working as a participating parent at her two daughters' parent participation preschool, she realized how much she enjoyed the company of three- and four-year-olds, mostly because of their honesty and sincerity. After completing her ECE certificate at Langara College, she worked for seven years at the University of British Columbia Child Study Centre, first as an assistant and then as head teacher. Following its closing, she worked with parents and colleagues to establish the Vancouver Child Study Centre, where she is currently working.

Chava Rubenson

Chava Rubenson was born in Amsterdam, Holland. As a young woman, she moved to Sweden, where she completed a bachelor's degree with a focus on childhood culture. She trained as an early childhood educator at the Stockholm Institute of Education, where she received her B.Ed. After moving to Canada, she worked at the UBC Child Study Centre for twelve years. When the UBC Child Study Centre closed, she joined forces with her colleagues to establish the Vancouver Child Study Centre in 1997. She lives with her husband and two sons in Vancouver.

Vivian Urquhart

Vivian has been committed to education for many years. She began her teaching career as a teacher of grade three. After raising her four daughters, she realized how much she enjoyed working with younger children. She recently received her master of education in early childhood. The topic of her paper was the challenges of young learners of English as a second language in the preschool setting. Today, Vivian enjoys the challenges of implementing Reggio practices in her preschool classroom.

MARPOLE OAKRIDGE PRESCHOOL

Michelle de Salaberry

Michelle de Salaberry has been teaching in the early childhood field for almost 30 years. She graduated in 1975 from Langara College in Vancouver, B.C., worked for several years in a child care setting, and for the past 24 years has been at Marpole Oakridge Preschool, a multiethnic, multilingual centre in southwest Vancouver. In the past five years Marpole Oakridge Preschool has provided a child-centred, emergent/negotiated curriculum, with particular attention to the environment as a third teacher, as well as used documentation to investigate the children's interests. Michelle was part of the Canadian delegation to Reggio Emilia in 2001. She continues to learn and implement many of the philosophies from Reggio in her day-to-day work. Michelle lives in Vancouver with her husband and enjoys being host parent to foreign students. She also enjoys travelling and photography.

Linda Murdoch

Linda Murdoch grew up in Victoria, B.C., and fondly remembers spending most of her early childhood exploring the great outdoors. After completing her ECE training at Langara College in the mid-70s, she worked for a few years in child care before choosing to stay at home to raise her own two children. In 1986 she started working at Marpole Oakridge Preschool, where she has worked ever since. She has helped establish a program at Marpole Oakridge with a strong focus on developing social success for children learning English as their second language. Over the last seven years she has been studying Reggio Emilia and trying to implement many of the Reggio Emilia principles in her program. She says, "It has been a very rewarding and exciting journey."

The views expressed in this publication are those of the author, representing her own interpretation of the philosophy and practices of the Municipal Infant-Toddler Centres and Preschools of Reggio Emilia. The content of this publication has not been officially approved by the Municipality of Reggio Emilia nor by Reggio Children in Italy; therefore, it may not reflect the views and opinions of these organizations.

Natsuko Motegi

Natsuko Motegi moved to Canada in 1999 to take the Master of Education program at UBC, and started to realize the joy and excitement of working with young children. After completing the program, she decided to take ECE training, and learned about emergent curriculum or the Reggio-inspired way of teaching/learning. After working with toddlers for three years, in 2005 she took a position at Marpole Oakridge Community Preschool and started to work with Linda in emergent curriculum. The excitement of working with children continues!

Pamela Wallberg

Pamela Wallberg is the founder and current pedagogista of Alderwood House School, a school for one- to five-year-olds in Richmond, British Columbia. Pamela holds her early childhood and infant toddler licences and has over sixteen years of experience in the field of youth, children, and early childhood through various roles working with families, schools, and child-care centres. Pamela's master's thesis focused on the development of democratic learning communities within two- and three-year-old classrooms. Attending study tours of the preprimary schools of Reggio Emilia, Pamela has been deeply inspired by the commitment to community and participation within not only the schools but the entire city of Reggio Emilia.

Appendix 2

THE COLLABORATIVE CRITICAL REFLECTIVE PROTOCOL

Alternative Method for Deconstructing and Co-Constructing the Image of the Child/Childhood, the Educator, and the School/Community

(Inspired in Rounds for Teachers, Project Zero, Harvard Graduate School of Education)*

1. The audience learns about **Documentation** that the documentors prepare for the session. **No explanation about the documentation is shared by the documentors at this point of the Protocol. Handouts** (copies of photos, children's productions, transcription of dialogues, description of actions, etc.) about the documentation are provided for the audience by the documentors (5 mins.).

2. Audience reflects on the documentation. This means that every participant (**individually and in silence**) writes **pedagogical documentation** (responses to the documentation). Pedagogical documentation includes **questions/assumptions/interpretations** of the children's learning (initiatives, thoughts, actions). Additionally, the audience offers "**readings**" using different theoretical lenses. The participants are encouraged to expand their questions, assumptions, and interpretations by referring to

*Alejandra Sánchez. Based on *Rounds for Teachers* by Steve Seidel, Project Zero. Harvard Graduate School of Education. Douglas College ECE Courses. Fall 2009.

the modernist perspectives (i.e., meaning-making discourse). The following questions might support the audience's contributions:

What is the image of the child/childhood, the educator, and the learning environment revealed in this documentation?

How and what is the child learning and making meaning of the world?

3. **Collaborative Conference:** The session is opened for discussion. The audience shares its pedagogical documentation (reflections written for #2). This is an opportunity to practise *deconstructive analysis and multiple readings* based on the documentation presented by the documentors (15 mins.).

4. The documentors share their pedagogical documentation/narration. In other words, the documentors explain their "**readings**" on how the modernist and poststructural perspectives (i.e., developmental psychology and the meaning-making discourses) support their interpretations of the image of the child/childhood, the educator, and the learning environment. Additionally the documentors respond to the audience's assumptions/interpretations and questions (they may or may not respond to all of them (15 mins.).

5. The documentors and the audience share **final thoughts** related to the **strengths and limitations** of using **Pedagogical Documentation**, as well as the ways to expand and enrich children's and educators' learning processes and productions (5 mins.).

Material produced by Alejandra Sanchez based on Rounds for Teachers by Steve Seidel, Project Zero, Harvard Graduate School of Education (used at Douglas College, ECE Courses).

References

Aska, Warabe. 1984. *Who goes to the park?* Montreal: Tundra Books.

———. 1986. *Who hides in the park?* Montreal: Tundra Books.

Asseline, Marlene. 1997. Bridging the gap: Family and community literacies. *Canadian Children* 22, 2:23–29.

Ball, Michael. 2000. *Wire magic.* Cincinnati: North Light Books.

Baumrind, D. 1967. Child care practices anteceding three patterns of preschool behaviour. *Genetic Psychology Monographs,* 75:43–88.

Bettelheim, Bruno. 1977. *The uses of enchantment: The meaning and importance of fairy tales.* New York: Vintage Books.

Biber, Barbara. 1972. Learning experience in school and personality: Assumptions and application. In *History and theory of early childhood education,* edited by Samuel J. Braun and Esther P. Edwards. Belmont, CA: Wadsworth.

Biber, Barbara, Edna Shapiro, and David Wickens. 1971. *Promoting cognitive growth: A developmental-interaction point of view.* Washington, DC: NAEYC.

Biesta, G. 2007. Education and the democratic person: Towards a political conception of democratic education. *Teachers College Record* 109, 3:740–769.

Bodrova, E., and D.J. Leong. 1996. *Tools of the mind: The Vygotskian approach to early childhood education.* Englewood Cliffs, NJ: Merrill.

Brazelton, T.B. 1981. On becoming a family: The growth of attachment. New York: Delacourte/Seymour Lawrence.

Bredekamp, Sue. 1993. Reflections on Reggio Emilia. *Young Children,* 49:13–17.

Bronfenbrenner, U. 1979. *The Ecology of human development: Experiments by nature and design.* Cambridge, MA: Harvard University Press.

Bruner, Jerome S. 1986. *Actual minds, possible worlds.* Cambridge, MA: Harvard University Press.

———. 1996. *The culture of education.* Cambridge, MA: Harvard University Press.

Cadwell, Louise Boyd. 1997. *Bringing Reggio Emilia home.* New York: Teachers College Press, Columbia University.

Cadwell, Louise Boyd. 2002. *Bringing learning to life.* New York: Teachers College Press.

Cagliari, Paola, and Claudia Giudici. 2001. School as a place of group learning for parents. In *Making learning visible: Children as individual and group learners.* Edited by Claudia Giudici, Carla Rinaldi, and Mara Krechevsky. Reggio Emilia: Reggio Children.

Carr, Anne. 2004. Changing teachers' beliefs and pedagogical practices. Unpublished doctoral thesis.

Ceppi, G., and M. Zeni (eds.). 1998. Children, spaces and relations: Metaproject for an environment for young children. New York: Reggio children.

Clay, M. 1975. *What did I write?* Auckland, NZ: Heinemann.

Curtis, Deb, and Margie Carter. 2000. *The art of awareness: How observation can transform your teaching.* St. Paul, MN: Redleaf Press.

Dahlberg, Gunilla, Peter Moss, and Alan Pence. 1999. *Beyond quality in early childhood education and care: Postmodern perspectives.* London, UK: Falmer Press.

Dahlberg, G. and P. Moss. 2006. Introduction: Our Reggio Emilia. In *In dialogue with Reggio Emilia: Listening, researching and learning* by Carlina Rinaldi. New York: Routledge.

Dewey, John. 1897. My pedagogic creed. *The School Journal* 54, 3 (January).

————. [1915] 1956. *The school and society.* Rev. ed. Chicago: University of Chicago Press.

Dixon, Glen. 1994. The first years of kindergarten in Canada. *Canadian Children* 19, 2:6–9.

Doll, William E. 1993. *A post-modern perspective on curriculum.* New York: Teachers College Press, Columbia University.

Edwards, Carolyn. 1998. Lecture at the Reggio Emilia Symposium, April, at Capilano College, North Vancouver, B.C.

Edwards, Carolyn, Lella Gandini, and George Forman, eds. 1993. *The hundred languages of children: The Reggio Emilia approach to early childhood education.* Norwood, NJ: Ablex Publishing Corporation.

————. 1998. *The hundred languages of children: The Reggio Emilia approach—advanced reflections.* 2nd ed. Greenwich, CT: Ablex Publishing Corporation.

Erikson, H. Erik. 1950. *Childhood and Society.* New York: W.W. Norton & Co. Inc.

Forman, George. 2003. *The Asian image of the child.* Detroit: Merrill-Palmer Institute, Wayne State University.

Forman, George, and Brenda Fyfe. 1998. Negotiated learning through design, documentation and discourse. In *The hundred languages of children: The Reggio Emilia approach—advanced reflections.* Edited by Carolyn Edwards, Lella Gandini, and George Forman. Norwood, NJ: Ablex Publishing Corporation.

France, A. 1998. 'Why should we care?' Young people, citizenship and questions of social responsibility. *Journal of Youth Studies* 1, 1:97–111.

Fraser, Susan. 1992. Talk to play and play to talk. *MC multiculturalism/multiculturalisme* XIV, 2/3:27–30.

Froebel, F. [1887] 1974. *The education of man.* Translated by W. Hailman. (Originally published in German 1827.) Reprint, New York: Kelly.

Fyfe, Brenda. 1994. Images from the United States: Using ideas from the Reggio Emilia experience with American educators. In *Reflections on the Reggio Emilia approach,* edited by Lillian Katz and Bernard Cesarone. University of Illinois, Urbana: ERIC/EECC.

———. 1998. Questions for collaboration: Lessons from Reggio Emilia. *Canadian Children* 23, 1:20–22.

Furth, H.G. 1969. *Piaget and knowledge: Theoretical foundations.* Englewood Cliffs, NJ: Prentice-Hall.

Gandini, Lella. 1994. Celebrating children day by day: A conversation with Amelia Gambetti. *Child Care Information Exchange* 100: 52–55.

Gandini, Lella and Carolyn Pope Edwards. 2001. *Bambini: The Italian approach to infant/toddler care.* New York: Teachers College Press.

Gandini, Lella, Lynn Hill, Louise Cadwell, and Charles Schwall (eds.). 2005. *In the spirit of the studio: Learning from the atelier of Reggio Emilia.* New York: Teachers College Press.

Gandini L. & Goldhaber. 2001. Two reflections about documentation. In *Bambini: The Italian approach to infant/toddler care,* edited by Lella Gandini and Carolyn Pope Edwards. New York: Teachers College Press, 124–125.

Gardner, Howard. 1983. *Frames of mind: The theory of multiple intelligences.* New York: Basic Books.

Gartrell, Daniel. 2001. *What the kids said today: Using classroom conversations to become a better teacher.* St. Paul, MN: Redleaf Press.

Gerst, Barbara. 1998. Further reflections upon the applications of the Reggio view in a kindergarten classroom. *Canadian Children* 23, 2:43–48.

Giudici, Claudia, Carla Rinaldi, and Mara Krechevsky (eds.). 2001. *Making learning visible: Children as individual and group learners.* Reggio Emilia: Reggio Children.

Goodman, Vera. 1998. The power of voice. *Canadian Children* 23, 2:49–50.

Harris Helm, Judy, Sallee Beneke, and Kathy Steinheimer. 1998. *Windows on learning: Documenting young children's work.* Columbia University, New York: Teachers College Press.

Harvey, D. 1989. *The condition of postmodernity.* Oxford: Blackwells.

Heberholz, Barbara and Lee Hanson. 1995. *Early childhood art.* 5th ed. Madison, WI: Brown and Benchmark.

Hendrick, Joanne (ed.). 2004. *Next steps toward teaching the Reggio way: Accepting the challenge to change.* 2nd ed. Upper Saddle River, NJ: Merrill/Prentice Hall.

Higgins, Mabel. 1999. Come join the journey: Bringing Reggio Emilia to the college community. *Canadian Children* 24, 1:33–40.

Hunt, J. McVicker. 1961. *Intelligence and experience.* New York: The Ronald Press.

Iannacci, Luigi and Pam Whitty (eds.). 2009. *Early childhood curricula: Reconceptualist perspectives.* Calgary: Detselig Enterprises Ltd.

Innovations in early education: The International Reggio Exchange. Detroit: The Merrill-Palmer Institute, Wayne State University.

Jones, E., and G. Reynolds. 1992. *The play's the thing: Teachers' roles in children's play.* New York: Teachers College Press.

Jones, Elizabeth, and John Nimmo. 1995. *Emergent curriculum.* Washington, DC: NAEYC.

Katz, L.G., and B. Cesarone, eds. 1994. *Reflections on the Reggio Emilia approach.* University of Illinois, Urbana: Eric/EECE.

Kaufman, Paul. 1993. Poppies and the dance of world making. In *The hundred languages of children: The Reggio Emilia approach—advanced reflections.* Edited by C. Edwards, L. Gandini, and G. Forman. Norwood, NJ: Ablex Publishing Corporation.

Krechevsky, Mara. 1993. Today's children: Our keys to tomorrow. *Canadian Children* 18, 2:6–12.

Krechevsky, Mara. 2001. Form, function and understanding in learning groups: Propositions from the Reggio classrooms. In *Making learning visible: Children as individual and group learners.* Edited by Claudia Giudici, Carla Rinaldi, and Mara Krechevsky. Reggio Emilia: Reggio Children.

Lee, Susan. 2004. The Asian image of the child. Interview. Vancouver, November 2004.

Lenz Taguchi, Hillevi. 2006. Reconceptualizing early childhood education: Challenging taken-for-granted ideas. In *Nordic childhoods and early education.* Edited by Johanna Einarsdottir and Judith T. Wagner. Greenwich, Connecticut: Information Age Publishing.

Lenz Taguchi, Hillevi. 2007. In *Contemporary/new critical issues in early childhood education*. Edited by Nicola Yelland, Victoria University. Melbourne, Australia: Open University Press.

Louv, Richard. 2005. *Last child in the woods: Saving our children from nature-deficit disorder*. Chapel Hill: Algonquin Books of Chapel Hill.

Luke, Anne. 2003. *Creating curriculum that empowers teachers and learners*. Toronto: IDEAS, Interaction, Canadian Child Care Federation.

Luke, Anne. 2003. Unpublished interview with Karen Westphal and Danica Sparvier, Early Learning Centre, Regina, Saskatchewan.

MacNaughton, Glenda. 2005. *Doing Foucault in early childhood studies: Applying poststructural ideas*. New York: Routledge.

Malaguzzi, Loris. 1993. For an education based on relationships. *Young Children* 49, 1:9–12.

Mouzard, Donna G. 1997. Building castles. *Canadian Children* 22, 1:38–39.

New, Rebecca. 1990. Excellent early education: A city in Italy has it. *Young Children* 45, 6:212–18.

———. 1994. Reggio Emilia: Its visions and its challenges for educators in the United States. In *Reflections on the Reggio Emilia Approach,* edited by Lillian Katz and Bernard Cesarone. Urbana, IL: ERIC/EECC.

———. 1997. Reggio Emilia's commitment to children and community: A reconceptualization of quality and DAP. *Canadian Children* 22, 1:7–12.

———. 1998. *Reggio Emilia: Some lessons for U.S. educators*. University of Illinois, Urbana: ERIC/EECE, EDO-PS-93-3.

Newsweek. The 10 best schools in the world and what we can learn from them. 1991. 2 December.

Pacini-Ketchabaw, Veronica, Laurie Kocher, Alejandra Sanchez, and Christine Chan. 2009. Rhizomatic stories of immanent becomings and intra-activity: Professional development reconceptualized. In *Early childhood curricula: reconceptualist perspectives*. Edited by Luigi Iannacci and Pam Whitty. Calgary: Detselig Enterprises Ltd. (p.87–117).

Parten, M. 1932. Social participation among preschool children. *Journal of Abnormal and Social Psychology*, 55:825–30.

Phillips, Lynda Jane. 2004. Unpublished doctoral thesis. Vancouver: University of British Columbia.

Piaget, Jean. 1952. *The origins of intelligence in children*. New York: International Universities Press, Inc.

———. 1971. *Science of education and the psychology of the child*. New York: Viking.

Piazza, Giovanni. 2002. Address to the Canadian delegation, February 12, 2002, Reggio Emilia.

Prochner, Larry. 1994. A brief history of daycare in Canada: The early years. *Canadian Children* 19, 2:10–15.

Reggio Children. 1995. The Fountains. In *A project for the construction of an Amusement Park for Birds*, English-Italian bilingual collection: The unheard voice of children no. 2. Reggio Emilia: Reggio Children.

Reggio Children. 2003. *Children, art and artists: The expressive languages of children: The artistic language of Alberto Burri*. Reggio Emilia: Reggio Children.

Reynolds, Gretchen. 1998. Reggio Emilia—an impossible dream? *Canadian Children* 23, 2:4–10.

Rinaldi, Carlina. 1993. The emergent curriculum and social constructivism: An interview with Lella Gandini. In *The Hundred Languages of Children: The Reggio Emilia Approach to Early Childhood Education*, edited by C. Edwards, L. Gandini, and G. Forman. Norwood, NJ: Ablex Publishing Corporation.

———. 1998. Projected curriculum constructed through documentation—progettazione: An interview with Lella Gandini. In *The Hundred languages of children: The Reggio Emilia approach—advanced reflections*. 2nd ed. Edited by C. Edwards, L. Gandini, and G. Forman. Greenwich, CT: Ablex Publishing Corporation.

Rinaldi, Carlina. 2001. Documentation and assessment: What is the relationship? In *Making learning visible: Children as individual and group learners*. Edited by Claudia Giudici, Carla Rinaldi, and Mara Krechevsky. Reggio Emilia: Reggio Children.

Rinaldi, Carlina. 2005. The whole school as an atelier: Reflections by Carla [sic] Rinaldi, edited by Lella Gandini. In *The spirit of the studio: Learning from the atelier of Reggio Emilia*. Edited by L. Gandini, L. Hill, L. Cadwell, and C. Schwall. New York: Teachers College Press.

Rinaldi, Carlina. 2006. *In dialogue with Reggio Emilia: Listening, researching and learning*. New York: Routledge.

Rodari, Gianni. 1996. *The grammar of fantasy: An introduction to the art of inventing stories*. New York: Teachers and Writers Collaborative.

Roskos, Kathy, and Carol Vukelich. 1991. Promoting literacy in play. *Day Care and Early Education* 19, 1:30–34.

Rubizzi, Laura. 2001. Documenting the Documenter. In *Making learning visible: Children as individual and group learners*. Edited by Claudia Giudici, Carla Rinaldi, and Mara Krechevsky. Reggio Emilia: Reggio Children.

Sanchez, Alejandra. 2009. Reconceptualizing ECE practices and training in B.C. *The Early Childhood Educator.* 29–32.

Seefeldt, Carol. 1995. Art—a serious work. *Young Children* 45, 3:39–45.

Seidel, Steve. 2001. The question cannot be satisfied with waiting: Perspectives on research in education. In *Making learning visible: Children as individual and group learners.* Edited by Claudia Giudici, Carla Rinaldi, and Mara Krechevsky. Reggio Emilia: Reggio Children.

Shanin, T. 1997. The idea of progress. In *The Post-Development Reader.* Edited by M. Rahnama and V. Bowtree. London: Zed Books.

Shearer, Branton (ed.). 2009. MI at 25. *Assessing the impact and future of multiple intelligences for teaching and learning.* New York: Teachers College Press.

Smilansky, S. 1968. *The effects of sociodramatic play on disadvantaged preschool children.* New York: Wiley.

Smilansky, S., and L. Shefatya. 1990. *Facilitating play: A medium for promoting cognitive, socioemotional and academic development in young children.* Gaithersburg, MD: Psychosocial and Educational Publications.

Smith, Cathleen. 1998. Children with special rights. *The hundred languages of children: The Reggio Emilia approach—advanced reflections.* 2nd ed. Edited by C. Edwards, L. Gandini, and G. Forman. Greenwich, CT: Ablex Publishing Corporation.

Smith, Dee and Jeanne Goldhaber. 2004. *Poking, pinching and pretending.* St. Paul, MN: Redleaf Press.

Sobel, David. 2008. *Childhood and nature: Design principles for education.* Portland, Maine: Stenhouse Publishers.

Spaggiari, Sergio. 1997. *Show and meter.* Reggio Emilia, Italy: Reggio Children.

Steele, Bob. 1996. A cornerstone of literacy: Children draw to express their deepest thoughts and feelings. *The Vancouver Sun,* 26 August, A19.

Sturges, Philemon. 1998. *Bridges are to cross.* Illustrated by Giles Laroche. New York: G.P. Putnam's.

Topal, Cathy Weisman and Lella Gandini. 1999. *Beautiful stuff: Learning with found materials.* Worcester, MA: Davis Publications, Inc.

Vecchi, Vea. 2001. What kind of space for living well in school? In *Children, spaces, and relations: Metaproject for an environment for young children.* 2nd ed. Edited by Giulio Ceppi and Michele Zini. Reggio Emilia: Reggio Children.

Vecchi, Vea. 2010. *Art and creativity in Reggio Emilia: Exploring the role and potential of ateliers in early childhood education.* New York: Routledge.

Vygotsky, L.S. 1962. *Thought and language.* Cambridge, MA: The M.I.T. Press.

Wien, Carol Anne. 1997. A Canadian in Reggio Emilia, May 1997, study tour. *Canadian Children* 22, 2:30–38.

Wien, Carol Anne (ed.). 2008. *Emergent curriculum in the primary classroom: Interpreting the Reggio Emilia approach in schools.* New York: Teachers College Press.

Yeates, Marilyn, Carolyn Warberg, Donna McKenna, and Karen Chandler. 1990. *Administering early childhood settings: The Canadian perspective.* Columbus, Ohio: Merrill Publishing.

Young, Kelly. 2010. Reconceptualizing literacies in ECE: An eco-justice approach. In *Early childhood curricula: Reconceptualist perspectives.* Edited by Luigi Iannacci and Pam Whitty. Calgary: Detselig Enterprises Ltd. (pp. 299–319).

VIDEOTAPES AND SLIDES

Detroit head start inspired by the Reggio approach. 1996. A 16-minute videotape that focuses on a staff development project launched in consultation with Reggio Children and sponsored by the Merrill-Palmer Institute of Wayne State University and the Head Start Division of the Detroit Human Services Department. $35 includes shipping.

Innovations in early education: The international Reggio exchange. Available from the Merrill-Palmer Institute, Wayne State University, 71 E. Ferry Ave., Detroit, MI 48202. http://www.mpi.wayne.edu/checkout.htm

Early learning in Reggio Emilia, Italy. 1993. A clear overview of the total programs in Reggio, presented with slides by Dr. Brenda Fyfe. Distributed by Project Apples, 27 Horrabin Hall, College of Education, Western Illinois University, Macomb, IL 61455, (309) 298-1634. $39 for *Innovations* subscribers.

100 Languages of children. 1995. A 30-minute videotape filmed at The Hundred Languages of Children exhibit in 1993–1994 at Dominican College, San Rafael, CA. Produced by Susan Lyon, coordinator of the exhibit at Dominican College. Available from M.S. Lyon, 101 Lombard St., 608W, San Francisco, CA 94111. $30 includes shipping.

The amusement park for birds. 1994. A 90-minute videotape that contains clips of the actual teaching practices used in La Villetta School of Reggio Emilia, Italy. Produced by George Forman and Lella Gandini. Available from Performanetics Press, 19 The Hollow, Amherst, MA 01002, (413) 256-8846, fax (413) 253-0898. Discount to *Innovations* subscribers.

The long jump: A video analysis of small group projects in early education as practiced in Reggio Emilia, Italy. 1991. Produced by George Forman and Lella Gandini. Available from Performanetics Press, 19 The Hollow, Amherst, MA 01002, (413) 256-8846, fax (413) 253-0898.

Children at the center: Reflective teachers at work. Setting sail: An emergent curriculum project. Thinking big: Expanding emergent curriculum projects. Featuring teachers from Hilltop Children's Center in Seattle. Produced by Margie Carter and Deb Curtis of Harvest Resources, PO Box 22106, Seattle, WA 98122-0106, (206) 325-0592, fax (206) 720-0494. www.ecetrainers.com; margie@ecetrainers.com

The Great Duck Pond video. Lynn Hill.

A Message From Malaguzzi. 1993. A one-hour video of an interview with Loris Malaguzzi. Produced by George Forman and Lella Gandini.

The creative spirit. 1992. PBS. Segment on Reggio Emilia in part 2 of this multipart video. Available from PBS Video, 4401 Sunset Blvd., Los Angeles, CA 90027. Companion volume: D. Goleman, P. Kaufman, and M. Ray. 1992. *The Creative Spirit.* New York: Dutton.

To make a portrait of a lion. 1987. Comune di Reggio Emilia, Centro Documentazione Ricerca Educativa Nidi e Scuole dell'Infanzia.

Not just anyplace. 2002. The first video entirely dedicated to the almost century-long history of the Municipal Infant-Toddler Centers and Preschools of Reggio Emilia. Also includes interviews with administrators, politicians, pedagogisti, teachers, atelieristi.

Colors of learning: Integrating the arts into the early childhood curriculum. Rosemary Althouse, Margaret Johnson, and Sharon Mitchell.

Open window. A portfolio of 36 slides from the municipal infant-toddler centres and preschools of Reggio Emilia.

ONLINE RESOURCES

Canadian Reggio Network
www.ucalgary.ca/~reggioca

Reggio Children
http://zerosei.comune.re.it/inter/rc_rechild.htm

NAREA
http://www.reggioalliance.org

Canadian Association for Young Children
www.cayc.ca

REGGIO-L is a discussion list co-owned by the Merrill-Palmer Institute at Wayne State University. To subscribe, send a message to: listserv@postoffice.cso.uiuc.edu. Leave the subject line blank. Just type: subscribe REGGIO-L YourFirstName YourLastName in the first line of the message area.

Project Zero

Making learning visible: Children as individual and group learners (produced in collaboration with Reggio Children) and *Making teaching visible: Documenting individual and group learning as professional development,* which explores how the Reggio Emilia approach might enhance preschool, elementary, and middle-school education in the U.S., are available from http://pzweb.harvard.edu.eBookstore

Resources related to Reggio Emilia are available from
Reggio Children USA
2460 16th St. NW, Washington, DC 20009
(800) 424-4310, (202) 265-9090, fax (202) 265-9161
www.cdacouncil.org

and also from
http://olivepressbooks.com
http://learningmaterialswork.com
http://ecetrainers.com

and in Australia through the Book Garden.

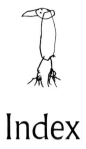

Index